Where to Retire

John Howells
with Teal Conroy

Where to Retire

America's Best &
Most Affordable Places

NINTH EDITION

Globe
Pequot
Guilford, Connecticut

Globe
Pequot

An imprint of The Rowman & Littlefield Publishing Group, Inc.
4501 Forbes Blvd., Ste. 200
Lanham, MD 20706
www.rowman.com

Distributed by NATIONAL BOOK NETWORK

British Library Cataloguing-in-Publication Information Available

Library of Congress Cataloging-in-Publication Data

Howells, John, 1928-
  Where to retire : America's best & most affordable places / John Howells. — Eighth edition.
      pages cm. — (Choose retirement series)
  Includes index.
  ISBN 978-1-4930-0639-7 (pbk.)
  1. Retirement, Places of—United States. 2. Quality of life—United States. 3. Social indicators—United States. I. Title.
  HQ1063.H6859 2015
  306.3'80973—dc23

                                                    2014038275

ISBN 978-1-4930-4366-8 (paperback)
ISBN 978-1-4930-4367-5 (e-book)

Contents

Introduction

This book is titled *Where to Retire*. As the title suggests, the focus is more on *where* to retire than *how* to retire. It is designed for those who are approaching retirement with a vague notion that they should move away from their hometowns after they retire but aren't sure where to go. Furthermore, we hope to help you decide what could be an equally important question: Why *should* you move away after retirement? Many people assume that relocation is an obligatory part of the retirement process. Contrary to common belief, most people do *not* move away when entering retirement. About 60 percent of those planning retirement intend to stay in the same neighborhood where they are presently living. Depending on the state, as many as 20 percent of those leaving the workforce might move to another town, yet only about 13 percent will actually move to another state or province. Also, a number of retirees prefer to stay right where they are, then escape harsh winters (or blazing summers) with part-time retirement, perhaps Florida for the winter, or Montana for the summer.

For most people, moving to a new city or a different state and starting over just doesn't make sense. But for others, finding a new hometown, making new friends, and creating a new lifestyle can be exciting and may contribute to a longer, happier life.

However, before pulling up the proverbial stakes to relocate to a Florida beach town, an Idaho ski resort, or an exotic foreign country, do a little self-examination. Often, it just isn't practical for those who have close family, dear friends, and wonderful neighbors to just pick up and leave all of that behind. On the other hand, you just might be one of those who barely recognize their neighbors, or whose kids have migrated to all directions of the compass. Maybe your closest friends are those you work with; when you retire, you'll be "out of the loop" and not part of the office gang anymore. If that's the case, maybe you should consider a new hometown, a new beginning, a new lifestyle. We hope this book will give you some ideas on how to go about it.

RETIREMENT IN THE 21ST CENTURY

This edition of *Where to Retire* appears in the year 2019, marking the date when large numbers of the baby boomer generation—children born between 1946 and 1964—will have reached the hallmark age of 65 years. A "hallmark" age, because that's when retirees can qualify for Medicare *and* Social Security. The youngest baby boomers will be 55 years old in the coming year. So for the next 7 years, those reaching the minimum retirement age of 62 should begin retirement planning.

The new millennium started out with a wave of confidence among those making retirement plans. Wages and employment levels were the highest in 30 years. Company retirement funds were prospering as stock market investments climbed steadily. Our 401K plans were gaining value every year. Early retirement seemed logical as well as affordable. After all, the equity in our homes had been increasing steadily to the point where, in most areas of the country, profits from a home sale were more than enough to finance a comfortable lifestyle when retirees cashed in on their generous and reliable company pensions.

All this changed with that disastrous 2008 Wall Street meltdown. A large number of baby boomers who were considering drawing Social Security at age 62 began taking a second look at their plans. The equity in their homes, counted on to finance their new lifestyles, began returning negative or underwater balances. A drastic rise in unemployment throughout the nation injected a feeling of uneasiness among potential retirees who were still holding down jobs. Not to mention the distress of those who appear to be permanently unemployed. Yes, the US economy has been making a recovery, although not nearly enough to restore the jobs lost since the recession bottomed out.

MEDICAL CARE & RETIREMENT

At the time of revising this edition of *Where to Retire*, the Affordable Care Act (aka ObamaCare) was still in place. We are hopeful that rule changes will eventually provide retirees *under* age 65 with full access to affordable and reliable health insurance. This will make early retirement more feasible. It's been estimated that as many as two million employees in the United States might take early retirement, were it not for the fear of losing employer-paid health care. Insurance companies have been famous for discovering preexisting conditions that can disqualify coverage—sometimes after years of the employee or the employer making regular monthly premium payments. This is not a trivial matter. One serious illness or accident can totally shred long-cherished plans for a dream retirement.

At this point the only other inexpensive health care alternative we can suggest would be moving to a retirement-friendly country such as Costa Rica or Mexico. Like many foreign countries, the Costa Rican and Mexican governments offer full health coverage, reliable and inexpensive, at *any* age. (For an example of a foreign retirement solution, see our books: *Choose Costa Rica for Retirement* or *Choose Mexico for Retirement*, both published by Globe Pequot.)

Now, just think about *this* happy thought: Wouldn't two million US workers taking early retirement translate into two million job opportunities for unemployed workers?

RESEARCH METHODS

One thing we are completely convinced of: You cannot find the right retirement location by studying statistics. A computer can't swallow a bunch of numbers and then spit out the "ideal" place for you to spend the rest of your life. It isn't that simple. Retirement guides based on statistics can give you only part of the story.

Over the years we've visited almost all the communities described in this book before evaluating them as suitable places for retirement. Of course, it would be impossible to visit *all* potential retirement locations in the United States. Instead, we travel to regions of the country where people tend to retire, then we critique a few key towns and communities typical of that region. This research has been ongoing for more than 20 years.

We visit neighborhoods, residential developments, and senior citizens' centers. We look at shopping, entertainment, recreational opportunities, and medical care. We regularly interview chambers of commerce, talk with managers and residents of retirement complexes, and chat with retired couples and singles. We visit real estate offices and interview salespeople. It turns out that many real estate professionals are retirees themselves. They enjoy the sociability of their jobs, the chance to meet new people, and, of course, the opportunity to pick up a few commissions. They're especially helpful because they understand the problems involved in moving to a new community.

We learn which neighborhoods retirees prefer, and we visit to see for ourselves. We use US government publications, drawing statistics from the US Census Bureau, the Department of Labor, and National Oceanographic Administration weather charts. The Consumer Price Index and the American Chamber of Commerce Researchers Association also supply us with trends.

Over the years we've investigated hundreds of popular retirement towns and examined many different lifestyles before making the final selections for this book. Just because a town is not described here, however, doesn't necessarily mean it wouldn't be a great place to retire. We hope this book will help you conduct your own research.

1

Finding Your Shangri-la

Most people eagerly look forward to retirement as a reward for toiling many long years, for getting up every morning and trudging off to the workplace whether you feel like it or not. You look forward to weekends off and dread going back to work on Monday, always wondering whether vacation time will ever arrive.

Then suddenly, you are set free! You can decide for yourself what you want to do today, tomorrow, and forever. You are free to create whatever lifestyle you can imagine. One exciting possibility for a new retirement lifestyle is choosing a new hometown. It's tempting to picture starting all over again, with new friends and new recreational opportunities, perhaps in a climate that doesn't involve snow shovels. That's the goal for many future retirees. But, *which* hometown? *Which* lifestyle?

Their parents' retirement styles will not be in the picture for the baby boomer generation. Choosing a new hometown involves much more than finding a nice climate and counting the number of nearby trout streams and golf courses. You'll need to do some research on your own.

Over the past several years, a growing trend was for workers to take early pensions or accept buyouts at younger ages. Downsizing, "golden parachutes," and "job outsourcing" reinforced this early retirement trend. Actually, "retirement" is not a term this younger crowd chooses to use. "Life transition" might be a better term. Of those retiring today, a large percentage would like to continue working, at least in a part-time or perhaps a consulting capacity. Some have plans to turn that extra bedroom into a home office.

Then, along came recession and massive unemployment to derail many well-thought-out retirement plans. Those who didn't lose their jobs began to look upon employment and a steady paycheck as a blessing. Another failure of many retirement plans was the collapse of the real estate market.

Those counting on inflated home equities to subsidize a luxurious lifestyle after retirement are finding themselves with negative mortgages, their expected profits vanished. Many are deciding to postpone retirement, at least for a while. Others, suddenly out of work with no job prospects, find themselves forced into early retirement. This shift of economic conditions makes careful planning essential.

BEST PLACES TO RETIRE?

Occasionally this writer gets a request from a magazine to write an article describing the "Twenty Best Places for Retirement." The editor expects me to rank towns and cities from 1 to 20, as if I were rating baseball teams. With a baseball team you can check wins, losses, and other statistics— people can't argue with statistics. But cities and towns don't score wins and losses, except in somebody's mind. What would be a perfect place for my wife and me could spell total disaster for you. (I always try to change the assigned magazine article's title from "Twenty Best Towns" to "Twenty *Great* Towns.")

Retirement writers often award favorable recommendations on the basis of factors that rarely affect retirees. For example, quality high schools and cultural amenities such as museums and operas receive high marks in retirement analyses. Yet how much will a secondary-school system matter to you? How many times a month will you be going to a museum or an opera? Would you rather live in a town with 10 golf courses and no museums, or 10 museums and no golf courses? Will you be satisfied living in a state where it's against the law for a restaurant to serve wine with dinner? Where you'll have to drive to a neighboring state to even *purchase* wine? Or where 98 percent of the population is of a different political persuasion than you?

Much is made of economic conditions, such as unemployment or state budget problems. Yet most retirees are not dependent on jobs to supplement their incomes. If finding work is a critical issue, retirees might be best staying where they are, where they have contacts for possible employment. Furthermore, a state government's budget won't affect a retiree nearly as much as the household budget.

Often retirement writers rank states by "tax burdens." This is misleading, because when a state gives you a break on income taxes, chances are it will make it up on higher property taxes, sales taxes, and so on. Yes, you might save a few hundred tax dollars a year by living in Kansas rather than Florida, but where would you be happier? Look at the tax table later on in this chapter, and you'll see how some states play games with taxes.

Rather than writing off a state as a retirement possibility because someone claims it's a "high tax" state, you should look at the *type* of state taxes and how these taxes will affect the kinds of income and assets that *you* have. For example, if you receive a substantial military pension, you might favor one of the 20 states that exempt military pensions. Of the states profiled in this book, the following do not tax military pensions: Alabama, Arkansas, Connecticut, Louisiana, Maine, Massachusetts, Mississippi, and Missouri. It's up to you to decide whether or not living in one of these states would be worth the taxes saved.

The bottom line: To find your ideal location, you're going to have to do your own ranking, to match your own preferences.

Ideally you'll start your retirement analysis early. A great way to do this is by combining research with your vacations. Instead of visiting the same old place each year, try different parts of the country. Check out each location as a possible place to retire. Look at real estate, medical care, and recreation. What about libraries? (An appalling number are closing because of lack of funds.) Does this town offer the types of cultural events you enjoy? Cultural events can be anything from concerts and stage plays to square-dance lessons, bowling tournaments, or chili cook-offs. Will you fit in culturally and socially and be accepted and welcomed by your neighbors? The point is: Will this be the ideal hometown for you?

The local chamber of commerce can be an excellent source of information. Make sure to ask if the community has a "retiree attraction committee" or "retiree welcoming committee." This growing concept of welcoming retirees into a community is sometimes coordinated through the chamber of commerce. A welcoming committee can be a marvelous way to make friends and to adjust to your new surroundings. At the end of each retirement town's review, we supply the chamber of commerce's telephone number and address, as well as its website.

If you can't or don't care to travel, you can do research on the Internet simply by searching the names of the towns that interest you. It's amazing how much you can learn. If you don't have a computer, use one in your local library. It used to be that libraries subscribed to a variety of out-of-town newspapers from larger cities. But with the decline of the newspaper industry, surviving newspapers are shrinking to the point where your best source of local information is the Internet.

You can learn much about a community by browsing a community's online newspaper. If drunk-driving arrests are top news stories, you have one picture of crime. If murders, home break-ins, and other mayhem are so common that they receive little attention, you get another image. Check real estate prices, rentals, and community events; compare them with your hometown expenses and activities and you'll begin to get a picture of relative costs and social life. If you don't know how to browse the Internet, ask your grandkids to show you. You'll love it!

WHAT TO LOOK FOR

Following is a list of requirements we personally consider essential for a successful retirement relocation. Your needs may be different; feel free to add or subtract from the list, and then use it to measure communities against your standards.

- **Safety.** Can you walk through your chosen neighborhood without fearful glances over your shoulder? Can you leave your home for a few weeks without dreading a break-in?

- **Climate.** Will temperatures and weather patterns match your lifestyle? Will you be tempted to go outdoors and exercise year-round, or will harsh winters and suffocating summers confine you to an easy chair in front of the television set?

- **Housing.** Is quality housing available at a price you are willing and able to pay? Is the area visually pleasing, free of pollution and traffic snarls? Will you feel proud to live in the neighborhood?

- **Nourishment for Your Interests.** Does your retirement choice offer facilities for your favorite pastimes, cultural events, and hobbies, be they hunting, fishing, adult education, art centers, or whatever?

- **Social Compatibility.** Will you find common interests with your neighbors? Will you fit in and make friends easily? Will there be folks with your own cultural, social, and political background?

- **Affordability.** Are goods and services reasonably priced? Will you be able to afford to hire help from time to time when you need to? Will your income be significantly affected by state income taxes? Will taxes on your pension make a big difference?

- **Distance from Family and Friends.** Are you going to be too far away or in a location where nobody wants to visit? Would you rather they don't visit? (In that case you might do better even farther away.)

- **Jobs and/or Volunteer Opportunities.** Will there be enough interesting volunteer jobs or paid jobs (if that's what you want) to satisfy your need for keeping busy? What about continuing-education programs at the local college?

- **Transportation.** Does your new location have intercity bus transportation or train connections? Many small towns have none, which makes you totally dependent on an automobile or taxis. How far is the nearest airport with passenger airline connections? Can friends and family visit without having to drive their automobile or spend a fortune on taxis from the airport?

- **A Lively and Safe Downtown.** Does your town or city have a town center with restaurants, shopping, and places to meet friends? Or it is a place of abandoned businesses with boarded-up windows, pawnshops, and secondhand stores? Will you be satisfied doing all your shopping out on the strip malls on the highway around town? For some people, this is not a problem.

- **Your Favorite Vacation Destination.** People often think of retirement as a permanent vacation. Nothing wrong with that. But before you pack up the proverbial lock, stock, and barrel to move to that beach town or mountain village where you've enjoyed spending your regular two-week vacations, ask yourself these questions: Will I be happy living there year-round? Will I become bored with trout fishing after a couple of months? Will I enjoy the beach during the winter, when my summer-resident friends have returned home, when most shops and restaurants are closed, and when northern winds sweep in with sleet, snow, and ice storms? *Think it over!*

EVALUATING HEALTH CARE

An important issue is the availability and quality of health care in your new hometown. Especially important is the quality of local hospital facilities. This is all but impossible to research objectively. Especially in smaller towns, the usual sources of information about health care quality are either the local chamber of commerce or the hospital's website. Understandably, both sources will claim that medical care and facilities in the community are top-notch and highly rated. Yet when we talk with local people, we sometimes get a different story.

Since local residents are rarely qualified to give expert opinions on medical issues, we've tried asking the hospital staff directly. That doesn't work either, because neither office personnel nor doctors are willing to criticize their employers or their colleagues. Of course, just about all larger cities have optimal hospital facilities to take care of major health problems, and smaller communities nearby can take advantage of the health care available in the population center. But in many smaller, more isolated communities, medical services can be limited to emergency care. (Sometimes the chamber of commerce fails to mention this.)

Here is a way to obtain reliable information about local health facilities via the Internet: Go to health.usnews.com/best-hospitals/rankings and enter the community's name and the state. This brings up a page listing all hospitals in that community, as well as those within a distance of 30 miles or so. When you click on the name of the hospital, you'll find a page that describes the hospital, its specialties, and rankings. Of special interest is the Patient Satisfaction Survey (a federal program), where recently discharged patients are asked to evaluate their stay in the hospital. If you are covered by Medicare, it's important to find out whether doctors in your community tend to accept Medicare patients. Medicare regularly monitors rates of reimbursement, which means doctors might earn less for office visits and various procedures. Also, there's often a delay before doctors are reimbursed from Medicare. Many doctors have dropped out of the program, leaving Medicare patients with fewer alternatives. This could narrow your choice of doctors.

Be aware that most HMOs will not offer coverage in unprofitable communities (especially those with low-density populations). Some HMOs have been known to discontinue their health care programs without notice, leaving clients in a precarious position of finding an insurance company willing to issue them coverage.

Finally, at the time of revising this book, the status of Medicare and Medicaid is in flux with changing government administrations. The revised versions of this insurance could possibly not only cover those age 65 and over, but *all* who join the program, no matter what their age. If this works out, millions of employees who cannot quit their jobs without losing health care could feel safe to retire early, without risking financial ruin from unexpected medical bills. This could change many retirement plans! (As well as provide openings for underemployed job seekers.)

OVER-50 COMMUNITIES

Over the years retirement has become a big business, prompting impressive corporate investment. Planned adult-only communities, some of astounding size, are popping up all over the country. These complexes are usually centered on a lake, golf course, or some natural attraction. Sometimes these are "gated" communities; that is, to enter the property you must be a member of that development or have good reason to be there. Round-the-clock guards often staff the gates, scrutinizing everyone who enters.

Sometimes private developments are "open" communities—without gates—yet are still age-restricted. Some are enormous. Arizona's Sun City West, for example, has more than 15,000 homes on 7,100 acres, with a population of well over 40,000. Its neighboring development, Sun City Grand, promises to be even larger. Most of these developments restrict buyers to those age 50 and older; youngsters may visit but may not live there. This affects the community in several ways. Obviously your lives will be more tranquil without gangs of kids riding bikes, playing loud music, or knocking baseballs through your living room window. You'll also enjoy a lower crime rate. Burglaries, vandalism, and theft usually occur in direct proportion to the number of teenagers in the neighborhood. Residents of over-50 developments report a secure feeling about their neighborhoods.

The other side of the coin is that many retirees relish the idea of living in mixed-generation neighborhoods. They find young children and teenagers fun to be with. You'll often hear them say, "I can't imagine a more dreary and stifling situation—living in a same-age community! We want to socialize with young people as well as those our own age and older."

However, they will find that mixed-generation communities tend to segregate into age groups anyway. How? When you want to play golf or go fishing, your younger neighbors have to go to work. When you have a barbecue and a few drinks in the backyard, they have a Cub Scout meeting scheduled. Instead of joining you for a concert or a play, your neighbors have to attend a PTA meeting or would rather relax in front of the television after a hard day's work. Just because they're called "mixed-generation communities" doesn't mean the mixed generations actually *mix* socially with each other!

Many organized adult-only communities have a built-in benefit: When you are unloading your furniture from the moving van, a social director will be there, asking about hobbies, sports, and recreational preferences, ready to put you in touch with kindred spirits in the community. You'll find instant friends with interests similar to yours. The bottom line is that age-restricted developments are selling a *lifestyle* as much as real estate.

MOVING TO THE COUNTRY

You might picture living in a rural or backwoods community as being the ultimate in get-away-from-it-all living. It's nice to enjoy an incredibly low cost of living, with housing at giveaway prices. Yet we have mixed feelings about recommending retirement in some inexpensive areas—particularly rural, farming communities—to folks from big-city backgrounds.

When you share few common interests with your neighbors, it's easy to feel left out. When almost everyone in the community is in some way involved in agriculture, ordinary conversations tend to dwell on the price of soybeans or the best way to de-worm hogs. When your agricultural experience is limited to watering houseplants, you find you have few words of wisdom others care to hear. When your accent sounds funny to your neighbors, when your tastes in movies, politics, and food are different (or when you don't even own a *pickup*), you could feel like an alien from another planet.

Seriously, in view of the polarized political climate in the United States today, it might be important for people with strong political views to investigate the political climate of small, isolated communities where conflict might be unavoidable. All too often, outsiders have difficulties becoming accepted in small-town society. Starting off as a maverick isn't going to help. You might find yourself very lonely. Of course, communities with large numbers of retirees from other parts of the country are usually much easier for outsiders to find their niche.

COLLEGE TOWN RETIREMENT

During the process of researching and selecting our favorite places for retirement, my wife and I began noticing something curious. Almost every one of our favorite locations happened to have a college or university as one of its features. At first we assumed this to be a coincidence. After all, we liked each of these places for its own personality and individual characteristics, conditions that scarcely seem connected with the presence or absence of a school.

Now, one characteristic of our favorite towns has always been a lively downtown business center, one that serves as the focus of the community, a place local residents use for shopping, entertainment, and socialization. A place to meet friends for lunch or dinner. Yet throughout the nation business districts of many towns and small cities have been practically abandoned as strip malls and megastores established themselves out on the highway bypass. Downtown merchants and businesses fled the city center in a mass migration, as they moved—lock, stock, and pizza parlor—to the outskirts of town. Left behind are shabby town centers with neglected buildings and boarded-up storefronts, with perhaps a few lonely secondhand shops. Often, the downtown is all but deserted.

For some very logical reasons, this seldom happens to a college town. Students are not overly fond of hanging out at strip malls. Instead, they patronize downtown restaurants, stores, and entertainment, preferably within walking or biking distance of the campus. With thousands of students, faculty, and college support staff as customers, most of them with money in their pockets, you can bet that successful merchants stay put and others eagerly rent any vacated stores.

Many a college town's historical central district is thus rescued from oblivion. Strolling down a college town's main street is like stepping back in time 50 years. People smile at you as you pass, stores are open and welcoming your business, and you might even find an old-fashioned movie theater—the Bijou or Rex—single screen, with the smell of buttered popcorn. In other words, things are pretty much as they were when we were kids.

Delightful side benefits of college town living include school sporting events, concerts, lectures, drama, light opera, and lots more, with many such offerings free to the public. And college towns are known for low crime rates: The yearly *FBI Uniform Crime Report* regularly shows unusually low incidences of crime in these communities.

Another occasional advantage to college town living is reasonable real estate. This isn't universally true, but many smaller college towns do offer bargain real estate prices compared with similar towns elsewhere. With perhaps 20 percent of the population being students on limited budgets and another large percent working as beginning teachers or support staff, housing prices can't be bid up past consumers' ability to pay. A tip: Choose a quiet neighborhood, away from fraternity-house row, where round-the-clock music can be so loud it peels wallpaper off your bedroom walls. (Just joking.)

COST OF LIVING

The most comprehensive research on the cost of living in the United States is done by the American Chamber of Commerce Researchers Association (ACCRA). They tabulate the cost of groceries, real estate, utilities, and other everyday necessities and publish them quarterly. Usually, this book presents cost of living statistics for each community profiled here. However, because of today's unsettled economic conditions, it's almost impossible to gauge the cost of living through normal statistical research.

For example, a major element in finding your ideal hometown is the price of real estate. Normally, home costs are estimated by reporting the median sales price of homes in a community. (Median sales price means that half of the homes being sold in an area are sold above the median sales price, and half of the homes are sold for less.) This gives you an indication of real estate trends and prices in a given town. At present, however, this figure is often meaningless. Why? Because at the time of this writing, many home sales are either foreclosures or distress sales because of job loss. If this isn't bad enough, many potential buyers are holding off, waiting for prices to hit the bottom.

But, how do we know when real estate prices have reached the bottom? As an example: We once noticed a small, upscale beach community reporting a median real estate sales index of only $85,000! (Normally, homes selling in that community would be priced above $400,000.) The $85,000 price brought the cost of living index way down for that community. Not understanding how property could possibly be priced so low, we called a real estate professional in that community for an explanation. The answer was: "For the month in question, the only real estate transaction was a mobile home on its own lot for $85,000!"

Local boosters too often place undue emphasis on a low cost of living and cheap real estate as the prime attractions of their communities. True, these items go hand in hand; that is, when you find low-cost housing, you'll usually find economical living costs in general. In our travels we've encountered places where $95,000 will buy a nice three-bedroom home, where carpenters will remodel for $12 an hour, and where haircuts are still $9.50. However, inexpensive living isn't necessarily the same as quality living. Although some low-cost areas are exceptional bargains—combining a high quality of life with welcoming neighbors and pleasant surroundings—other low-cost areas can be intensely dreary and boring, and, even worse, high-crime areas.

Why is the cost of living and housing dramatically less in some localities? Basically you'll find two reasons for cheap real estate and low rents. The most common reason: an undesirable place to live. These towns steadily lose population because they have absolutely nothing going for them—no jobs, no charm, no nothing. Homes sell for rock-bottom prices because eager sellers outnumber reluctant buyers. Unless you are sincerely dedicated to boredom, bad weather, and cable TV, these may not be places you would seek out for retirement.

The second reason: an unforeseen and disastrous business slump or other circumstances that suddenly cause the job market to disintegrate. When this happens, people don't necessarily want to leave and seek work elsewhere, but they find they have to. Homes go on the real estate market at giveaway prices because sellers have no other choice. This doesn't necessarily make a desirable community turn into a lemon. It's always possible that this could be an opportunity for those looking for an affordable place for relocation. Two examples of this type of disaster for local residents, but a possible bonanza for those seeking real estate bargains, would be a factory closing and production being shipped overseas, or a proposed military base closure.

As an aside, I might mention that a few years ago, Fort Ord, near our home in California, was closed, and all personnel were relocated to Fort Lewis, Washington. A friend of ours bought a condo from a departing military family at a bargain price. Today its value has increased fourfold.

Although situations like this are personal tragedies for displaced families, they open windows of opportunity for retired folks. Because jobs and regular weekly paychecks aren't essential for many retired couples, quality real estate could become theirs for a fraction of what similar housing would cost elsewhere. As younger couples with growing children move away, older people often move in and raise the ratio between retired and working people to unusual levels. Retirees occasionally become a majority of voters, and can wield appreciable influence over local government and political processes.

WORKING DURING RETIREMENT

A generation ago the question of working when retired would seem out of place in a book on retirement. Used to be, most people worked until age 65 or older, then eagerly looked forward to the day they no longer had to get up every morning, down a cup of coffee, and drag themselves off to work. The ideal was a house on the golf course or a home by a bass lake. If someone merely changed jobs or went into business for himself or herself, how could that person be retired?

How things have changed! For one, the average age of those leaving the workplace has rapidly decreased as early baby boomers achieved financial success. Ironically, finding themselves underemployed in a sluggish economy, baby boomers trend toward early retirement. Not necessarily because they *want* to retire early. Often it's because their jobs disappear or move overseas, and they have to either retire or find another job.

As mentioned previously, many consider themselves *relocating* rather than retiring. They often relocate within striking distance of their former employer's business base, or similar enterprises, to keep their hand in the job market, if only on a consulting basis. This is why some southern states are popular with those leaving jobs in the industrialized areas of New England and the Great Lakes regions. If they are planning on consulting jobs, vacation-replacement employment, or other connections with former employers, it's much more convenient to commute to New York from North Carolina or Florida than from California or Arizona.

Many people just *think* they need a job. The real problem is, they've always worked and are horrified at the prospect of suddenly not having anything meaningful to do. The curse of the work ethic is all too real; after all those years of toil, folks tend to feel guilty or even decadent when they no longer leap out of bed at 6:30 a.m. and scurry off to a job. Too often those who don't really need the income end up working just for the sake of working.

This work ethic is understandable and difficult to leave behind. Our recommendation is that if you cannot find enough to do around the house, then volunteer. As a volunteer, you will not only be doing meaningful work, but also you'll meet others in the community, widen your network of friends, and lay the groundwork for later years when you may need volunteers to help you. A special bonus is that your services will be sincerely appreciated and valued more highly than if you were to work in a fast-food restaurant or some other high-competition, low-paying job, trying to please an employer you don't like in the first place.

Let's take the case of our friend Katharine, a retired librarian who lived in a tiny apartment in Monterey, California. Her rent was $1,400 a month. To supplement her retirement income, she took a part-time job in a bookstore that paid $100 a month after taxes. When she moved to a small town in coastal Oregon, she found another small apartment for $900 a month, with a view of the Pacific Ocean. Part-time jobs in small towns like this often pay minimum wage, or less, but even so, the part-time jobs were all filled. However, Katharine discovered that the $500 she saved in rent made up for the $500 she had been earning at her bookstore job. In other words, she had been working just to pay higher rent. Now she devotes her time to art classes and satisfying volunteer work in the community, and manages to live just fine on her retirement pension and Social Security.

TAXES

Property taxes vary by state and locality, with states like Arkansas or Alabama taking less than Arizona or California. But choosing retirement in Alabama over Arizona simply to save a few dollars a year would be foolish, unless Alabama has everything you want in the way of retirement and Arizona lacks something important. Taxes are just one component of many elements.

Just because a state has no individual income taxes or sales tax doesn't necessarily mean the total tax burden will be less. States have ways of making up the difference. No income tax? Don't rejoice so quickly—higher property taxes and sales taxes will make up the deficit. No sales tax? You can be sure the state will figure out another way to tax you.

If you are like most retirees, much of your income will be lower. A lot of it will come from tax-deductible pensions and Social Security benefits. In that case, state income taxes may not be all that serious. (Of course, some states tax Social Security and pensions.) On the other hand, if you're in a high-income bracket, elevated tax rates could be significant, so you might consider a state that taxes income lightly or not at all. Those states without individual income taxes are Alaska, Florida, Nevada, New Hampshire, South Dakota, Tennessee, Texas, Washington, and Wyoming.

According to the Tax Foundation (a Washington, D.C., think tank), New Jersey, California, New York, Hawaii, and Minnesota are the least taxpayer-friendly states, while Alaska, Florida, South Dakota, and Wyoming are the most taxpayer-friendly. However, except for Alaska, I'm not sure I agree with their conclusions.

Take a look at the tax burden table on page 15, and compare the tax burdens on citizens in different areas. (The table is based on a couple with an income of $60,000 a year, living in a home assessed at $225,000.) For example: Taxpayers in Oregon—where state income taxes are collected—pay state and local taxes of $4,777. Taxpayers in Washington—where there is no state income tax—pay $4,548; a difference of $237 a year, or about $20 a month. Not likely to affect a budget. (By the way, Oregon doesn't collect sales tax, so the state makes up the difference elsewhere in the property tax structure.)

Another example: A couple living in Texas—which does not collect income taxes—will pay $41 a month *more* to live in Texas than just across the state line in New Mexico, where state income taxes *are* collected! Look at the figures for Florida, another state that doesn't tax income. Even so, Florida is one of the highest-tax states listed in our chart, second only to Texas. So much for saving on income taxes! The bottom line: It costs money to operate a state government, and the state *will* collect that money, one way or another.

Certainly, if you are living in a high-tax state such as New Jersey or Indiana, where you are paying double or triple what you might pay in another state, this could influence your move. Or you might have an unusually high income, such that a no–income tax state would make sense. But aside from that, don't allow tax bills to be your main concern. Think about climate, nearness to friends and relatives, recreation, and outdoor activities. Consider cultural events, medical care, access to transportation, and all the other items that will affect your lifestyle. It would be an enormous mistake to relocate in a community where you could be unhappy, simply for the sake of saving a few dollars a month.

EXAMPLES OF TAX BURDENS IN VARIOUS STATES

State	City	Property Tax	Personal Tax	Sales Tax	State Tax	Total Burden
AL	Dothan	$731	$240	$2,055	$1,322	$4,358
AZ	Lake Havasu City	$1,842	$563	$1,736	$594	$4,735
AR	Fayetteville	$2,252	$383	$2,362	$1,129	$6,125
CA	San Diego	$2,407	$360	$1,714	$155	$4,636
CO	Boulder	$1,575	$539	$1,930	$437	$4,481
FL	Fort Lauderdale	$4,707	$81	$1,327	No Tax	$6,115
GA	Athens	$2,604	$406	$1,655	$98	$4,763
ID	Boise	$2,259	$159	$1,284	$784	$3,446
KY	Danville	$2,222	$371	$1,327	$1,512	$5,432
LA	Baton Rouge	$1,579	$24	$2,134	$455	$4,192
ME	Camden	$2,785	$681	$1,156	$891	$5,725
MA	Cape Cod	$1,229	$508	$1,010	$1,466	$4,213
MS	Hattiesburg	$2,733	$845	$1,915	$269	$5,762
NV	Carson City	$1,990	$557	$1,576	No Tax	$4,123
NM	Albuquerque	$3,278	$124	$1,586	$956	$5,944
NC	Asheville	$2,512	$398	$1,564	$1,510	$5,984
OK	Grand Lake	$2,185	$185	$2,286	$918	$5,574
OR	Portland	$2,765	$75	No Tax	$1,937	$4,777
SC	Aiken	$1,926	$571	$1,505	No Tax	$4,002
TN	Crossville	$1,317	$48	$2,469	No Tax	$3,834
TX	Austin	$4,476	$145	$1,825	No Tax	$6,446
UT	Cedar City	$1,523	$372	$1,575	$1,374	$4,844
VT	Burlington	$3,870	$120	$1,629	$56	$5,678
VA	Charlottesville	$2,120	$709	$1,296	$141	$4,266
WA	Seattle	$2,347	$234	$1,959	No Tax	$4,540
WV	Princeton	$1,695	$523	$1,505	$1,094	$4,817

Data from Eve Evans and Elizabeth Niven, *America's Best Low-Tax Retirement Towns* (Houston: Vacation Publications, 2008)

REAL ESTATE PRICES

Throughout this book you will find references to real estate prices somewhat vague, and deliberately so. The problem with quoting specific home prices in a book on retirement is that prices can, and possibly will, be out of date before the book is delivered to the bookstores! Since the last edition of *Where to Retire*, the market has stabilized in most areas of the country. The wave of foreclosures has smoothed out, and most areas of the country are seeing a steady increase in value.

To get an idea of current real estate trends for possible retirement communities, you can find some interesting and up-to-date charts furnished by the National Association of Realtors website at: realtor.org/research/research/metroprice. The figures are revised every quarter, and you can see how much prices have changed over the past three years.

However, do *not* make retirement decisions on the basis of surprisingly low-cost home prices. Allow me to point out that there could be a very good reason why homes are so inexpensive in some towns: Anyone in their right mind would *not* choose to live there. Your job will be to keep abreast of trends. Then decide whether to invest in a home before prices recover, or rent until asking prices take an even more significant dip. Don't rely only on what you read here—this writer has been predicting the collapse of the California real estate market for 30 years! In the meantime our very ordinary California home, purchased 35 years ago, has increased in value many times over.

THE MOBILE-HOME ALTERNATIVE

Why are they called "mobile homes"? That's a good question. For years manufacturers have struggled to change the terminology to "manufactured homes." Obviously they are anything but *mobile*. Few of them have any trace of the wheels that were used to move them to their locations. Since "manufactured" never caught on, we'll continue saying "mobile."

For people searching for a magic, low-cost path to home ownership, we recommend investigating the possibility of mobile-home living. Now before you turn up your nose and start visualizing a "trailer park" inhabited by welfare recipients, allow me to explain. Those classically rundown facilities, ravaged by screaming children and indigent parents, are easy to avoid. Simply look for those advertising high-quality *adults-only* facilities.

They'll have names ending with "Mobile Estates" or "Village" or "Manor." Avoid places with signs such as "Jake's Trailer Park and Motorcycle Repair." Do *not* consider mobile-home parks where monthly rentals are allowed. (The park's management has no control over who might be renting there.) Check out the ambience, and remember that it's worthwhile to pay a higher monthly rent in a higher-quality mobile-home park.

To sum up: For those who cannot afford to buy a conventional home, or those who have just gone through a foreclosure, a mobile home could be a practical alternative to renting conventional housing. You might be astounded at the wide range of lifestyles made possible by mobile-home living.

Top-end facilities offer luxurious, country club–style surroundings, professional landscaping, swimming pools, and deluxe clubhouses. We've looked at developments with customized mobile homes that are almost impossible to distinguish from conventional homes you might expect to see in a gated golf course development. (Actually, many mobile-home parks *are* golf course communities.) We've seen these deluxe homes priced as high as $350,000. At the other end of the spectrum are small, economical, no-frills parks with little more than laundry facilities and a club room for socializing and playing bridge. Depending on the setting, inexpensive mobile-home parks can be just the ticket for those on limited budgets. We've checked out double-wide units in quiet adult parks where $40,000 would buy an adequate home. An advantage is, in *some* states, mobile homes are not subject to property taxes. Instead, a yearly license plate or fee is an economical substitute for property taxes.

Both styles of parks can be in the same area of town, often within a mile or two of each other. Nothing wrong with the lower-rent, no-children places if you cannot afford the luxury layout. Sometimes the smaller and simple places have the most friendly neighbors. But, do your research!

From our point of view, a mobile home is a viable alternative for those who cannot afford to buy a conventional home and do not care to rent. However, our firm opinion is: If you cannot pay *cash* for your mobile home, you cannot afford to buy it! Always remember that, unlike a conventional home, mobile homes *depreciate* over the years, rather than appreciate. Fortunately, the wide range of mobile-home prices and park rents make it possible for most people to buy without financing.

Apart from the money you have invested in your mobile home, your monthly budget outlay for park rent could be less than half of what you'd have to pay to rent an ordinary house or apartment. This assumes that you take our advice and do not buy something you cannot afford, and end up making stiff mortgage payments.

CHOOSING YOUR CLIMATE

All your working life you've heroically put up with whatever inconveniences, insults, and misery your local weather dumped on you. The good news is that when you retire, you no longer have to take it. You can search for a perfect climate and live happily ever after. The bad news is that there is no such thing as a *perfect* climate!

Retirees in Maine love their summers but think it's too cold in the winter. Their retired friends in Miami love Florida winters but complain because summers can be hot and muggy. Florida newcomers say they miss the change of seasons. Parts of California have what we consider the best overall climate—sunny, relatively bug-free, and comfortable, with low humidity most of the year. Yet native Californians grumble when occasional winter days drop below 50 degrees and winter rains keep them from walking along the beach or sunning beside the pool.

Even though you can't find the perfect climate, you certainly can find one that suits you best. And chances are, you'll find one far superior to the weather you've had to put up with all those working years. One of the exciting things about retirement is that, for the first time in your life, work doesn't dictate where you must live. You now have a choice in the matter.

Another advantage of being footloose and fancy-free is you needn't lock yourself into one weather pattern. You can choose any combination of climates that fits your new lifestyle. Many people use their hometowns as base camps, enjoying a glorious spring and a lazy summer, and then head south to Florida, Southern California, or Arizona to enjoy a warm and sunny fall and winter. Some retirees choose Mexico or Costa Rica for their second homes as an escape from the coldest winter months.

It takes a little gumption to get started "following the sun," but many thousands do just that, and they love it! (To consider foreign retirement alternatives, check out our books: *Choose Costa Rica for Retirement* or *Choose Mexico for Retirement*, both published by Globe Pequot.)

PERSONAL SAFETY

Most people agree that crime can be a major problem in some areas of the United States. It's true that crime rates are dropping dramatically in most parts of the country, but there are still neighborhoods where people are practically prisoners in their own homes. Instead of criminals being behind bars, some law-abiding citizens find themselves hiding behind barred windows and chained doors.

There is little we, as private citizens, can do about any of this. Your only solution is to find a safe place to live. Curiously, in neighborhoods not so very far away from high-crime areas, people can leave their doors unlocked and walk home from a late movie without anxiety. There are still places almost as calm as they used to be when we were children. Remember when kids used to play outside long after dark? Remember when people seldom locked their front doors? In our research we've come across many locations with *almost* that same safe feeling of those good old days. (I say *almost* because conditions have changed, even in the best of places.)

A few years ago this writer and his wife bought a summer home in a small Oregon town (population less than 100). When we inquired about safety, we discovered that most residents never locked their cars. And some even left their keys in the ignition so they wouldn't lose them! On the other hand, friends who lived in a nearby, much larger city also didn't lock their cars—but for an entirely different reason. Automobile break-ins were so common in their neighborhood that a locked car was an invitation for a thief to break the window to see if something valuable might be inside. Yet in the better neighborhoods of that same city, auto break-ins were rare.

FINDING A SAFE PLACE TO LIVE

The bottom line is, there is no such thing as a crime-free area. As long as people live in social groups, there will always be individuals who don't care to distinguish between their belongings and those of their neighbors. It just stands to reason that the larger the social group, the more deviant individuals it produces. Therefore, you'll find much higher crime rates in Washington, D.C., than in Walla Walla, Washington, and more crime in New York City than in New Madrid, Missouri. On the other hand, just because a town is peaceful doesn't make it a great place to live. It could also be so boring that burglars and robbers can't stand working there, or perhaps it's so cold in the winter that auto thieves can't get the cars started.

Generally speaking, the larger the city, the higher the crime rate. Yet most big cities have neighborhoods just as safe as nearby suburbs and smaller towns. These are usually middle-class, low-turnover neighborhoods, places where residents know each other and where most people are over the age of 50. For example, Hermosa Beach, an affluent suburb in the Los Angeles metropolitan area, ranks exceptionally high in safety—often at the top of the FBI's list of safest towns—yet it's just 20 minutes away from some of the most crime-ridden neighborhoods in the country.

You can learn a great deal about a community by simply driving around and observing. Are the homes neat, with trimmed shrubbery and mowed lawns? Or are they shabby, obviously owned by absentee landlords? Do foreclosure signs and boarded-up windows draw your attention? Do you see old junk autos parked around the neighborhood in various states of repair, with teenagers trying to repair them? Or do you see folks your own age working in their yards, walking the dog, or polishing the car? The best way to ascertain a neighborhood's safety is to simply ask the residents. If folks feel safe living there, they're happy to tell you all about it. If they offer to lend you a weapon to protect yourself, it's probably not a safe neighborhood!

In this book we've used the latest version of the FBI's annual publication "Crime in the United States" to help analyze personal safety of a community. Although FBI statistics are quite detailed, they often do not provide a solid basis for comparing crime rates among communities. This is because not all police departments file crime reports with the FBI. Therefore, our analysis of personal safety for a community is based partly on FBI reports, but is also influenced by our personal observations and interviews with folks living in the community.

WHY NOT MY STATE?

Occasionally we receive letters from readers demanding to know why we didn't include their home states: Iowa, Illinois, or Indiana, for example. "What do you have against my state?" they inquire. "It's a wonderful place to retire." Other readers complain that we don't cover places in North Dakota, Montana, or other cold-weather states that often receive lavish praise from retirement writers.

Aside from the obvious explanation that it would be impossible to cover all communities in one book, there are two reasons for limiting coverage. Let's take Montana as an example. We've been there in the summer and can vouch for the fact that it's a delightful place, in an exceptionally beautiful part of the country. Places like Glacier National Park make the Big Sky country a wonderful place to visit. And most of those who were born and raised in Montana will surely retire there when they leave their jobs, just as most retirees in Pittsburgh, Omaha, and Milwaukee probably will never move away from their home states.

However, we think it's irresponsible to encourage those from Pittsburgh, Omaha, or Milwaukee to leave one cold-winter climate to move to an equally cold and frigid environment just for the sake of a few glorious summer months. If you've decided to relocate, why not choose someplace comfortable? For those who love snow, surely the 40 to 45 total inches per season in hometown Pittsburgh or Omaha should suffice. But in places like Montana or North Dakota, winter often begins in October, with an average 3-foot snowpack that can remain until April. From our point of view, it's far better to stay in your hometown or move to a place with a pleasantly warm winter climate, and then make summer visits to the northland when you can really enjoy it.

Weather aside, our retirement selections are mostly communities where people actually *do* relocate, places most people consider appropriate for a new beginning. To take book space away from well-liked retirement destinations and dedicate it to describing places that few people would be interested in would be counterproductive. Of course, there is nothing wrong with the idea of retiring in Iowa, Minnesota, or South Dakota. However, very few future retirees from these states harbor a burning passion to move to Iowa, Michigan, or North Dakota. Statistics clearly show that for every thousand retirees who move out of northern, cold-winter states, only a tiny handful relocate to other cold-winter states. Even then, most moves are for a specific reason, such as returning to the old hometown, to where family members live, or to a college town where weather and location aren't all-important.

THE MOST POPULAR STATES FOR RELOCATION

The three most popular states for retirement or relocation are Florida, California, and Arizona, in that order. All three have one thing in common:

pleasant winter temperatures. This tells us that climate is a major factor in deciding where to relocate. Also popular are the states of Oregon and Washington, where coastal communities enjoy mild winters as well as cool summers. The southeast coastal states of North Carolina and South Carolina are narrowing the gap as preferred places for retirement. This is partly because they are not far from the northeastern industrial and commercial centers and the developing high-tech facilities in the Carolinas, where retirees can be closer to family and possible work connections as part-time employees or consultants for their companies.

With a goal of presenting the most popular retirement locations first, and because Florida is the most fashionable place for out-of-state retirement, we will begin by looking at Florida, the "Sunshine State."

2

Florida: A Retirement Tradition

When dreaming of retirement, many people automatically picture Florida. They've vacationed there for years, so relocation there seems logical. Visions of warm weather, snow-free streets, and easy living flow through their fantasies. Soft, sandy beaches with swaying palm trees and balmy January days complete the vision. Beginning in the 1920s, retirees moved south in such numbers that Florida retirement became almost a tradition.

Because Florida is a high-profile state, it receives a lot of media attention. Sometimes it seems that the only news coming out of the state deals with oil spills, hurricanes, wildfires, overcrowding, and disrepair. Does this mean you should write off Florida as a viable choice? Not by any means! From our research we are convinced that of all the states, Florida still offers some of the best bargains in quality living and affordable retirement for the average retiree. Regardless of what you see on television or the Internet, most Florida communities are as safe as other popular retirement destinations. If this book were to give ratings, many Florida towns would receive ratings far above towns of similar size elsewhere, both in livability and safety. Even though Florida isn't for everyone, it's still a great place to retire.

ISN'T FLORIDA OVERCROWDED?

Florida is now the third most populous state in the Union and still growing. New residents move here at the rate of more than 900 a day, most of them retirees, and Florida soon will displace New York as the country's third-largest state population. Since the 2000 census, Florida's population has expanded by about six million people!

Florida Tax Profile

Sales tax: 6% to 9.5%; food, drugs exempt
State income tax: no
Property taxes: approximately 1.6% on 100% of valuation; permanent residents eligible for additional exemptions
Social Security taxed: no
Pensions taxed: no
Inheritance tax: no
Estate tax: limited
Gasoline tax: 53.4¢ per gallon

With all those retirees moving in, isn't Florida overcrowded? That depends upon which part of Florida you're talking about. Certainly some parts of Florida are heavily populated, with high-rise apartments and condos clustered together and nothing but shopping centers and parking lots to break the monotony. Yet other sections of Florida are somewhat sparsely populated. Thousands of square miles have practically no human presence at all. Herons, egrets, ducks, storks, and wildfowl of all description share vast expanses of land with other wildlife ranging from panthers to rabbits and alligators to turtles and pythons. Deer abound in the open countryside and in the state's large system of national forests.

Lightly populated central Florida features rolling, wooded terrain dotted with small towns and crossroads communities comparable to those in small-town Ohio or Illinois. They are quiet, safe, and rural. Were it not for an occasional palm tree, you could easily forget this is Florida. These places are often overlooked in retirees' enthusiasm for living close to beaches and glittering excitement. Yet most of these remote locations in the interior are less than an hour's drive from a beach. No place in the entire state is much more than 70 miles from salt water. In some towns in the center of the state, you have a choice: An hour's drive can take you either to the Atlantic Ocean or to the Gulf of Mexico. You can spend a day playing in the sand and return home in time for dinner. And the state is well endowed with coastline—almost 9,000 miles of it!

Florida offers a wide range of relocation choices. You can select the convenience and excitement of a city, or you can choose a small-town community with slow traffic and rural tranquility. Florida has it all, except perhaps mountain climbing and downhill skiing.

FLORIDA WEATHER

The near-tropical climate of Florida's peninsula has always been a major attraction for those from the North and Midwest who want something better to do with their winters than shoveling snow and staying indoors, watching television. January afternoon temperatures generally climb into the 60s or low 70s, with nights dropping into the 50s and even into the 40s on occasion. Summers are hot, to be sure, but aren't summers in the Midwest and North scorchers, too? If you insist upon cool summers *and* mild winters, you need to think Pacific coast—California, Oregon, or Washington. But that's another chapter. In the summer Florida's early-morning temperatures are usually in the 70s, giving you plenty of opportunity to exercise outdoors. Summer afternoons are why God gave Florida swimming pools and iced lemonade.

Florida's tropical setting is an accident created by a huge flow of warm water—a kind of oceanic river—known as the Gulf Stream. This balmy current sweeps up from the Caribbean, hooks around the Florida Keys, and then brushes along Florida's east coast. Its benevolent warmth flows close to shore, bestowing its blessings on the Atlantic coast until a point near Vero Beach, where it swerves a few miles farther out to sea.

While Florida has been hit hard in recent years by hurricanes and tropical storms, the entire state benefits from the Gulf Stream, but an 80-mile stretch of southeastern coast known as the Gold Coast is the biggest beneficiary. Summers here are slightly cooler than in most Florida locations, because of the ocean's constant temperature and the frequent cloud cover. The winters are warmer than anywhere else in the continental United States. This dreamy weather explains why you see several million people crowded together along Florida's Gold Coast.

FLORIDA REAL ESTATE

Florida offers almost every kind of housing imaginable. Condos, town houses, and apartments are popular along the coasts or wherever land costs are high; multiple units bring the per-condo cost down. Traditional subdivisions are everywhere, as are custom homes and apartment buildings. Gated communities—usually reserved for folks over age 55—often feature a clubhouse and tennis courts, and sometimes a private golf course.

For many folks, tourists and retirees alike, Florida's beaches are what it's all about. Although beaches draw throngs of tourists, just a few miles away from the beachfront crush, even just a few blocks away, a different world presents itself: the world of residents. It's entirely possible to live in a quiet, normal neighborhood and then, whenever you choose, slip away to join the hedonistic, suntan-crazy tourist world just a few blocks from home.

A Florida innovation is boat-canal living: homes built along a waterway, with sailboats, powerboats, yachts, or canoes tied up in their backyards. Residents of canal developments enjoy the ocean or gulf in ways that beachside folks cannot. Some boating communities are locked-in or gated arrangements, but most are in open neighborhoods. We're continually surprised to find homes backing up to a canal are sometimes priced not that much higher than similar places in "dry" neighborhoods.

NORTH-CENTRAL FLORIDA

Although attractive retirement locations can be found all over the state, an area that is often overlooked for retirement possibilities is Florida's interior. The north-central part of Florida is a different world, as different from either coast as you can imagine. Instead of being ironing-board flat, as is most of the state, central Florida sits at a higher elevation, on rolling hills covered with woods, meadows, and numerous lakes. Forests of oak, pine, maple, flowering dogwood, and azalea make this a place where palm trees and other tropical flora almost seem out of place. Yet the fun beaches of either coast are within easy driving distance. Because of its slightly higher altitude and distance from the water, you'll find true changes of season, with cooler summer nights and a rare dusting of snow in the winter.

This part of Florida attracts more retirees from the Midwest and north-central states than from New York and New England (whose residents seem to prefer Florida's Gold Coast). By and large, the state's interior is peaceful, more rural, and safer. The hectic beachfront zones seem to be a universe away.

Residents here tend to duplicate the home styles and ambience of their Midwest hometowns. Generous lawns and single-family dwellings make this a re-creation of small-town America, with a slight Florida flourish. Homes come equipped with the pools, hot tubs, sundecks, and screened patios so important for Florida outdoor lifestyles. Were it not for an occasional orange grove, many neighborhoods would look right at home in Peoria or Terre Haute, places where their owners retired from. Part of this openness

NORTH-CENTRAL FLORIDA WEATHER

| | IN DEGREES FAHRENHEIT | | | | ANNUAL | |
	Jan.	April	July	Oct.	RAIN	SNOW
Daily highs	72	84	92	84	48"	—
Daily lows	49	60	73	65		

is due to affordable rural land costs that encourage larger building lots, which are routinely measured in acreage rather than square feet.

The climate is different here, too. In this region the weather-stabilizing Gulf Stream is farther off Florida's coast. Consequently, summer days are a few degrees warmer and winters a few degrees colder. Slightly less rain falls as well. These temperature differences can be significant when you consider Florida's high humidity. Miami averages 30 days a year with temperatures higher than 90 degrees, whereas inland it's more like 100 days of 90-degree-plus weather. Nevertheless, if you love warm weather (as we do), 90-degree days aren't bad, even with the 75 percent humidity you find in most of Florida. As one person from Rochester, New York, pointed out, "Coping with hot weather is simply a matter of changing my living patterns. Back home in New York, I stayed indoors all winter. I only went outside to go to work or to shovel snow. Here, I stay indoors during summer afternoons, yet every morning and evening it's comfortable outdoors for golf or bicycling."

It is important to note that the period from the year 2000 to the present writing of this book has been marked with a series of devastating hurricanes, including Hurricane Irma in 2017 and Category-5 Hurricane Michael in 2018, the latter of which served as the strongest since Hurricane Andrew in 1992. The Atlantic hurricane season starts in June and last through November. Just like earthquakes on the West Coast or tornados in the central states, preparedness for natural disaster must be considered.

Orlando Area

At one time we considered Orlando one of Florida's better retirement ideas. That was before it became so busy. In a surprisingly short time it made a remarkable transition from a sleepy crossroads of citrus orchards and residential neighborhoods into one of the fastest-growing cities in the state. Actually, for such a booming economy, Orlando managed to make this transition fairly painless by diversifying commerce and concentrating on clean, high-tech industry. It gained the nickname "Silicon Swamp." Another nickname for Orlando is "Hollywood East," because of the film industry's focus on this area. Disney, MGM, and Universal Studios have invested millions in soundstages, production entities, and tourist attractions.

Newcomers do not appear to be put off by growth; metropolitan Orlando has doubled over the past few decades, to boost the population to over two million. Many more have settled in the smaller towns scattered around Orlando's city limits. Even though Orlando has grown into a real city—and the best places to live are near, rather than in, the city—there are nevertheless some tranquil neighborhoods not too many blocks from downtown. Residents live quietly and oblivious to the hubbub of the tourist attractions, which are mercifully some distance from the city. Ancient oak trees arch over the streets, and restored homes from the early 1900s qualify some neighborhoods for historical status. ("historical" meaning 100 years ago, when the city's population was 2,481.)

Orlando's major problem, as far as retirement is concerned, is that it grew too much and too fast. With tourist super-attractions like Disney World and other Hollywood-style promotions, throngs of visitors create traffic jams and encourage the proliferation of fast-food joints, souvenir stands, motels, and business areas—which can be depressing to those who live here year-round. This shouldn't detract from the fact that Orlando has many wonderful services and attractions that are worth day visits for local residents.

Orlando is a golfer's paradise, with more than 80 golf layouts in the metropolitan area and another 60 or so within driving distance. Some courses were designed by golf greats such as Arnold Palmer, Jack Nicklaus, Tom Fazio, Dick Wilson, and Gary Player. It's no coincidence that numerous PGA Tour players have made Orlando their home, including Tiger Woods, Mark O'Meara, and Nick Faldo.

The Orlando metropolitan area is surrounded by small, pleasant towns that are almost pastoral, yet close enough to downtown to take advantage of big-city offerings. Orange groves and lemon blossoms sweeten the air of the rolling countryside. More than 50 lakes dot the landscape, their tropical shores edged with cypress, pines, and tall palm trees. Fish abound in the lakes, along with an occasional alligator.

An inviting place for retirement just outside Orlando is Winter Park, a scenic little college town with curving brick streets and charming Mediterranean-style architecture. The town boasts a chain of 17 lakes with a parklike setting of Spanish moss–draped live oaks. A little more expensive than some neighborhoods in Orlando, the town demonstrates its quality in a downtown that features a main street bustling with alfresco cafes, upscale boutiques, arts-and-crafts galleries, posh clothing shops, and other shopping pleasures.

One benefit of retirement living in or near the Orlando complex: When grandkids visit, you'll have no problem finding enough entertainment attractions to keep them occupied and looking forward to the next visit. The area is loaded with exciting theme parks of all descriptions, such as the Disney Magic Kingdom, crammed with themes of adventure, fantasy, and scary rides. The area is full of museums of all descriptions, as well as the famous Sea World Theme Park, Legoland, and Universal Studio's Islands, both featuring thrill rides and attractions.

For some of your more mature guests, there's always the Congo River Golf and Exploration Golf Course, which features two 18-hole courses in a lush tropical setting, complete with waterfalls, caves, and—just to make it interesting—25 live alligators. (I suppose that gives a new meaning to "water hazards.") Furthermore, you don't have to choose Orlando as your retirement hometown to enjoy these amenities; dozens of pleasant communities are within a half hour or so drive.

Two good-size health care centers serve the region: the Orlando Medical Center (general medical and surgical, pediatrics, heart and heart surgery), with 1,356 beds, and Florida Hospital (general medical and surgical), with 2,204 beds.

Orlando Chamber of Commerce: 301 E. Pine St., Ste. 900, Orlando, FL 32814; (407) 425-1234; orlandochamber.org.

DeLand

Some interesting retirement possibilities near Orlando are found north of the city in a fan-shaped area starting at Orlando's northern edge. A dozen small towns are scattered throughout this triangle, from DeLand on the east to Leesburg on the west, places little publicized as retirement destinations. Most of these towns are long settled, with established neighborhoods and mature shade trees along quiet streets. DeLand is the largest of these communities, with a local population of approximately 24,000 and about 53,000 in the shopping area. The town serves as the county seat as well as a busy commercial hub.

An important feature of the town, which distinguishes it from similar communities in the region, is the presence of Stetson University. Even though it's a small undergraduate school, the presence of its 2,200 students has a beneficial impact on the community. This happens to be Florida's first university, public or private. It was founded in 1883 by a New York philanthropist, Henry DeLand—who also founded the town. In 1887, when DeLand convinced John B. Stetson (who made his fortune manufacturing Stetson hats) to contribute, the school was named Stetson University. Because of the school and its distinctive campus, with dramatic Greek and Tudor architecture, the town likes to claim the title of the "Athens of Florida." DeLand sits on Lake Wales Ridge, a range of hills that runs north and south through the heart of the Florida peninsula. Nearby is a wildlife refuge, Blue Springs State Park, as well as the DeLeon Springs State Park. The latter is so named because legend has it that this is where Ponce de León should have been looking for his prized "Fountain of Youth." (Ol' Ponce probably missed the DeLand turnoff from the interstate.)

Unlike many older Florida towns—those that trace their beginnings to the 1920s—many of the historic buildings are still intact. DeLand's origin dates back to the late 1800s. (Actually, the oldest commercial structure in the sedate downtown section is said to date from 1775, when Florida was still part of the Spanish empire!) The city is trying to preserve the historic town center, which has many turn-of-the-20th-century Victorian and brick buildings. The goal is to encourage the establishment of antiques shops, boutiques, art galleries, quaint cafes, and coffeehouses.

Throughout the region you'll find wonderful outdoor recreational opportunities. The countryside is dotted with many lakes, and the crystal-clear St. Johns River is great for fishing, kayaking, and hiking. (By the way, the river is navigable all the way to the Atlantic coast at Jacksonville.) DeLand and surrounding towns offer good tennis facilities, and there are 16 public golf courses within 17 miles of DeLand's civic center.

For amenities and entertainment not found in DeLand, residents have only a 25-minute drive to Daytona Beach. There they'll find amenities, cultural activities, and entertainment not usually found in a town of 28,000 population. This is not to mention the many miles of wide, uncrowded beaches all along this section of the Florida coast.

Most homes in these smaller towns are in conventional neighborhoods, while larger retirement developments can be found in the surrounding countryside. As an example: We looked at a very impressive retirement complex near Leesburg. Because country property is relatively inexpensive in this area, a local developer was able to purchase a tract of land—a mixture of rolling hills, pastures, small lakes, and marshland—to create an interesting development. Because homes can't be placed on wetlands, much of the land is open, giving most homes unobstructed views and privacy. The facilities (completely owned by the homeowners' association) are top quality and include an Olympic-size pool, a huge clubhouse, tennis courts, and large areas of parkland. The development has its own golf course.

The AdventHealth DeLand Hospital, with 156 beds, serves the community's health needs. Hospitals in both Daytona and Sanford (about 20 miles away) have larger facilities.

DeLand Chamber of Commerce: 120 S. Florida Ave., 2nd Floor, DeLand, FL 32720; (386) 734-4331; delandchamber.org.

Winter Haven

Another possibility that shouldn't be neglected is the area southwest of Orlando and east of Tampa, a group of small communities around Winter Haven. Lakeland (pop. 108,000) is the largest and newest of the cities, while Frostproof (pop. 3,200) is the smallest and probably the oldest.

Winter Haven (pop. 41,000) is the best known of these communities because of the positive publicity it receives as a potential retirement destination. Like DeLand, Winter Haven traces its roots back to the 19th century. As Florida boomed in the 1920s, the town gained a reputation as a retirement destination for those leaving behind the frigid winters and snow of the midwestern states. By the mid-1930s tourism became one of the major components of the local economy.

Besides holding a sense of nostalgia about its former years as the MLB spring training camp of the Cleveland Indians and serving as the home of famous tourist attraction Cypress Gardens (now incorporated into Legoland), Winter Haven bills itself as the waterskiing capital of the world. For good reason: A series of 18 spring-fed lakes known as Chain O' Lakes, interconnected by navigable canals, provides unlimited opportunities for waterskiing, boating, fishing, and swimming. Ospreys, egrets, and other birds roost in the moss-covered cypress and oaks and flowering plants by the shores of the lake. Forty percent of the area within the city limits is covered by lakes or canals, which contributes to cooling in the summer and warming in the winter.

About 40 golf courses make the Winter Haven region ideal for enthusiasts. Many PGA tournaments are hosted here. It is an outstanding golfing area with a good number of uncrowded courses.

Regional housing is affordable, with homes routinely selling below national averages. Winter Haven was recently ranked as the 40th most-economical city in the nation and possibly the lowest cost of housing in Florida with regard to real estate. Much of the lakefront is open and park-like, yet boat access is almost unlimited. Lakes away from Winter Haven commonly have homes with private docks.

Health care is a major industry, with 5 hospitals and 10 medical centers scattered about the county. The largest of the medical facilities is Winter Haven Hospital, with 519 beds. Four smaller hospitals are within a 16-mile drive.

I-4 hustles traffic to Tampa or Orlando for serious shopping in short order. Shopping is more than adequate in Winter Haven and environs, however, with a large mall that rivals those in bigger cities. The area is lucky to have daily Greyhound bus service to Tampa, Orlando, Jacksonville, and Miami. When family comes to visit, they will be thrilled to know that Disney World is 35 minutes away, Sea World a 45-minute drive, and Busch Gardens 60 minutes away.

Winter Haven Chamber of Commerce: 401 Avenue B NW, Winter Haven, FL 33881; (863) 293-2138; winterhavenfl.com.

Gainesville

Originally developed as a health resort and described as the "Eden of the South" by its founder, Gainesville was visualized as a health-resort community with a "regular body of skilled physicians in attendance." In a way this dream was fulfilled, because Gainesville ranks very high when it comes to Florida health care. Today's population is about 130,000.

The home of the University of Florida (the university system's first and largest state-funded university), Gainesville is one of the most culturally stimulating cities in the state. It's interesting how much one university town can resemble another, with the same kinds of businesses, services, students, even similar street names. Large old homes on tree-shaded streets, some converted to fraternity houses, along with unobtrusive university construction, recall memories of this writer's own college days. The city's official nickname, the "Tree City," is certainly appropriate. You needn't be a student to participate in the many activities connected with the university. Theater for all tastes is highlighted by the Hippodrome, one of only four state theaters for the performing arts. Miracle on 34th Street is a cultural complex with museums of art and natural history as well as an 1,800-seat performing-arts center. The university's ongoing program of public lectures and other cultural events entertains many retirees in the area. Everything from symphony concerts to Broadway plays, choral music, and dances invite the public to enjoy.

As in most college towns, rentals are at a premium, except for the summer quarter, when many students leave town. If a town of 130,000 is too large for you, the nearby communities of High Springs and Archer are 15 minutes by automobile. Housing costs less there, and small farms can be affordable. Haile Plantation, an upscale golf-course development, offers miles of walking/bicycle trails, tennis courts, swimming pools, and other recreational amenities in addition to a new 18-hole golf course. This is but one of several such entities.

Besides the 52,000-student university, Gainesville is home to the two-year Santa Fe College, with a student body of about 15,000. A walk through its pleasant campus reveals a large percentage of students here with gray hair. Tuition is free under most circumstances to those age 60 and older. The extensive curriculum includes classes as diverse as dog training, computers, and antiques collecting. If you're looking for Florida relocation in an intellectual climate, Gainesville is the place to investigate.

For outdoors people there's plenty to do. A dozen nearby lakes invite anglers—six of the lakes have boat ramps. For golf, Ironwood, an 18-hole, par-72, public golf course, is one of six public or semiprivate links. Thirty municipal parks, some with tennis courts, are publicly maintained. And, of course, either the Gulf or the Atlantic is a short drive away. The closest saltwater fishing is in Cedar Key, a 49-mile drive to the Gulf. Driving time on I-75 is about 2 hours to Tampa Bay.

The University of Florida Gators football team draws fans from all over the nation and creates great excitement with local residents. If indoor shopping is your favorite sport, there's the million-square-foot Oaks Mall, an enclosed shopping facility with five department stores and 150 other shops and boutiques. Nearby wildlife areas provide great pleasure to birders and to those interested in ecology. About 65 percent of the county's 965 square miles is a wilderness of forests and wetlands dotted with scenic lakes.

Winter Haven Hospital is the major medical center for the Gainesville area, a facility with 519 beds. There are 6 hospitals, 10 clinics, and more than 900 physicians and dentists in the county.

Gainesville Chamber of Commerce: 300 E. University Ave., Gainesville, FL 32601; (352) 334-7100; gainesvillechamber.com.

Ocala

Another of Florida's fast-growing areas, Ocala (pop. 59,000) is home to a rapidly expanding retiree population. About one in four adults is age 65 or older. The town's laid-back lifestyle attracts those who hate northern winters yet want to avoid the traffic jams and insanity of crowded beach cities. Ocala styles itself as the "Horse Capital of the World" and is famous for its rolling hills and beautiful horse farms. Here you'll find 15 golf courses, several freshwater lakes, and dozens of crystal-clear rivers with outstanding bass fishing. The cost of living here is usually among the lowest in Florida.

Ocala's downtown business district is rather orthodox, looking very much like a typical midwestern agricultural town, with a traditional downtown square. This isn't surprising, because Ocala actually *is* an agricultural center. Modern malls and chain stores haven't totally killed the town center, as they have in some small cities.

The countryside is checkered with farms, especially horse farms. The area around Ocala is one of the most important thoroughbred-breeding areas in the country. There are even "farm subdivisions"—developments where you can buy a few acres, a barn, and a house and do small-scale farming or horse raising as your retirement hobby.

One retiree told us that he chose to live here because Ocala reminded him of the countryside where he grew up in northern Illinois. "The only thing it lacks is the ice and snow in the wintertime," he added. When asked about northern Florida summers, he replied, "I don't believe they are any hotter than they were back home. Anyway, whenever we get the notion, the wife and I drive an hour and twenty minutes to Daytona Beach and cool off in the Atlantic Ocean. We can get there by nine in the morning and be home with sunburns by suppertime!"

Real estate in and around Ocala is affordable, with a trend toward restored homes in the historic district and new developments away from the town center. Single-family homes in nice neighborhoods sell for what condominiums go for elsewhere, and a lakeside home on a golf course is not too much more. Prices like these account for the influx of retirees. Not only do Ocala's mobile-home parks range from ordinary to deluxe, but it's also possible to buy a few acres, or just a small lot, and install your own mobile home instead of building a house. (This would be against local building codes in most Florida communities.) Many small farms of 5 to 50 acres dot the countryside, with nothing but a mobile home and a barn on the property.

Two medium-size hospitals serve the area: AdventHealth Ocala and Ocala Regional Medical Center.

Ocala Chamber of Commerce: 319 SE Third St., Ocala, FL 34471; (352) 629-8051; ocalacep.com.

FLORIDA'S ATLANTIC COAST

Florida's eastern-most coast is characterized by probably the most comfortable weather in the eastern United States. Cool ocean breezes keep summer temperatures from getting much above 80 degrees. Winter afternoons usually top the 70-degree range, with the warm Gulf Stream flowing up the coast. Frost and cold spells are so rare, they make headline news across the country. Outdoor activities such as golf and boating are enjoyed year-round. This is the Florida that many retirees dream about.

Palm Coast

Let's take a look at one of those multiple-use communities, one with beach, golf, tennis, and boating facilities all in one. This is not to be considered an advertisement or an endorsement of this particular community, but rather an example of similar communities found all over the state. Some are much more expensive, and most are smaller. Palm Coast is interesting in that it evolved from a large-scale development into an actual city of more than 86,000 residents. It is now a conventional community with no ties to the original developer.

Palm Coast is located halfway between St. Augustine and Daytona Beach—22 miles each way. A private ocean beach club (open to residents)

ATLANTIC COAST WEATHER

	Jan.	April	July	Oct.	RAIN	SNOW
	IN DEGREES FAHRENHEIT				ANNUAL	
Daily highs	68	80	89	81	48"	—
Daily lows	47	59	72	65		

is an easy walk or bike ride across the Intracoastal Waterway Bridge. The planned community was developed by ITT Community Development Corporation over a two-decade span and is still under way.

As you exit I-95 to enter the Palm Coast development, you immediately feel as if you have entered a park. The landscaped, four-lane parkway through residential and commercial areas is bordered by lush forests of oak and native palms. Bicycle and jogging paths meander through the landscaped commons and are fully used by Palm Coast residents and visitors.

Great care was taken to preserve the semitropical landscape, with its magnificent tall trees, tangled vines, and indigenous palm trees. Housing and businesses are skillfully hidden behind the vegetation so that it appears to the casual visitor that most of the development is natural parkland. The business district and shopping centers are tastefully landscaped and surrounded by a buffer of trees to keep noise and traffic away from residential areas. Of the original 42,000 acres in the development, 5,000 acres are set aside as a nature reserve.

This development wasn't planned solely as a place for retirement. Provisions were made for business parks and light, technology-oriented industry to provide jobs for Palm Coast residents. These businesses are located near the interstate and screened from the residential areas by nature preserves, yet close enough for workers to walk or ride bicycles to work. The infusion of young couples and children adds freshness to the face of Palm Coast, taking it out of the category of a retirement center.

Scattered through the complex are five championship golf courses, two of them designed by Arnold Palmer. The community tennis club is one of only four clubs in the country with clay, grass, and hard-surface courts within the same complex. Sixteen courts draw players of all skill levels. The club is complete with an aerobics room, lockers, and restaurant.

Boating enthusiasts can have their own private marinas at their back door. The canals vary from 60 to 125 feet wide and are about 8 feet deep.

Homes here are, of course, priced higher than houses on ordinary streets but are surprisingly good values, considering the amenities.

All Florida retirement communities are not created equal. Across the Intracoastal Waterway is another development (also by ITT Community Development Corporation) called Hammock Dunes. It also features golf courses and natural Florida landscaping, but on a lavish scale, along 5 miles of oceanfront. An impressive 32,000-square-foot clubhouse overlooks the Atlantic and a spectacular golf course.

Flagler Chamber of Commerce: 20 Airport Rd., Palm Coast, FL 32164; (800) 881-1022; flaglerchamber.org.

Daytona Beach

Daytona Beach, about 65 miles south of St. Augustine, is one of Florida's nicer-looking Atlantic cities, with graceful buildings on both the peninsula side and across the Intracoastal Waterway on the mainland where the commercial district is located. It's situated partly on the peninsula and partly on the mainland. As you drive across the connecting causeway, rows of mature tropical trees outline a pleasant view of downtown in the distance. Daytona Community College offers interesting courses that seniors enjoy, with more than 28,000 adults and continuing-education students using the facility.

Not surprisingly, Daytona Beach's main tourist section is on the peninsula's ocean side rather than facing the mainland. The city's population is around 68,000, with more than 120,000 in the metropolitan area. The 23-mile-long white sand beach is the area's most famous feature, one of the few places in Florida where autos are permitted to drive along the beach. The only time to drive it is during low or outgoing tide, when it is hard packed and pavement-like. Many speed records have been posted on this beach back in the days of Barney Oldfield and high-speed, steam-powered race cars.

Years ago, to keep tourism alive during the slow tourist months, the city decided to renew automobile and motorcycle racing to bring in the crowds. Over the years these events have gained wide media recognition, drawing racing enthusiasts from all over the nation. During important races visiting race fans outnumber the resident population. This creates welcome revenue for Daytona Beach and the surrounding communities but also produces some marvelous traffic jams. Local people pay close attention to the schedules and try to avoid the peninsula during races. The famous tourist area—on the peninsula—has a wide promenade, an amusement park, and a fishing pier to entertain vacationers.

The Halifax River is part of the Intracoastal Waterway, which stretches from the Florida Keys north to New Jersey. It's wide and sheltered—a perfect place for learning how to handle a sailboat before venturing into open water. Everything from fishing dinghies to freighters uses this channel to follow the coast. You can make it to the Florida Keys with very little exposure to the open ocean. A recent development in Daytona Beach is the Halifax Harbor Marina, which is now the largest marina between Baltimore and Fort Lauderdale.

Rents in the tourist sector vary widely, depending upon the season, the view, and access to the beach. When buying something near the beach, always make sure you aren't buying into a party pad. Any complex where most units are rented to tourists by the week is liable to mean trouble. A clean-cut college student can invite the whole fraternity house for an around-the-clock animal party. Retirement-type housing is available on the peninsula, but most retirees prefer to live in the comparative peace and quiet of the mainland.

Some nearby communities worth investigating are Ormond Beach—where the famous daredevils like Barney Oldfield raced automobiles in attempts to break the one-time 60-mile-an-hour speed barrier—and New Smyrna Beach, which is as far as autos can be driven on the sand. This is where the Canaveral National Seashore wildlife preserve begins, the refuge of alligators, turtles, manatees, and a marvelous variety of birds.

Where the wildlife preserve ends, the Canaveral Peninsula and the John F. Kennedy Space Center begin. New Smyrna Beach, by the way, is one of the oldest settlements in America. Historians believe Ponce de León landed here in 1513.

Daytona Beach's largest hospital is Halifax Health, with 678 beds. Two other hospitals are located within 15 miles of Daytona Beach.

Daytona Beach Chamber of Commerce: 126 E. Orange Ave., Daytona Beach, FL 32114; (386) 255-0981; daytonachamber.com.

COCOA BEACH TO MELBOURNE

The "Space Coast" derives its name from the John F. Kennedy Space Center on the Canaveral Peninsula. All along this section of coast, from Cocoa

Beach down to Melbourne and Melbourne Beach, you'll find an attractive group of towns just made for retirement.

Cocoa Beach's commercial center is much larger than the city's actual population of 16,000 might indicate. The downtown streets are lined with flower boxes and old-time village shops where folks can watch potters at work, leathersmiths making belts and hats, and skilled craftsmen restoring antiques. Cocoa Beach serves as a focal point for nearby cities such as Cocoa, Merritt Island, and Rockledge. The Canaveral Pier at Cocoa Beach extends almost 800 feet into the ocean and is a great place for fishing, dining, and nightlife.

The area is home to many space-center workers and military families from nearby Cape Canaveral and Patrick Air Force Base. Cocoa Beach and the nearby towns have attracted a large share of military retirees, folks who liked the area when stationed here.

According to the local chamber of commerce, a good percentage of the population are retirees, and quite active in politics. The number of services available to senior citizens reflects this. Thirteen apartment and housing complexes are reserved for senior citizens. A good public transportation system is augmented by the free wheelchair-accessible van service provided by a local surfing shop.

Broward Community College offers continuing-education classes, including subjects such as beginning-level sailing, windsurfing, and navigation. There's also a state university branch located here.

The Cape Canaveral Hospital, with 145 beds, is located in Cocoa Beach, and 7 miles away, in Rockledge, is the Weustoff Medical Center, with 291 beds.

Melbourne

Sitting at the lower end of this famous coast is its largest city, Melbourne, with a population of 80,000. Palm Bay, Merritt Island, and Satellite Beach are also part of Melbourne's shopping area. This is a relatively quiet area, at least compared with the hectic, tourist-clogged pace of nearby Orlando.

Melbourne itself is on the mainland; a causeway takes you to the beach town of Indiatlantic. And what a beach it is, with 33 miles of sandy, uncrowded Atlantic shore! At one time this beach was nicknamed the "Treasure Coast" because when a hurricane shipwrecked a fleet of Spanish ships against the shore, thousands of Spanish doubloons spilled into the sea. The survivors spent years trying to recover the treasure. Today divers still keep their eyes peeled for coins and bullion that were overlooked.

From May until September loggerhead turtles visit the beaches to dig nests and lay eggs. As many as 12,000 nests are dug each season. Retirees are invited to join the Sea Turtle Preservation Society. The elusive manatee is occasionally sighted around here as well.

Holmes Regional Medical Center, with 514 beds, takes care of the region's health care needs.

Cocoa Beach Chamber of Commerce: 400 Fortenberry Rd., Merritt Island, FL 32952; (321) 459-2200; cocoabeachchamber.com.

FLORIDA'S GOLD COAST

It all started back in the 1880s when two starry-eyed brothers, John and James Lummus, bought a barren spit of sand that jutted from the southern Florida mainland. Lying in the indigo waters between Biscayne Bay and the Atlantic Ocean, their new purchase inspired a dream. They were convinced they could turn this worthless piece of land into a fabulously productive coconut plantation. They planted thousands of trees and sat back, waiting for them to mature, and for tropical winds to shake the harvest to the ground.

However, things didn't work out that way. Blight cut the harvest potential, and tree rats harvested more coconuts than the plantation owners did. Mosquitoes and other insects drove workers away, and finally the dream died. But the coconut trees survived. Later, promoters saw a different promise: tourism and retirement. They called their new development "Miami Beach."

The boom started in the 1920s and enthusiastically spilled from Key Biscayne north to Fort Lauderdale, Pompano Beach, Boca Raton—all the way to Palm Beach and beyond. By the 1930s the area was in full swing as a winter retreat and retirement haven. This is Florida's famous Gold Coast. A drive along the coastal highway will explain how it received its name. It certainly took a lot of gold to build it and even more to maintain it.

Individually, the cities from West Palm Beach down to Coral Gables don't appear to be particularly large. But together, the more than 40 towns and cities form one long, enormous metropolitan area of almost

GOLD COAST WEATHER

	IN DEGREES FAHRENHEIT				ANNUAL	
	Jan.	April	July	Oct.	RAIN	SNOW
Daily highs	75	82	89	84	60"	—
Daily lows	56	65	74	70		

three million people. These communities spread along the beach have no chance of having a central focus or a common downtown area. Broken into a string of suburbs without an urban area to be suburban to, each has its own shopping center, stores, businesses, and its own small political entity. In this unconsolidated way Florida's Gold Coast resembles greater Los Angeles.

Except for the spiffy residential sections along the beaches, much of the housing consists of single-family bungalows, low-profile condominiums, and expansive apartment complexes. In some of the less intensely developed areas, where housing isn't so tightly packed, it's easy to forget that you are part of an urban sprawl. People commonly don't go shopping away from their self-contained area; they have no need to.

Along the Gold Coast you'll see some of the biggest contrasts in all of Florida. Tall forests of condominiums and apartment complexes remind you of New York's Park Avenue. Then rows of suburban bungalows are reminiscent of Los Angeles. You'll find every imaginable type of housing and neighborhood—all within miles or sometimes yards of each other. Then, in stark contrast, just 10 to 20 miles to the west, the land can be totally uninhabited, the domain of alligators, bobcats, and herons.

The Miami Complex

This is the Florida you usually read about in your newspaper's travel section, the Florida you see on television and in movies. For some folks, the thought of living in such a crowded area is a turnoff. But for others the amenities of a metropolitan area—combined with a mild climate and gorgeous beaches—add up to ideal retirement living. They adore everything about the Gold Coast. They love the convenience of well-stocked shopping centers, good medical facilities, and a wide array of restaurants. Folks here enjoy apartment and condo living. They enjoy having someone else wash windows, mow lawns, and trim shrubs. As one lady put it, "We've lived all our lives in or near Manhattan. We couldn't survive in some dinky, one-horse town where they roll up the sidewalks after dark!"

Curiously, in the midst of this densely packed, tropical replica of Manhattan, distinct concepts of neighborhood and community emerge. We've visited several large condominium developments and are always fascinated by the way folks create their own islands of interests and community. A typical complex, this one in Pompano Beach, has a dozen eight-story buildings set apart in a parklike setting. Each building has complete laundry facilities and an exercise room. Jogging paths, swimming pools, and tennis courts are strategically placed about the grounds, and a clubhouse dominates the center. In effect the development corresponds to a small town, or an intimate neighborhood in a larger city. The condo owners' association substitutes for city politics back home. Residents have a great time voting for officers, running for election, lobbying for pet projects, or trying to recall from office those who aren't doing their job. "I feel like I have a helluva lot more control and say-so about my neighborhood now than I ever could hope for back in New York," said one resident who was in the middle of a political fight to redecorate the clubhouse and install more outdoor lighting.

Century Village East

Another example is a condo development in Deerfield Beach, a place called Century Village East. It seems to be populated primarily by former New Yorkers, many of whom knew one another back home. Century Village is not only large, but also well organized—so much so that it puts out an impressive monthly newspaper that's circulated to the several thousand residential units, covering activities and news at the development. Residents have their own shopping center, golf course, even buses and trolleys. They elect members to serve in positions analogous to mayor, city council, and so on.

Like any metropolitan area, the Gold Coast area has its drawbacks. Higher crime rates, traffic jams, and crowded stores are pretty much standard. The crime picture, however, is somewhat distorted in the Miami area because of the vigorous commerce in illegal drugs. Presumably you are not into drug dealing and won't be participating in car chases, revenge killings, and shoot-outs as featured on television shows. Therefore, statistics on drug busts, drive-by shootings, and gang-related activities should not affect you—as long as you stay away from the dangerous neighborhoods.

One important point: What metropolitan areas lack in peace and quiet, they more than make up for in services and conveniences for retirees. The larger the population, the more and better senior citizen centers, libraries, educational opportunities, and other advantages. For example, there are nine health care facilities within 10 miles of Century Village.

Miami Chamber of Commerce: 1601 Biscayne Blvd., Miami, FL 33132; (305) 350-7700; miamichamber.com.

FLORIDA KEYS: THE END OF THE LINE

Except for Hawaii, this jumbled string of islands and reefs known as the Florida Keys is the most tropical part of the United States. The main highway follows the route of an old railway line—an engineering marvel in itself—110 miles to the last of the accessible islands, Key West. The highway skips from one coral atoll to another over numerous causeways and bridges, across islands festooned with palm trees, hibiscus, and bougainvillea and bearing such romantic names as Key Largo, Islamorada, and Matacumbe. This is as close to living in a tropical paradise as you'll find this side of Costa Rica.

Substantial numbers of retirees, both snowbirds and regular residents, populate these islands. Boating and fishing are top attractions, with year-round tropical weather the frosting on the cake. When it comes to snorkeling and diving, these islands are a virtual paradise. Folks here boast of the longest living reef in the Western Hemisphere, crystal-clear waters with visibility up to 100 feet, and more than 500 wrecks to explore.

Yachts are "in" throughout the Keys, large ones and small ones. Resident sailors often cut berths into the coral and limestone backyards of their homes and tie up their boats. Many houses are set back against networks of canals, where their occupants can dock after a day's adventure of fishing or treasure hunting in the warm waters of the Gulf Stream. You'll even find mobile homes with sloops moored at their floating patios.

In the 1900s Key West developed a reputation as a retreat and retirement spot for writers and artists. Wallace Stevens fell in love with Key West back in 1922, and his poem "The Idea of Order in Key West" described living here as "a summer without end." Having let the cat out of the bag, Stevens soon found himself in the company of other intellectuals who wanted to participate in this "summer without end." Ernest Hemingway, John Dos Passos, and Tennessee Williams all maintained houses in Key West. Some of their homes are now major tourist attractions.

The tradition of an artist colony continues, but in a somewhat diminished form. Key West has become incredibly crowded and overrun with tourists and weekending college students. Finding a parking place becomes a treasure hunt. Key West's tolerant openness to varying lifestyles and its "live and let live" attitude has encouraged the establishment of a considerable gay community.

Because it's such a long drive from the mainland, over a snail's pace, two-lane highway, and because housing costs in Key West are hardly bargains, our recommendations lean toward retirement farther up the line, in places such as Key Largo, Marathon, and Big Pine Key. Property here isn't exactly cheap, but certainly less than in Key West.

One of the major complaints by residents of Key West, besides the continual influx of newcomers, has been a steadily rising real estate market (although the disastrous housing crash of 2008 has clearly taken its toll on property values). At one time, residents reminisce, you could rent an apartment or small home for next to nothing, but today the tariffs have become higher than on the mainland. This is particularly so in the town of Key West, where space is at a premium and tourists arrive to become residents at an alarming rate. I once saw a bumper sticker there: "Key West: A Drinking Town with a Tourist Problem."

Key West residents are famous for their independence and stubborn refusal to conform. Their reaction to a recent hurricane season was typical: When ordered on several occasions to evacuate in the face of oncoming hurricane-force winds, there was an almost unanimous refusal to obey. As they have in the past, residents preferred to weather the storms by calmly nailing plywood over the windows and finding second-story refuges from possible storm surges. It's an opportunity for another hurricane party! Besides, Key West residents figure it's more dangerous to drive the snail's pace, two-lane highway north to the mainland (the bridge sits only a few feet above the water) than to simply stick around home and watch out for their property.

Lower Keys Medical Center, a general medical and surgical facility with 100 beds, handles health care for Key West.

Key West Chamber of Commerce: 510 Greene St., Key West, FL 33040; (305) 294-2587; keywestchamber.org.

FLORIDA'S WEST COAST

For some unknown reason central Florida and the state's west coast seem to draw an unusual number of emigrants from the Midwest, whereas newcomers from New York and New England seem to prefer the Atlantic side of the peninsula. Therefore, it isn't surprising that west coast Florida architecture and lifestyles are more disposed toward midwestern values. Instead of tall condos and apartments, the preferred style is low profile, informal, and conservative. Single-family homes are the norm, sometimes sitting on lots measured in quarter acres rather than in square feet, with generous areas of lawn and landscaping.

The climate is different here, too. The weather-stabilizing Gulf Stream misses Florida's west coast. The result: Summers along the Gulf are hotter and winters a few degrees cooler than along the Gold Coast. But the folks who've retired here say it's worth it, and they point out that the relative humidity is lower than on the other coast.

Another thought: For many people (including this writer), living by the beach is a delightful part of retirement. Actually, my wife and I have two retirement homes: our original home on the Pacific Ocean in Monterey, California; the other home, also on the Pacific, in Costa Rica. We live about 100 yards from the beach in both locations, with views of the ocean from both houses. Yet how many times have we dipped our pinkies into the Pacific Ocean in the last 20 years? Zero in Northern California (it's way too cold), and only occasionally in Costa Rica. It's the beach *ambience*, not the water, that counts.

This southwestern part of the state is one of our favorites. From Fort Myers/Cape Coral on down to Naples and Marco Island, you'll find a wide assortment of neighborhoods as inexpensive as any developed part of Florida, or as luxurious as you might wish. Cape Coral's average sales price for existing homes is usually average, whereas Naples and Marco Island rank among the most expensive in Florida. Sanibel Island also ranks up there in expense and carries an added handicap of not having any place to park.

		WEST COAST FLORIDA WEATHER				
	IN DEGREES FAHRENHEIT				ANNUAL	
	Jan.	April	July	Oct.	RAIN	SNOW
Daily highs	74	85	91	85	54"	—
Daily lows	53	62	74	68		

Fort Myers and its sister city of Cape Coral are separated by the Caloosahatchee River. (No, I'm not making that up.) Neighboring Pine Island lies across a saltwater pass from Cape Coral. Fort Myers Beach is also an island, one of a string of them that shelter the coastline most of the way south to Naples. In the middle are Bonita Springs and Bonita Beach, two excellent choices for in between expensive and affordable relocation.

This was formerly a cattle-raising area, and population growth here is nothing short of phenomenal—an astonishing 600 percent in the last 25 years! Good transportation accounts for some of this growth; I-75 shoots through the area, making it a snap to drive east to the Gold Coast or north to the Tampa Bay area in 2.5 hours. Fort Myers also boasts an international airport. Medical care is excellent with the new Gulf Coast Hospital's discounts for senior citizens. A half dozen other hospitals and several nursing facilities serve the area as well.

This is definitely a winter snowbird haven—the population doubles between the first of November and Easter week. Then, when summer's humidity and 90-plus-degree weather sets in, the comfort-loving snowbirds fly home to cooler northern climes. But year-round residents protest when I suggest that summer might be harsh. "Check it out; it's just a little bit warmer than Miami Beach," they point out, "and it's a lot safer living around here!"

Fort Myers/Cape Coral

Discovered early in the 20th century by Henry Ford and Thomas Edison, Fort Myers has been booming ever since. The city's landscaping is a unique heritage left by Thomas Edison. He loved to experiment with trees and shrubs, particularly palm trees. Older residential areas are full of them, grown tall and mature over the decades since the great inventor planted them around town. It's claimed that more than 70 varieties of palms grace the streets of Fort Myers. Some stand tall and stately; others are short, with bottlelike trunks. A few trees flaunt astonishing leaf patterns that look as if they were created by fashion designers.

The overall theme of this area is prosperity, with very few sections of town looking seedy. Well-manicured lawns, flowering bushes, and magnolia trees give residential areas of Fort Myers a quiet, homey look. Edison Community College offers a profusion of classes, almost free, at its Lifelong Learning Center. Naturally, landscaping is one of the more popular courses.

Fort Myers and North Fort Myers have a combined population of approximately 165,000, about the same as sister city Cape Coral. The island of Fort Myers Beach—population around 17,000—fronts the city of Fort Myers and provides open access to the Gulf, making it a popular place for homes with boat docks. The 7-mile-long island is tightly packed with small homes, condos, and beachfront properties. The island is only about three-quarters of a mile wide. Given how close it is to such a popular beach, prices are affordable, but winter traffic on the island can be horrific, and the number of tourists along the beachfront appalling. Be aware that the Fort Myers Beach population *triples* during the winter. A few blocks off the beach, confusion and noise greatly diminish, that's true, but this is a place for the young at heart and possibly the hard of hearing.

Throughout the area is a profusion of condos, some sitting on the edge of their own 9-hole golf courses. Condo styles seem quite practical: mostly two stories with bedrooms upstairs and no other families living overhead or underfoot. Developers have been generous in providing spacious lawn areas between the condos, so you don't have the cramped, hemmed-in feeling that comes with east Florida multistory skyscrapers and asphalt parking lots.

Mobile-home parks are plentiful. Most are beautifully landscaped and offer organized activities in their clubhouses as well as recreational facilities. Some are downright luxurious, some super-expensive, and others quite affordable.

Pine Island

For quiet, rural island retirement, Pine Island is the place. Seventeen miles long and about 2 miles wide, this is the largest of the barrier islands in these parts. Its shores are almost completely ringed with mangrove estuaries, many in wildlife preserves. As its name implies, the island is rustic, covered with pines, and retirement housing is inexpensive. Approximately 10,000 year-round residents are joined by another 6,000 during the winter months.

Pine Island is accessed from Cape Coral via a fishing bridge that crosses over to Matlacha and Little Pine Islands. This is known as "Florida's Fishingest Bridge," and at almost any time, day or night, you are apt to see anglers dipping their lines into Matlacha Pass. This area is a throwback to the time when tiny fishing villages were the norm along the southwest coast. The western shore sits in the lee of Captiva Island, which makes the water safe for sailing and peaceful fishing.

Fort Myers Beach Chamber of Commerce: 2450 Estero Blvd., Fort Myers Beach, FL 33931; (239) 454-7500; fortmyersbeach.org.

Tampa/St. Petersburg

Separated by Tampa Bay, the twin cities of St. Petersburg and Tampa are connected by three causeways. I-275, the area's main link to southern Florida, crosses the wide mouth of Tampa Bay on yet another long causeway as it heads south to Bradenton. Together the cities and their suburbs have more than 2.5 million people, making it the second-largest metropolitan area in Florida. Although many retire here, the best retirement places are nearby, an easy drive from the metropolitan center.

St. Petersburg is famous for its proclaimed year-round sunshine; the local newspaper has a standing pledge to give away a newspaper every day the sun doesn't peek out at least some. On one of our visits, it was overcast all day. We're still waiting for our free newspaper. According to the US Weather Bureau, the Tampa–St. Petersburg area can expect an average of 127 cloudy days a year and 107 days of rain. This surprised me, especially when I compared these figures with San Francisco, a place famous for foggy and overcast days. Turns out that San Francisco averages 100 cloudy days and only 67 days with rain.

St. Petersburg entered into the retirement business long ago, advertising in newspapers around the country, stressing its great climate and emphasizing the pleasant retirement possibilities here. It worked so well that the city soon became overrun with senior citizens. The city fathers then changed the advertising campaign to attract industry and younger people. The story goes that the city even removed park benches in an effort to discourage senior citizens from "hanging out." Perhaps they were concerned about gangs of geriatric delinquents getting out of hand. That didn't discourage retirees; they kept on coming, probably bringing their own park benches.

The focus on retirement here is not necessarily either St. Petersburg or Tampa, but surrounding, smaller locations, using the metropolitan area as a central focus. The nearby towns of Sarasota and Bradenton to the south and Clearwater, Indian Shores, Tarpon Springs, and a dozen other communities north of St. Petersburg are all pleasant places for relocation. Clearwater is famous for its stretch of pure white sand beach. North of Tampa, along I-75, you'll find another series of great prospects, particularly for inexpensive mobile-home living, in farming communities with affordable acreage and a down-home country atmosphere, yet minutes from big-city life.

Sarasota is our particular favorite in this area. Apparently others agree, because *Money* magazine usually ranks Sarasota among the "Top 20 Places to Retire" and on its "Best Places to Live in the US" list. *Southern Living* magazine calls Sarasota County "the nation's per capita arts capital."

With its own opera and symphony, bolstered by the Ringling Museum and School of Art and the Asolo Theater, Sarasota can be considered the culture capital of the state, attracting a population—many of them retirees—that supports the arts. A portrait artist friend who resides here has lived in and visited just about every part of the country, including Hawaii, but chooses to live here because of the city's comparatively low population density and leisurely pace.

You'll find a wide selection of housing choices here, from small cottages in renovated neighborhoods to luxury condominiums and mansions on the Gulf, to smaller apartment complexes throughout the city. Miles of beaches are within a few minutes of almost any residential area, and a protected bay and marina make boating and fishing popular activities. Golfers and tennis enthusiasts enjoy the city's many public and private golf courses and tennis courts.

Saltwater fishing is one of Tampa Bay's outdoor attractions. Anglers are out in early summer for silver king tarpon and then kingfish in early fall. By the way, fishing licenses aren't required in Florida for residents over age 65. Baseball fans might be interested to see the Tampa Bay Rays in action or catch the Yankees during spring training. For golf addicts about 70 golf courses dot the surrounding area.

For cultural balance the metropolitan area supports two theater groups, a ballet, and an opera company. Nine art museums, including two at the university and the Museum of Fine Arts, complete the schedule. Numerous hospitals and medical specialists ensure excellent health care. The largest hospital is Lee Memorial, with 1,574 beds.

Tampa Chamber of Commerce: 201 N. Franklin St.; (813) 228-7777; tampachamber.com.

Sun Coast

North of Tampa/St. Petersburg is another area that's been largely ignored by retirement writers. Local public relations folks call this area Florida's "Sun Coast." Originally it was known as "Pirate Coast," until the local chambers of commerce did a little public relations work, thus renaming the area "Sun Coast." The region is known for miles and miles of prime beaches and sunny days from early December through May. More than 35 miles of white sand beaches line eight offshore barrier islands. Quality beaches are found on nearby Caladesi Island, which locals claim to be America's fourth-best-rated beach, and Clearwater Beach, ranked number one for city beaches in the Florida Gulf area.

As US 19 goes north from Clearwater, it passes through several moderately settled areas and occasionally thins out into farmland and forest. Parts of it are as rural as you'll find in the state. New housing developments and livable mobile-home parks spice up pleasant small towns such as Hudson, Crystal Springs, and Homosassa. Nearby is the uniquely named Weeki Wachee Springs State Park; Weeki Wachee was named by Seminole Indians, meaning "little springs" or "winding river." The spring is of significant depth—so deep that the bottom has not been located.

Roadside signs and billboards clearly affirm the Sun Coast's dedication to retirement services. Large billboards announce items of interest to senior citizens: cataract surgery, arthritis clinics, hearing aids, cardiac care. One billboard announces a large-print book fair; another advertises supplementary Medicare policies.

From Clearwater north, stores and businesses crowd the main route (US 19) and begin thinning out past New Port Richey. Even though much of this portion of the route seems to be one long shopping center, just a block off the highway in either direction, you will find quiet residential areas. As you drive farther north, population becomes sparse, a clear invitation for more development. The construction of I-75, which parallels US 19, draws the flow of tourist traffic onto its faster, 65-mile-an-hour route, leaving the slower, divided highway for residents. The most important roadside signs caution motorists to watch for deer crossing.

The major hospital here is Morton Plant Hospital, with 560 beds. Within a 10-mile radius there are at least six other smaller hospitals and a Veterans Affairs Hospital. Some nearby St. Petersburg and Tampa hospitals are also available.

Clearwater Chamber of Commerce: 401 Cleveland St., Clearwater, FL 33755; (727) 461-0011; clearwaterflorida.org.

FLORIDA'S PANHANDLE

Starting from Tallahassee, the state's capital, and stretching westward to Pensacola, Florida's Panhandle is markedly different from most of the state. Pure white sand beaches and enterprising resort towns clearly remind you that you're in Florida, but the Panhandle also borrows from nearby Georgia and Alabama. There's a down-home atmosphere here; the native accent is Deep South, the thinking is pure country. Many southerners and midwesterners feel especially comfortable with this combination of resort-country retirement living. Our research shows many Panhandle locations have personal safety statistics similar to those of Alabama and Georgia, which contrasts pleasantly with statistics for the Gold Coast.

The main tourist and retiree attraction is a 100-mile length of beach that begins at the little town of Mexico Beach and runs westward to Pensacola. Many folks who eventually retire along this coast are those who regularly spent their summer vacations here with their families. They fondly remember summers on the white sand beaches and fishing expeditions far out on the Gulf's blue waters.

As much as I would like to avoid using the "H" word, I need to point out that the entire Gulf Coast, from Florida to east Texas, suffered hurricane damage, to some degree at least, during the record 2005 hurricane season through the present day. Florida's Panhandle, especially around Pensacola, was hit even harder in 2004, when Hurricane Ivan struck, and again in 2018, when hurricane Michael brought on significant devastation.

In terms of property damage, these were among the costliest hurricanes in US history. Those who insist on having houses on stilts, as close to the salt water as possible, are advised to keep up their flood and storm damage insurance.

Face it: Hurricanes are a fact of life anywhere in the Gulf of Mexico, or along the Eastern Seaboard. They aren't confined to this region by any means. From 1938 to 1960 seven hurricanes *missed* Florida entirely, blasting north along the East Coast, from North Carolina to New England, even as far north as Labrador! A couple of heavy storms in 2010 also swerved and went up the East Coast as far north as Newfoundland, leaving the Gulf practically untouched.

The Florida Panhandle jogs northward 20 miles west of Tallahassee. The land ends abruptly at Cape San Blas, where the highway makes a right-angle turn north toward Port St. Joe. From here all the way to the Alabama state line, two main features dominate: military bases and powder-white beaches. Many people decide on retirement here on the basis of their regular snow-bird vacations that they enjoyed during their working careers.

From Port St. Joe to Pensacola, more than a dozen little towns cater to tourists and retirees. Sometimes no more than a few blocks wide, the towns string along the highway and beach in a very laid-back manner. Single-family homes, duplexes, and small apartments are available for either seasonal or year-round rental. Some stretches of high-rise construction would do justice to Florida's Gold Coast, however. During the winter months these little towns are quiet, waiting for summer to make up for this hustle-bustle deficit.

Panama City

The largest population center between Pensacola and Tallahassee is Panama City (pop. 38,000). Like many towns in this area, Panama City has a dual personality. One side is that of a happy summer resort, the other a peaceful

PANHANDLE AREA WEATHER

	IN DEGREES FAHRENHEIT				ANNUAL	
	Jan.	April	July	Oct.	RAIN	SNOW
Daily highs	61	77	90	79	61"	—
Daily lows	43	59	74	59		

winter retreat. From November until March the 27 miles of emerald-green waters and stunning white sand beaches are uncrowded and quiet. About the only tourists you'll see are speaking French with a Quebec accent. So many French Canadians congregate here in the winter that one begins to wonder who's tending to business in Montreal. But with warmer weather the French Canadians go home, just as midwesterners arrive for their turn at the beaches.

An offshoot of the Gulf Stream known as the Yucatan Current moves close to Panama City. It tends to warm the water in the winter just a tad. This flow also brings nutrient-rich waters from the Caribbean and, with it, schools of sport fish. Anglers haul in marlin, sailfish, tuna, and dolphin, as well as buckets of panfish. A fishing pier extends about 1,600 feet into the Gulf for the convenience of anglers. To a certain extent the Yucatan Current moderates summer temperatures, but not to any appreciable amount. This doesn't deter the tourists, because as one of the natives pointed out, "It flat cain't get too hot for tourists!"

You needn't live on the beach to enjoy Gulf Coast living. Many folks reside in towns just a 20-minute drive from the sand and surf. Callaway, Springfield, Lynn Haven, and others are preferred by many retirees, particularly those who aren't captivated by the busy beach scene.

Part of the dual personality is the question of seasonal apartment and home rentals. In the off-season most rents drop rapidly, just as you would expect, but beach condos vary wildly, depending on season and demand. Housing prices along this coast are traditionally among the lowest in the state. At times residential real estate has been an amazing 19 percent below the national average. However, the market has seen a spike in recent years due to supply and demand following the damage of Hurricane Michael.

Of several hospitals in the region, Panama City's largest is the Bay Medical Center, with 368 beds.

Panama City Chamber of Commerce: 235 W. 5th St., Panama City, FL 32401; (850) 785-5206; panamacity.org.

The Emerald Coast

Between Panama City and Pensacola stretches a selection of towns ranging from ordinary to luxurious. A particularly interesting area circles a large body of water known as Choctawhatchee Bay. This is the self-styled Emerald Coast. It includes the town of Navarre and a dozen other little towns, but does not include Seagrove Beach. Some places look very comfortable, and the cost of living is comparatively inexpensive. Some towns look as if they coddle tourists to the nth degree. A few of the skyscraper-type condo towers would look right at home on Miami Beach. Despite the tourist factor, the area enjoys an unusually low crime rate.

Major towns on the bay are Fort Walton Beach and Destin, which seem to blend together into one city with a combined population of approximately 40,000. Valparaiso is the second city across the bay. Personnel at Eglin Air Force Base account for much of the off-season business activity as well as the high numbers of retired military who live around Choctawhatchee Bay. The long string of beaches here is famous for having some of the whitest, cleanest, and softest sand in the world. According to geologists, the beaches are composed mainly of quartz washed down from the Appalachians via the Apalachicola River, some 100 miles east of Fort Walton Beach. By the time the sand reaches Fort Walton Beach, the grains have been polished into tiny ovals that cause the sand to squeak when you walk along the dry part of the beach. Local residents are conservation minded and are working hard to prevent erosion. Fishing is said to be wonderful both on the beach side and in the bay itself. A fishing pier at Navarre Beach, on Santa Rosa Island, is a popular loafing place for local retirees.

Okaloosa Island, where Fort Walton Beach and Destin are located, is one of several barrier islands that protect the mainland. The bay is sheltered and makes for great swimming, boating, and picnicking. This is the place to look if you insist on living within blocks of the water. Winter rentals are relatively inexpensive and plentiful during the off-season, but expect to pay your dues during the rest of the year.

For the area's best bargains in housing and rentals, check around Niceville and other communities on the mainland side of the bay. About a 25-mile drive along a divided highway is Crestview, near I-10. Real estate

FLORIDA GULF COAST WEATHER

	IN DEGREES FAHRENHEIT				ANNUAL	
	Jan.	April	July	Oct.	RAIN	SNOW
Daily highs	61	77	90	79	61"	—
Daily lows	43	59	74	59		

prices here are also favorable for retirees, and the interstate brings Pensacola's hospitals and services within a 45-minute drive. Four small hospitals serve Fort Walton Beach and Destin.

Destin Chamber of Commerce: 4484 Legendary Dr., Ste. A, Destin, FL 32541; (850) 837-6241; destinchamber.com.

Pensacola

The Spanish recognized Pensacola as an excellent seaport when they settled here in 1559. With both an offshore island and a peninsula barrier to protect against storm-driven tides, the town is relatively secure from the scourge of hurricanes. This didn't help much, however, when Hurricane Ivan scored a direct hit on Pensacola in 2004, damaging about 70 percent of the homes. Then, just 10 months later—in 2005, as the city was celebrating getting back to normal—Hurricane Dennis struck. Nearby Navarre Beach took the brunt of the hurricane's fury, but Pensacola suffered extensive roof damage, with many houses destroyed by falling trees. The damage was quickly repaired.

Pensacola is one of the oldest towns in Florida, predating St. Augustine. Its famous historic district is not only one of the oldest, but also one of the best preserved in the state. Pensacola has a checkered history, its political allegiance changing 13 times—between Spain, France, England, the Confederacy, and finally the United States in 1810. (Flag making must have been a bustling cottage industry.) Its growth from the time this writer worked here many years ago (on the *Pensacola News-Journal*) has been phenomenal, changing it from a sleepy little town into a modern city of about 60,000.

Pensacola is proud of the title "Cradle of Naval Aviation." Countless naval fighter pilots received their training here and served in every major military conflict for generations. Five military bases are located in the Pensacola area, with an estimated 36,000 Navy, Marine Corps, and Coast Guard aviators undergoing training here. Eglin Air Force Base, Whiting Field Naval Air Station, and the Pensacola Naval Air Station ring the town.

Upon retirement, pilots who have served here naturally recall the attraction of the Panhandle's "Riviera" beaches and the convenience of military medical and base-exchange privileges. The end result is an estimated 30,000 retired military living in the Pensacola area.

Other nearby Panhandle towns also have military bases. Tyndall Air Force Base, with over 6,000 personnel, starts just west of Mexico Beach and extends to Panama City. There's also a Naval Coastal Systems center in Panama City, with about 2,300 personnel. The military presence in the area is significant indeed, with large payrolls supporting the economy because many civilians work on the bases.

Baptist Hospital and Sacred Heart Hospital, each with over 400 beds, serve the Pensacola area, along with West Florida Hospital, with 339 beds.

Pensacola Chamber of Commerce: 890 S. Palafox St., Ste. 202, Pensacola, FL 32502; (850) 438-4081; pensacolachamber.com.

3

California

A friend of ours, originally from Manhattan, once made this observation: "People on the West Coast are different from people back east. They think differently, they act differently, they view the world in different ways." He went on to explain that folks in the East have a sense of neighborhood; they feel they *belong* to the neighborhood or district where they live. They identify with those living there. When in a different neighborhood, they somehow feel like strangers, as if they don't quite belong. "But in the West Coast and especially California, I feel as if I belong everywhere," he said, "I have no sense of neighborhood or district."

Maybe it's because the western states have so much open space. Unlike the East Coast, where just about every square foot of land is fenced and posted as private property, a huge percentage of western land is public and open for anyone to enjoy. Almost 50 percent of California and Oregon belongs to the US government. Nevada is 85 percent federally owned and Arizona, 44 percent. Compare this with under 4 percent federally owned land on the Eastern Seaboard and in the Midwest.

Western seashore and ocean beaches are also considered public property. Unlike the Atlantic and Gulf shores, where property

California Tax Profile
Sales tax: 7.5% to 10.50%; food, drugs exempt
State income tax: 1.00% to 1.55%; can't deduct federal income tax
Income brackets: lowest, $8,544; highest, $1,000,000
Standard deduction: single, $3,841; married filing jointly, $7,682
Property taxes: typically within range of 1.1% to 1.6% of assessed value
Social Security taxed: no
Pensions taxed: all
Inheritance tax: no; limited estate tax related to federal estate tax
Gasoline tax: 57.8¢ per gallon

owners often own the beach in front of their homes and can post No Tres-
passing signs, Pacific beaches, generally speaking, belong to everyone. By
law, property owners are supposed to provide public access to the beachfront. You can usually stroll along almost any beach you please, secure in
the feeling that it is as much your property as anyone's. This law also applies
to many rivers, where the first 10 feet of riverbank is open to the public.

Because most West Coast weather is mild and generally pleasant year-
round, people tend to find outdoor things to do. Most live within a few
hours' drive of excellent ski country, golf courses, or swimming beaches.
They can enjoy snow sports in the afternoon, then drive back down the
mountain to dip in the swimming pool or relax in a hot tub the same evening. Outdoor living is the hallmark of western lifestyles.

THE PACIFIC COAST

The West Coast offers the most amazing assortment of retirement choices
imaginable. Choose from mountain communities with alpine winters,
deserts that look more like the Sahara, or farmlands reminiscent of Iowa.
You'll also find rocky coasts as rugged as Spain's Costa Brava and beaches
as smooth and surf as high as Hawaii's (albeit with colder waters). Within
an hour or so of many cities, you can be hunting deer, fishing for trout, or
trolling for salmon. From a rustic home deeply isolated within a forest, you
might be able to drive 45 minutes to an art museum or to a high-tech job in
a city. Within reason, just about any ecological, environmental, or climatic
feature can be found on America's West Coast.

The Pacific Ocean tempers the weather here. Especially near the
ocean, from San Diego to Seattle, temperature variations between winter
and summer are not extreme. This is partly due to a chain of low, coastal
mountains that runs along the entire West Coast, separating the coastal
plains from the inland valleys. A natural "air-conditioning" system occurs
when the sun heats up the inland valley air. This warm air rises, creating
low pressure that then draws air from the ocean across the coast and over
the mountains to cool things off. If it weren't for this phenomenon, the
coast areas would be as hot as the interior valleys. In the winter, air currents are stable and the cooler air stays offshore, allowing both beaches
and inland to bask in the sunshine. Often the "heat waves" of the coastal
lands occur in November, with 80 degrees common, as opposed to the

70-degree days of August. Therefore, the coastal towns are for those who don't like air-conditioning and also hate freezing weather. Los Angeles is a good example of this: pleasantly warm in the winter, never extremely hot in the summer. This climate is a compelling reason why so many people live there.

Contrary to popular stereotype, California is not all palm trees, movie stars, and surfers. Much of the state is almost midwestern in character, with small towns set among broad expanses of agriculture. (Without the typical midwestern climate, I might add.) Small towns set in national forests or in the wine country are pretty much like small towns anywhere when it comes to cost of living and lifestyles. Forest-covered mountain areas provide settings for those looking for skiing, hunting, and fishing. Inland farmlands and high Sierra snow-covered peaks contrast with the Mojave Desert and Death Valley. California has a relocation destination for every taste. Hundreds of thousands of retired folks will tell you they wouldn't consider living anywhere else.

California is not the place to look for bargain-basement living, although you'll find some wonderful communities where housing is comparable to other parts of the country—not next door to movie stars, but certainly in pleasant, safe neighborhoods. Some of the most expensive places to live are found here as well. In some communities around Los Angeles and San Francisco, home prices can be as much as 80 percent higher than the national average!

SOUTHERN CALIFORNIA

When most folks think about Southern California, they conjure up images of Hollywood, surfboards, swimming pools, and convertibles. They picture Southern California towns such as Santa Barbara, Beverly Hills, or Palm Springs with broad, palm-lined boulevards, pastel-colored mansions, and ultramodern apartment buildings.

There is that, but most of us cannot afford to relocate in such elegant surroundings. There are plenty of Southern California locations where living costs aren't necessarily out of line. After all, groceries, clothing, and automobiles cost much the same no matter where you live. Competition for consumer business keeps prices competitive. You'll find the Los Angeles area usually offers the lowest gasoline prices in the state. Because the climate is mild to warm, neither air-conditioning nor heating costs make drastic dents in the budget.

Why do people keep coming to Southern California? Primarily because of the weather, but also the wide variety of things to do and sights to see. Places like Los Angeles and Santa Barbara owe much of their early growth to retirees coming to visit and deciding to stay. Land promoters used to run cross-country passenger trains with free tickets just so retirees could investigate Southern California as a retirement haven. When the unsuspecting retirees were hooked on the lovely orange-grove dreamland, the slick promoters sold building lots for as much as $175 per parcel, with a house for another $3,000. These original homes could sell today for as much as a million dollars!

San Diego Area

With a population of more than a million, San Diego is the epitome of Southern California living. With tasteful architecture, city landscaping with semitropical plants, and neighborhoods of Spanish-style pastel homes with tile roofs, this is a dream place for relocation. Be prepared for sticker shock, however, when it comes to real estate.

The attraction here is the superb weather. Statistically, San Diego has the best climate in the continental United States. It never freezes or snows, and it rains a scant 11 inches a year, just enough to keep shrubbery and flowers fresh. A constant breeze from the Pacific pushes heat into the desert and nullifies cold snaps. Smog or air pollution is not a problem here, and you'll have little need for air-conditioning.

San Diego's downtown center is an excellent example of a city in transition from the 1930s to the 21st century. The downtown, once rather ordinary and deteriorating, has been transformed into a vibrant, welcoming business and entertainment center. Trees, landscaping, and careful planning are doing the trick.

The San Diego area has an unusually large percentage of retirees. There are more than a hundred senior citizens' organizations, with membership totaling more than 100,000. Numerous life-care centers and seniors-only apartments and housing complexes are scattered around the region.

The big drawback with San Diego is expensive housing, some of the costliest in the nation. The median price of a single-family home is often more than 60 percent above the national average. You can find affordable neighborhoods if you look for them, but few places that could be considered bargains.

It isn't necessary to live in the city of San Diego itself to enjoy the weather and ambience. At the eastern edge of San Diego, the country becomes rolling desert hills, with dramatic boulders and rock formations garnished with cactus and desert brush. Within easy shopping distance from San Diego are the towns of El Cajon (pop. 101,000), Alpine (pop. 14,000), Lakeside (pop. 21,000), and several other smaller communities that are popular as relocation destinations. Land is far less expensive. Building lots tend to be spacious, sometimes large enough to keep horses. Riding trails take off in all directions to wander through the empty mountain country. The tradeoff is slightly warmer summers and cooler winters. Still, there is never ice or snow.

From your suburban home you can run into San Diego to enjoy professional sports: the Padres, the Hawks, or the Farmers Insurance PGA Open. San Diego State and the University of San Diego bring collegiate football as well as the usual artistic presentations, and the opera, theater, and symphony are nationally renowned. For your grandkids or visiting family, Sea World and Legoland hold a day of fun and amusement. El Cajon, for example, is only 15 miles via interstate to downtown San Diego. Senior citizens account for more than 20 percent of El Cajon's population and enjoy numerous services provided by the East County Council on Aging and Grossmont Hospital in La Mesa. Two other hospitals are here, including a Kaiser Foundation facility.

About 30 miles northeast of San Diego is the town of Escondido (pop. 151,000). The climate is similar to El Cajon's—dry and pleasant—but you're now in rolling grass country. Low mountains loom in the background, and ranches and homes on acreage lots dominate the outlying areas here. Many homes have horse stables. Houses and condos rent for considerably less here than in San Diego, and homes sell for 15 to 30 percent less than similar homes in the city. Escondido offers most amenities retirees demand: a hospital, an excellent senior service center, a community college, and adult education programs that are free to those older than 60.

San Diego Chamber of Commerce: 402 W. Broadway, Ste. 1000, San Diego, CA 92101; (619) 544-1310; sdchamber.org.

SOUTHERN CALIFORNIA COASTAL WEATHER

	IN DEGREES FAHRENHEIT				ANNUAL	
	Jan.	**April**	**July**	**Oct.**	**RAIN**	**SNOW**
Daily highs	65	67	75	74	12"	—
Daily lows	47	52	63	59		

Los Angeles Region

This is where the Southern California dream started. Retirement became big business back in the 1880s when promoters began capitalizing on the ideal climate. From that time on, retirement growth remained big as the town grew larger and larger. But Los Angeles didn't simply grow larger as most cities do; it grew quite unpredictably, spreading out in this direction and that, until the result is a city that looks different and is different from any other metropolis in the world.

Not long ago, friends from Argentina came to visit us. We met the couple at the Los Angeles airport and treated them to a sightseeing tour. They were thrilled at finally seeing fabulous Los Angeles, but after some time driving around, they were puzzled. "But where is the city?" they asked. "We were expecting tall buildings. Everything here is small." We had driven through Hollywood, Beverly Hills, and all the other obligatory areas, yet they found few places that matched their image of what Los Angeles should be. To them a real city should resemble Buenos Aires or Manhattan. There should be tall, elegant apartment buildings, graceful skyscrapers, fancy restaurants with sidewalk cafes, and all the metropolitan delights that combine to make a real city. Instead they found single-family homes, one- and two-story commercial buildings, and spread-out shopping malls. The occasional tall building seemed lonely and out of place.

In most large cities of the world, land is at a premium, far too valuable to waste on lawns and landscaping. Buildings start at the sidewalk and rise as high as possible. When room is left over for a lawn, it is placed behind the house and jealously guarded for the family's personal use. To be sure, the Los Angeles city center does have a group of high-rises, but they are for commerce, not for people to live in. They stand out like lost visions, mistaken attempts to create something impossible: a real city in the Los Angeles collection of suburbs.

There is, of course, a "downtown" section, but it isn't the same as in other big cities. People don't go downtown for Christmas shopping or to seek out those special restaurants as they do in New York, San Francisco, or Buenos Aires. People avoid the central downtown and go to the nearest shopping mall, or to shopping districts in neighborhoods such as Beverly Hills, Hollywood, or Santa Monica instead. Like satellites, a garland of smaller cities surrounds Los Angeles.

This ring of small towns is where retirement is best considered, not in Los Angeles proper. FBI crime charts show that most of the towns circling Los Angeles are quite safe. Hermosa Beach, Agoura Hills, and Redondo Beach, for example, rank in the top levels of personal safety. People who live here seldom if ever venture into less safe zones; they have no reason to do so.

There are so many delightful communities here that it's impossible to list them. It's worth spending time driving and looking from Capistrano in the south to the San Gabriel Mountains to the north, or out to the desert-like settings in the east as far as San Bernardino. Nice mobile-home parks are increasingly plentiful the farther you travel from Los Angeles.

The area's superb year-round climate makes outdoor recreation practical, with golf, tennis, and swimming available in most every neighborhood. Wilderness areas are but 1 or 2 hours' drive from city hall. Gold panning in the San Gabriel Mountains, skiing and trout fishing at Lake Arrowhead and Big Bear, or rockhounding in the desert—all these and more are available. Fishing off the piers, jogging, walking, or loafing on the beaches adds another facet of outdoor recreation. The ocean can be enjoyed to the limit. Sailboats and fishing craft can be berthed at numerous places along the coast.

As for Los Angeles itself, it offers cultural advantages found only in big cities. World-famous art galleries, museums, and symphonies are easily accessible, as are theaters, universities, and all types of senior activities. The area is home to many professional sports teams, including the L.A. Lakers, Clippers, Dodgers, and Galaxy, and top-ranked collegiate play from USC and UCLA. There are many attractions for children, like Six Flags Magic Mountain, Knott's Berry Farm, Universal Studios, and, of course, Disneyland in neighboring Orange County. It's a great place for short visits.

The Los Angeles area is not an inexpensive place to retire, yet it doesn't have to be prohibitive. It takes some shopping to find a comfortable niche, a place where housing prices aren't off the wall. But it's important to look beyond housing prices here; the quality of a neighborhood is far more important than affordability. The bottom line around Los Angeles is: If you can't afford to live in a safe neighborhood, forget it.

Los Angeles Chamber of Commerce: 350 S. Bixel St., Los Angeles, CA 90017; (213) 580-7500; lachamber.com.

Pismo Beach/Five Cities Area

Once the butt of many Jack Benny jokes, Pismo Beach is today having the last laugh. People are discovering that it's a very pleasant place to spend a vacation, plus it's a great place to retire. Located about 200 miles north of Los Angeles, the Pismo Beach area has a population of approximately 110,000. However, this population figure is misleading. This is because Pismo Beach is just one of five adjoining towns spread along the beach and near-inland areas that give the Five Cities its name. Together the towns blend into one good-size city spread along the beaches. You'll find all the conveniences available in much larger towns, yet you can enjoy a pleasant small-town ambience, no matter which of the Five Cities you choose for retirement. By the way, the word *pismo* comes from the famous pismo clams that at one time seemed to almost pave the long stretches of sandy shoreline. Until 1985 or so, the favorite sport here was digging into the sand at low tide in search of these large, succulent clams. Both locals and tourists still do, but today's clam diggers aren't like the crowds of a few years ago. Too many clam forks and increasing hordes of voracious sea otters have thinned the mollusk population considerably. Yet clams are still there for the persistent, and fishing is still great from the long pier that juts out past the surf (no license required on the pier). Ling cod, red snapper, and sand dabs are favorite catches. Fishing and clamming are year-round sports.

Pismo Beach is one of the few places along the California coast, and the only state park (Oceano Dunes), where it is permissible to drive a motor vehicle onto the sand. You'll find 5.5 miles of hard-packed sand and huge undulating dunes for both sport and easy passenger car driving. Huge, undulating dunes are meccas for four-wheel-drive vehicles and dune buggies. Converted Volkswagens, Jeeps, and other souped-up contraptions zip up and down the dunes like motorized roller coasters (away from the more quiet beach crowd, of course). Another favorite beach activity is horseback riding. A couple of stables rent horses for leisurely rides along the surf line. Golf is popular, with several courses in the area.

The loosely connected communities that together make up the sprawling Five Cities area are Shell Beach, Oceano, Grover City, Arroyo Grande, and Pismo Beach itself. Arroyo Grande, with a population of 18,000, is the largest of the Five Cities. Housing is naturally more expensive along the cliff tops, or anywhere an ocean view fills your picture window.

When we first started writing about Pismo Beach and the Five Cities complex, we considered the area one of the best real estate buys on California's central coast. One reason for this was the exodus of workers who labored on the nearby Diablo Canyon nuclear-power project when the facility was completed. Eventually, a wave of popularity and economic growth boosted prices to the level of similar California locations. New developments with upscale housing have been competing with large, luxury homes. The hills overlooking the beaches are becoming filled with elegant-looking, Spanish-styled homes, complete with tiled roofs. This isn't to say this is now an outrageously expensive area. You'll find plenty of inexpensive neighborhoods (of course, without the ocean view), especially in the older sections of Pismo Beach, which are just a few blocks' walk to the beach, rather than sitting up on a hill, which requires a drive to the beach.

As you might expect, where there are large numbers of retired folks, you will find active senior citizens' organizations. Pismo Beach supports several organizations, ranging from grandmothers' clubs to a singles' club for people older than 60. You'll find an active RSVP chapter, Meals on Wheels, and a senior citizens' ride program—plus plenty of opportunities to get involved in volunteer projects. Younger retirees and semiretired people commute to San Luis Obispo for part-time jobs with Cal Poly University as well as in the private sector.

Because of the close proximity of San Luis Obispo, most people go there for hospital care. However, there is one hospital located in Arroyo Grande, the 65-bed Arroyo Grande Community Hospital.

Pismo Beach Chamber of Commerce: 581 Dolliver St., Pismo Beach, CA 93449; (805) 773-4382; fax (805) 773-6772; pismochamber.com.

San Luis Obispo

The university town of San Luis Obispo is just a 15-minute drive north of the Five Cities area. This is a real charmer and, from our perspective, perhaps one of the best places for retirement in the entire state. Like the Pismo Beach/Five Cities area, San Luis Obispo's 46,000 population is a bit misleading. San Luis Obispo County has a population of almost 300,000 and is considered 81 percent urban and only 19 percent rural. A conglomeration of smaller towns contributes to a viable business center. But the major influence is from California Polytechnic State University and its almost 20,000 students' and 2,500 faculty members' and administrative staff's involvement with the communities in and around San Luis Obispo.

A city beautification program, started some 30 years ago, has paid off handsomely, making the downtown center a treat for the eyes. Mature and massive trees arch over commercial avenues lined with prosperous businesses and stores with tastefully designed exteriors. San Luis Obispo was not long ago awarded the distinction of having "the best downtown in the Western United States" by *Sunset* magazine. Nationally known outlets you would expect to find only in shopping malls—fashionable clothing stores, large drugstores, and boutiques of all description—are located right in the center of town, instead of all being in a strip mall a 10-minute drive away.

Like most university towns, San Luis Obispo enjoys school-related services and facilities that benefit students and retirees alike. Interesting yet affordable restaurants, bookstores that stock more than just bestsellers, and foreign and award-winning movies that you'd seldom find in other towns are among the qualities that retirees appreciate about San Luis Obispo living. Another downtown tradition is the Thursday night farmers' market, a delightful hubbub of organically grown local greens and flowers, street musicians, and barbecued ribs. There's also a burgeoning wine-growing area on the outskirts of town, with tours and tasting rooms galore.

Residential neighborhoods present enticing retirement scenarios, with nicely landscaped properties and views of mountains in the distance. Although San Luis Obispo property values never were cheap, homes and condos appear to be bargains when compared with some other quality central coast locations, such as Monterey or Santa Barbara. For slightly less expensive real estate, take a look at the nearby communities of Grover Beach, and Nipomo in the Five Cities area and Atascadero, Templeton, and Paso Robles to the north and inland.

The university sponsors a multitude of cultural events such as plays, lectures, and concerts, many free to senior citizens. The Performing Arts Center on the Cal Poly campus attracts Broadway shows, concerts, plays, pop singers, and more. Mission Plaza, once just a street in front of the mission, is now the cultural heart of the city—a place for craft fairs, promotional events, and special events such as the Festival Mozaic (formerly known as the Mozart Festival), wine festivals, and free Friday evening concerts in the plaza.

All of this makes San Luis Obispo a pleasant retirement location for those who don't feel the need to be within walking distance of the beach (although the ocean is only a 15-minute drive). The advantages of living close to, but not right on, the ocean include abundant sunshine and comfortable evenings with shirtsleeve weather, rather than the typically cool evenings by the ocean, where sweaters are routinely required.

As the health care center for the region, San Luis Obispo has several medical facilities: Sierra Vista Regional Medical Center, French Hospital (with an outstanding cardiac unit), and the county-operated General Hospital, as well as several outpatient clinics, including a Veterans Administration clinic. Because the area is a draw for professionals from all walks of life, there is a full range of medical practitioners to ensure good care.

San Luis Obispo Chamber of Commerce: 895 Monterey St., San Luis Obispo, CA 93401; (805) 781-2777; slochamber.org.

THE CALIFORNIA DESERT

Most of Southern California is desert, starting only a few miles from the ocean beaches and covering the lower part of the state. One of the world's most famous deserts, Death Valley, is in California, and the Mojave Desert covers a good portion of Southern California with multicolored sand dunes, volcanic cinder cones, Joshua tree forests, and mile-high mountains. You'll find some great relocation towns that will appeal to some people, perhaps not to others. Many relocate here from the Los Angeles area, attracted by low crime rates, cheap land, and wide-open spaces.

Traditionally, California deserts are divided into two types: high desert and low desert. As you would expect, the higher country has colder winters and more pleasant summers. However, "colder" winters doesn't mean

CALIFORNIA DESERT WEATHER

| | IN DEGREES FAHRENHEIT | | | | ANNUAL | |
	Jan.	April	July	Oct.	RAIN	SNOW
Daily highs	72	87	109	92	5"	—
Daily lows	43	54	75	60		

continual freezing weather; it means that when cold winds blow from the north, it can get downright chilly, sometimes cold enough to snow. But most of the time, whenever it's sunny, daytime temperatures climb to either shirtsleeve or light sweater weather, even in the midst of winter.

Palm Springs

When people speak of Palm Springs, they could mean any of a half dozen towns scattered along I-10, from Palm Springs to Indian Wells. The city of Palm Springs has a population of about 48,000, but the surrounding complex of towns probably doubles this figure.

The playground of millionaire industrialists, movie stars, and other rich and famous types, Palm Springs is synonymous with class. Over the years well-known personalities such as Bob Hope, Bing Crosby, Gerald Ford, and a host of others have made golf fans aware of the great, year-round golf courses. When people with enough money to live anywhere in the world choose the Palm Springs area for their homes, there must be something special going on!

Sheltered in the lee of the rugged San Jacinto Mountains, with abundant irrigation water, Palm Springs is verdant and livable year-round. Green landscaping, huge palm trees, and manicured golf courses convert the desert into a botanical wonderland. The area supports more golf courses than most cities have supermarkets, 93 in all. Many are private, belonging to residents of the surrounding developments, but there are plenty of public courses.

Winters are as delightful here as summers are hot. As one real estate salesperson put it, "Which is worse, a low-humidity, hot summer—or an icy, freezing winter?" As this writer worked on his notes, it was the middle of January in Palm Springs. I was outdoors—barefoot, wearing shorts and a T-shirt—listening to radio reports of 18-below-zero storms savaging the Midwest and eastern states, with snowdrifts deeper than our swimming pool! Instead of snowstorms, Southern California deserts have windstorms. However, Palm Springs is spared many of the windstorms because nearby mountains block most of the wind, creating a haven of calm and turning roaring winds into light breezes. A significant number of people routinely flock to the desert for half of the year to escape from cities hit hard by harsh winter climates. They may live in Palm Springs to take advantage of the mild winters, and then depart the dreaded hot summers for more pleasant weather in other parts of the country. In recent years Palm Springs has been noted for its large and vibrant LGBTQ community. In 2019 the city boasted the nation's first all-LGBTQ city council, which has furthered its draw as a destination where residents and vacationers alike can live out and proud at gay-friendly clubs, bars, and events.

A drive through expensive neighborhoods can be overwhelming: one street after another competing for the title of the most fancy and opulent. Shopping centers that look as if they were built for sultans or nobility offer any kind of luxury item you can afford (and many that you can only dream of). Clean desert air and a rugged mountain backdrop give Palm Springs an aura of pristine beauty combined with regal affluence.

The curious thing is, although this is one of the more expensive retirement areas in the country, it's not necessarily out of reach for folks with moderate incomes. The bottom line is, most residents are *not* rich. They work for ordinary wages and cannot afford a super-expensive lifestyle. The most common occupation here is support services: restaurants, stores, hotels, or gardening for wealthy families, and other jobs of that nature. Wages for grocery clerks, auto mechanics, or waiters are never so high that they drive up the housing market.

The most-fancy homes are found in adjoining towns, places such as Rancho Mirage, Palm Desert, or Indian Wells. Yet interspersed with these exclusive enclaves are affordable neighborhoods for ordinary wage earners and retirees, often just a few blocks away. Mobile-home parks also provide moderate-cost alternatives. Some are elegant, complete with golf privileges; others are less fancy, with competitive rates.

At times, real estate prices in Palm Springs can fluctuate wildly. Why would that be? Because the real estate market here goes up or down according to the health of the national economy, and particularly in response to Southern California's business ups and downs. It turns out that the Palm Springs real estate market crashes every time there is an abrupt downturn in Los Angeles's economy. When defense industry jobs dry up, when lucrative businesses go bankrupt, when high-paid executives go on unemployment, one of the first things to be sacrificed is that second home in Palm Springs. None of this affects people who maintain their main residences here; nothing much changes except home prices. The trick is to buy at one of the low cycles, because you can be sure property values will return to the top before long.

Medical care in the region is said to be excellent, which isn't surprising considering the large numbers of wealthy residents who can afford the best. The Desert Regional Medical Center is located in Palm Springs, and the Eisenhower Medical Center is located in Rancho Mirage, about 9 miles away.

Desert Hot Springs

If the posh atmosphere of Palm Springs is a little intimidating, you'll find a "Poor Man's Palm Springs" just across I-10, about a 15-minute drive away. This is the town of Desert Hot Springs (pop. 24,000). Its name comes from the hot water that seeps beneath the town from nearby mountain slopes. Homeowners commonly tap the steaming water and enjoy it in their backyard swimming pools and hot tubs. Much smaller than Palm Springs or any of the ritzy sections on the other side of I-10, Desert Hot Springs has a lot to offer in pleasant, relatively economical desert retirement.

Desert Hot Springs bestows many of Palm Springs's advantages without the higher prices. The fabled restaurants, golf courses, shopping, and social life of Palm Springs are just a few minutes away. With an elevation about a thousand feet higher than Palm Springs, Desert Hot Springs enjoys summer temperatures a smidgen cooler than communities on the valley floor. Winter days are often warmer because of the mountains, which block north winds that occasionally bring cold down from Alaska. The most common weather complaint concerns annoying westerly winds that hit Desert Hot Springs but circumvent Palm Springs.

Like Palm Springs, a large percentage of the residents live here year-round. Many are retired, but there's also a large balance of younger people who work in Palm Springs but can't afford its prices. The downtown area is low-key, as is the rest of the town.

Palm Springs Chamber of Commerce: 190 W. Amado Rd., Palm Springs, CA 92262; (760) 325-1577; pschamber.org.

SAN FRANCISCO BAY REGION

One of our most favorite cities in the country—in the world, in fact—San Francisco has become one of the more expensive cities in the country. Although real estate prices took a sharp hit in the 2008 crash, they've recovered and then some. San Francisco real estate most likely will never again become what most families might call affordable.

This is unfortunate, because for many people there's a certain magic aura about San Francisco. Probably something that originated back in the gold rush days, when San Francisco was the West Coast's center of civilization and sophistication in the countryside of wildcat mining camps, boomtowns, and rough-and-ready tent communities. When visiting "the City," we often look at people walking along the street and wonder: "*Do they really appreciate how lucky they are to live in San Francisco?*"

It's difficult to explain this to someone who has never experienced the sophisticated mellowness of San Francisco. More than just a "city," it's a collection of unique and intimate neighborhoods, all blending into a small self-contained metropolitan area. In some ways San Francisco is a miniature New York City. Each neighborhood has its own personality and distinctive restaurants waiting for discovery. There's a huge Chinatown and a separate Japan town. There's an Irish neighborhood, and a little Italy area, as well as two neighborhoods with a strong LGBTQ+ identity. Everything is covered in "the City."

For those who love San Francisco as we do, the solution is to live in a smaller, nearby community where one can own or rent a retirement base, then visit whenever the urge overtakes you. You'll find a dozen or so suitable satellite towns within an hour's drive or less, in a half circle around San Francisco. Few of them could be called "inexpensive," but most are definitely more affordable. The below examples are to the north of San Francisco.

Sonoma County

About an hour's drive north of the high-priced real estate of San Francisco is one of the world's top wine regions—Sonoma County. Multiple airports allow for easy access to the region: San Francisco International, Oakland International, Sacramento International, and Sonoma County Airport.

Because of their close proximity, cities in Napa and Sonoma Counties are often referred to nationally as "wine country" and are intermixed and

SONOMA COUNTY WEATHER

	IN DEGREES FAHRENHEIT				ANNUAL	
	Jan.	April	July	Oct.	RAIN	SNOW
Daily highs	57	67	82	75	29"	—
Daily lows	46	42	54	47		

confused with each other. While it is true that the region produces internationally recognized libations, the towns within the two counties hold distinct personalities and offerings. Real estate has hit a high in certain cities within the area, particularly in Napa County, but there are still opportunities for retirement in some of the yet-to-be discovered jewels for those that can't afford the sky-high prices of San Francisco or Silicon Valley.

Weather in the region is conducive to agriculture in the valleys that surround it. The summers can be quite hot, yet they receive the cooling benefit of coastal breezes. Temperatures dip in the winter, bringing moderate rainfall but, of course, no snow. The mild climate lends to year-round comfortable living.

Santa Rosa

Just off the US 101 freeway in central Sonoma County, Santa Rosa (pop. 175,000) provides the modern conveniences of a well-populated city with the scenic beauty of the region. The city is the largest in Sonoma County and the fifth most populated in the Bay Area. Many buildings in Santa Rosa have kept their historical charm, which led Hollywood to seek out the city as a location for films as far back as 1943, when Alfred Hitchcock filmed *Shadow of a Doubt*.

The region was hit hard by the Tubbs Fire in October 2017. Over 5,300 homes in Sonoma County were destroyed by the wildfire and half of those homes were in Santa Rosa. Home prices surged in the aftermath as residents sought to invest their insurance money back into real estate. The city is still recovering from the extensive damage and the market has begun to level out as of the writing of this book.

Santa Rosa neighbors the Russian River Valley, Alexander Valley, and Dry Creek Valley, all of which have been heralded for producing some of the finest wines to come out of Northern California. To the east, you can find Napa County–based towns such as Calistoga and St. Helena. These are vacation spots for the business elite and celebrities alike due to their upscale spa retreats and delectable restaurants. Michelin-rated restaurants have drawn in the most dedicated "foodies." Many restaurants take pride in using locally grown and organic produce, breads, and livestock.

The even climate provides ample opportunity for outdoor activities. You will commonly find dedicated cyclists hitting the streets and off-roading on trails. The Bennett Valley Golf Course provides an outlet for those who like to hit the links. The Russian River runs nearby, and people take advantage of the easy river access for boating, fishing, swimming, and canoeing.

Cultural and entertainment opportunities are easy to come by. The Wells Fargo Center for the Arts and the new Green Music Center in neighboring Rohnert Park hold world-class performances. Continuing-education opportunities exist at Santa Rosa Junior College, Sonoma State University, and the University of San Francisco's regional campus.

Santa Rosa Memorial Hospital provides a wide range of services. It serves multiple cities outside of Santa Rosa, such as Sonoma and Petaluma, with a state-of-the-art facility with 278 beds for acute care.

Santa Rosa Chamber of Commerce: 50 Old Courthouse Square, Ste. 110, Santa Rosa, CA 95404; (707) 545-1414; santarosametro chamber.com.

Petaluma

Southern Sonoma County holds much of the quaint feel you will find in northern parts of the county with a blend of urban offerings. Thirty-two miles north of San Francisco, the city of Petaluma (pop. 60,000) sits just off US 101, south of Santa Rosa. Petaluma has roots in the gold-mining surge and became a significant business center for manufacturing and shipping in the mid- to late 1800s. At the turn of the 20th century, the city picked up the nickname "The World's Egg Basket" due to a large population of chicken and dairy farms. This history is still celebrated each year with the annual Butter and Eggs Day parade in the spring.

The downtown area is nestled against the riverfront of the Petaluma River. A variety of locally owned shops, bookstores, and restaurants are housed in unique architecture that provides the atmosphere of a 1950s throwback. In fact, Petaluma has served as the backdrop for films such as *American Graffiti* and *Peggy Sue Got Married*.

The city prides itself on its dedication to the arts. The Petaluma Arts Center offers lectures, classes, and even art exhibitions throughout the year. Antiques fairs and art festivals are commonplace. Film festivals are held at the historic Mystic Theatre annually.

The Petaluma Community Center offers regular classes, such as fitness, dance, and health courses. The Petaluma Senior Center also offers a variety of activities geared toward those 55 years and older. For those seeking additional educational opportunities, Santa Rosa Junior College has a campus in Petaluma, and the main campus is a short drive away from Santa Rosa.

Multiple hospitals are within close proximity. Petaluma Valley Hospital holds 80 beds for acute and critical care, with a highly respected cardiology center. Additionally, Novato Community Hospital and Santa Rosa Memorial Hospital are within 15 miles south or north, respectively.

Petaluma Chamber of Commerce: 6 Petaluma Blvd. N., Ste. A-2, Petaluma, CA 94952; (707) 762-2785; petalumachamber.com.

GOLD COUNTRY

In 1847, in a part of Mexico called Alta California, a group of workers labored to construct a sawmill on a rushing stream that flowed down from the Sierra Nevada range. This was not far from what is now Sacramento. As workers dug into the riverbank, a man noticed something curious in his shovel's blade. Sparkling pebbles of metal mixed with the gravel. Gold!

This event touched off one of the most exciting chapters in US history. News of the discovery spread. The rush was on. People came by covered wagon and horseback; others sailed around Cape Horn to join in a frenzy of prospecting. Eager miners attacked streams with gold pans and sluice boxes to fill their pockets with heavy nuggets of gold. Deposits were so rich, the miners called the area the "Mother Lode."

Within a short span of time, rude mining camps became towns, then small cities. Paved streets, brick buildings, theaters, and businesses flourished, creating replicas in miniature of midwestern and eastern towns of that era.

When their claims finally played out, gold miners drifted on to other enterprises. Some moved to fertile California valleys to seek fortunes on

GOLD COUNTRY WEATHER

	IN DEGREES FAHRENHEIT				ANNUAL	
	Jan.	April	July	Oct.	RAIN	SNOW
Daily highs	54	62	85	71	40"	5"
Daily lows	35	38	54	44		

the land. Others settled in the growing coastal cities. When miners moved away, Mother Lode towns became virtual ghost towns. Luckily, this abandonment preserved these towns in time-capsule form, providing fascinating pictures of life as it was during California's romantic past. The old mining towns with narrow streets and buildings of native stone and old brick harmonize perfectly with nearby green-clad mountains. The state jealously preserves the sites as a charming part of California's past—the country of Brett Harte, Mark Twain, and John Frémont.

This area of the state encompasses a 300-mile stretch of rolling-to-rugged country that runs from Downieville in the north to Coarsegold in the south. From gentle hills studded with black oaks and manzanita to the majestic peaks of the Sierra Nevada, the Mother Lode encompasses a unique scenic wonderland. Here you'll find not only a true four-season climate, but variation on the seasons, depending on the altitude you choose. From mild winters and warm summers in Jackson and Angels Camp to deep snowpack and cool summers in Lake Tahoe, you have a complete selection of climates and seasonal colors. Trout streams are well stocked, with rare golden trout waiting to be hooked in the higher lakes.

By the way, the forty-niners didn't get all the gold. They left enough to keep hundreds of weekend prospectors and amateur miners working at their dredges and sluice boxes. With much of the countryside designated as public land and national forest, you'll have ample opportunity to try your luck if you wish. A favorite family outing is to take a picnic lunch and a couple of gold pans and spend the afternoon working one of the many creeks and streams that traverse hills covered with oak, pine, and cedar. Some people do quite well, but you can expect them to be very close-mouthed about where they found their private bonanzas. Others are ashamed when they can't locate much gold, so they tell lies about how much they found. (That's what we do.)

Amador County

As an example of Gold Country, let's look in detail at one area in the center of the Mother Lode. Amador County straddles historic CA 49, which follows the trail that once connected the mining towns from north to south. One of the richest gold-mining districts, Amador County accounted for more than half of all the gold harvested from the Mother Lode. Here we find such fascinating towns as Jackson, Sutter Creek, Volcano, Fiddletown, and Plymouth, all of them popular places for relocation.

In the mountains climate varies with altitude, and the altitude varies widely in Amador County. Elevations start at 200 feet and climb all the way to more than 9,000 feet. Magnificent views of snow-covered peaks, mountain lakes, and meadows are everywhere. With low summer humidity even the warmest days are comfortable. Winters are short and mild in the lower regions. January highs average 56 degrees. The entire region enjoys true spring and colorful fall seasons.

Jackson, the largest town in the county, has a population of 4,600. Founded as a gold rush camp in 1848, the town was destroyed by fire in 1862. It was rebuilt, and many existing historic Main Street buildings date from that reconstruction era. The town of Jackson works hard at maintaining the historical atmosphere and is the shopping center for nearby Gold Country retirement communities. All is not historical architecture here, though; modern ranch-style homes and subdivisions are plentiful on the outskirts of the city.

Amador County has dozens of suitable places for retirement: not only towns and villages, but also small farms or wooded acreage. Among the towns are Plymouth, which straddles CA 49 on the northern edge of the county, and Sutter Creek, which was named for famed gold discoverer Captain John Sutter, who arrived here in 1844 to establish a lumber mill. Then there is Fiddletown (pop. 1,000) and Pine Grove (pop. 2,600), both settled in 1849. During the height of the gold rush, Fiddletown had the largest Chinese settlement outside San Francisco.

A growing population created the need for better medical facilities in Amador County. The Sutter Amador Hospital recently underwent major enlargement and now offers a new 93,000-square-foot, 66-bed facility with 24-hour emergency services.

Amador Chamber of Commerce: 70 West Ridge Rd., Sutter Creek, CA 95685; (209) 223-0350; amadorcountychamber.com.

Grass Valley/Nevada City

Other popular relocation towns are found to the north of Jackson, places like Grass Valley and Nevada City, which are a bit more sophisticated and offer a more cosmopolitan charm than Jackson. The area teems with a sense of history and abundant natural beauty. Gold rush architecture sets the tone, with white church steeples and Victorian buildings shaded by century-old sugar maples and liquidambars that early settlers brought with them from New England. Thousands of miners came here in the 1800s—this was one of California's richest gold-producing regions—and today retirees are finding their personal bonanzas in quality living.

The towns of Grass Valley and Nevada City sit in the Sierra Nevada foothills at an average elevation of 2,500 feet. The surroundings vary from rolling hills to rugged peaks, with plentiful forests of oak, pine, cedar, and fir. Residents enjoy four gentle seasons, with homes perched above the fog line yet below the heavy snow line.

Grass Valley is the larger town, with almost 14,000 residents, and nearby Nevada City adds another 3,000. I-80 is conveniently close, making trips to Reno (90 minutes), Sacramento (1 hour), or San Francisco (3 hours) a piece of cake for those who crave city life from time to time. Cultural activities are available right here, too, including classical music festivals, concerts, and theater. Several theater companies mount productions almost year-round. A community college is the latest addition to the cultural scene.

Gold-mining technology, for which Nevada County was famous, today has been replaced by 21st-century computer technology, earning the area the nickname "Silicon Valley of the Sierras." Many high-tech companies, some of them quite small, have relocated here. Some are involved in design and production of digital video, multimedia, and robotics equipment, as well as medical data processing. It is claimed that as many as 1,000 hardware and software development professionals call Nevada County home. It isn't surprising that many high-tech residents here use the Internet to telecommute, and many operate their own high-tech companies without ever leaving their homes.

For outdoor recreation the region is filled with lakes, streams, parks, campgrounds, and hiking trails. Winter skiing is only an hour away at half a dozen resorts, and the short drive makes returning home after a hard afternoon's skiing less of a chore. Summers see very little rainfall, so you'll have plenty of sunshine to accompany you on fishing trips and picnics. There are four golf courses—one public and three private.

Nevada City, by the way, has an exceptionally active senior center, with activities and volunteer opportunities galore. The Gold Country Telecare network keeps folks in touch by phone for problem solving, assistance, and counseling. Telecare volunteers are available for seniors who can't afford to hire someone to fix a leaky faucet or repair porch steps. Legal and tax questions are covered by other volunteers, and still others make sure seniors don't miss shopping, recreational activities, or an appointment with the dentist. Medical care is excellent, with the Sierra Nevada Memorial Hospital, a 124-bed, acute-care facility, offering state-of-the-art diagnostic, surgical, and therapeutic equipment.

Scattered around the countryside are any number of smaller communities—historic places such as Rough and Ready, Gold Run, or Colfax—away from town but only a few miles from shopping. Before you settle on a gold-mining location, you must see 'em all!

Grass Valley/Nevada County Chamber of Commerce: 128 E. Main St., Grass Valley, CA 95945; (530) 273-4667, (800) 655-4667; grass valleychamber.com.

Lake Tahoe

A short drive from Reno up a wide, four-lane highway is a beautiful, bustling area in a forested lake setting that many consider a prime retirement place. This is South Lake Tahoe, a sprawling community that straddles the line between Nevada and California. Well known for luxurious hotels and gambling casinos, Lake Tahoe is also celebrated for beauty; it sits next to one of the most gorgeous lakes in the world.

Snow is an important part of Tahoe's winter. If there isn't at least a 6-foot pack on the ski slopes, skiers feel cheated. From anywhere in the area, it is a matter of minutes to a ski lift, a joy to those who enjoy the sport. The snow typically falls in isolated, heavy storms that dump up to 3 feet in one night, then the weather turns sunny for days or weeks until the next snow. From my perspective the best thing about Lake Tahoe snow is that it takes only a 20-minute drive to be out of it! You can be skiing at Incline Village in the morning and wandering through Carson City casinos in shirtsleeves that same evening.

HIGH SIERRA WEATHER

	IN DEGREES FAHRENHEIT				ANNUAL	
	Jan.	April	July	Oct.	RAIN	SNOW
Daily highs	42	58	85	65	37"	105"
Daily lows	26	33	51	37		

Because the Lake Tahoe economy is basically tourist oriented, many normal cultural and entertainment activities are lacking. But those lacking elements are more than compensated for by the top-notch talent presented by the casinos. Hollywood stars and entertainers regularly appear at the gambling emporiums, usually at a fraction of the entrance fees you'd expect in a noncompetitive economy. Also, the area is served by Lake Tahoe Community College, which offers various courses oriented toward seniors, from computers to exercise classes.

The cost of living here is clearly higher than in nearby Reno or Carson City. With tourist dollars floating around freely, you can expect that prices will float with them. Housing is expensive as well. But for many people a higher cost of living is a reasonable tradeoff for the quality of the surroundings and the excitement of the lake area and its outdoor wonderland. Those who aren't ready for a rocking-chair retirement will usually find plenty of part-time work opportunities in the casinos or local tourist-oriented businesses.

One medium-size hospital, Barton Memorial, with 119 beds, serves the medical needs of the area. The facility is equipped to handle most cases, but when it can't, transportation is available to nearby Carson City, the University of California Hospital at Davis, near Sacramento, or the Washoe Medical Center in Reno.

Why would folks consider retiring in the Tahoe area? "Living here is like being on permanent vacation," said a friend of ours who owns a lakefront cottage near North Shore. Like many residents he bought his home several years ago in anticipation of retirement. He rented out his second home by the day or week at premium rates to regular visitors—vacationers, skiers, and gamblers—and by the time he was ready to retire, a good portion of his retirement home had been paid off. The deductions and depreciation as a rental also helped ease his tax burden. Long-term rentals, however, are usually available at rates one would expect to pay in most

California urban areas. That can be expensive, and may be worth it only if you cannot consider living anywhere else because you love Lake Tahoe so much. Many people living here feel just that way.

Lake Tahoe Chamber of Commerce: 100 N. Lake Blvd., Tahoe City, CA (530) 581-6900; gotahoenorth.com.

Oroville

About 100 miles to the north of Amador County, the Feather River yielded another rich harvest of shining metal. Scattered above the canyon on a place called Nimshew Ridge, a collection of little villages and mining camps sprang up, with vivid names such as Dogtown, Toadtown, Poverty Ridge, and Whiskey Flats. At Dogtown (now Magalia) a prospector uncovered a 59-pound gold nugget back in 1859. Several nuggets weighing up to 9 pounds each turned up later, but after the Dogtown nugget, everything else seemed anticlimactic.

Previous versions of this book outlined the beauty and the history of the town that grew from these early gold-mining roots: Paradise. Unfortunately, the 153,000-acre Camp Fire of 2018 was the most devastating and deadliest wildfire in recent history, and it completely decimated the entire city. Paradise, formerly with a population nearing 30,000 and a total of about 45,000 clustered about the city limits, had homes tucked away in quiet, wooded neighborhoods, most of which burned.

Thousands of modern-day retirees, many of whom came from San Francisco and Los Angeles, believe they'd found their paradise here. After all, 49 percent of the residents were over 55. On a personal note, the destruction of Paradise hit very close to home for one of our authors, who was born there and who lived there until she was five years old.

While there are people who are working to rebuild and proudly declaring "Paradise Strong," many have been forced to relocate, and nearby Oroville has proven to be an attractive option. It is situated on the Feather River on what was one of the first gold-mining sites, known as Bidwell Bar, where thousands of prospectors once flocked to seek their fortune.

Oroville is home to over 20,000 people, and upwards of 55,000 when you include outlying neighborhoods.

Housing ranges from stately homes with views on lots shaded by tall pines to individual mobile homes hidden from view of the road. Clever landscaping can make them practically indistinguishable from conventional housing.

The city is not far above sea-level, so heat can certainly rise in the summer months. Overall, the climate is fairly moderate with an average of 243 sunny days per year. Outdoor opportunities are abundant; Oroville has multiple parks with picnic grounds and play structures. Riverbend Park boasts 201 acres with four separate pavilions available for rental. Two local, public golf courses will get you out on the links.

If you are looking to continue your education, you need look no further than 30 minutes away at CSU Chico and their ElderCollege program, where people over the age of 60 may sit in on any regular university course on a space-available basis for a $60 per semester fee.

As would be expected within a city that holds many retirees, Oroville Hospital offers state-of-the-art services.

Oroville Chamber of Commerce: 1789 Montgomery St., Oroville, CA 95965; (530) 538-2542; paradisechamber.com.

Chico

In contrast, only a 25-minute drive from the suburb city of Oroville, the more urban city of Chico is a popular relocation town with affordable real estate in a university setting. Chico (pop. 88,000) is a typical Sacramento Valley town, located on the banks of the Sacramento River, with live oak and huge ash trees shading quiet streets on topography as flat as a card table. What lifts Chico above other agriculturally centered valley towns is Chico State University and its vibrant academic life. The campus dominates the city center, and, like all California state universities, Chico State encourages senior citizen participation with free and reduced tuition rates. Cultural events, such as concerts, plays, lectures, and foreign films, are plentiful and, more often than not, free.

Many good home buys in Chico are found in older neighborhoods and in some more recent developments on the edge of town. Typical construction is frame with a stucco finish, favored because of its resilience in earthquakes.

Chico residents point out the advantage of being close to the mountains: good fishing, hunting, and camping. A short drive takes you to the natural beauty and the recreational opportunities of the Feather River

SACRAMENTO VALLEY WEATHER

| | IN DEGREES FAHRENHEIT | | | | ANNUAL | |
	Jan.	April	July	Oct.	RAIN	SNOW
Daily highs	54	73	98	79	22"	1"
Daily lows	36	44	59	47		

Canyon Recreation Area. Skiing is enjoyed at Inskip, about 40 minutes away, and some of the best striped bass in the West are caught in the nearby Sacramento River. Incidentally, anglers haul monster sturgeon from this river, many fish tipping the scale at more than 200 pounds! Because sturgeon is a game fish and not sold commercially, few people have ever tasted a succulent steak from one of these large creatures. It's like no other fish you've ever tasted—as firm as lobster, as juicy as a filet mignon, yet with a flavor closer to frogs' legs than fish.

The weather in Chico, as in all Central Valley towns, is both a blessing and a drawback, depending on your opinion of how hot summers should be. You can find days on end with temperatures approaching 100 degrees. Balance that against mild, seldom-frosty winter days, and I believe Chico's weather comes out a winner. After all, when the summer gets going, that's the time for you to get going to the nearby mountains for a picnic beside a cool stream or a day's prospecting and panning for gold in the Feather River.

Chico Chamber of Commerce: 180 E. 4th St., Ste. 120, Chico, CA 95927; (530) 891-5556; chicochamber.com.

Dunsmuir

The Sacramento River, which passes through Chico on its way to San Francisco Bay, has its origins farther north, past Redding and beautiful Lake Shasta, in the mountains not far from the small but intriguing town of Dunsmuir (pop. 1,800).

Dunsmuir sits in a canyon, overshadowed by ridges covered with Christmas-tree pines and segmented by streets that climb steeply from the river bottom to the interstate highway above the town. Residents enjoy a spectacular year-round view of snow-covered Mount Shasta in the distance.

This ancient volcano is one of the highest peaks on the continent and offers some pretty fair skiing at a place called Snowman's Hill.

Dunsmuir is a town this writer knows quite well! Years ago I spent a year working for the *Dunsmuir News*, a weekly paper serving the mountain communities of Dunsmuir and the sister town of Mount Shasta. This was back in the days when newspapers were produced by clanking linotype machines and hand-fed cylinder presses. (Sadly, like small-town newspapers throughout the nation, the *Dunsmuir News* faded away many years ago.)

The town of Dunsmuir was as antique as the newspaper office, both frozen in time. The town hasn't changed much over the years. Many (if not most) homes date to the early 1900s. A sense of history permeates the old-fashioned downtown section and its two main streets. The bus station is still referred to as the "stage stop" by some older residents, and the Greyhound bus is often called the "stage."

Although some mining went on in the area, Dunsmuir originated as a roundhouse and service station for passing trains, providing fuel and water for the locomotives and food for the dining cars. With the decline of steam engines, the original purpose of the town faded. Today retirees find this a great place for small-community relocation. Property is affordable, with great trout fishing, gorgeous views—especially the view of Mount Shasta from your front porch every morning—and unforgettable sunsets.

Dunsmuir's northern location and 2,300-foot elevation ensures at least a couple of good winter snowstorms every season. The canyon turns into a billowy white winter fantasyland for a day or two until a warm rain clears it all away.

Dunsmuir Chamber of Commerce: 5915 Dunsmuir Ave., Dunsmuir, CA 96025; (530) 235-2177.

Mount Shasta

Dunsmuir's slightly larger cousin is reached by a short drive up I-5 through the Sacramento River Canyon, where the landscape changes into a plateau of gently rolling hills. The town of Mount Shasta sits at an elevation of 3,500 feet, at the foot of its majestic namesake peak. This ancient, snow-covered volcano is one of the highest mountains on the continent, at 14,162 feet. The stark cinder cone of Black Butte presents another ever-present landmark to the north. Because of the increased altitude, Mount Shasta receives much more snow than Dunsmuir; 96 inches of the stuff falls every winter, compared with Dunsmuir's 38 inches. And it stays on the ground longer here, too.

Mount Shasta is the larger of the two towns, with a population nearing 4,000. It sits on a wide expanse of more-or-less-level land, in contrast to Dunsmuir's narrow canyon. Room for expansion means you'll find more contemporary housing and upscale residences here. The commercial district is also much larger. This is where Dunsmuir residents come for serious shopping purchases.

The College of the Siskiyous offers stage and musical presentations, including internationally renowned performing troupes, making Mount Shasta the cultural center of Siskiyou County. The school's learning resources center is geared toward continuing education for older students.

Five golf courses are within driving distance: one in Mount Shasta, one in McCloud, one in Weed, and two in Lake Shastina. On the southern slope of Mount Shasta, between the town and McCloud, Mount Shasta Ski Park is a full-service winter resort featuring alpine and cross-country skiing as well as snowboarding in one convenient nearby location.

In recent years tourism has increased due to the oversaturation of seasonal inhabitants in Lake Tahoe, flocking from all over Northern California. Mount Shasta provides robust outdoor opportunities with a similar drive time from the Bay Area with less congestion.

Mount Shasta's Mercy Medical Center is an 80-bed hospital with 20 doctors on staff and a 24-hour emergency care center. The hospital covers a wide range of services.

Mount Shasta Chamber of Commerce: 300 Pine St., Mount Shasta, CA 96067; (800) 926-4865; mtshastachamber.com.

CALIFORNIA MOUNTAIN WEATHER

	IN DEGREES FAHRENHEIT				ANNUAL	
	Jan.	April	July	Oct.	RAIN	SNOW
Daily highs	42	58	85	65	37"	105"
Daily lows	26	33	51	37		

Fall River Mills/Burney

One last example of a Gold Country relocation destination is known as the Intermountain Area, nestled between the Sierra Nevada and Cascade ranges in the northeast corner of California. The highway east from Redding winds past several abandoned mines as it makes its way to the towns of Burney and Fall River Mills. Actually, gold mining was only a brief interlude in the development of these towns; when the mines played out, local people switched to agriculture without missing a beat. Besides tourism the local economy now includes cattle ranching and wild rice and wheat farming in Fall River Mills, and lumber mills in Burney. Lately, farmers have started growing mint, which is distilled into mint oil and sold to chewing gum manufacturers.

"Fall River Mills?" I hear you saying. "Never heard of it. Why would anyone want to live there?" Well, you've heard of one of Fall River Mills's earlier residents: Bing Crosby? With all of the country to choose from, Bing bought a ranch there as a place to raise his boys. (Another Hollywood personality owns the ranch now; I won't say who, because local people don't like to bring attention to the area that way.)

Bing's favorite sports were golf and fly fishing. The superb trout streams throughout the region satisfied the latter interest, but Bing could not survive without golf. This explains the existence of a beautiful 18-hole championship golf course located just west of Fall River Mills. It's reputed to rank among the top 10 public courses in California.

Fall River Mills and nearby McArthur are widely spread out, with most homes built on an acre or more. The setting is a wide, grassy valley circled by tree-clad mountains. A remarkably clear stream (the Fall River) wells up from the depths of a volcanic formation a few miles away and collects the waters of a dozen sparkling trout streams as it meanders through the valley. The views are enhanced by Mount Lassen (10,457 feet) to the southeast and by majestic, snowcapped Mount Shasta (14,162 feet) to the northwest.

It's difficult to get a handle on the population of Fall River Mills because the area is 100 percent unincorporated, with homes scattered throughout various communities and informal groups of residences. In the Fall River Valley, if we include the areas of McArthur, Glenburn, Day Road, Eastman Lake, Soldier Mountain, and Pittville, there are between 5,000 and 6,000 residents.

The town of Burney is officially credited with a population of 3,500, but its unincorporated area should include the communities of Old Station, Hat Creek, and Cassel, bringing the actual population to around 12,000 to 13,000.

Those seeking low-cost retirement living will find better housing bargains in Burney, with large three-bedroom homes selling for a third of the cost of many California tract homes. Land is inexpensive, so again, large building lots are the norm. Fall River Mills property is priced a bit higher because of a recent real estate land rush. In smaller communities like this, just a few people moving in at once can create a housing scarcity.

Between Burney and Fall River Mills, you'll find all the basic services necessary. Burney has a small downtown, complete with a shopping district. Fall River Mills is scattered over several miles of highway and ends at an even smaller town, McArthur. The nearest city of any size, Redding, is an hour's drive away, the place to go for really heavy shopping. But for all practical purposes, the Intermountain Area is self-sufficient, with shopping centers, banks, restaurants, and a hospital.

The Mountain Senior Center, located in Burney, is a complex consisting of single-family homes and one-bedroom apartments within easy walking distance of shopping and medical facilities. It also features a park, community center, and RV storage, all designed for use by people age 55 or older. Free bus transportation is also available to seniors throughout the Intermountain Area for special needs.

The waterways of the Intermountain Area offer many varieties of fishing. Choose from deep, cold lakes or mountain streams for bass and trout; try the warmer waters for catfish and crappie. Lakes Britton, Eastman, Fall River, Baum Crystal, and Iron Canyon are a lure to all types of anglers. With a short drive to the northwest, anglers will find hot spots on Bear Creek, Medicine Lake, and McCloud River. Two wild trout streams—Hat Creek and the Fall River—offer trophy trout to the dedicated fly fishers or those fishing with artificial lures. (Live bait is prohibited.)

Fall River Mills Chamber of Commerce: P.O. Box 475, Fall River Mills, CA 96028; (530) 336-5840; fallrivervalleycc.org.

NORTHERN CALIFORNIA COAST

The northern California coast is highlighted by the urbanity and sophistication of the San Francisco Bay area. But the City by the Bay shouldn't be your only stop on a tour of this area's relocation possibilities. After you cross the Golden Gate Bridge going north, CA 1 winds through some of the most peaceful and rural landscapes to be found anywhere. The towns are small, neighborly, and uncrowded.

California's Napa Valley wine-producing country and its delightful little towns and villages are great for relocation. People choose places like Healdsburg, Angwin, or American Canyon, just to name a few. For quality living at moderate cost, the Napa-Sonoma region merits closer investigation. But there's a lesser-known wine country—just as pretty, much less crowded, and not far away. It's known as the Mendocino Coast, with small towns and tiny villages on the edge of the Pacific Ocean, with low coastal mountains to the east, sometimes only a half mile distant. Small, family-owned wineries and their tasting rooms make for interesting visits. If you are looking for discos, beach parties, and tourist traps, you are much too far north.

The only town of any size on this northern stretch of California coastline is Eureka, with the next "metropolitan" area being way up the Oregon coast at Coos Bay. The string of inviting towns and villages is interspersed with forest and grazing land and small family farms, sleepy and laid-back, just as they should be. The traditional industry here has always been lumbering, which appears to be in a permanent state of depression all over the West. The second industry is fishing, much of which is done by amateurs or people just out for fun. Because neither industry is hiring workers, jobs are scarce, and younger people are leaving for the cities. That means housing is affordable. The moral of this story is, if you need to work part-time to make ends meet, forget about the northwest coast. If you can satisfy your need for work through meaningful volunteer jobs, you will do just fine.

If you are members of that class who hate hot summers and cold winters, however, you've come to the right place. Frost is all but unheard-of, with 40 degrees just about as cold as it ever gets in January. Highs in January in Eureka, for example, average 53 degrees, but the July and August highs rarely top 70 degrees! Compare that with your town's average July temperatures. Every night of the year you will sleep under blankets; an air

NORTHERN CALIFORNIA COASTAL WEATHER						
	IN DEGREES FAHRENHEIT				ANNUAL	
	Jan.	April	July	Oct.	RAIN	SNOW
Daily highs	53	55	60	60	39"	—
Daily lows	41	44	52	48		

conditioner would be an absurd waste of money here. On the other hand, because lows are never subfreezing, many homes don't bother with central heating systems, depending upon a wall furnace and/or a fireplace for comfort.

Mendocino/Fort Bragg

The Mendocino Coast is accessed only by a slow, two-lane, coastal high-way; most casual tourists and hurried travelers choose to travel inland, along multilane, high-speed US 101. This leaves the towns along the coast untouched by those who aren't specifically interested in enjoying the special ambience of this area.

Founded in 1852 as a mill town, Mendocino started with a Cape Cod flavor that has been carefully preserved. This Cape Cod look didn't come about by accident. The tradition dates to California gold rush days, when fishermen and loggers from New England found the region very much to their liking. They brought New England–style architecture with them. Many homes were prefabricated in Massachusetts and shipped around the tip of South America, then reassembled here. So many, in fact, that the Mendocino region is sometimes described as "Cape Cod Shipped 'Round the Horn."

Like many settlements along the coast, Mendocino has a community of artisans, which accounts for the many art galleries and boutiques. In fact, the basic business here deals with art in one form or another. Mendocino is a small place, unincorporated, with approximately 1,100 residents, although more than 8,000 live in the surrounding area. The village sits high on a bluff, surrounded on three sides by the Pacific Ocean. Hollywood studios have filmed several motion pictures here, taking full advantage of the region's picturesque setting.

Housing prices are not as inexpensive as you might expect; well-off San Franciscans like their weekend homes here. Real estate can be pricey in the village, but when you leave the immediate vicinity of the town center, prices drop considerably.

For more inexpensive real estate, look toward Fort Bragg, which is 10 miles north of Mendocino on CA 1. This is a working community, a lumbering and fishing town of around 7,000 residents. A no-nonsense business section makes Fort Bragg the place where people come for necessary services and shopping. It's an exceptionally clean and attractive place, more modern in appearance than Mendocino. A local performing-arts company produces concerts, stage plays, musicals, and revues. San Francisco Symphony musicians join local musicians for the Mendocino Music Festival in July.

Housing costs are in line with local wages, thus less expensive than in Mendocino. Both communities are attracting retirees as well as artisans, many coming from the San Francisco and Los Angeles areas.

The Mendocino Coast District Hospital in Fort Bragg is a small 25-bed facility. The hospital operates an ambulance service with air service for emergency transfer. The nearest larger hospital is Ukiah Valley Medical Center, with 75 beds, about 37 miles away.

Fort Bragg–Mendocino Chamber of Commerce: 217 S. Main St., P.O. Box 1141, Fort Bragg, CA 95437; (707) 961-6300; mendocino coast.com.

Eureka

This is another area that owes its origins to the gold rush, even though gold was never found here. In the 1850s Eureka's location on Humboldt Bay made it ideal as a port to supply gold miners working to the east in Trinity County. Eureka flourished overnight as gold seekers poured into the port fresh from San Francisco. Arcata, on the north side of Humboldt Bay, flourished at the same time. Brett Harte put in a brief stint as editor at a newspaper here until some local toughs took exception to his writing. He hopped a steamboat for San Francisco, where he achieved fame for his tales of life in the mining camps.

After the gold fields played out, prospectors stayed and accepted steadier work as fishermen, farmers, and lumberjacks. The stately redwoods became the backbone of the economy in the late 1800s. Victorian homes built of almost indestructible redwood grace the landscape of

Eureka and the surrounding communities. These old homes are showcases for now-forgotten arts of carpentry. Since many of them were the homes of lumber barons, you can imagine the care and attention to detail that went into their construction. For this reason the town has been declared a State Historical Landmark.

Humboldt Bay fishing highlights Eureka's economy nowadays. More than 300 fishing vessels call this port home and land more rockfish, crab, oysters, and shrimp than any other place in California. Strolling along Eureka's quaint Old Town waterfront is a favorite activity, breathing in the fresh sea air, watching boats returning with catches of salmon and tasty Dungeness crab.

With a population of around 26,000, Eureka is the center, culturally and commercially, of another 48,000 residents in the immediate urban area. In fact, 86 percent of Humboldt County's population lives within a 20-mile radius of Eureka. The famous Redwood Empire forests begin near the edge of town and climb the mountains high into the Trinity Alps, with backdrops as high as 6,000 feet. Although this is primarily a mountainous region encompassing six wild and scenic river systems and stands of majestic redwood groves, Eureka itself is on a level coastal plain. Eighty percent of the county is forested public lands.

The weather here, typical of beach towns along the coast north to Washington, makes this a place for those who hate the thought of hot, steamy summers or icy, frigid winters. Except for a lot more rain in the winter months, there's little difference in the weather year-round. A sweater feels comfortable almost every evening of the year, and noonday weather is seldom, if ever, hot enough to make you sweat. Air-conditioning is something people here read about. Winters are mild enough that many homes heat with fireplaces or woodstoves. Many older houses have fireplaces in every room. Annual rainfall here is around 38 inches, a lot for California but much less than most midwestern and eastern cities. Snow shovels are as unnecessary as air-conditioning.

Located on US 101, a main north-south artery, the Eureka area also has an airport with regional carriers for short flights to San Francisco and other important local cities. The airport is a few miles north of Arcata, about 15 miles from Eureka, and is served by a shuttle bus.

Three excellent hospitals serve the area, one each for Eureka and the neighboring communities of Arcata and Fortuna. Arcata's hospital can boast that its staff makes house calls, because the hospital operates a home-care service for those who need ongoing treatment outside the hospital. The service is carried out by registered nurses, home health aides, and physical therapists under the direction of a physician.

The Humboldt Resource Senior Center, housed in an old grammar school, is one of the most extensive and comprehensive we've seen. From classes such as arts and crafts to an Alzheimer's day-care center, the services are superb. The Retired Senior Volunteer Program counts on more than 700 retirees who contribute their skills and interests in service to the community.

Fishing, of course, is a favorite sport here, with salmon, albacore, and Dungeness crab all waiting to be harvested. With generally benign weather some kind of fishing, crabbing, or clamming is possible all year. For those who get seasick, the country immediately behind the town, continuing 100 miles or so, is full of great trout streams. Deer, river otters, herons, and other wildlife are plentiful because much of the Coast Range and inland Klamath Mountains are jealously preserved as wildlife areas.

Eureka Chamber of Commerce: 612 G St., Ste. 101, Eureka, CA 95501; (707) 442-3738; eurekachamber.com.

Arcata

Nearby Arcata (pop. 17,000) is the home of Humboldt State University, one of the area's economic mainstays. With a good reputation as a serious school, the university is also the source of many cultural and intellectual events open to the public. There's also the College of the Redwoods, a two-year community college, and Eureka Adult School, with several community locations around the county. The academic atmosphere complements the old-fashioned, Victorian atmosphere of the area, a place where mountains, forest, and blue Pacific all come together.

Along this northern coast, all the way to Washington State, lower wages and low living costs are the rule. As a result, housing is quite reasonable—probably as low as you'd expect to find anywhere on the West Coast. We looked at several Victorians in the region, our favorite being one priced for what a garage would cost in San Francisco. It had high ceilings, a claw-foot bathtub, an antique wood cookstove, and some stained-glass windows. Mobile homes are located away from the city's residential sections and seem to be in abundant supply because they sell at very reasonable prices. In the countryside many people place mobile homes on spacious wooded lots. Except for Arcata, where students compete for housing, rentals are readily available.

Arcata Chamber of Commerce: 1635 Heindon Rd., Arcata, CA 95521; (707) 822-3619; arcatachamber.com.

Ferndale

We feel it mandatory to mention the fascinating little town of Ferndale while describing this northern region of California. Just a short drive south of Eureka, with a population of no more than 1,400, Ferndale is famous for its fancy gingerbread Victorian mansions. The town was founded in the late 1800s as a prosperous dairy farm center. The farmers prided themselves on their splendidly ornate homes built with their dairy-farming profits. The homes were called "Butterfat Palaces."

Like the other towns around Eureka, Ferndale preserves a small-town atmosphere of neighborliness with a bed-and-breakfast economy. Even though Ferndale is a tourist attraction, it's mostly a "stop-for-lunch, look-around, let's-get-going-again" sort of tourism. Retirees find it a great place to visit, but it's doubtful that many will decide to settle in. Although it does have a certain appeal for us.

4

Arizona

The third most popular state for retirement relocation is Arizona. This is a state with amazing scenic variety: evergreen-clad mountains, peaks covered with winter snow, deserts with forests of cactus, mineral-rich winding valleys, and gentle brooks and rapidly flowing streams and rivers. Here's where one of America's greatest natural wonders, the Grand Canyon, is visited by tens of thousands every year. Arizona is also a state with human variety: One-seventh of the US Native American population resides here. There are also generous numbers of Spanish speakers and newcomers from across the United States and Canada. Add to this the benefits of mild winters and a strong senior citizen political presence and support structure, and you have a state where retirement is a growth industry.

Speaking of growth, the US Census report shows that while most states grew in population over the past decade, Arizona added an astounding 30 percent to its population, an increase of more than a million and a half new residents! It's interesting to note that of all the states sending retirees here, the two top retirement states, California and Florida, send the *most* retirees! Because California is conveniently located nearby, this isn't surprising. Yet a large number of those retirees coming from Florida are making a second relocation move—choosing Arizona after having first tried Florida retirement. So many retirees throughout the country decide on Arizona that more than one-quarter of the state's residents are over the age of 55. Most people that age tend to vote—so you can be sure senior citizen issues garner a fair share of attention, from the local city council to the governor's office.

Arizona has three basic choices for retirement lifestyles. The first is in the low-desert climate found in the southern portion of the state, actually an extension of Mexico's great Sonoran Desert. As you would expect, the summers are hot and winters pleasant. The second type of climate is high

Arizona Tax Profile

Sales tax: 6.6% to 13%; food, drugs exempt

State income tax: 2.59% to 4.54%

Income brackets: lowest, $10,346; highest, $155,160

Property taxes: range from 0.8% to 1%

Social Security taxed: no

Pensions taxed: government pensions $2,500 exemption

Inheritance tax: no

Gasoline tax: 19¢ per gallon

desert, where you'll find more pines than cactus, and light snowfall in the winter to create postcard scenery. And finally there are the mountains and plateaus of the northern regions, where winter snows can be deep and the summers cool and refreshing. Tall pines and deep canyons make northern Arizona as different from the southern parts as day from night. You have many choices here!

CENTRAL ARIZONA: BETWEEN PHOENIX & FLAGSTAFF

Between the enormous urban sprawl of Phoenix and the modest northern city of Flagstaff, you'll encounter some of the most varied, spectacular desert scenes in the West. From Phoenix's urban landscape mixed with cactus and sagebrush, through mountains clad with majestic pines, Indian reservations, and ski resorts, the variety seems unending. Higher altitudes are often covered with forests of pine and juniper, great habitat for deer, raccoons, and other denizens of the woods. The best part about both desert and mountain landscapes is they're accessible to everyone. About 45 percent of Arizona's land is owned by the federal government; it belongs to all of us. It isn't fenced, and you'll not see "Keep Out" signs. If you feel like strolling through government-owned deserts or forests, you can darn well do it.

Each of these Arizona regions offers its own temptations and advantages as relocation destinations. Nevertheless, when considering retirement in Arizona, most people automatically think of the Phoenix area. Over the past two decades, population growth here has been enormous, almost as astounding as Las Vegas (another desert community). "Retiring in Phoenix" usually means any one of a dozen communities on the expanding fringes of the metro area rather than Phoenix itself. Retirees choose places like Mesa, Tempe, Scottsdale, and many more.

ARIZONA LOW-DESERT WEATHER						
IN DEGREES FAHRENHEIT					ANNUAL	
	Jan.	April	July	Oct.	RAIN	SNOW
Daily highs	65	83	105	88	7"	—
Daily lows	39	53	80	59		

Years ago the most popular places—such as Scottsdale, Sun City, and Apache Junction—were stand-alone towns. Today you often can't tell when you leave one and enter another unless you see a city limits sign. The combined population of this mega-metropolitan area is around 1.5 million. With a large percentage of the populace near or past retirement age, health care servers have responded by providing some of the best facilities in the West. In addition to several excellent hospitals scattered over the Phoenix area, this is now the home of the world-famous Mayo Clinic's basic research center.

Given all the retirement choices offered in the Valley of the Sun, you'll need to do some in-depth investigation to find the community that suits your personality and desired lifestyle. Let's take a look first at a couple of organized, seniors-only retirement communities in the Phoenix area: Sun City and Sun Lakes. Next we'll discuss two open, multigenerational communities: Scottsdale on the high end of the scale and Apache Junction on the economical end. When you visit, by all means do not confine your investigation to these communities. Take your time and make sure you're making the correct decision.

Sun City

The concept of seniors-only, self-contained communities with homes clustered around recreational and social facilities began right here in the Arizona desert. About 45 years ago the Del Webb Corporation unveiled its first retirement-oriented model homes in a community called Sun City. This was a non-gated adult community that promised "an active way of life" for retirees. Before a single home was offered for sale, a shopping center, golf course, and other recreational facilities were in place. The shopping center provided space for a supermarket, variety store, Laundromat, barber shop, drugstore, and a service station. These facilities were essential, because at that time Sun City sat out in the desert, a long way from the city.

Today it is one solid metropolis, with the Sun City complexes extending miles past the original location.

This highly popular concept of age-restricted and socially organized communities has changed the way many people view retirement. This pre-arranged lifestyle particularly suits those moving from another area, who have no acquaintances, and who don't want to invest time and energy trying to make new friends and develop hobbies and recreational interests. It's all right here, in one package. As soon as the moving van unloads the furniture, a social director is interviewing you about your hobbies, sports, and lifestyles. Before long you'll be out playing golf with your neighbors, being invited to play bridge, or perhaps working in the arts and crafts center. You are buying a lifestyle, not just a house.

The original Sun City was so successful that thousands of additional acres were purchased, and soon three more Sun Cities appeared on the Arizona desert. Today more than 75,000 retirees are enjoying the benefits of four multimillion-dollar recreation centers, probably a dozen 18-hole golf courses, a 200-bed hospital, and a large performing arts center.

Home buyers have choices of model homes that vary from large four-bedroom places to small two-bedroom town houses. Because these homes are mass produced, they can be priced to sell. However, as the communities expand and people snap up the tempting new models, prices in the original Sun City developments decline. For retirees looking to join this lifestyle, homes in the older sections can be real bargains.

Sun City West Chamber of Commerce: P.O. Box 9303, Surprise, AZ 85374; (623) 282-9300; northwestvalleyconnect.org.

Sun Lakes

Not far from Phoenix is another example of a Sun City–style, adults-only development. However, Sun Lakes is a *gated* community, on a somewhat more luxurious level than Sun City. Accommodating more than 17,000 residents, Sun Lakes is divided into five country-club neighborhoods, each with its own golf course and clubhouse. Although golf is Sun Lake's central theme, residents can enjoy a multitude of other activities such as tennis, swimming, fitness, and arts and crafts. More than just a retirement community, residents find a resort-vacation lifestyle and country-club living.

However, a surprising number of residents do *not* play golf. They simply like the secure feeling of living in a luxurious, gated community. Of course, you pay a premium for these amenities. An impressive number of nearby shopping facilities make it unnecessary to travel to Phoenix, not even for major purchases. But when you want to go to the big city, I-10 access is just 2 miles away.

Nearby, Sun Lakes residents can enjoy a public library; casinos featuring blackjack, poker, and slots; and attractions such as Firebird International. This is just one of many communities in the Phoenix area for those who enjoy secure country-club living.

Sun Lakes Chamber of Commerce: 25 S. Arizona Pl., #201, Chandler, AZ 85225; (480) 963-4571; chandlerchamber.com.

Scottsdale

The Sun City and Sun Lakes design appeals to those retirees who appreciate and need structured social and recreational environments. However, not everyone wants this. Many retirees prefer to choose neighborhoods in which they may blend with residents of mixed ages, similar to the settings they left in their hometowns. Scottsdale provides this different look, a distinct residential flavor that avoids mile after mile of similar dwellings.

Scottsdale has some of the most elegant and opulent shopping districts and residential neighborhoods we've encountered anywhere in the country. Majestically landscaped boulevards are lined with so many fabulous, prestige-name stores that your credit card vibrates as you drive past. Sumptuous residential neighborhoods display homes so elegant and palatial that you'll hate yourself for not being able to afford one. Scottsdale is a synonym for high-class, luxurious, and expensive, yet you'll find areas where housing costs aren't very much different from Sun City–type developments or ordinary neighborhoods in average communities.

If Phoenix and vicinity sounds like a golfer's paradise, with more than 130 golf courses around the area, consider that 37 public courses are located in Scottsdale, and several new layouts are always under construction. At least 14 of them are public, including the Tournament Players Club of Scottsdale.

Cave Creek and Carefree, on Scottsdale's northeastern edge, epitomize tasteful, desert-living lifestyles. The area is in the foothills, sitting above Scottsdale and Phoenix. The extra altitude provides an appreciable difference in the temperature as well as scenery. Most homes sit on large lots beautifully landscaped by natural desert plants. Large cactus of all description, flowering desert trees, and gnarled shrubbery surround upscale homes. Mountains loom in the background, and the air is pristine. This is one of our favorite retirement locations of all; we highly recommend it for those who can afford it.

Scottsdale Chamber of Commerce: 7501 E. McCormick Pkwy., Ste. 202-N, Scottsdale, AZ 85258; (480) 355-2700; scottsdalechamber.com.

Apache Junction

For those who consider Sun Lakes, Cave Creek, and Scottsdale to be too expensive, a lower-cost possibility for Phoenix area retirement is Apache Junction. It doesn't have the charisma or charm of Scottsdale (few places do), but it also doesn't have the price tag or higher property taxes. Conventional housing sells for what are probably the lowest prices in the Phoenix area.

One of Phoenix's many commuter bedroom communities, Apache Junction is fast acquiring a dual personality in its role as a popular retirement destination for both permanent and temporary residents. A variety of lifestyles are offered in Apache Junction including urban, single-family, residential neighborhoods; adult-only retirement clusters; and plenty of mixed-age-group living areas. Desert rural acreage, not far from the town center, is popular with many retirees.

Retirees from the Midwest and East are ending their retirement search when they discover Apache Junction's laid-back attitude and the area's year-round summer. Over the last 25 years, the permanent population has doubled, to 40,000. Much of this increase can be attributed to retirees.

Only a half-hour drive via the fast-moving Superstition Freeway from downtown Phoenix and Sky Harbor Airport, the town can almost claim rural status because of its position on the border between city and open desert. In the distance the Superstition Mountains rise above the desert floor, presenting a mysterious fortress-like appearance. Once the stronghold of fierce Apache warriors, these mountains also are the source of the most famous "lost gold mine" story of all times. The Lost Dutchman's Mine has drawn adventurers for a century to search and explore the canyons and cliffs of the Superstitions, hoping to find the treasure. According to legend, at least eight men have died mysteriously in their quest for the Lost Dutchman. But don't let this discourage you—by all means, have a look. (By the way, the *mine* was lost, not the Dutchman.) Every February the Lost Dutchman Days festival is celebrated with concerts, a rodeo, a parade, and a carnival.

Apache Junction's second role in retirement is with RV enthusiasts and snowbirds who travel to Arizona each winter. They enjoy it here because the town welcomes them (and their money) so warmly and because the city of Phoenix is easy to visit. More than 70 mobile-home and RV parks accommodate these visitors. Many of the winter snowbirds bring their RVs to stay in one of the dozen luxury RV parks in Apache Junction, which have swimming pools, social centers, organized activities, and more.

The medical center for Apache Junction is located in nearby Mesa. The Banner Baywood Medical Center is a 336-bed facility, a 14-mile drive from Apache Junction.

Apache Junction Chamber of Commerce: P.O. Box 1747, Apache Junction, AZ 85219; (480) 982-3141; ajchamber.com.

Wickenburg

About an hour's drive northwest from Phoenix, the town of Wickenburg is attracting retirees who don't want to accept the neatly arranged, orderly, and secure life of Sun City or the bustle of traffic-bound Phoenix. In small-town Wickenburg they savor the tang of the Old West. This was the location where Henry Wickenburg discovered gold back in the 1860s. Some 80 mines were in operation in the old days. The downtown section, along the railroad tracks, has several historic buildings, one of which houses the local chamber of commerce.

The town has been famous for years for its guest ranches (they used to call 'em dude ranches), which go way beyond being simply ranches. They come complete with amenities such as swimming pools, tennis courts, or even an 18-hole golf course. Although guest ranches are still popular with tourists, the retirement emphasis here is on small-acreage places where you can keep and ride your own horses.

Wickenburg has a population of about 6,500—which doubles in the winter—and is the shopping center for more than 21,000 residents of the surrounding countryside. Health care, like many desert communities far from the big cities, is somewhat inadequate, with a 19-bed hospital facility. It's necessary to drive 30 or 40 miles to excellent Sun City hospitals, with medical professionals who specialize in and cater to problems of the elderly.

Land here is abundant and inexpensive, so lots are typically sold by the acre. You may keep horses in your yard if you care to; the local horse population is considerable. You can saddle up and go for a ride through open desert and brush country in almost any direction you care to ride. Because almost all the surrounding land is owned by the federal Bureau of Land Management, nobody can interfere with your rides. You don't know how to ride horseback? No problem—local saddle clubs with friendly members will help you get started. The clubs organize numerous social activities centered on horseback riding, from afternoon rides for beginners to the grueling Desert Caballeros Ride for seasoned horsemen, who come from all over the country to participate. Other outdoor recreation activities include golf, tennis, hiking, exploring old mining locations, birding, and jeep tours in the desert.

Wickenburg has several mobile-home parks, with many units used only part of the year, their owners choosing to live elsewhere during the hot summer months. At one time it was possible to buy a lot and install a mobile home on your own property, but nowadays this is frowned upon by the city council.

It does get hot in the summertime, with July and August posting daily highs of 100 degrees and above. But like most Arizona desert country, low humidity takes much of the sting from the high temperatures. Winter nights can be cold, with frost common, but daytime temperatures are quite pleasant, with shirtsleeve weather being the noonday norm and January highs averaging 63 degrees at midday.

Wickenburg Chamber of Commerce: 216 N. Frontier St., Wickenburg, AZ 85390; (928) 684-5479; wickenburgchamber.com.

Sedona

Some folks choose their retirement locations because of beautiful surroundings. Sometimes people make decisions because of the weather. Occasionally you'll run across a town that combines both attributes in one neat package. Sedona is such a gem: mild four-season weather plus beautiful surroundings. Endowed with incredibly gorgeous views from any place in the area you might choose to live, Sedona is something you'll never get used to, even if you live there for the rest of your life. A friend who retired on the outskirts of town said, "Every morning when we wake up, we look through our kitchen window and drink in the view. We feel joyous, and we congratulate ourselves for being so lucky to live in Sedona." It's true. Enormous, jagged red-rock formations, framed by a deep blue sky, sprinkled with rich green Arizona cypress and piñon trees, all majestically towering over the desert countryside—one can't help but draw in a deep breath and sigh.

On our first visit to Sedona several years ago—after taking our obligatory deep breath and emitting a long sigh—we experienced a curious feeling of déjà vu. The view seemed strangely familiar, as if we'd visited here often. This odd feeling kept nagging at us until it suddenly hit us: *Western movies!* Sedona has been the location for hundreds of western-themed films. We'd seen these jagged cliffs and red bluffs over and over again, as cavalry troops chased Apaches or ran from them, as masked bandits robbed stagecoaches. Sedona has been a Hollywood tradition since the 1920s. In fact, Hollywood artists and technicians came here so often that many decided to relocate here, either between films or as retirees. Several well-known personalities live here and don't hesitate to participate in local politics and community affairs.

The number of retirees who select Sedona as their home base is truly impressive. The head of the senior citizens' center estimates that around 40 percent of the population is retired. Sedona's total population is more than 12,000. "This makes for an interesting mix of retired folks, artists, New Age devotees, and serious corporate people," he said. Sedona is the place to cultivate latent talents or to appreciate the artistic talents of others. Between 200 and 300 artists reside here, accounting for the 35 art galleries and an exceptionally active community art center. Two theater groups present year-round performances, and there are several ad hoc performances by a senior citizens' center group. Another theater group presents outdoor performances on summer evenings.

A local arts and cultural commission tries to focus the efforts of all talented people in the community into interesting, year-round projects. The theater and music wing of the Artists and Craftsmen Guild presents

---

ARIZONA MID-DESERT WEATHER

	Jan.	April	July	Oct.	RAIN	SNOW
	IN DEGREES FAHRENHEIT				ANNUAL	
Daily highs	51	68	90	74	13"	116"
Daily lows	24	36	61	42		

---

programs ranging from jazz to the classics, and the art center holds monthly art exhibitions to augment the many art galleries in town.

The altitude at Sedona is 4,300 feet—that's 3,200 feet higher than Phoenix, only 2 hours away by car, and 2,700 feet lower than Flagstaff, which is less than an hour away. This altitude means warmer winters than Flagstaff and cooler summers than Phoenix. (Some guidebooks list Sedona's elevation at 4,400 feet. Because the town slopes downward, it all depends upon where you measure.)

The area's housing is predominantly single-family residences, with several condominium developments and many subdivisions toward and beyond the city limits. Several nice mobile-home parks provide alternative housing opportunities. Don't expect to find bargain real estate prices here, because the overall quality is high, and this is a very desirable location. On the other hand, when you consider what your dollar buys in Scottsdale and other high-quality and popular Arizona locations, Sedona looks somewhat reasonable in comparison.

Lest I make Sedona sound like paradise on earth and start a stampede, let's take a look at two downsides frequently mentioned by residents: first is the expensive real estate and second is the traffic. Congestion on Sedona's main thoroughfares is aggravated by the continual flow of tourists gawking at the scenery, maneuvering for parking spaces, and generally getting in everybody's hair. The other side of the coin: Sedona's quality of life and stunning landscape greatly lessen the impact of these minor inconveniences.

The best medical care in the region, the Verde Valley Medical Center, is located in Cottonwood, about 18 miles from Sedona.

Sedona Chamber of Commerce: 331 Forest Rd., Sedona, AZ 86336; (800) 288-7336; sedonachamber.com.

Prescott

Sedona's rival in Arizona mountain retirement is the small city of Prescott, about 70 miles to the southwest. Its setting is as spectacular as Sedona's but with a different flavor. Instead of desert scrub, cactus, and dramatic red-rock formations, Prescott views jagged peaks in the distance, sometimes snow covered, while a forest of ponderosa pines (reputedly the largest in the world) overlooks the city. Prescott's movie-set panorama not only rivals Sedona's, but residents claim their weather is better because the four seasons are more sharply delineated.

The elevation here is about 1,000 feet higher, which means even cooler summers, with daily highs rarely climbing out of the 80s, and temperatures dropping to the 60s every evening. On the other hand, winters are cooler, with several good storms every year. One of our visits to Prescott was in January, two days after a 3-inch snowfall. The sky was brilliant, and clumps of snow were clinging to the branches of the ponderosa pines. Very impressive. By the next day most of the snow had disappeared.

Founded back in the 1860s as a gold-mining camp, the town today preserves its past. Prescott has neighborhoods of stately Victorians and a downtown that is a mixture of Old West and formal government buildings, suitable for a county seat. The town center features shops and restaurants in an area known as Whiskey Row, named for its colorful past in the frontier days. Nearby are several neighborhoods of modest homes. Away from the city center, new subdivisions with modern ranch-style homes and western landscaping mix with homes on acreage and horse barns. We found housing prices much lower than in Sedona, with an abundance of rentals for those who want to try the area for a few months before making any decisions.

Prescott is much larger than Sedona, with more than 43,000 inhabitants, and shopping facilities to match the 70,000 people in its surrounding countryside. The city provides a multitude of services, including museums, art galleries, a concert hall, and a 110,000-volume library that would be the envy of many larger cities. Yavapai College, a two-year institution, offers a noncredit "retirement college" with usually 900 students over the age of 62. A liberal arts college and an aeronautical university are also in the area.

Six public golf courses are part of the outdoor recreational scheme, along with hiking trails, camping, fishing, and horse trails. Should you be unable to control the urge, 7,600-foot Granite Mountain offers an exciting rock-climbing opportunity.

Health care is above average here, with nearly 100 physicians and surgeons and a 129-bed hospital, the Yavapai Regional Medical Center, as well as a 236-bed Veterans Administration facility. The area also shares medical facilities with Sedona at the modern Verde Valley Medical Center in Cottonwood, about 24 miles from Prescott.

Prescott Chamber of Commerce: 117 W. Goodwin St., Prescott, AZ 86303; (928) 445-2000; prescott.org.

Flagstaff

Twenty-six miles north of Sedona, and close enough to be a strong cultural influence, is the city of Flagstaff, with a population of about 67,000. It's the largest city in northern Arizona. At 7,000 feet in altitude, the region receives full mountain winters, averaging 97 inches of snow annually. Yet it also averages 300 days of sunshine! Because of warmth during clear and sunny days following the storms, the melt-off is often rapid. Summer highs seldom top 80 degrees, while Phoenix cooks at more than 100 degrees. Summer evenings are always cool, while low humidity takes the bite out of brisk winter days.

Flagstaff is a beautiful, modern city with lots of tall pines throughout the residential neighborhoods. The historic downtown area features picturesque stone buildings dating back to the days when the railroad arrived. At one time Flagstaff was the largest town between New Mexico and California. You'll find interesting shops, galleries, and restaurants in the historic district. Flagstaff also benefited from construction of the now famous Route 66 in the 1920s, bringing many tourists and travelers into the city.

The San Francisco Peaks in the distance rise 12,670 feet and provide a breathtaking backdrop. For the outdoor enthusiast, fishing and hunting opportunities are without equal. With the snowfall here, golf is definitely *not* a four-season sport. Instead the emphasis is on skiing. On nearby Mount Humphrey, the popular Arizona Snowbowl Resort is a ski area with a vertical drop of 2,300 feet, more than 30 trails, and several chairlifts—a great place for skiing, snowboarding, and snowshoeing. However, there are six golf courses in the area, three of which are public.

Northern Arizona University is situated on 730 acres, with about 27,000 undergraduate students and more than 5,000 graduate students.

About half of the students live on campus, and the rest are integrated into the community. There is also a community college and trade schools for those wanting to dabble in specific fields.

Flagstaff Medical Center, with 271 beds, is a regional referral center for northern Arizona. It offers a wide range of medical services, including a trauma center and a cancer center.

Flagstaff Chamber of Commerce: 101 W. Rte. 66, Flagstaff, AZ 86001; (928) 774-4505; flagstaffchamber.org.

SOUTHERN ARIZONA'S SONORAN DESERT

Even though you have alternatives to Arizona's hot desert weather, the heat is exactly why many people retire here; they are fed up with battling ice and snow. Lovers of hot weather can't do much better than southern Arizona, short of moving to Death Valley. Sure, you'll spend many summer days enjoying indoor air-conditioning when it's 100 degrees outdoors, but those warm and balmy winter days with 70-degree January temperatures make up for it. No matter how hot it gets in the daytime, Arizona's dry air allows the heat to radiate rapidly so that the nights are usually pleasant, if not exactly cool. Your air-conditioning system often shuts down at night. With more than 300 days of sunshine each year and almost no rain, you have loads of opportunities to get outdoors. And just think about it: no snow shovels, no tire chains, no rubber boots, no windshield scrapers!

Bisbee

Economic disasters—such as a failing industry, a military base closure, or any other condition that causes a community to lose its vitality and residents to abandon ship—are bound to happen from time to time. An economic crash will be looked on as a disaster by those affected, yet those looking for retirement bargains can be the winners. Families pack up and move away, home prices fall, and businesses fail from lack of customers.

Two such clouds descended on Arizona some years ago, clouds with silver linings for those searching for inexpensive retirement destinations. The towns affected were Bisbee, in the southeastern part of the state near the Mexican border, and Ajo, a good deal farther west. Both were mining towns, and both saw prosperity vanish when the mining company, without warning, ceased operation. Despair and pessimism reigned for a time but changed to optimism when the word got out and retirees began visiting to see what they were all about. Both towns regained their places in the sun and are admittedly grateful for their discovery and rescue by retirees.

A word of caution has to go with these recommendations: Not just any community can be rescued by an influx of retirement money. There needs to be suitable infrastructure, plus something that makes the idea of living there attractive. Cheap real estate isn't enough. Our feeling is, these two retirement suggestions would require serious introspection, to make sure that the personalities and inhabitants of the town will match yours. Remember that an inexpensive lifestyle isn't necessarily an ideal lifestyle.

Bisbee's colorful history matches its picturesque desert-mountain setting. Tucked away in a canyon only a few miles from the Mexican border, Bisbee has narrow, winding streets that evoke a classic style of the late 19th-century mining towns. Because of its steep hills and ornate Victorian construction, people often describe the town as having a certain San Francisco atmosphere—without the cable cars, of course.

When we first wrote about Bisbee years ago, the town had just suffered financial disaster. At that time completely furnished homes sold for as little as $1,000. Homes were sometimes abandoned with doors left unlocked, furniture and fixtures intact. By the time we visited, things had taken a turn for the better, with retirees coming in to buy the cheap real estate and help rebuild the town. Bisbee made a dramatic switch from an abandoned mining town to its newer role as a retirement "discovery."

Be aware that the days of super-bargain homes are long gone. Of course, fixer-uppers can still be found, and satisfactory housing can easily be had for far below national averages. Bisbee's surge of popularity initially sent its population up to 8,000. Ironically, after the initial rush the number of inhabitants began to decline. Today's population is estimated at 6,000 residents—a drop of 25 percent from 1990. Meanwhile, the nearby town of Tombstone—of Wyatt Earp and the O.K. Corral shootout fame—increased population almost 25 percent. Apparently the retirement boom didn't sustain its momentum. Today Bisbee's median resident age is 43 years, higher than most places, but clearly not a predominantly retired population.

Bisbee's Copper Queen Community Hospital provides basic 24-hour emergency care, with slightly more extensive medical services found in nearby Douglas. By the way, Douglas is a border town, so the usual prescription bargains are available when buying in Mexican pharmacies.

Bisbee Chamber of Commerce: 1326 State Hwy. 92, Bisbee, AZ 85603; (520) 432-5421; bisbeearizona.com.

Sierra Vista

Near Bisbee—just 26 miles west—the high-desert town of Sierra Vista is emerging as a popular retirement destination and one of Arizona's fastest-growing communities. With abundant sunshine, crystal-clear air, and an elevation of 4,600 feet, Sierra Vista enjoys an enviable climate. July high temperatures here average 89 degrees (compared with Phoenix's 105 degrees), and July low temperatures are 67 degrees (compared with Phoenix's 80 degrees).

The town's picturesque setting among the Huachuca, Dragoon, Mule, and Whetstone Mountains justifies Sierra Vista's Spanish name: "mountain view." The town owes its existence to Fort Huachuca (pronounced waa-CHOO-ka), established in 1877 as a cavalry post to secure the southern border to protect settlers from Native American attacks by the Apache chieftain Geronimo. This was also the home base for the famous black troopers known as buffalo soldiers of the Ninth and Tenth Cavalry. They pursued Pancho Villa's army in the 1916 expedition into Mexico led by General John H. Pershing.

From a small town around the fort, Sierra Vista has grown to 44,000 residents, including about 11,000 military and civilian workers employed at Fort Huachuca. Several major commands now operate at the fort, including the Army Information Systems Command, the Army Intelligence Center and School, and the Electronic Proving Grounds. Because of the military presence and amenities available to retired personnel, Sierra Vista is understandably popular with military retirees and families.

Sierra Vista is the commercial center for Cochise County and parts of northern Mexico. To meet the area's growing needs, a 400,000-square-foot mall opened a few years ago, with many major retailers represented. Fine dining is also available throughout the area.

Sierra Vista's mild winters and warm summers encourage outdoor sports such as golf, tennis, hiking, and bike riding. Two championship golf courses are located here, and nine other golf facilities are within easy driving distance. You'll also find first-class bowling lanes, public and private tennis courts, and an Olympic-size swimming pool.

Housing is affordable and diverse, including ranchettes, apartments, and condos, as well as traditional neighborhoods and country-club settings with homes bordering fairways. Generally, real estate sales are about 7 percent below the national average. A gated retirement community for age 55-plus residents is available, as are seven mobile-home parks that many retirees use for either summer or winter getaways (spending the rest of the year in retirement in their hometowns).

Medical care is provided by the Sierra Vista Regional Health Center, a small facility with 88 beds. The military facilities are open to veterans with health problems.

Sierra Vista Chamber of Commerce: 21 E. Wilcox Dr., Sierra Vista, AZ 85635; (520) 458-6940; sierravistachamber.org.

TUCSON

Sitting at an elevation of 2,375 feet in a high-desert valley surrounded by mountains, Tucson can guarantee an agreeable year-round climate. Its dry air and rich desert vegetation qualify it as one of the nation's finest winter resorts. Its more than 530,000 inhabitants make Tucson a moderately large city, and it is still growing. The fastest-increasing age group here is the 60-plus crowd, which used to account for 20 percent of the population but is now pushing 30 percent. Because this is the group most likely to vote, it's no surprise that senior citizens get fair treatment in this city. The well-appointed Tucson Senior Citizens' Center clearly shows the attention that city politicians show retired people.

The University of Arizona, located in Tucson, greatly enriches the community's educational, cultural, and recreational life. Classes, lectures, plays, and concerts are an ongoing boon to retirees. The state's only opera company is based in Tucson, and a light opera company stages Broadway musicals.

Another favorable aspect of Tucson retirement is usually below-average housing prices. Buyers have a wide selection of neighborhoods, ranging from inexpensive to out of touch with reality. Tucson's warm and pleasant winters don't demand much in the way of heating costs, but this will be offset by air-conditioning in the summer.

Tucson is a popular place for mobile-home living. The newspaper's classified section usually has listings from mobile-home parks advertising spaces for rent, something rare in many metropolitan areas. A space in one of Tucson's adult mobile-home parks can often be found for half of what a nice two-bedroom apartment might cost. With so many mobile-home parks to choose from, you would be well advised to do some shopping. Some parks are primarily for working people, and their interests and social lives are intertwined with friends who live somewhere else. Other parks have mostly retired folks, where you'll find plenty of activities and neighborly retirees. Visiting a park residents meeting or attending one of the bingo sessions can tell you worlds about who your new neighbors might be.

Tucson is also known for its organized retirement and adults-only complexes. With beautifully designed homes, shopping and medical facilities, and extensive sports centers, these complexes are small cities in themselves. One adult community, Saddlebrooke, calls itself the "youngest adult community" because it sets its lower age limit at 45 instead of the usual 55. These complexes typically feature 18-hole golf courses, shuffleboard, bocce and tennis courts, card rooms, jogging tracks, exercise rooms, and, of course, the ubiquitous swimming pools.

The Armory Park Senior Citizens Recreation Center in downtown Tucson is a model of its kind. Senior citizens take an energetic part in running the center and have no trouble getting all the volunteer help they need. At any one time several hundred volunteers are on call as they try to use everyone's special skills. For example: Retired accountants and tax professionals give free income-tax assistance. Others teach handicrafts such as jewelry making, crocheting, and painting. A senior citizens' housing authority high-rise is across the street from the center and another is planned, making it convenient for everyone to participate.

Medical care here is exceptional. No less than eight hospitals serve the area, plus a 283-bed veterans' facility. The largest hospital is Tucson Medical Center, with 555 beds.

Tucson Chamber of Commerce: 65 West St. Mary's Rd., Tucson, AZ 85701; (520) 792-1212; tucsonchamber.org.

Green Valley

Green Valley started off as an unlikely development dream on a somewhat elevated piece of desert land, miles from anywhere, a long way from a city or even a shopping center. The Green Valley concept turned out to be not so unlikely after all. Today about 22,000 people call Green Valley home, the overwhelming majority of them retired. One source reports the average age here to be in the upper 60s.

Located 25 miles south of Tucson on I-19 and 40 miles north of the Mexican border, Green Valley sits at an altitude of 2,900 feet at the foot of the Santa Rita Mountains (an Apache hangout in the olden days). There are four shopping centers and more than 350 businesses serving residents here, including supermarkets, two major drugstores, discount department stores, apparel stores, restaurants, and other specialty stores. Tucson International Airport is only 23 miles away.

Green Valley is unincorporated, and folks seem to prefer it that way: fewer taxes, fewer bureaucrats, more time for golf. Residents boast that summer temperatures are consistently five degrees cooler than Tucson and 10 degrees cooler than Phoenix. On the hottest July and August days, low humidity permits night temperatures to cool as much as 30 degrees below the afternoon's high. Green Valley winter temperatures are similar to those in Tucson or Phoenix, ranging from the mid-60s to the low 70s.

At one time a study of the local telephone directory clearly demonstrated the melting-pot character of Green Valley. In addition to phone numbers and addresses, the local directory listed the residents' former hometowns as well as their occupations before retirement. The directory listed retirees from all 50 of the United States and 10 Canadian provinces, as well as residents from 26 foreign countries, including Costa Rica, England, France, Ireland, Germany, and Sweden. Not all of Green Valley is restricted to 50-plus folks. There's a sprinkling of youngsters around, just enough to keep the makeup of the community from becoming one-dimensional.

Recreational facilities at Green Valley are complete—it even has a bowling alley. For golf you have the choice of nine courses (seven of which are public) to satisfy that urge for hunting lost golf balls some retirees cannot shake. The rec center is quite comprehensive, with facilities for arts and crafts, sewing, lapidary art, and photography. A swimming pool, Jacuzzi, sauna, and exercise room complete the recreational picture.

Green Valley has two highly rated nursing homes and a 24-hour emergency clinic, as well as two private clinics and a 60-bed health care center. Tucson hospitals are 20 miles away via I-19. There is also a volunteer organization called Friends In Deed (FID), which assists seniors in sharing their lifetime experiences and skills with one another.

Green Valley Chamber of Commerce: P.O. Box 566, Green Valley, AZ 85622; (520) 625-7575, (800) 858-5872; greenvalleysahuarita.com.

WESTERN ARIZONA: COLORADO RIVER RETIREMENT

After the wild Colorado River exits the Grand Canyon, it winds its way south toward Mexico and the Sea of Cortez. Along the way its waters are captured by a series of dams that provide peaceful lakes, contrasting nicely with the desert hills and shaded canyons that enclose the river.

Along this stretch of waterway—from Parker on the south to Bullhead City on the north—growing numbers of retirees and snowbirds settle in each winter. The numbers increase every year, with more and more buying homes and staying year-round. Places such as Lake Havasu have grown from small clusters of trailers and fishing shacks, with catfish and mallards as the only major attractions, practically into cities with all the facilities needed for desirable relocation choices.

Lake Havasu City

In the late 1930s, when a dam across the Colorado River created a long body of water separating the states of Arizona and California, the lake became a best-kept secret among snowbirds. Along the banks of the lake, where Lake Havasu City stands today, a collection of fish camps sprouted, drawing ever more seasonal retirees. At first they were nothing more than

WESTERN ARIZONA WEATHER

| | IN DEGREES FAHRENHEIT | | | | ANNUAL | |
	Jan.	April	July	Oct.	RAIN	SNOW
Daily highs	69	86	107	90	3"	—
Daily lows	43	56	80	62		

a few rustic RV parks, campsites, and shacks selling bait and beer—a quiet and inexpensive place to escape the rigors of winter. Snowbirds would arrive by late fall, enjoy the summerlike winter, acquire a deep tan, then pack up their tents and head home in the spring.

From these unpretentious beginnings Lake Havasu City has boomed from nothing more than a fishing camp to a city of more than 53,000 full-time residents. Houses and condos, trailers and mobile homes, and businesses and services of all descriptions appeared as if by magic. Today an estimated 12,000 winter residents swell the population and add to the general prosperity.

A surprise for tourists here is the sight of the original 140-year-old London Bridge set up in the Arizona desert, complete with a mile-long channel and a replica English village! Accompanying the village is a large shopping center. (No medieval English village should be without a shopping center.) The historic bridge was bought several years ago at a London auction by the original developer of Lake Havasu City. He had the 130,000-ton bridge dismantled and shipped through the Panama Canal and then trucked 300 miles to be reassembled brick by brick, granite arches, and iron sections. (We're not making this up!)

When we first visited here, many years ago, we thought the treeless bank of a desert lake a highly unlikely place for year-round retirement. Every time we returned, we've been impressed by the growth of business and residential neighborhoods. The residential community has grown gracefully, not just a quick-and-easy expansion, with new developments tastefully done with quality construction. New businesses, shopping facilities, and nice restaurants quickly appear to keep up with the increasing population.

Adding touches of scenic splendor, spectacular erosion sculptures—cliffs, canyons, and ragged peaks—never fail to draw gasps of astonishment as we pass through the region. True, in July and August you'll bake. But not much worse than in Phoenix. And as in Phoenix, winter's balminess and gentle warmth makes you forget the rotisserie of summer.

The cost of living here is usually about the national average. High utility bills and medical care costs are offset by below national average home prices (sometimes as much as 15 percent below average).

Mobile-home and RV parks still dot the riverbanks, each with its own boat-launching ramp and nearby bait shop. The quality of these accommodations is vastly improved today. By the way, boating and fishing aren't the only sports enjoyed in Lake Havasu. Several golf courses and at least one bowling alley will keep you active. A bustling senior center provides a dial-a-ride service in addition to the customary bridge games, arts and crafts, and nutrition facilities. A community college offers fee discounts to senior citizens, and some activities are coordinated with Arizona State University, including drama performances, concerts, and lectures.

Because of the high number of retirees, the Lake Havasu area enjoys a more complete health care system than ordinarily found in communities of similar size. A 138-bed acute-care hospital staffed with 35 physicians and a nursing center serves the community. The hospital expanded by 50 percent a few years ago to keep up with the increasing population.

Lake Havasu Chamber of Commerce: 314 London Bridge Rd., Lake Havasu City, AZ 86403; (928) 855-4115; havasuchamber.com.

Bullhead City/Laughlin

Bullhead City is a potpourri of several miles of boomtown strip malls, inexpensive housing, and mobile-home parks, all hugging the riverfront. Much nicer housing developments are perched in the hills to the east of the highway, yet only a few minutes from the commercial district. Jagged peaks and ravines, created by volcanic activity eons ago, provide a wonderfully rugged, almost alien backdrop to the region. As is usual in the Colorado River Valley, the temperature routinely climbs over the 100 mark during the summer, just about every day. But winters are delightful.

You're just far enough north here so that the west bank of the Colorado is in the state of Nevada instead of California. The very southern tip of Nevada touches here, allowing a bevy of glittering gambling casinos—more than 10, at last count—to add an interesting dimension to the region's social life. Speedy little ferryboats shuttle residents, tourists, and casino employees back and forth across the river between Laughlin and Bullhead City. Most people choose to live on the Arizona side, although several upscale housing developments have appeared on the southern edge of Laughlin. An added benefit of being a Nevada resident is no state income taxes on all those gambling winnings. (Yes, but don't hold your breath.)

Facing each other across the river, Bullhead City and Laughlin are an odd-couple combination of staid residential and high-life gambling personalities. Both places are booming to the point that it's difficult to know precisely how many people are living there. Bullhead City's population keeps growing, with about 41,000 at latest estimate. Laughlin's population is about 7,500. Until the casinos began riding high, Bullhead City was a sleepy fishing village, not much more than a scattering of winter retirement places and fishing marinas. But with Laughlin constantly needing more employees for its motels and casinos, Bullhead City's growth kept pace as workers and retirees increased their numbers. Today the casinos employ thousands. Many early retirees enjoy full-time or part-time jobs doing everything from cleanup to dealing blackjack.

The Bullhead Chamber of Commerce is continually trying to think up activities to keep residents and tourists on the Arizona side of the river. As a result, their activity calendar is generally full, with something going on every week, from chili cook-offs to jazz dance combos. When they promote a Harley-Davidson rally, as many as 30,000 bikers show up! Another cultural event on the schedule is the "Country Fair & Burro Barbecue." Not being overly fond of burro spareribs, we passed on that one.

Real estate costs vary widely in Bullhead City, as does the range of quality. At the low end of the scale are ordinary, single-wide mobile homes with prices to match the caliber. At the top of the line, elegant riverfront homes and spiffy houses perched in the hills command views of both mountains and river. Newer houses on the Nevada side of the river are often more expensive and located in tasteful neighborhoods, sometimes gated communities.

Recreational opportunities include eight golf courses, six of them 18-hole layouts, and water recreation that includes waterskiing and boating, as well as fishing in the river for bullhead catfish. The region is said to offer some of the finest desert hiking in the world. However, most of the trails in the area are for serious and/or experienced hikers. The hiking areas do not have restroom facilities, drinking water, or first aid. You are on your own when hiking in these remote, yet extremely fascinating areas.

The Bullhead City Regional Medical Center, with 139 beds, provides 24-hour emergency service with full-time emergency physicians on duty. About 6 miles away, in Fort Mohave, is the Valley View Medical Center, with 66 beds.

Bullhead City Chamber of Commerce: 1251 Hwy. 95, Bullhead City, AZ 86429; (928) 754-4121, (800) 987-7457; bullheadchamber.com.

Yuma

Yuma, the last of our Colorado River towns, anchors Arizona's southwest corner, where the mighty Colorado crosses into Mexico on its way to the Sea of Cortez. At this point the river loses its majesty; much of its water has been siphoned off along the way to irrigate truck farms, supply drinking water to dozens of communities, and make ice cubes for gambling casinos.

A sleepy little desert town just a few years ago, Yuma has undergone development that can be described as explosive. Since 1980 its population increased from 39,000 to today's estimated 93,000. Low-cost real estate helps the growth process. Only the center part, or old town, shows evidence of the city's historic past. The rest seems brand new. Originally described as "the great crossing place of a very wide and treacherous river," Yuma was the regional trading center for early-day adventurers and settlers.

Because of Yuma's low-desert altitude (only 138 feet), summers here are exceptionally hot. Throughout the year residents expect just a little more than 3 inches of rain. Make no mistake, this is the desert!

Yuma's winter population triples, as snowbirds from all over the country descend upon the area, bringing motor homes, trailers, and campers. Just like the Rio Grande Valley area, Yuma becomes a year-round nest for many snowbirds.

Many of these retirees take advantage of nearby Mexico for inexpensive prescription drugs, dental care, and experimental medications not yet approved in the United States (although most have been in Europe). Allow us to give our routine warning about crossing the border into Mexico for shopping or dining: Always make local inquiries about safety before crossing the border. Although it has been relatively rare for tourists to be harmed or involved in the occasional border disputes, that doesn't mean you can't be an exception. When you visit, ask at the border; when you live there, ask your neighbors.

A Marine Corps base is located in the city limits, sharing its runways with private and commercial aircraft. Residents are treated to an interesting display of Marine fighter jets and airliners alternating on takeoffs. This base provides PX, commissary, and medical care for military retirees.

For gaming activity there's the Cocopah Gaming Center, a tribal casino south of Yuma on US 95. For the academically inclined a state college, a state university, and two private colleges fill educational needs.

Medical care is available at the Yuma Regional Medical Center. The facility has 333 beds.

Yuma Chamber of Commerce: 180 W. First St., Yuma, AZ 85364; (928) 782-2567; yumachamber.org.

5

The Southeast Coast States

For those who live in the Midwest or on the East Coast, the idea of a West Coast retirement is a pleasant thought, but often seems too far away from friends and family. Florida, too, may be out of the question, for any number of reasons. The search is then narrowed to an affordable location with a mild, four-season climate that isn't too far to return "home" periodically and where friends and family can reasonably be expected to visit from time to time. Of course, the setting should be attractive, so that friends and family will look upon visits with joyful anticipation rather than with dread. The southeastern seaboard states—Virginia, the Carolinas, and Georgia—fulfill these requirements for a growing number of families.

From earliest times southern colonists who owned plantations in the warm and muggy coastal regions enjoyed escaping to the cool highlands when summer drew near. To this day, mountain sections of Georgia, the Carolinas, and Virginia are noted for a growing population of "part-time" retirees, often from Florida, who come here to cool off in the summer. After spending a couple of seasons in the upland hill country, many visitors become ex-Florida retirees, choosing to settle here permanently. One North Carolina native said, "Northerners are discovering our part of the country by going to Florida first and then making a second retirement move here. We call that 'making a J turn.'"

These coastal Atlantic states offer a rich variety of both part-time and full-time relocation settings: sandy beaches, rolling green hills, and forested mountains brightened with azaleas, mountain laurel, and myrtle trees. From fertile agricultural lands with neat farms and white fences to rugged mountains where bears and herds of deer roam unmolested by humans, the Atlantic Coast region has it all. The ocean yields harvests of fish, crabs, and oysters; inland streams and lakes offer superb sport opportunities for trout, bass, and other game fish. Modern cities with full conveniences and cultural attractions are but short distances from rural villages steeped in 19th-century atmosphere and country friendliness.

SOUTHERN HOSPITALITY

"Southern hospitality" is an oft-tossed-about phrase, but one with more than a kernel of truth. It's interesting to note how southerners interact with one another as well as with strangers. You'll notice an open friendliness and sharing that differs from the general custom in other parts of the country. For example, when visiting friends or relatives in the South, I am always surprised at how often people drop in unannounced for a visit. Sometimes it's a steady procession of acquaintances coming and going all day long. Close friends sometimes don't bother to knock. They'll just open the door and call out, "Anybody home?" They know they're always welcome for a chat. "Just passin' by," they'll explain. "Thought I'd stop in to say hello." An extra cup of coffee is usually on the kitchen table before they can pull out a chair.

In other parts of the country, this would be unheard of. In my California neighborhood, before you visit someone other than a close friend, you telephone first and see if it's okay to come over for a visit. In still other parts of the country, you either wait for an invitation or you suggest meeting for lunch at a nearby restaurant. For some folks southern-style hospitality would take some getting used to. Some might feel abused if casual acquaintances drop in and expect them to interrupt whatever they're doing to chat awhile.

Having given you the bright side of southern hospitality, be aware that small-town prejudices sometimes can be an issue. It doesn't seem to be a matter of South versus North; it's more of rural values versus urban values. Newcomers from northern states can sometimes find a reluctance of small-town southerners to accept outsiders as close friends. Rural communities tend to be conservative politically and religiously, being impatient with outsiders who do not conform to community values. This rejection is rarely overt, usually in the form of ignoring newcomers.

Our recommendation is to make exploratory visits to your desired community and test the waters. Either make sure there are enough like-minded individuals living in town to provide a friendship base, or be assured that your future neighbors are accepting newcomers into their social milieu. The last thing you would want would be neighbors who consider you to be a permanent outsider, or a hated liberal in a vigorously conservative neighborhood. (Or vice-versa.)

CHURCHES IN THE SOUTH

In most sections of the country, religion plays a minor role in people's social lives. They'll attend church sporadically, on Christmas Eve and Easter, and whenever someone gets married or buried. An estimated 28 million people in the United States almost never go to church. They aren't all atheists; many just prefer to catch up on weekend chores, go fishing, or play golf. For them, attending church is a personal choice, not a social obligation.

In a typical southern town, however, churches play an important role in most residents' social as well as spiritual lives. Church on Sunday is as much a part of the weekly routine as mowing the lawn. Close friends almost always belong to the same church. Another thing northerners aren't used to is the way churches in the South can be politically active. When a congregation decides to pressure local politicians, the message gets across. This is why so many parts of the South are "dry" and why the local bootlegger is such an esteemed southern institution. "Vote dry, drink wet" is the motto. (By the way, bootleggers, enthusiastic about prohibition, are always happy to financially support the local preachers in their campaign to stamp out liquor stores.)

On the other hand, churches can make relocation easy by welcoming and introducing newcomers to a community. The moment strangers show up for a Sunday visit, churchgoers begin shaking their hands, inquiring where they are from, and welcoming them to their new hometown (and, of course, inviting newcomers to become members of their church). We've interviewed numerous retirees who seldom, if ever, attended church where they came from, but are now regular members of a congregation. A church can be the doorway to the community's social life.

A GEOGRAPHY LESSON

The Southeast Coast states are divided into three distinct regions. The first is a broad coastal plain that rises from the Atlantic, often with low, marshy ground, studded with palmettos and scrub oak. Several hundred miles of beautiful white sand beaches are convenient for those who need to include the seashore in their relocation schemes. Farther inland, fertile fields and comfortable small towns offer a quieter, more introspective lifestyle.

These flat lowlands end at the fall line, where the foothills of the Blue Ridge and Great Smoky Mountains begin. Rivers, creeks, and streams, gentle in the lowlands, suddenly change into rapids and low waterfalls at this point, hence the term "fall line." This is called the Piedmont or foothill region, a country of rolling hills covered with hardwood forests and dotted with more than 400,000 acres of lakes.

Finally we come to the Blue Ridge and Great Smoky highlands, where the Appalachians lift to an elevation of around 3,000 feet. This mountain chain runs in a northeast–southwest direction from just north of Atlanta all the way to the Canadian border. Crystal-clear rivers and streams cascade through canyons and tumble over waterfalls into deep pools. Yet the Appalachian country isn't so high that it catches severe winters. Snow is a regular winter occurrence, but it seldom sticks around more than a day or two (except for higher elevations and skiing areas). The mountains have other functions besides being picturesque. They deflect or delay cold air masses approaching from the north and west and thus protect coastal areas from arctic blasts.

NORTH CAROLINA

Many changes took place across the nation over the last half of the 20th century, and North Carolina may be the state that changed most of all. Until the middle of the 20th century, North Carolina was a sleepy, underdeveloped place whose main industry, other than agriculture, seemed to be military bases: places such as Fort Bragg, Camp Lejeune, and others. The state's social and economic doldrums lasted so long that in addition to North Carolina's nickname, the "Tarheel State," it was also dubbed the "Rip Van Winkle State."

This began to change as northern manufacturers relocated their facilities to North Carolina to take advantage of lower costs and inexpensive labor. Later, new high-tech industry followed suit, stimulating local economies and starting a chain reaction of northerners moving into North Carolina to follow their jobs, which in turn attracted more industry because of the abundant skilled-labor pool.

The turning point came in the 1960s with the success of the huge Research Triangle Park in the Raleigh-Durham area, which quickly developed into the nation's largest governmental and industrial research laboratories. The facility required an army of laboratory scientists, technicians, business experts, and academics of all descriptions. New manufacturing processes were introduced to the state: electronics plants, rubber and plastic factories, and fabrication of light machinery. High-tech jobs drew more northerners into the state as North Carolina's top universities turned out highly qualified graduates.

North Carolina has clearly shed its Rip Van Winkle image, now ranking as the South's most highly industrialized state and one of the nation's leaders in technology. Many of today's "early-bird retirees" are relocating here as a place for part-time or consulting work within driving distance of their retirement homes.

> **North Carolina Tax Profile**
>
> **Sales tax:** 4.75%; drugs exempt
> **State income tax:** flat rate of 5.75%
> **Property taxes:** about 1.2% on 100% of appraised value
> **Social Security taxed:** no
> **Pensions taxed:** excludes $4,000 government, $2,000 private pensions
> **Gasoline tax:** 35.4¢ per gallon

Fortunately, technological progress and the growth of "clean industry" means these changes have had little impact on the beauty of the state. Actually, the increased population has opened previously isolated communities in the Blue Ridge and Great Smoky Mountains and turned them into ideal places for retirement.

Blue Ridge & Great Smoky Mountains

We're convinced that some of the most beautiful and scenic places in the country are found in the Blue Ridge and Great Smoky Mountains. October, when leaves are turning, is a marvelous time for a visit. Hardwood trees display a full explosion of color, with brilliant reds, yellows, purples, lavenders, and all colors in between to dazzle the eye, while evergreens provide a

BLUE RIDGE MOUNTAIN WEATHER

	IN DEGREES FAHRENHEIT				ANNUAL	
	Jan.	**April**	**July**	**Oct.**	**RAIN**	**SNOW**
Daily highs	48	69	84	69	48"	17"
Daily lows	26	43	62	43		

conservative background of year-round green. We've also made the rounds in the spring, when the dogwoods, azaleas, and mountain laurels are in full bloom. The sight and smell of spring make one forget winter.

Driving the Blue Ridge Parkway is an experience not soon forgotten. The parkway starts at the small town of Front Royal in northern Virginia and wends its way southwest until it ends at Great Smoky Mountains National Park, which is partly in Tennessee and partly in North Carolina. The scenic highway winds through beautiful mountain terrain, past wild rivers and thick forests. Hikers and river rafters love this country. Golf is a top sport here, with more than 20 first-quality courses throughout the Great Smoky Mountains area alone.

Asheville

Three North Carolina towns in this region form a triangle, with Asheville as the apex and Hendersonville and Brevard forming the triangle's base. All three towns consistently receive praise as retirement locations in magazines, newspapers, and retirement guides. Because there's only about 20 miles or so between one city and the next, it would seem they could be treated as one subject, but we feel they are different enough to deserve separate consideration. We are describing Asheville here, the best known of the three.

Asheville is the queen city of North Carolina's western region, the wedge-shaped projection of the state that forces its way between Tennessee and Georgia. Nestled where the Great Smoky and Blue Ridge Mountains meet, Asheville sits 2,340 feet above sea level. This elevation accounts for the city's pleasant summer weather as well as its brisk, but not harsh, winters.

As the largest city in western North Carolina, Asheville (pop. 84,000) is the region's cultural and commercial center. The region is characterized by prosperous farms and forest-covered foothills, rounded and green, growing steeper toward the north. Its natural setting, surrounded by a million acres of national forest, combines with the convenience of city living to make Asheville and its environs one of North Carolina's most desirable retirement destinations. Not surprisingly, Asheville was famous as a resort town, attracting tourists and retirees, long before Thomas Wolfe described his hometown in his novel *Look Homeward, Angel*, and even before George Vanderbilt thought about creating America's largest home here, the 255-room Biltmore House. Since the turn of the 20th century, famous Americans such as Henry Ford, his friend Thomas Edison, F. Scott Fitzgerald, and William Jennings Bryan enjoyed summers here. Many came for the summer and stayed on for retirement. They now come in ever-increasing numbers, with a surprising number of "second-chance retirees" moving here after having tried Florida, California, or Arizona.

Because of its distance from a truly large metropolitan center, Asheville enjoys many services and amenities normally absent in a small city. No fewer than 16 shopping centers—four of them indoor malls—ensure wide selections of merchandise. Two interstate highways (I-40 and I-26) intersect in Asheville, as well as the Blue Ridge Parkway and 10 other US and state highways. This maze of freeways, plus an airport with daily flights and connections to several major cities, makes Asheville a transportation hub for this area.

The University of North Carolina at Asheville sponsors a unique resource for seniors living in the region. It's called the North Carolina Center for Creative Retirement. The center consists of several programs designed to introduce retirement-age people to a wide variety of learning experiences as it integrates them into the community. The center should be one of the first stops on your pre-retirement tour of Asheville, and, should you decide to move here, the center should become part of your retirement scenario for continuing education.

One of the center's programs is called College for Seniors. Drawing on retirees' professional expertise and life experiences, curricula and classes are designed and taught by students as well as university faculty. Classes range from Chaucer to computers, from foreign affairs to opera. Another is the Senior Academy for Intergenerational Learning, which matches retired professionals with university students to work as research partners, tutors, and career mentors. The Leadership Asheville Seniors program brings seniors together to explore ways to link their talents and expertise with community needs.

A concentration of hospitals and related facilities firmly establishes the city as a medical center for the entire region. Eight hospitals ensure excellent medical care for the Asheville triangle. Among them are Mission Hospital, with 730 beds, and a veterans' hospital with 200 beds.

Outdoor recreation here is enhanced by Asheville's nearness to some of the prettiest Appalachian country imaginable. Always within view, the Blue Ridge and Great Smoky Mountains soar to heights greater than 5,000 feet. Hiking, fishing, camping, and winter skiing make for year-round outdoor recreation within walking or driving distance. Several public and private golf courses challenge players, with good weather in all but the two coldest months of the year.

A few years ago Asheville was known for its low-cost, high-quality real estate market. But Asheville's popularity as a retirement destination has boosted prices until they are among the highest in the state, usually well above the national average. Nearby Hendersonville offers some of the same attractions as Asheville, but with lower property price tags.

Asheville Chamber of Commerce: 36 Montford Ave., Asheville, NC 28801; (828) 258-6101; ashevillechamber.org.

NORTH CAROLINA'S HIGH COUNTRY

The rugged mountain country to the north of Asheville is appropriate for those demanding the best in Appalachian settings. This was Daniel Boone country. The famous pioneer was supposedly born and raised in Boone, one of the major towns in this area.

For more than a century, wealthy families from all over the nation have traditionally used these mountains as summer hideaways, secluded places where they could slip away for quiet vacations. Industrialists from Chicago and Pittsburgh, socialites from New York and Boston, and southern aristocracy from Charleston, Charlotte, and other affluent cities maintained summer retreats deep in the mountains. Places like Linville, Banner Elk, and Blowing Rock are unknown to most of the country but quite familiar to the wealthy.

The first resorts and retirement homes appeared on the scene in the 1890s, but it wasn't until the advent of the automobile and good roads that retirement began in earnest. Then anyone who could afford a Chevy could

HIGH COUNTRY WEATHER

	IN DEGREES FAHRENHEIT				ANNUAL	
	Jan.	April	July	Oct.	RAIN	SNOW
Daily highs	45	68	84	68	49"	18"
Daily lows	25	41	62	44		

visit and settle in these formerly exclusive areas. And they did. This turned out to be a natural retirement haven, with inexpensive property, a mild climate, and gorgeous surroundings.

The latest retirement wave began around 40 years ago when a few developers bought small valleys of wooded land and built golf courses. Golf was the irresistible bait to entice northern buyers to these parts. The ones with money built posh homes, at first for summer getaways, eventually for retirement.

Boone

Nestled in a scenic valley amid some of the oldest mountains in the world, Boone is the region's largest town, with a population of about 18,000. Boone likes to be referred to as the "Heart of the High Country." The town has a surprisingly large downtown business district and an expansive strip mall that belie its population figure. This is partly because Boone serves as the major commercial center for surrounding towns, but also because of Appalachian State University's 18,000 students, who almost match the town's resident population. Not all students live in town, of course; at least 25 percent commute daily from surrounding communities. We've enjoyed watching Boone grow from a small town into a small city over the years that we've been visiting. It boasts a historic downtown with turn-of-the-20th-century brick buildings that fit in perfectly with the Blue Ridge setting. The city center is healthy and bustling, as most college towns are.

Nearby you'll find numerous small towns and villages where you can blend into the daily routine among friendly neighbors. The local folk, who proudly refer to themselves as mountain people, are famous for their hospitality to "flatlanders." However, the large number of outsiders moving in from various parts of the country is growing larger every day. Before long flatlanders will probably outnumber the mountain people.

We flatlanders must remember to be extra hospitable to mountain people at that point.

The town of Boone is the health care center for the region. A recently expanded 127-bed hospital has a critical care unit and a new outpatient surgical facility, resulting in more than adequate medical care.

Boone Chamber of Commerce: 870 W. King St., Boone, NC 28607; (828) 264-2225; boonechamber.org.

THE UNIVERSITY TRIANGLE

Between the flat coastal region and the Appalachian foothills, a stretch of gently rolling countryside, strewn with farms and hardwood forests, is interspersed by crossroads villages, small towns, and sophisticated cities. The region is known as the Midlands. The terrain is too rolling to be considered plains yet not hilly enough to be foothills. The Midlands present a unique combination of cultural choices: from Beethoven to bluegrass and from stock-car racing to scholarly research. Just about any kind of intellectual and recreational pursuit imaginable can be found here.

Because three of North Carolina's top universities are clustered in the Midlands in three of the state's best-known cities, the region around Chapel Hill, Durham, and Raleigh is rightly labeled the University Triangle. The University of North Carolina is located in Chapel Hill, Duke University is in Durham, and North Carolina State is in Raleigh. Besides these three major universities, five four-year colleges plus eight two-year colleges are grouped within a few miles of the others. The University Triangle has more than 64,000 students in attendance, deeply influencing the region's culture, social structure, and worldviews.

Unlike some sections of the South, where outsiders are rare curiosities, outsiders are pretty much in the majority here. The Triangle's famous universities—plus numerous research labs, think tanks, and other academic institutions—draw new residents from all over North America and beyond and from all walks of life. It's claimed that per capita, more academics, PhDs, and scientists live in the University Triangle than in any other part of the country. This is arguably the least "southern" place in the Carolinas, maybe in the entire South. Finding neighbors from your old hometown is highly possible.

NORTH CAROLINA MIDLANDS WEATHER

	IN DEGREES FAHRENHEIT				ANNUAL	
	Jan.	April	July	Oct.	RAIN	SNOW
Daily highs	50	72	88	72	42"	2"
Daily lows	30	47	67	48		

Universities and colleges profoundly influence lifestyles here, with a large percentage of the community either working for or with educational institutions and others benefiting from the many stimulating events connected with academic life. Dramatic performances, lectures, and a host of other presentations are open to the public, and collegiate sports, of course, are perennially popular.

Research Triangle Park

High technology and research are big business here in the Carolina Midlands with Research Triangle Park. One of the nation's major centers for industrial and governmental research, this enormous facility is located on a 6,800-acre wooded tract between the three cities. It employs almost 50,000 people, including some of the nation's top scientists. This recession-proof industry has a beneficial impact on the economics, as well as the social makeup, of the community. Because of the vast number of employment opportunities in the high-tech field, this area is a popular retirement destination for engineers, electronic technicians, and computer experts, who can live just about anywhere within driving distance of any of the Triangle cities. Part-time work and consulting jobs are readily available for those who do not view retirement as a career in itself.

Medical care in the region is outstanding. Six major hospitals, all within easy driving distance, with a total of over 3,000 beds, serve the three cities that make up the University Triangle. Two of the hospitals are university sponsored and nationally acclaimed.

Raleigh

Raleigh was founded in 1792, designed from the very beginning to be North Carolina's state capital. The state's congressmen grew weary of holding sessions in whatever town they could find accommodations, so they purchased 1,000 acres for their headquarters. They designed a town complete with a statehouse, building lots, and even a town cemetery, and named it after the English explorer Sir Walter Raleigh. Today Raleigh has 125 local historic landmarks and five historic districts within its boundaries, as well as numerous fine examples of early modernist architecture.

The city grew slowly over the years, reaching a population of 94,000 by 1960 when the Research Triangle Park was established. Twenty years later, in 1980, Raleigh's population had climbed to 150,000, making it the largest city in the region. Today the population has increased to more than 465,000! This accounts for the many neighborhoods of new homes and developments that are perfect for relocation.

We have friends who moved here from New York City, from a small but expensive rented Manhattan apartment into a spacious five-bedroom Raleigh home on 2 wooded acres. "Our entire apartment could easily fit in the space of our new dining room, living room, and kitchen," they said. "Never in our wildest dreams could we have afforded to buy an apartment in New York." Because they bought when interest rates bottomed out, their monthly mortgage payments were one-third of what they paid in rent for a tiny Manhattan apartment. For some reason real estate here has remained below the national average in cost.

In addition to the cultural benefits bestowed on it by colleges and universities, Raleigh also has a major-league hockey team, the Carolina Hurricanes.

Raleigh Chamber of Commerce: 800 S. Salisbury St., Raleigh, NC 27602; (919) 664-7000; raleighchamber.org.

Chapel Hill

Chartered in 1789 the University of North Carolina has helped Chapel Hill to retain the essence of what a true college town should look like. Because the population of Chapel Hill is only around 59,000, the university—with 29,000 students, 3,200 faculty members, and many support personnel—exerts an enormous influence on the lives of the town's inhabitants. The school and the city have acquired a reputation as an island of a somewhat liberal shape, conflicting with North Carolina's moderately conservative political currents.

Chapel Hill's downtown is user-friendly, with the casual, laid-back pace one would expect from a community that hosts a world-class university. The school is set on a 687-acre campus that is as beautiful as the institution is prestigious. The city's residential neighborhoods seem to compete with the school's famous landscaping in beautifying Chapel Hill. Nonstudent residents are encouraged to participate in the university's agenda via interesting, noncredit adult classes.

Chapel Hill Chamber of Commerce: 104 S. Estes Dr., Chapel Hill, NC 27515; (919) 967-7075; carolinachamber.org.

Durham

Needless to say, medical care in the Triangle is as good as it gets. All three cities and universities are loaded with hospitals, clinics, and medical schools, but Durham leads the way. It has adopted the motto the "City of Medicine." (It used to be nicknamed "Tobacco Town" because tobacco money founded Duke University—but that name seems to be politically incorrect today.) Five excellent hospitals serve the area, and Durham is famous for the university's teaching hospital. In fact, this is a larger city, with a population of about 267,000.

Duke University's two impressive campuses also influence the community, not only financially but culturally. Whether it's black-tie or blue jeans, ballet or beach music, the entire area has something for everyone. The school's cultural programs can amount to an astounding 500 presentations a year.

Greater Durham Chamber of Commerce: 300 W. Morgan St., #1400, Durham, NC 27701; (919) 328-8700; durhamchamber.org.

Pinehurst, Southern Pines & Aberdeen

The villages of Pinehurst, Southern Pines, and Aberdeen, in the central part of the state, have long enjoyed the distinction of being premier golf destinations. Located within minutes of each other, this triangle of towns contains 43 superb championship courses within a 16-mile radius, some of which are among the most highly rated in the world. It's said that this area, known as the Sandhills, offers nearly 700 holes of golf. With a mild climate (July high temperatures average 79 degrees), you'll have every opportunity to play as much golf as you care to.

Many who now have retired here at one time considered Pinehurst and Southern Pines merely as convenient stopover places on their way to

Florida vacations. This was the logical place to break up the trip—about halfway for many easterners. Why not stay over a day or two and get in a few rounds of golf? As retirement time drew nearer, some folks naturally began thinking more about Pinehurst and the Sandhills and less about Florida.

Of course, membership in Pinehurst Club was mandatory for those who bought lots in the many subdivisions ringing the golf-tennis complex. Those who buy here today automatically inherit memberships as part of the purchase price of their lots or homes. (They inherit the monthly fees as well.) This is an important feature, because some golf-club developments have a long waiting list for membership.

Southern Pines is an offshoot development, separate from Pinehurst. Southern Pines is larger, with a population of 12,800 and a downtown area somewhat less touristy than Pinehurst's Village Center. Southern Pines is basically a residential community, liberally endowed with golf facilities and shopping malls, and with a quaint town center. The homes we looked at were superbly designed to fit into the Sandhills's pine and oak ambience.

Aberdeen, with almost 7,000 inhabitants, is the third village in this grouping. In its early days it was a bustling center of trade and commerce. Then came quieter years as the downtown saw businesses moving out. But Aberdeen has emerged from its slump, and Main Street is lively once more, with its fine antiques shops, boutiques, and other shopping. Our impression of Aberdeen is that it's a place for relatively more affordable housing, but it's still in the golf-club circuit.

Because the elevation here is higher than most of Florida, summers aren't quite as warm or humid. Furthermore, the 55-degree January days permit plenty of outdoor activities. "Any day it's not raining, I can golf, hike, or ride horseback," said a retiree here. "When I lived in Florida, it was too damned muggy in the summer."

Pinehurst and Southern Pines are clearly upscale residential communities with a focus on golf courses and quality homes, yet they are not gated as are many country club–type developments. The neighborhoods are open; anyone can cruise through the streets without having to be a resident. This is not much of a problem, because crime levels in the Pinehurst–Southern Pines region are exceptionally low. Because of the large percentage of out-of-state retirees, newcomers don't feel that they stand out as they might in other small southern towns.

More than adequate health care is covered by a 397-bed regional hospital with a medical staff of 112 physicians and 1,400 employees, assisted by 500 volunteers. A 24-hour mobile intensive care unit provides up-to-date life-support treatments.

Moore County Chamber of Commerce: 1295 Old US Hwy. 15, Ste. 13, Southern Pines, NC 28387; (910) 692-3926; moorecountychamber .com.

SOUTH CAROLINA

The Carolinas have much in common. They share 500 miles of scenic Atlantic coastline on one side and the spectacular Appalachian Blue Ridge Mountains on the other. As in North Carolina, the South Carolina coast and Blue Ridge foothills are separated by sandhill formations, rich farmland, and forested acreage. The coastline here is more accessible than farther north, with ocean and freshwater recreation readily available. Aristocratic low-country cities, based on the plantation culture dating from colonial days, offer unique retirement lifestyles.

South Carolina Tax Profile
Sales tax: 6%; food, drugs exempt
State income tax: 3% to 7%; can't deduct federal income tax
Income brackets: lowest, $2,970; highest, $14,861
Property taxes: 4%
Social Security taxed: no
Pensions taxed: $3,000 exclusion
Gasoline tax: 22¢ per gallon

South Carolina is much less industrialized and high-tech than its northern neighbor and is perhaps a bit more laid-back. Like the other Atlantic coastal states, South Carolina can be divided into three regions. The first is the coastal plain, including South Carolina's many miles of tidal shoreline and barrier islands and its colonial cities. Next is the Piedmont region, whose rolling hills and rich farmland make up about two-thirds of the state's area. The third division is the Appalachians, with the highest elevation in the Blue Ridge Mountains in the northwestern part of the state.

Columbia

Columbia, the capital of South Carolina, combines all the graces of a rich past with the vibrancy of the emerging Sunbelt. With an estimated population of 133,000, Columbia is a good-size city, yet small enough to feel almost like a small town. A surprising number of northerners have found this to be a great place for retirement. In fact, Columbia claims to have a higher percentage of retirees than anywhere else in the state. Columbia is also the region's center for military, academic, government, and commercial activity.

Columbia sits right in the center of the state, at the point where the coastal plain meets the Piedmont. The rolling foothills begin at the western edge of the city, while from the opposite edge of town, the country is flat all the way to the ocean. This is a comfortable city, with the vast majority of the housing owner-occupied. Streets are shaded with large trees, adding to a quiet charm that comes with ordinary people living in ordinary neighborhoods. Yet Columbia has its sophisticated side as well, with a cosmopolitan feeling that goes with being a university town.

Many colonial cities grew haphazardly, without much planning of any sort. But Columbia is different. The British needed a capital city, so in 1686 they designed the first planned city in the colonies. The city's broad boulevards and architectural gems attest to its early beauty. Robert Mills, one of the pioneers of American architecture, designed several buildings here as well as many in Washington, D.C. (One of his more famous works is the Washington Monument.)

Another educational center of the South, Columbia has the University of South Carolina as its focal point. The university, with almost 30,000 students, is a major source of cultural enrichment. Along with a nearby two-year college, the school attracts academics from around the nation, many of whom later join the ranks of Columbia's retired. All South Carolina state colleges and technical institutes waive tuition for residents older than 60 years of age on a space-available basis.

This is a popular retirement location for military families because of the town's proximity to Fort Jackson. Many who were stationed here fondly recall the mild weather and friendly South Carolinians. These memories are bringing the ex-GIs back to Columbia for their retirement careers. These two out-of-state groups, academic and military, contribute toward making the Columbia area heterogeneous, with open, accepting feelings toward newcomers.

We found several retirees who had started out intending to retire elsewhere. One retired couple admitted that they had always planned on retirement in Florida. "Every year, as we made our annual trip to Florida, we broke our trip up with a stopover in Columbia," they explained, "and again on the way back. Then, one day, just before retirement, we realized that we really liked Columbia better than Florida!" They decided to rent an apartment, just to "see how Columbia feels." They found low living costs and friendly, cultured neighbors. "We never made it to Florida," they said with satisfied smiles. "We still go there for vacations, though."

I asked the husband how he felt as a Yankee moving into a Deep South town. Did he find any prejudices? "To tell you the truth, I haven't noticed anything like that," he said. "My neighbors are just as nice as the ones we had back home, but they're definitely more friendly. Other northerners warned us, 'They'll be neighborly, yes, but they'll never invite you to their daughter's debutante party unless you were *born* in Columbia.'" He shrugged his shoulders and said, "That's a relief to me, because the last place I'd want to be invited would be to some teenager's debutante party! I'd have to invent an excuse why I couldn't go."

Another advantage they pointed out—aside from the low cost of quality housing—is the excellent medical care available. (As a pharmacist, he was aware of such things.) Three major hospitals, plus 10 smaller ones, serve the area with more than 500 doctors to treat your ills.

There's always something happening around Columbia. Fifteen public golf courses can be found in the area. For spectator sports there is a minor-league baseball team, a recent 18,000-seat basketball/entertainment arena, and a 142,500-square-foot convention center. Open-air concerts and festivals are held at frequent intervals, and the nation's oldest community theater presents drama productions.

Columbia Chamber of Commerce: 930 Richland St., Columbia, SC 29201; (803) 733-1110; columbiachamber.org.

SOUTH CAROLINA MIDLANDS WEATHER

| | IN DEGREES FAHRENHEIT | | | | ANNUAL | |
	Jan.	April	July	Oct.	RAIN	SNOW
Daily highs	50	72	88	72	43"	5"
Daily lows	32	50	69	50		

Aiken

Aiken (pop. about 30,000) is a genteel Old South town located in the western corner of South Carolina's Piedmont region, with the majestic Blue Ridge Mountains a short drive away. Aiken's robust business district makes it look larger than it actually is, because it's the shopping and employment center for a large area. Aiken County has about 168,000 people.

One way Aiken differs from many other southern towns is that so many out-of-state people have moved here that distinctions between natives and newcomers have blurred. Townspeople are used to different accents and other lifestyles; a cosmopolitan mix has broken through all but the most inbred social barriers. Where did these outsiders come from? Initially people came to work for the Department of Energy's high-tech, atomic-energy facility in Aiken. The department imported engineers, physicists, technicians, bricklayers—you name it—from all over the country.

When the energy project was finally up and running, many workers moved elsewhere to new jobs. Others—some nearing retirement anyway—elected to stay. The word soon got around about this beautiful little city with mild winters, friendly people, and low real estate prices. This brought even more outsiders into Aiken. The result is an eclectic collection of people from all over the country.

Aiken isn't all single-family homes, mansions, and honeysuckle. Modern condominiums, apartments, and gated communities are home to many families. Away from town you'll find small farms and homes on acreage for horses or garden hobbies. Luxury communities—Kalmia Landing, Woodside Plantation, Midland Valley, Cedar Creek, and Hounds Lake—offer country-club retirement accommodations and an atmosphere of studied elegance.

From its inception Aiken was known as a health resort. Wealthy people from Charleston and the coastal plantations came here to escape the sultry, lowland summer heat and malaria-bearing mosquitoes. The Civil War and its aftermath of poverty put a temporary halt to Aiken's role as a resort. But by the 1890s Aiken entered a new golden age when wealthy northerners, seeking pleasant, quiet places for their winter homes, "discovered" the town. At an altitude of only 527 feet, the town had a climate mild enough to permit year-round grazing and was a perfect place to raise thoroughbred horses. Soon the ordinary rich, the filthy rich, and the disgustingly filthy rich bought old mansions and built new ones of their own designs. They bought farms for their racehorses and enclosed pastures with white fences. They established the Palmetto Golf Club in 1893 and were slicing drives into the lake by the time the first thoroughbred colts were frisking in the meadows. (Residents here today are still into horses, and it's common to see riders in town. In fact, this may be the only city in the country providing stoplights with pushbuttons that enable mounted riders to stop traffic while the horse crosses the street!)

Aiken's wealthy early-day retirees quickly established the area as a rich man's playground, mostly a haven for wealthy Yankees from New York and Connecticut. These newcomers brought prosperity to Aiken and, with it, a return to a genteel lifestyle that had disappeared with the Civil War. Aiken's old, aristocratic families quickly accepted the winter residents into local society despite different customs and accents. This established a tradition of openness and hospitality that has characterized Aiken ever since. Today the super-rich northerners have gone elsewhere, but the legacy of hospitality and friendliness remains.

Aiken is home to a campus of the University of South Carolina and Aiken Technical College. This means many inexpensive courses for senior citizens and entry into the academic community of the town. Aiken Regional Medical Centers includes a 256-bed, state-of-the-art acute- and mental health–care hospital, with a staff of more than 100 physicians. Veterans Administration hospitals are located in both Columbia and nearby Augusta for military retirees and their dependents.

Recreational choices abound; because the weather is generally mild, year-round outdoor activities are possible. There are 19 golf courses within a 20-mile radius of Aiken; several feature senior citizens' clubs. The famous Masters Tournament is played every year in nearby Augusta. Each autumn on the shores of Lake Hartwell, Clemson University conducts a camping program for senior citizens. Fishing, swimming, even waterskiing, for all those old-timers who go for that sort of nonsense, are available at any number of nearby ponds or lakes. Lifetime hunting and fishing permits are available for $9 to residents age 64 and older.

Aiken Chamber of Commerce: 121 Richland Ave. E., Aiken, SC 29801; (803) 641-1111; aikenchamber.net.

ON THE OCEAN

Most of South Carolina's coastal region is lowland country, sparsely populated and mostly suitable for rice cultivation. Generally the major roads
and highways run far inland, with occasional roads meandering toward
the ocean. Except for Hilton Head, the Charleston area, and a few isolated oceanfront towns, the state's most logical beachfront retirement
choices occupy a 60-mile stretch of fascinating coastline known as the
Grand Strand. It begins at Little River, on the North Carolina–South
Carolina border, and stretches south to the Santee River, just beyond
Georgetown.

The warm waters of the Gulf Stream flow only 40 miles offshore, which
explains the Grand Strand's unusually mild weather. It's said that winter
temperatures here are only two degrees cooler than the northern Florida
coast. Local residents qualify this, however, by saying, "We do get some
right smart cold spells from time to time." Snows are rare.

Sparsely settled a few years ago, the Grand Strand today is blooming
with new residential developments. Timber plantations along the shore
are being replaced by upscale resorts, some complete with golf courses and
clubhouses. Some of the developments are priced well within the average
retiree's budget.

Myrtle Beach

Myrtle Beach sits in the center of the accessible beach areas of the Grand
Strand. With about 32,000 year-round inhabitants, Myrtle Beach doesn't
sound like such a big town, but seasonal visitors can double the population.
The full length of the Grand Strand has a permanent population of about
60,000, a large percentage of whom are retired, but visitors expand the
population to more than 300,000. Spring and fall have always lured golfers to enjoy the more than 100 golf courses along the Grand Strand. And
summer traditionally draws crowds of vacationers to delight in beach sun

SOUTH CAROLINA COASTAL WEATHER

	IN DEGREES FAHRENHEIT				ANNUAL	
	Jan.	April	July	Oct.	RAIN	SNOW
Daily highs	60	75	89	75	51"	2"
Daily lows	40	53	71	53		

and fun. Each summer seems to bring more and more tourists. Retirement here means you will be living in a really busy tourist resort. The compensation is that you don't have far to go for golf or other tourist attractions.

When we first researched Myrtle Beach about 25 years ago, we described the town as South Carolina's equivalent of a Florida Panhandle resort: tourist-frenzied in the summer and somewhat relaxed in the winter. In fact, many restaurants and small businesses closed down when tourists went home for the winter. Inexpensive homes were almost the rule, and rentals were plentiful. I reported that after Labor Day, "the town drops its frantic, super-hero role and changes to its mild-mannered, sleepy identity for the rest of the year."

Since that time the population of the Grand Strand has more than doubled. All seasons are now busy. Myrtle Beach has become one of the South's premier golfing meccas, drawing visitors from all over the country. According to the chamber of commerce, Myrtle Beach has the greatest number of golf courses per square mile in the world! People who live in country-club developments in other parts of the South routinely organize excursions to play golf on the Grand Strand. Besides golf courses you'll find an assortment of golf schools, golf shops, and a wide range of golf vacation packages should you decide to come here to test the water (or the sand traps, for that matter).

A proliferation of country-and-western entertainment centers, modeled after Missouri's Branson and Tennessee's Grand Ole Opry, have joined golf to make full-tilt tourism a year-round business. Adding to the momentum are events like the annual Harley-Davidson motorcycle rally and the Sun Fun Festival. The increased tourism is nice for commerce, but it creates traffic congestion and additional strain on summer-season facilities already under pressure. With an increased workforce and long-term visitors competing for housing, bargain real estate is out of the picture today.

Despite the aforementioned drawbacks, folks are still coming here to retire. A look around tells why. Between Myrtle Beach's main thoroughfare (which used to be US 17) and the ocean, several blocks of beautiful homes on spacious, well-landscaped lots provide neighborhoods of gracious living, and other equally nice areas are found away from the business centers. Other choices are golf-course communities and upscale subdivisions, as well as more modest homes between the main street and the US 17 bypass.

Three medium-size hospitals manage the care for Myrtle Beach and nearby communities. Another half dozen scattered along the Grand Strand service the other communities along the coastline.

Myrtle Beach Chamber of Commerce: 1200 N. Oak St., Myrtle Beach, SC 29577; (843) 626-7444; myrtlebeachareachamber.com.

Charleston

After its settlement in 1670, Charleston quickly became one of the most prosperous cities in the 13 colonies. Charleston was the standard against which people measured other cities in terms of beauty, culture, and riches. Its expansive harbor port served what is today called the Low Country, a land that was rich and fertile. Planters, acquiring wealth from fantastically productive rice plantations worked by slaves, began designing mansions as lavish as money could provide. They built with such loving attention to detail and devotion to quality and style that future generations of Charlestonians have resisted all temptations to exchange those prizes for new fashions. At least 240 homes still standing are known to have been built before 1840, and 76 predate the American Revolution, with some dating back to the 1720s. Hundreds more date from the time of the Civil War and Reconstruction.

Today Charleston (pop. 130,000) vies with Savannah for the title of most beautiful city on the Atlantic Seaboard. Each scores high marks, and each claims to be the "cultural center of the South." It's difficult to choose between them. Charleston is so steeped in history that a walk through its downtown is an adventure in time travel. It's easy to imagine fine carriages jaunting along cobblestone streets or fashionably dressed women and nattily attired men strolling the sidewalks. A pause in front of a home built in 1720 evokes a feeling of humility as you mentally re-create the setting, almost three centuries in the past. (In the California town where my wife and I live, any home built before 1910 is considered a priceless antique!)

Built on a narrow peninsula between two rivers, Charleston's downtown section isn't very large. The emphasis today is on private homes rather than on commercial activity. The most important enterprise (from my standpoint as a lover of seafood) in this old section is the superb collection of fine restaurants. As major tourist attractions, Charleston's restaurants fully live up to their reputation for southern gourmet dishes of all descriptions. (We can never pass through town without a pause for our favorite culinary delight: she-crab soup!)

Charleston living isn't for everyone. It can be terribly formal, paced with the tempo of old-time southern society, intellectual pursuits, and traditional manners. We've been told that the social whirl is a closed affair, with few outsiders ever invited in. (Depending upon your personality, this could be a drawback.)

Even if you aren't interested in buying a historic mansion and entering the social whirl, you might be tempted by the possibility of a part-time living arrangement. You can do as the old-time planters did: live in Charleston most of the year and somewhere else for the summer. Many old mansions in Charleston's historic district were long ago converted to apartments, which at one time rented at unusually affordable rates, given the enchanted atmosphere. Carriage houses behind the mansions were remodeled into studio apartments or charming cottages, with lofts converted into upstairs bedrooms. As historic district real estate becomes more and more valuable, however, more homes are being restored to their former glory, and prices for rentals have risen to match the more expensive housing.

All is not lace curtains and fresh paint in old Charleston. As in many cities, the curse of urban blight hovers. Not very far from the prosperous streets described here, you'll find rows of abandoned houses, so old and uncared for that they look as if they might collapse from age and decay. It's unfortunate there's not some way to preserve these old mansions. Some stand three stories high, with beautifully crafted balconies and balustrades rising the full facade. Porches, high columns, and carved woodwork add to the impression of museum pieces from an irretrievable past. Within a decade these will probably all be gone. Most neighborhoods bordering the downtown area do not look to be appropriate retirement possibilities.

More than half the city's population lives in West Ashley and James Island, which lie just to the west of the peninsula. Here old mixes with new: neighborhoods with older brick homes and graceful oak trees settled in with subdivisions and commercial centers.

If you don't care to live in or near a city center, or if you can't afford one of the historic places, you should check the outskirts of Charleston or one of the outlying towns, within easy distance of the old town for dinner or a play any time you feel like it. Nearby places where people choose to retire include Charleston's islands or towns such as Summerville.

With five major hospitals, including the University of South Carolina's 656-bed facility, the Charleston area enjoys some of the finest medical care in the region. The University of South Carolina's Medical University is a leading biomedical, teaching, patient-care, and research center. A veterans' facility with almost 100 beds is also located here.

Isle of Palms

Just east of Charleston, bordered by the Atlantic Ocean and the Intracoastal Waterway, two semitropical islands, with one luxurious resort community, are popular places for relocation. Miles of sandy beaches, pastel homes, and warm, friendly people make relocation pleasant. The Isle of Palms is a classic family-oriented beachfront community offering a wide variety of accommodations and recreation options. Wild Dunes, located on 1,600 acres at the northeastern end of the island, is a premier resort community with championship golf and tennis facilities, a full-service marina, and a full selection of homes and villas for sale.

Sullivan's Island

This is the Isle of Palms's sister island. More of a residential beach community, Sullivan's Island is located just south of the Isle of Palms, across Breach Inlet. There are beautiful beaches and an impressive selection of homes on this island. Natives describe the difference between the two islands this way: Isle of Palms is "more of a resort island," whereas Sullivan's Island is "more of a beach town."

Sullivan's Island offers much more, however, than a quiet beach-town atmosphere. Here you'll find a quaint restaurant area, historic Fort Moultrie, a working lighthouse, public tennis courts, and an old-fashioned community playground complete with a grandstand gazebo. Of course, Sullivan's Island offers all the natural amenities you could want: wide sandy beaches, fishing, swimming, boating, sunning, and more.

Charleston Chamber of Commerce: 4500 Leeds Ave., North Charleston, SC 29405; (843) 577-2510; charlestonchamber.org.

Hilton Head Island

Still in South Carolina, just 40 miles north of Savannah, Georgia, Hilton Head Island is the epitome of a luxury retirement area. The island is divided into eight gated developments (called "plantations") centered on active living—golf, tennis, boating, and 12 miles of white, sandy beach. Present-day population is about 38,000.

This semitropical island is defined by its tidal rivers and streams and its unspoiled forests of moss-draped live oak, magnolia, and palmetto. Its white, sandy beaches, quiet lagoons, meandering creeks, and expanses of sea marsh embody the romance and mystery of the Carolina coastline.

Hilton Head Island—named for an English sea captain in the 1600s—was developed early on into plantations and was occupied by Union troops during the Civil War. Through all the years, it has managed to preserve its pristine beauty. Its latter-day development has been a model for forward-looking planning and conservation. Custom homes and villas are interspersed with open areas and wildlife preserves. Commercial zones are free of garish signs and billboards, and the beaches are pristine. The good news is that all the Hilton Head beaches are public, from the ocean to the high-water mark. The bad news is that access to the beach is often private.

More than a million visitors come here every year, yet the island is refreshingly tranquil. Traffic, commercial, and recreational facilities are coordinated to allow visitors and residents to coexist nicely. One of the big attractions is golf; in fact, the island is one of the nation's foremost golf meccas. I counted 40 golf courses in the area, with almost 500 holes spread over 12 locations on Hilton Head and nearby Daufuskie Island. Courses range from spectacular oceanfront layouts to settings along rivers, beside lakes and lagoons, and in forests and tidal marshes, with most of the layouts designed by the PGA's most noted players.

For tennis buffs there are more than 250 courts, ranging from major complexes that host national championships to one or two courts adjoining a condo or apartment complex. Five hundred acres are set aside as a forest preserve with an astonishing 260 species of birds, alligators, deer, raccoons, and wild turkeys. (A small gate fee is required to enter.) Hiking, shrimping from the shore, biking, and boating fill out the menu of outdoor activities. The list of gourmet restaurants is also impressive. According to the chamber of commerce, about 200 restaurants, cafes, and fast-food emporiums serve everything from gourmet cuisine to stand-up pizza and egg rolls.

The bottom line: This is a place for those who can afford to pay top dollar for a high-quality lifestyle. Housing prices, although not the most expensive in the country, are certainly not for the fainthearted, although a friend who has a vacation home on the island told me there are some inexpensive alternatives available.

Hilton Head Island supports a large community of doctors, dentists, and other health care professionals. The local 68-bed Hospital Medical Campus has a medical staff that represents more than 30 specialties and subspecialties, a number frequently found in hospitals several times its size.

Sun City Hilton Head

The Del Webb Corporation's Sun City retirement development began in the Southwest several decades ago and quickly became synonymous with planned retirement concepts. Before long Sun City clones began appearing in other parts of the country. Now South Carolina has its own Del Webb development: Sun City Hilton Head.

Actually located on the mainland on 4,300 acres of what had once been a pine forest, Sun City Hilton Head has 35 percent of the land dedicated to lakes, lagoons, and woods. Since its beginning in 1994, almost 10,000 residents have moved here, and construction is under way for more homes. Sun City Hilton Head is 13 miles from the island of Hilton Head, 6 miles off I-95. Like other Del Webb projects, this one features golf and tennis and emphasizes an active community lifestyle.

This new development fulfills much of the original Arizona concept, but with a motif adapted to South Carolina's gracious southern traditions. The community is focused on a town center designed to resemble a traditional southern town square, complete with a picturesque clock tower. The Village Center offers indoor/outdoor swimming pools, a tennis club, bocce courts, a bowling center, a huge fitness complex, and other amenities you would expect to find in a Sun City. Four medical facilities are within a 15-mile radius of the development.

Two 18-hole golf courses are in place, with a 10,400-square-foot clubhouse; another clubhouse and an additional 9 holes are in the planning stages. Cultural offerings include live theater, dance, and a variety of galleries. The well-respected Savannah Symphony and other cultural delights of Savannah are a short drive away, and those of Hilton Head Island are even closer. The advantage to this type of retirement—besides quality surroundings and excellent facilities—is the carefully planned social structure already in place when newcomers move in. You'll find instant involvement in bridge clubs, golf foursomes, hobbies, travel clubs, and much more. It eases the effort of making new friends in the adopted community. Everything is in place for you to start a new life.

Hilton Head Chamber of Commerce: 1 Chamber of Commerce Dr., P.O. Box 5647, Hilton Head Island, SC 29938; (800) 523-3373; hilton headchamber.org.

GEORGIA

The state of Georgia is trying hard to tempt out-of-state retirees into moving here rather than continuing on to Florida, and a growing number of folks are discovering that they like the state's varied menu of locations and its Sunbelt climate. The largest state east of the Mississippi, Georgia stretches from the golden beaches of the Atlantic to the foothills of the Appalachians. The Blue Ridge Mountains taper off in the northern end of the state, but not before rewarding the region with rich valleys, forested hills, and scenic mountains.

A good prospect for retirement is Georgia's Atlantic coast, characterized by sea islands with moss-draped oaks and magnificently preserved colonial towns with affordable retirement choices that once were the domains of millionaires. To the south is the Plantation Trace with its early spring, delightful small cities, and nearness to both the Gulf and Atlantic. Also popular for retirement is around Augusta, which enjoys the benefits of two

Georgia Tax Profile

Sales tax: 4% to 7%; drugs exempt
State income tax: 1% to 6%; can't deduct federal income tax
Income brackets: lowest, $750; highest, $7,000
Standard deduction: single, $2,700; married filing joint return, $3,000
Property taxes: typically 0.98%, plus variable local taxes on 40% of assessed value
Social Security taxed: no
Pensions taxed: excludes first $10,000 for older taxpayers
Inheritance tax: limited estate tax
Gasoline tax: 31¢ per gallon

geographical areas: the Piedmont plateau and the Atlantic coastal plain. This is golf and thoroughbred country.

Savannah

Although Georgia was the last of England's 13 colonies to be settled, Savannah was the first British settlement in the colony of Georgia. It all started in 1733, when England was anxious to secure her claim to the territory against Spanish encroachment from Florida. General James Edward Oglethorpe selected a spot to settle on the Savannah River, 10 miles from the Atlantic, on the edge of Yamacraw Bluff. Savannah's historic city hall now sits on the same bluff where Oglethorpe landed. Besides a military outpost, Oglethorpe hoped to create a planned city—a center of agriculture, manufacturing, and export. He was eminently successful. Instead of allowing a traditional, haphazard village layout to develop, Oglethorpe designed a system of street grids, broken by a series of public squares. From the beginning, Savannah was designed to be beautiful as well as defensible.

Instead of Charleston's ostentatious one-of-a-kind showpieces, which were built as winter residences for inland planters, Savannah's antebellum mansions were owned by merchants, shippers, and townspeople. They preferred the dignified, formal expression of Italianate, English regency, and Gothic revival. Homes in Savannah were designed to harmonize with one another, precisely arranged around parklike squares. Many homes in Savannah's historic district are so well preserved and fit so perfectly in the scheme of things that they look as if they were constructed last year. Of the original 24 squares in the master plan, 22 still exist. Today these squares—tastefully landscaped with live oak, azaleas, fountains, and statues—give Savannah that charming flavor that sets the city apart as unique as well as beautiful.

Our first research visit to Savannah was about 25 years ago, when the historic city center was in the first stages of renovation. At that point Savannah had a long way to go. Crime statistics looked dismal, the downtown was not someplace you would care to walk after dark, and rehabilitation seemed all but impossible. How things have changed!

With loving care and determined community action, Savannah's downtown historic district (the largest of its kind in the country) has been not only restored, but made exceptionally livable. It changed from an area of above-average crime to a safe place to be. In fact, *Walking Magazine* once nominated downtown Savannah as one of the "Ten Top Walking Cities in the US." You can stroll the historic district, the cobblestone riverfront area, or City Market.

Four blocks in the heart of Savannah's historic district have been renovated to capture the atmosphere and character of the old marketplace. Restaurants, open-air cafes, jazz clubs, theme shops, and crafts and gift shops blend to create a pleasant place to pause during a walk, have lunch, and enjoy the scene. The market features artists working in their lofts and exhibiting their works for sale. Savannah's determination to protect and improve its historic sites presents a model for historic-preservation efforts.

For a flavor of Savannah, read John Berendt's book *Midnight in the Garden of Good and Evil*, which is set in the heart of the historic district. Tourism in Savannah increased more than 13 percent in 1996; folks wanted to see the places described in the novel. The motion-picture version of the book was filmed on location in Savannah, with lovely old mansions as backgrounds.

Savannah has 143,000 inhabitants and is surrounded by some very livable communities, possibly a bit more suitable for retirement than the city's historic center (as well as more affordable). The greater Savannah area comprises a 50-mile radius of Chatham County and has a total population of almost 600,000. Real estate varies from the very expensive on Skidaway Island, where building lots run into six-figure prices, to livable neighborhoods in nearby towns, where acceptable homes can be purchased for the price of a building lot elsewhere. Most of the cost-of-living indicators are usually well below national averages here.

One of Savannah's fastest-growing residential areas is on the fringes of the south side, only 6 miles from the historic district. A collection of attractive neighborhoods offer quality single-family housing as well as a number of apartment complexes, town houses, and shopping centers. To zip downtown is a matter of minutes.

Savannah's Islands

Eighteen miles east of downtown Savannah, Tybee Island could be the prototype of a summer beach community. People from Savannah and tourists from all over come here to enjoy sunning and shell collecting on the island's 2 miles of white sand beaches. However, the 3,000 year-round residents enjoy the vacation atmosphere all year long. Accommodations are

GEORGIA COASTAL WEATHER

	IN DEGREES FAHRENHEIT				ANNUAL	
	Jan.	April	July	Oct.	RAIN	SNOW
Daily highs	60	75	89	75	51"	2"
Daily lows	40	53	71	53		

divided into short-term rentals of condos and apartments and permanent-resident housing, which tends to be older and not fancy. Other island communities on the way to Tybee Island are Wilmington, Whitemarsh, and Talahi. Like most Georgia islands, they are not crowded and have several nice-looking developments.

The ultimate in upscale living hereabouts can be found at Skidaway Island, the Isle of Hope, Southbridge, and a few other developments. Many of these are gated communities, very posh, and usually offer private golf-course membership as a part of ownership fees.

Savannah Chamber of Commerce: 101 E. Bay St., Savannah, GA 31402; (912) 644-6400; savannahchamber.com.

Brunswick & the Golden Isles

A hundred years ago—when being a millionaire meant more than having equity in an above-average Connecticut home—millionaires from all over the country converged upon the Golden Isles and encouraged their contractors and interior decorators to enter the competition for the fanciest homes possible. The objects of their affection were the islands of St. Simons and Jekyll on the south Georgia coast. The mainland base camp and supply station for the islands is the conservative old town of Brunswick. Compared with its rich island cousins, Brunswick is a rather ordinary community of approximately 20,000 inhabitants. But there's a charm about the place that money can't buy. All in all, Brunswick looks like the place to live for those who want to enjoy the fishing, beaches, and amenities, if not the ambience, of nearby Jekyll and St. Simons without paying the cost of actually living on the islands.

Development on the islands began in the 1880s when opulent families like the J. P. Morgans, Rockefellers, and Goulds formed the Jekyll Island Club. Only club members were permitted to live on the island, making this one of the most exclusive resorts in the entire world. Historians estimate that at one time Jekyll Island Club members represented one-sixth of the world's wealth!

Because Jekyll Island is now a state park, and because all the lovely homes here are situated on state-owned land, the homes are purchased, but the land itself must be leased from the State of Georgia. Although homeowners don't pay property taxes (after all, they don't own the property), their lease payments for the land equal what taxes would normally be. Technically, a real estate transaction on Jekyll Island involves buying a lease instead of a deed. But this doesn't affect the price, because the cost of the lease is equal to the value of a home on a conventional piece of land.

Nearby Sea Island is another mind-boggling upscale development, this one dating from the 1920s. The country's most successful barons of industry and finance constructed enormous mansions in the style of the Roaring Twenties that the Great Gatsby would have adored. These gorgeous homes are the island's hallmark, but since the end of World War II, a few less ambitious homes have made their appearance (less ambitious in style, perhaps, but not in price!).

Homes on Jekyll Island and Sea Island are not places the average retiree can afford, especially Sea Island. But St. Simons Island is another story. Here you'll find many affordable neighborhoods and charming rural areas interspersed with the higher-cost spreads. The population is about 15,000.

Originally named San Simeon by 16th-century Spanish explorers, St. Simons is the largest of Georgia's fabled Golden Isles. Britain took over in 1736, and the island flourished as rice, indigo, and cotton plantations expanded. Later, islanders actively participated in the revolution against British rule. The revolutionary warship *Constitution* ("Old Ironsides") was clad with iron-hard planks from live oak trees hewn on St. Simons Island.

Today sprawling plantations of the 19th century have become beautiful residential areas, golf courses, tennis courts, and quaint commercial areas with numerous shops and restaurants. The island's original town center is called the Village, a quaint district at the island's southern tip. The Village includes a 200-year-old working lighthouse, a great fishing pier, shops, boutiques, and a coastal history museum. Many handsome homes—both large Victorians and cute cottages—sit within walking distance from the Village, often set back from the road under spreading oak trees festooned with

Spanish moss. The northern portion of St. Simons Island is less crowded, with homes set on wooded acreage along the lightly traveled road. Several developments are underway here, with upscale housing set among oaks and palmettos. Instead of rice or cotton, the major harvest today is tourists. They come here year-round to swim and sail along St. Simons's miles of lovely beaches, to challenge its 81 holes of golf, and to dine in gourmet restaurants. Island residents manage quite well coexisting with tourists. Several shopping areas hide behind shrubbery, partially hidden from view from the main road that curves along the beach side of the island. Several miles of fine public beach invite picnics and sunbathing.

There are no hospital facilities on Jekyll Island, the nearest being the Southeast Georgia Hospital in Brunswick. The facility has 273 beds and is about 9 miles from the island.

Brunswick–Golden Isles Chamber of Commerce: 1505 Richmond St., 2nd Floor, Brunswick, GA 31520; (912) 265-0620; brunswickgoldenisleschamber.com.

Georgia's Blue Ridge Mountains

The Appalachian range pushes into north-central and northeastern Georgia with a mountainous plateau that rises to the state's highest elevations. Covering about 1,400 square miles, this picturesque and uncrowded three-county area has about 73,000 residents, many of them retirees who have come from all parts of the country to relocate in this beautiful Blue Ridge setting.

With lovely mountain scenery everywhere, you're never far from lakes, rivers, and state parks. The Chattooga Wild and Scenic River is nearby, with dramatic waterfalls and spectacular rapids and other natural beauties. Deep canyons like the 1,200-foot chasm of Tallulah Gorge, high peaks like the 3,600-foot Blue Ridge Crest, and the spectacular 729-foot plume of Amicalola Falls all combine to create some of the most dramatic and stirring scenery of the Appalachian chain. The famous Appalachian Trail traverses the counties. All this wilderness thrives here, yet is 90 miles or less from Atlanta. South of here the Blue Ridge Mountains dwindle into foothills and finally change into gentle hill country as you approach the fringes of metropolitan Atlanta.

GEORGIA BLUE RIDGE MOUNTAINS WEATHER

| | IN DEGREES FAHRENHEIT | | | | ANNUAL | |
	Jan.	April	July	Oct.	RAIN	SNOW
Daily highs	52	69	84	69	60"	10"
Daily lows	32	45	65	46		

Over the past decade retirement writers have dedicated much of their attention and enthusiasm to the region, more because of the lovely mountain scenery rather than actual numbers of retirees relocating here. Successful publicity has taken its toll in northeast Georgia, considering the number of people who've decided to relocate here. Although not overwhelming, the influx of newcomers to a sparsely settled area naturally pushed up formerly bargain-basement real estate prices. In fact, the campaign to attract retirees was so successful that the Clayton Chamber of Commerce had to start charging money to send out its relocation packets. It was besieged by so many requests that the printing costs, postage, and handling got out of hand. But this doesn't mean homes are expensive; they're just not bargains any longer.

Rabun, Lumpkin, and Habersham Counties have several delightful towns suitable for retirement. Clayton, in Rabun County, has attracted the most attention, probably because it's one of the more picturesque in Blue Ridge Mountain country. Other locations—such as Clarkesville, Demorest, Helen, and Dahlonega—haven't achieved quite the same popularity. The terrain around these latter towns can be more accurately described as Blue Ridge foothills rather than Blue Ridge Mountains, but this doesn't detract from their charm. None of the dozen locales that make up this region are very large. Clayton is the largest town with about 2,300 inhabitants, and the entire county has 16,000 residents.

A natural getaway near the town of Clayton is an area called Sylvan Falls. Next to the Chattahoochee National Forest, several hundred homes are tucked away in the forest here, some with lookout vantage points from a 2,500-foot-high ridge. Not all homes are blessed with such breathtaking views, but each enjoys its own little natural paradise of rustic beauty. We once visited a couple, retired here from New Orleans, who live on the apex of the ridge. As we gazed out over the view, our friend Marjorie said, "We feel like we're on the edge of heaven here in the Blue Ridge Mountains of northeast Georgia. It has to be one of the most beautiful spots in the country!"

One feature all residents point out proudly is their four-season weather with gentle summers. As local boosters say, "This is where spring spends the summer." Flowering trees in the spring, delightful summers, and fall colors keep you aware of the seasons, yet comfortable enough to enjoy them.

Another interesting retirement possibility is Dahlonega (pop. 5,000), the location of the first full-blown gold strike in the United States. Gold was discovered here in 1828 and can still be panned today. The restored county courthouse now has a gold museum. Dahlonega boomed until gold was discovered in California in 1849. Immediately, local miners deserted their claims en masse and hot-footed it out west to find fame and fortune. (Those who couldn't find gold became real estate developers and surfers.)

A tourist brochure claims the region is just an hour's drive from Atlanta, but I would hesitate a long while before getting into a car with someone who routinely makes the 75-mile drive in one hour! The countryside here is made up of rolling hills rather than low mountains, and, although not as picturesque as Clayton, it has a rural charm.

Dahlonega has a small hospital, with 49 beds, to serve the county's population. For a larger facility, about 20 miles away is Gainesville's 471-bed Northeast Georgia.

Clayton Chamber of Commerce: 301 E. Main St., Clayton, NC 27520; (919) 553-6352; claytonchamber.com.

GEORGIA LOWLANDS

The southern half of Georgia is known as the Lowlands. This region easily fulfills the Hollywood stereotype of the Old South—enormous plantation homes surrounded by fields of cotton with forest in the background. Many of these plantations are still operating and play host to dignitaries and celebrities. Because of a moderate year-round climate and many outdoor recreational offerings, this part of Georgia is attracting the attention of retirees who are seeking a favorable cost of living as well as affordable real estate.

Long before the plantations were constructed, the region was known for its abundant wild game, thick pine forests, and wetlands. One of North

GEORGIA LOWLANDS WEATHER

	IN DEGREES FAHRENHEIT				ANNUAL	
	Jan.	April	July	Oct.	RAIN	SNOW
Daily highs	62	75	91	74	48"	2"
Daily lows	33	51	70	51		

America's largest Indian populations flourished here, evidenced by seven large ceremonial mounds that date back seven centuries or more.

Today the historic districts of the towns and cities of the Lowlands display dramatic evidence of the wealth created by cotton. Beautiful mansions and public buildings are living museums of antebellum lifestyles.

Athens

The city of Athens began as a tiny settlement and trading post that took root at Cedar Shoals, where an ancient Cherokee trail crossed the Oconee River. The settlement grew into a large town, and in 1785 the Georgia General Assembly created the University of Georgia, the first state-supported university in the United States. The city is a delight for the eyes, with a beautifully restored downtown center and many historic districts with period homes and other buildings. Athens has 14 separate neighborhoods listed on the National Register of Historic Places.

In recent years Athens has become nationally famous for its music scene. The result is an unusually lively nightlife, popular with students and residents alike. According to the chamber of commerce, Athens has spawned notable bands such as R.E.M., the B-52s, and Widespread Panic. (I have to take the chamber's word for this, seeing as I know zilch about popular bands.) The international success of these hometown heroes has caused the city to call itself the "Liverpool of the South," while *Rolling Stone* magazine has dubbed Athens the "Best College Music Scene" in the country.

Athens is yet another excellent example of how the presence of a university can transform an ordinary city with an exciting blend of academia, cultural events, and entertainment, all leading to a quality lifestyle. The population of 115,000 here includes more than 26,000 students, creating a demand for a high level of services and nice shopping facilities. Because students are chronically short of money and because retirees don't like to be extravagant, prices naturally remain at reasonable levels. Athens is located approximately 70 miles east-northeast of Atlanta—a little over an hour's drive on the interstate.

Downtown Athens looks exactly like a university town's downtown should. The main street is called College Avenue and is arched over by large trees, with old-fashioned, wrought-iron lampposts with globes, and sidewalk tables and chairs in front of cafes. Exotic restaurants specialize in everything from traditional southern-style cooking to wood-fired pizza, from Mexican enchiladas and Indian tandoori to exotic Japanese cuisine. Folks from nearby towns come to downtown Athens to browse bookstores and specialty shops for articles not normally found in small Georgia cities. A mixed crowd of students, residents, and tourists stroll the streets browsing stores and restaurants, or lounges on wrought-iron benches, observing the passing world with the unhurried casualness only students and retirees can afford to have. Downtown Athens is the central focus of activity for students and residents alike.

A university atmosphere also pervades Athens's residential districts. Lovely neighborhoods packed with Greek revival mansions and Victorians are interspersed with modern ranch-style homes and bungalows. You'll also encounter an occasional antebellum homestead with massive columns and magnolia-shaded gardens reminiscent of the way of life enjoyed by the planter class of the Old South. Because of the large student population, visiting scholars, and temporary faculty, Athens offers an ample supply of apartments, condos, and rental homes. Two private golf-course communities, with upscale homes peering over the fairways, provide alternative housing for golf nuts. Several other golf courses are open to the public. Of course, the University of Georgia can be relied upon as a source of year-round athletic events, everything from football and basketball to intramural sports.

Medical care here is superb. Two major hospitals in Athens support more than 150 physicians in all medical specialties. Both facilities provide 24-hour emergency care. Of interest to military retirees, the Navy Corps Supply School provides medical and dental facilities to veterans.

Athens Chamber of Commerce: 246 W. Hancock Ave., Athens, GA 30601; (706) 549-0095; athenschamber.net.

Valdosta

In their haste to get to Florida, many vacationers zip right past Valdosta (pop. 58,000), never suspecting that a delightful little city sits undiscovered just a short skip away from I-75. Some tourists stay overnight in motels, maybe getting in some shopping at the manufacturers' outlet stores before steering their cars back onto the interstate to resume the high-speed parade to the saltwater beaches a couple of hours down the cement pavement.

Valdosta is set in Georgia's Plantation Trace, a region marked by fertile plains, bountiful woods, and hundreds of blue lakes. Steeped in Victorian history and architecture as well as modern subdivisions, Valdosta stands out as south Georgia's dominant city. Featuring immaculately maintained neighborhoods shaded by enormous trees and enhanced by landscaping that emphasizes flowering plants, Valdosta's residential sections are exceptionally inviting. One retiree affirmed that this well-groomed, upscale ambience influenced his decision to choose Valdosta as a place to settle, saying, "You can tell Valdostans respect their town by the way they treat it. It's a joy to live among people like that."

To be fair I'll have to admit that our first Valdosta research coincided with the first riotous days of spring in the midst of an outrageous explosion of blossoms splashing color from every tree, bush, and garden. It's no coincidence that Valdosta calls itself the "Azalea City." Yet the overall quality of these neighborhoods transcends mere flower beds and magnolia trees.

As we visited neighborhoods, noticing beautiful, quality brick homes on half-acre lots, a theme kept recurring: This is a place where a couple cashing in equity in overpriced sections of the country could move up and live in a fabulous neighborhood, in a style never dreamed of—and probably still bank some of their profits from the sale of their house.

The downtown area, too, shows that Valdosta residents care. An ambitious renovation of an already nice-looking town center is under way to make this one of the showplaces of the South. To finance this project a special sales-tax measure passed with an overwhelming margin, a refreshing vote of confidence in Valdosta and its future.

An important consideration for those retiring from other parts of the nation is Valdosta's cosmopolitan retiree community; they come from everywhere! Large numbers of Air Force officers spent training time at Moody Air Force Base. Naturally when retirement draws near and military families begin discussing favorite towns, they remember this area with fondness.

This is a university town, too, and Valdosta State University's grounds and campus are in keeping with the upscale look of its surroundings. The university offers continuing education, with low-cost fees, in classes ranging from calligraphy to tai chi. Transportation is another strong point here, with good bus service oriented toward serving the student population.

Valdosta's cost of living is generally less than national averages, with housing costs (during normal economic conditions) ranking 10 percent or more below average. The region benefits from a recession-resistant economy based on military and university payrolls, which don't vary a great deal when the national economy stumbles. Because of a high turnover of Air Force families (mostly officers) who are transferred in and out for training, there's a wealth of apartment complexes scattered about town—more than 100.

The surrounding countryside's woodlands and numerous lakes make hunters and anglers happy. The federally owned Grand Bay Wildlife Area provides 5,900 acres of hunting preserve. With a wildlife-management stamp firmly affixed to their state hunting licenses, hunters easily bag their limits of ducks and geese making their way south each fall.

Three hospitals provide excellent health care services to the Valdosta area, totaling more than 359 beds and about 125 doctors. Several health-related firms and nursing homes provide auxiliary care as needed. Smith Hospital is a 71-bed, acute-care hospital in nearby Hahira, with 24-hour emergency services.

Valdosta Chamber of Commerce: 416 N. Ashley St., Valdosta, GA 31601; (229) 247-8100; valdostachamber.com.

VIRGINIA & WEST VIRGINIA

Originally one state, Virginia and West Virginia became separated during the Civil War. In some ways they blend together, with Virginia starting at an Atlantic coastline, moving westward with a gradually rising landscape, and becoming more hilly as the foothills of the Appalachians rise higher and higher. Then West Virginia takes over to complete the scenic scheme, with some of the loftiest mountains east of the Rockies. Driving from one extreme to the other takes you through not only some of the East's most varied panoramas but also a wide variety of communities and possible lifestyles. You'll see everything from stretches of Atlantic beaches, tidewater wonderlands, rolling fields and farms stocked with thoroughbred horses, and, finally, the legendary Appalachian Mountains majesty.

The state of Virginia is the more diverse. Lifestyles include the international sophistication of the Washington, D.C., suburbs, modern cities, university towns, tidewater communities on coastal inlets and bays, and small towns tucked away in the Blue Ridge Mountains. Yet curiously, Virginia, as a rule, doesn't attract a large

> **Virginia Tax Profile**
>
> **Sales tax:** 5.3%; drugs exempt
> **State income tax:** 2% to 5.75%; can't deduct federal income tax
> **Income brackets:** lowest, $3,000; highest, $17,000
> **Property taxes:** average 1.2% of assessed value
> **Social Security taxed:** no
> **Pensions taxed:** excludes $6,000 for people age 62 to 64, $12,000 for 65 and older, minus Social Security and railroad retirement benefits
> **Gasoline tax:** 16.2¢ per gallon, plus sales tax

number of retirees. In fact, Virginia has one of the highest ratios of *outbound* retirees compared with incoming retirees of any state. This exodus can be explained partly by the fact that large numbers of out-of-staters come here to pursue careers in Washington, D.C., and vicinity. When they retire, or when their political party is voted out of office, they tend to pack up and return to their home states.

Once away from the hustle and bustle of the capital, the scene quickly morphs into pristine rural areas with small towns and villages tucked away between wooded ridges and fast-running rivers. Several tempting examples of retirement lifestyles can be found throughout the two-state region. And—important for those who plan on working occasionally during retirement, maintaining consulting connections, or keeping a hand in political affairs—many locations are within a feasible commuting distance from the capital.

Charlottesville

The central regions of Virginia are similar to the Carolina Midlands: stretches of rolling hills covered with grassy fields, interspersed with hardwood forests and well-tended farms. The area is famous for thoroughbred horse farms, with picturesque pastures surrounded by neat white fences. More than a dozen wineries dot the surrounding countryside.

We can recommend a particularly attractive candidate for relocation in this region: historic Charlottesville, a small city of 46,000 inhabitants, almost in the shade of the Blue Ridge Mountains. Three early-day US presidents made their homes in the vicinity: Thomas Jefferson, James Monroe, and James Madison. Two of the most famous landmarks here are Jefferson's famous hilltop home, Monticello, and Madison's mansion, Montpelier. Charlottesville is regularly listed among *Money* magazine's 100 best places to live in the United States, and it's usually the most highly ranked city in Virginia.

Jefferson especially loved Charlottesville; he called it the "Eden of the United States." Not only did he build his own home here, but he designed and constructed it, too. Charlottesville is also where he founded the University of Virginia in 1819. Several campus buildings were designed by Jefferson and are still in use. They are considered to be among the finest examples of neoclassical American architecture. Today the University of Virginia consistently ranks in the top 10 of public universities in the United States.

Charlottesville is one of the prettiest and best preserved of all early American cities, as well as a model of what college towns should look and feel like. Charlottesville's residents aren't enough to overwhelm the influence of the university's 19,000 students and a sizable faculty and staff, who participate fully in the city's economy and its social life.

The university reaches out to the community with a wide range of cultural amenities: drama, concerts, lectures, visiting dance troupes, and summer opera. Many events are open to the public free of charge. Art exhibits, film festivals, and jazz festivals round out the offerings.

Charlottesville itself offers an impressive variety of cultural, social, and recreational opportunities, including 23 neighborhood parks, several museums, and a year-round ice-skating rink. A thriving art, music, and theater community keeps the creative spirit alive.

CENTRAL VIRGINIA WEATHER

	IN DEGREES FAHRENHEIT				ANNUAL	
	Jan.	**April**	**July**	**Oct.**	**RAIN**	**SNOW**
Daily highs	62	75	91	74	48"	2"
Daily lows	33	51	70	51		

Other popular activities in the area include tennis, golf, hiking, horse-back riding, fishing, biking, camping, hunting for antiques, and wine tasting at local vineyards. Hiking and backpacking on the Appalachian Trail are just minutes away from town, and winter skiing is not much farther.

Medical care is superb here. The University of Virginia Health Sciences Center, a 600-bed hospital, and the 150-bed Martha Jefferson Hospital are more than ample in supplying the most modern health care.

Charlottesville Chamber of Commerce: 209 Fifth Street NE, Charlottesville, VA 22902; (434) 295-3141; cvillechamber.com.

Tidewater Region

The Tidewater is one of Virginia's more interesting regions. It is defined as that area bordered on the north by the Potomac River and extending south almost to the North Carolina state line. Several tidal rivers crucial to early American history run through the region as they flow into Chesapeake Bay. The James, York, and Rappahannock Rivers served as highways of commerce for early British colonists, providing their plantations easy access to markets in Europe, the West Indies, and the other colonies. The Tidewater region became the keystone of colonial trade, and the region is rich in history.

Of course, the ill-fated but ultimately first successful British colony in the New World was established at Jamestown. And nearby is Yorktown, where the British suffered the final defeat that resulted in the independence of the United States. And from the beginning to the end of the Civil War, major battles and campaigns were fought in the Tidewater region, which is covered with historic battlefields.

The countryside is naturally oriented toward river and sea. Every cove and bay appears to have docks where commercial and pleasure fishing boats tie up. Good seafood restaurants are more than a tradition here; they're considered essential to quality living. Boats and yachts are ubiquitous.

Tidewater living offers several distinct lifestyle possibilities, depending on the locale. You'll find a historical and intellectual flavor near Colonial Williamsburg, as well as outdoors-oriented, gated golf developments scattered throughout the region. But we found our favorite lifestyle in a wonderfully rural and sparsely settled area along the James River. The countryside there looks pretty much as it might have appeared in colonial times, or during the Civil War era. Many homes and buildings indeed date from those periods. You'll frequently see remains of tobacco barns or what might have been slave quarters falling into disrepair behind stately old plantation homes, now occupied by couples recently moved in from out of state.

Instead of reporting on a particular retirement community here, let's investigate living in one of the many tiny crossroads villages in this region. These are special places within easy commuting distance to a city, where folks may enjoy rural living yet not cut ties to employment, places where out-of-state retirees can feel comfortable and welcome. We combined our research with a visit with some friends we made while interviewing residents of this rural Virginia region.

The couple lives in one of many tiny crossroads communities within a 45-minute commute from the city of Richmond. Its population is probably less than 75. (It's probably too small to find on a map, so the name doesn't matter.) Our friends dearly love their home, a 150-year-old farmhouse sitting on 5 partly wooded acres. The property includes a barn, a chicken house, and a rabbit hutch. One small parcel is cultivated as a truck garden, supplying fresh veggies for their kitchen. Their pride and joy are an asparagus patch and adjoining lettuce bed.

Normally an isolated, rural location like this could be culturally stifling. All too often native residents and newcomers find little in common with each other; their worldviews and backgrounds are worlds apart. Not here. It turns out that almost everyone here is a newcomer, an escapee from an urban or suburban environment. Almost all homeowners in the community relocated here as commuters or for retirement, to enjoy the peace and quiet of the Tidewater countryside. Socially they are little different from those who still live in city neighborhoods and therefore share much in common—except that neighbors here are much closer than they would ever be in a city neighborhood.

The downside of living in an isolated Tidewater crossroads community is the total lack of services. Purchasing a can of tomato sauce or a roll of paper towels entails a 20-mile round-trip. The nearest doctor is 15 miles away, the same distance as the video-rental store. But as one resident said, "It's worth it. We don't have many neighbors, but the ones we have are quality. They're more than neighbors, they're friends we can count on when we need them. We don't need a big city to be happy."

VIRGINIA TIDEWATER WEATHER

	IN DEGREES FAHRENHEIT				ANNUAL	
	Jan.	April	July	Oct.	RAIN	SNOW
Daily highs	62	75	91	74	48"	2"
Daily lows	33	51	70	51		

Williamsburg

Near here is where it all started, 400-plus years ago. On May 14, 1607, Captain John Smith and a band of 108 settlers from England landed at Jamestown to establish Britain's first lasting colony on the American continent. The settlers put ashore on the banks of the James River, 60 miles from the mouth of the Chesapeake Bay, in the heart of Tidewater country. Their settlement was on the narrow neck of a peninsula about 10 miles from the York River and about 8 miles from the present-day site of Williamsburg. The community was named for King William III of England and became the first colonial capital of Virginia in 1699. (In 1780 the capital was moved to Richmond.)

Few places in the United States have witnessed such a panorama of historic events as this region. Yorktown, just a half dozen miles from Williamsburg, was the site of the decisive battle of the Revolution, where British General Cornwallis surrendered to George Washington, effectively ending the war—in our favor, of course.

All of this is commemorated by one of the first historical parks in the country. More than 9,000 acres encompass the Jamestown colony, the Yorktown battlefield, and historic Williamsburg. Especially famous is the colonial village of Williamsburg, an authentic re-creation of what typical village life was like back in the earliest days of our nation. A visit here is like stepping back in time two and a half centuries. Yet few tourists bother to visit the modern-day town of Williamsburg.

The town was settled in 1632, and the College of William and Mary was founded about 60 years later, in 1693. That makes it the second-oldest college in the nation. Today you can stroll along the same pathways traversed by Presidents Thomas Jefferson, James Monroe, and John Tyler when they were students here. Williamsburg is probably where Jefferson incubated the idea of the university he later created in Charlottesville. Famous people of the time, such as Patrick Henry, George Washington, and James Madison, were no strangers here.

Williamsburg today is the epitome of college town ambience. The town's population is around 15,000, but students and faculty add another 9,000 or so to the community, exerting a profound influence on the social and commercial atmosphere. As might be expected, the presence of the college provides many cultural and social benefits to all residents. A life-long learners' program, with classes taught by the college faculty, encourages retirees to participate. Lectures, concerts, and plays are often open to the public free, or for a small donation. Regular courses are tuition-free for residents over the age of 60, space available.

When family and grandchildren visit, they'll find plenty of family entertainment. The Historic Triangle offers plenty of outdoor recreation with parks that offer hiking, fishing, canoeing, and biking. The city maintains 10 tennis courts, 7 of which are lighted, all-weather facilities. The area boasts over a dozen notable and challenging golf courses. Take in a concert, browse an art museum, or indulge in serious shopping at any of hundreds of shops and stores in the area. There are myriad Williamsburg attractions suitable for the entire family.

Williamsburg General Hospital, a 120-bed facility, takes care of most medical needs, with more specialized care in Hampton, about 20 miles away. A Veterans Administration hospital is in Newport News, about 10 miles from Williamsburg.

Williamsburg Chamber of Commerce: 421 N. Boundary St., Williamsburg, VA 23185; (757) 229-6511, (800) 368-6511; williams burgcc.org.

Virginia Beach

Virginia Beach is a retirement destination that receives frequent endorsements describing "Top Ten Places to Retire" or "Best Places to Live in America" in publications such as *Ladies' Home Journal, Money* magazine, and *Entrepreneur* magazine. Residents are drawn to Virginia Beach for a variety of reasons, not the least of which is an outstanding, water-oriented, high quality of life. Residents enjoy 38 miles of shoreline on the Atlantic Ocean and the Chesapeake Bay, 28 miles of public beaches, and even more miles of scenic waterways. They find plenty of opportunity for water sports, boating and sailing, fresh- and saltwater fishing, and tennis. The city has 11 public golf courses, 18 marinas with public access, 3 fishing piers, and 60 miles of biking trails. Virginia Beach takes much pride in its many well-preserved 17th-, 18th-, and 19th-century homes, historic churches, and public buildings.

All of this is somewhat offset by an above-average cost of living. Housing is pretty much upscale here, although neighborhoods with affordable housing can be found. Since many retirees are ex-military officers, with decent retirement benefits, the housing market hasn't received the hits that similar communities in the area have.

Virginia Beach's temperate maritime climate benefits from the nearby Gulf Stream, which explains its mild winters that rarely drop below freezing. Swimmers enjoy great beach weather that extends from spring through fall. Residents like to point out that personal safety is high here; for several consecutive years Virginia Beach has had the lowest crime rate in the nation for a city its size. And the area enjoys an outstanding reputation for quality health and medical care. Nearby Hampton Roads also has a well-coordinated regional health care system with state-of-the-art equipment and facilities and specialists in every field.

Virginia Beach residents enjoy cultural amenities such as symphony, opera, performing arts, and museums. The Virginia Marine Science Museum in Virginia Beach not long ago completed a $35 million expansion and is one of the most attended aquariums in the nation. Education plays a prominent role in the region, with 11 colleges and universities serving the community.

Virginia Beach Chamber of Commerce: 500 E. Main St., Norfolk, VA 23510; (757) 622-2312; hamptonroadschamber.com.

Appalachian Discovery in the Virginias

Sometimes we discover a "sleeper" (a location where quality retirement lifestyles can be enjoyed on exceptionally low budgets and where nice homes sell at rock-bottom prices). Our latest discovery is a charming Appalachia locale, straddling the borders of Virginia and West Virginia. Four towns—two on the Virginia side, two on the West Virginia side—have joined forces to lure retirees into their communities to replace residents who moved away because of an economic slump. The cost of living is among the lowest in the country, and quality housing is going for a song—truly a buyer's market. The four towns call themselves the Four Seasons Country, and they are serious about attracting people for relocation.

The idea of communities luring newcomers into their midst as a way of bolstering the economy is becoming rather common in today's small-town America. Yet Four Seasons Country's two-state, two-county, and four-city pooling of resources to attract retirees is unique. It's awfully nice to feel wanted! And the low cost of living is just one of the enticements here.

What happened here to make retirement living a bargain? Two conditions: one, an economic disaster; two, a public relations dilemma. The economic meltdown began about 20 years ago, when the region's major industry, coal mining, decided to automate, installing elaborate, labor-saving devices that displaced workers and decimated the workforce. As jobs were eliminated, families moved away in search of work. The economy never fully recovered.

The public relations problem is battling the stereotype of what coal-mining towns look like. The image is poverty and substandard living conditions: ramshackle trailers and tumbled-down shacks, dreary company stores. This probably is an accurate picture in some areas, but to our delight we found this not true here. Instead we found exceptionally nice-looking communities with housing ranging from above average to elegant. The countryside is dotted with small farms with lovely Victorian mansions and modern ranch-style homes. You'll find gated golf-course developments as well as lovely, tree-shaded neighborhoods with friendly small-town ambience.

So what happened to the stereotype? It turns out that coal miners in this particular region had long been unionized and always earned exceptionally high wages. With incomes equal to middle-management personnel elsewhere, coal-mining families had sufficient disposable income to afford any kind of housing they desired. It's no surprise that they preferred high-quality homes on spacious lots, suitable to affluent, middle-class lifestyles.

As jobs evaporated, workers received generous severance pay and ample pensions. Some retired here; others took the cash and moved away to take other jobs. Real estate prices plummeted; the market never fully recovered. Nice 1,500-square-foot homes often sell for about half the median price of homes in Florida, Arizona, or California—sometimes less than that. Larger, more upscale homes on landscaped and wooded parcels can be found for double that amount. At the time of our last visit, a stately five-bedroom brick home on an acre of land could be had for what a suburban tract home in California might sell for.

CENTRAL APPALACHIAN WEATHER

| | IN DEGREES FAHRENHEIT | | | | ANNUAL | |
	Jan.	April	July	Oct.	RAIN	SNOW
Daily highs	40	65	84	68	39"	13"
Daily lows	18	36	59	40		

Excellent medical facilities are another legacy of the old days, before machines displaced people. The miners' union negotiated for excellent company-paid health plans with comprehensive benefits for coal-mine employees. This created a high demand for medical services that was filled by a surprising number of hospitals and clinics accustomed to using high-tech technology. Five hospitals serve the four towns described here, with 870 beds plus specialized physicians of all types providing a level of medical care found in few nonurban areas anywhere in the country.

Four Seasons Country

Let's take a look at the four communities in West Virginia and Virginia that are so eager to have you come and visit: the West Virginia towns of Bluefield and Princeton and the Virginia towns of Tazewell and Richlands.

Bluefield, Virginia/West Virginia

Straddling the Virginia–West Virginia state line, Bluefield is technically two separate cities, one on each side of the state line, each with its own municipal government. The two Bluefields nevertheless consider themselves as part of the same community. Originally known as Higginbotham's Summit, Bluefield was renamed in honor of the profusion of blue chicory flowers that cover the surrounding countryside each spring.

Bluefield is the region's largest town, with about 17,000 inhabitants (counting both sides of the state line). For years it was the

West Virginia Tax Profile

Sales tax: 6%; drugs exempt
State income tax: 3% to 6.5%; can't deduct federal income tax
Income brackets: lowest, $10,000; highest, $60,000
Property taxes: average 1% of assessed value
Social Security taxed: no
Pensions taxed: yes
Inheritance tax: no
Gasoline tax: 33¢ per gallon

business center for the other communities. However, like many similar small cities around the nation, Bluefield saw its downtown steadily lose ground to the inevitable strip-mall shopping centers. Yet Bluefield still has a downtown center that looks as if it belongs in a much larger city. Residential neighborhoods are neat and attractive, with plenty of affordable homes in quiet surroundings. Many stunning Victorian mansions stand as reminders of the affluent era when coal was king. Several newer subdivisions of upscale homes have been built on rolling hills on the outskirts of town, with lovely views.

The 2,600-foot elevation here creates such a pleasant summer climate that the city calls itself "Nature's Air-Conditioned City."

Tazewell & Richlands, Virginia

On the Virginia side the towns of Tazewell and Richlands combine efforts to entice new, out-of-state residents to relocate in the Four Seasons Country. They have a combined population of 9,000 residents within their town limits. Many people prefer to live out in the country, in rolling foothills or crossroads communities close to Tazewell and Richlands, so the area's total population is just over 21,000 inhabitants.

Although both towns are sophisticated on one level—with plenty of modern services, shopping, and cultural activities—they are also small enough to be places where neighborhood picnics and the friendliness of small-town living are still enjoyed by all. One retiree remarked, "As long as I've lived here, I still can't get used to perfect strangers saying 'hello' when we pass on the street." The social norms, customs, and accents seem to be more midwestern than southern.

We were impressed by some upscale developments under way in and around the town of Tazewell. Our favorite is a group of high-quality homes, each surrounded by a half acre or more of wooded land bordering a golf course, complete with country-club facilities and a restaurant, all included with ownership. Selling prices for a 3,000- to 3,500-square-foot home are about what an ordinary tract home would sell for in Southern California.

People here are justifiably proud of Richlands's Southwest Virginia Community College. The school does an excellent job of providing cultural events of a quality normally found only in much larger metropolitan areas. Regular drama and musical productions are sponsored by the college—everything from ballet to satire and comedy. The 50-plus crowd is welcome to participate in classes tailored for their needs, with such courses as pottery, jewelry, leatherworking, and computers.

Tazewell Chamber of Commerce: 230 Tazewell Mall, Tazewell, VA 24651; (276) 988-5091; tazewellchamber.com.

Princeton, West Virginia

Princeton, on the West Virginia side, was settled in the early part of the 1800s. Largely destroyed during the Civil War, the town was slow to rebuild. Most of its older buildings date from the early part of the 1900s, with a handful of earlier Victorian homes. Princeton enjoyed great prosperity during the heyday of coal mining but, like neighboring communities, saw its population leave as efficient machines began replacing skilled labor. According to the latest census, Princeton has a population of approximately 6,500.

Some lovely wooded residential developments are located here—dating from the affluent boom era—and they feature tastefully designed homes that make quality lifestyles somewhat affordable. Starting on the outskirts of town, many country roads meander through woods and fields where ranch-style homes sit on huge lots or on small farms just minutes from Princeton's town center.

Princeton–Mercer County Chamber of Commerce: 1522 N. Walker St., Princeton, WV 24740; (304) 487-1502; cityofprinceton.org.

Lewisburg, West Virginia

This region never ceases to provide us with surprises and discoveries. The historic town of Lewisburg (founded in 1751 as Lewis Spring) is one of our more interesting retirement surprises. Nestled in the heart of West Virginia's Allegheny Mountains and close to the Greenbrier, with its famous and historic golf course complex, Lewisburg is one of the region's retirement success stories. The town plays a delightful role as a time capsule, steeped in traditions of colonial and federal architecture. Artists, shopkeepers, residents, and, of course, retirees casually reside in homes built of native stone, some dating from the time of the Revolution. A stroll along Lewisburg's tree-shaded streets takes you past native limestone buildings built in the 1700s, antebellum mansions, Victorians, and cottages so old they defy dating. Antiques stores, excellent restaurants, boutiques, and art galleries seem to be the only modern touches. You almost expect to see horse-drawn carriages and powdered wigs here.

Of course, newcomers to Lewisburg fully appreciate the ambience, and some hope to keep it a best-kept secret. As we interviewed one lady, she smiled and held a finger to her lips as she whispered, "We love it here, but don't tell anybody else!" I solemnly promised her I wouldn't tell. (But everyone knows how we travel writers lie!)

Retirees come to Lewisburg from all sections of the country and from all walks of life, often from artistic or professional endeavors. Some find an excuse to keep busy by dealing in antiques, creating artwork for galleries, or starting some small, laid-back business enterprise. So many artists have relocated here that Lewisburg occasionally makes the ranks of "100 best small art towns in America." All of this makes for a sophisticated mix of people and an interesting social milieu. No matter where you are from, you could very possibly find your neighbors come from the same part of the country.

With a population of less than 4,000, Lewisburg is large enough to have all needed services and shopping, yet still retains an elegant, small-town feeling. Home prices here reflect the general higher-class neighborhoods and antique quality of some homes. Yet not far from the town center, you'll find truly affordable homes, and a 10-minute drive over a narrow highway, winding through rolling farmlands, leads to 19th-century farmhouses and manor houses, as well as modern ranch-style homes surrounded by large parcels of semiforested land.

Lewisburg Greenbrier Chamber of Commerce: 905 W. Washington St., Lewisburg, WV 24901; (304) 645-2818; greenbrierwvchamber.org.

6

The Gulf Coast States

Five states curve around the Gulf of Mexico's 2,000 miles of northern shoreline, forming a sort of private sea. Western Florida and the Panhandle account for more than a third of the Gulf's coastline; westward are Alabama, Mississippi, Louisiana, and Texas. Long strands of white sand beaches alternate with miles of saltwater marsh, the home of egrets, herons, roseate spoonbills, and dozens of other shorebird species. Wildlife sanctuaries abound. Fishing ports, sheltered bays, and natural harbors protected by offshore islands make saltwater sports convenient and productive. Gulf waters teem with life: shrimp, pompano, flounder, speckled trout, plus weird specimens like blowfish, rays, and robbin fish. No telling what might attack your bait.

Sometimes a highway will run along the coast, just a few yards from the beach; it might be lined with restaurants, businesses, and even casinos. Venerable old live oak trees can arch over the road, limbs draped with solemn Spanish moss. Other places are accessible only by boat or swamp buggy. Some towns are tourist oriented, drawing throngs of summer vacationers that crowd the beaches. Other towns are quiet and reserved primarily for the enjoyment of residents. Not everyone chooses to live by the beach; more find their retirement inland, where other, non-marine attractions entice them to live.

The last edition of *Where to Retire* reported on two disastrous hurricanes that ravaged the Gulf Coast states—Irma in 2017 and Michael in 2018, following Ivan in 2004 and Katrina in 2005. At that time we had second thoughts about recommending beachfront retirement along the Gulf of Mexico. Several delightful towns that we profiled in previous editions of *Where to Retire* are missing from this book because of horrendous damage to the Florida Panhandle, Alabama, Mississippi, and Louisiana coastal areas. Fortunately, with help from federal and state governments, plus determined actions from Gulf Coast communities, the region is recovering from the recent disasters. Most victims immediately began rebuilding their destroyed homes, gambling that it won't happen again. Optimism may not be enough. Were it me, after those enormous wave surges pushed by 120-mile-an-hour winds did their damage, I would choose to build a few miles away from the beach. The world must be filled with optimists, however, because beachfront home rebuilding has once again negated the effects of nature.

Throughout the Gulf Coast states, modern cities provide cultural and medical facilities prized by retirees. Quaint towns with friendly neighbors make transitions into retirement easy. Gracious old southern mansions, moss-draped bayous, and southern hospitality are all part of the setting. To all this, add a four-season climate that varies from semitropical to warm temperate, and you have a formula that spells successful relocation for many people.

The cost of living in these states is favorable, with some areas of the Gulf Coast offering the most inexpensive housing we've ever seen. Wages are lower, to match the living costs. These economic benefits are offset somewhat by above-average utility costs in some locales. Personal safety in the smaller towns is also reassuring.

Many people have images of the South that aren't so idyllic. The news media years ago highlighted a dramatic struggle for civil rights—complete with violence and tragedy—as African Americans fought for the right to vote and to be treated with dignity as equals under the law. These vivid impressions of conflict, social injustice, and poverty remain highlighted in recent years as the fight for social equality continues.

This lingering bad impression is unfortunate, because the South has undergone tremendous change over the past six decades, resulting in a remarkable turnabout in the conscience of the region—a significant turn from a world in which US citizens were restricted to designated sections of buses and theaters or who had to drink from separate water fountains.

I'm not suggesting that all southerners have suddenly changed into color-blind liberals, free of racism and full of brotherly love. My point and opinion are that the overall southern attitude toward race relations has taken a dramatic turn for the better, despite any racist organizations that try to stoke fires of hatred.

ALABAMA

This is one of the nation's most active states when it comes to seeking out retirees and creating a welcoming environment for them. According to state officials, over the past several years, Alabama's share of retirement immigrants has increased dramatically. Part of the credit is due to a state-funded program called Alabama Advantage for Retirees, which works intensively at getting the news out about retirement opportunities within the state.

Alabama's convenient location to the northern and midwestern states and Florida, its mild winter climate, and crime rates as much as 20 percent lower than the national average are important to many potential retirees, but there's much more. Among other enticements Alabama combines quality living with one of the country's most favorable living costs. Tax burdens are lowest in the nation. For example, the property tax on a $130,000 home

Alabama Tax Profile

Sales tax: 4% to 12%; drugs exempt
State income tax: 2% to 5%
Income brackets: lowest, $500; highest, $3,000
Property taxes: homeowners 65 and over exempt
Social Security taxed: no
Pensions taxed: most pensions exempt from taxes
Inheritance tax: no
Gasoline tax: 18¢ per gallon, plus possible local taxes

(approximately the average price in Alabama) is about $707—and can be less, depending on the community. No, that isn't $707 each *quarter*, it's $707 for the *year*! And real estate here is among the most affordable in the nation. Other economic advantages for retirees include most pensions being exempt from taxes, and free fishing and hunting licenses for residents 65 years of age and older. Alabama's colleges and universities offer free or reduced tuition to residents 60 or older. Some private schools offer tuition discounts, special classes, and access to recreational and cultural programs for retirees.

But Alabama is more than just a low-cost place to live; it's a state of multiple lifestyle choices and retirement opportunities. As more and more "outsiders" take up residence, the population becomes more cosmopolitan, making transition into the community easier. No, it isn't for everyone, but Alabama deserves consideration, should your needs match what the state offers.

Each Alabama community mentioned in this book has a welcoming committee to help newcomers assimilate into the social whirl of the town. Although this won't ensure that you'll find successful retirement, you know you'll be welcomed and won't be considered a stranger. For information call (800) 235-4757 or visit alabamaadvantage.com, for a free Alabama Advantage guidebook.

Gulf Shores/Orange Beach

Because of the rude manner in which Florida's Panhandle elbows Alabama aside to hog the Gulf of Mexico shoreline, you wouldn't expect Alabama to have any beach at all. Look at a map and you'll see what I mean. Florida's Panhandle runs from the Georgia state line almost to Mobile in the west. However, visitors are flabbergasted at the quality and beauty of Alabama's 32-mile beach that fronts the Gulf between Pensacola and Mobile. It clearly matches anything Florida has to offer, and it's peaceful and relatively uncrowded.

Mobile—Alabama's only large Gulf Coast location, with almost 200,000 inhabitants—like most large cities is best considered as a commercial center, a place for serious shopping and entertainment, with ideal retirement away from the metropolitan area. Traditional candidates for nearby retirement are Fairhope and Daphne. But because the city of Mobile is only about 15 miles distant, these towns have become "bedroom communities" for those working in the city. As such, property has become more costly.

On the other hand, the two small towns that comprise Alabama's Gulf Coast "Riviera" are fast becoming a choice destination for retirees, particularly with golf nuts and anglers. Traditionally a roost for thousands of snowbirds each winter season, Gulf Shores (pop. 5,000) and Orange Beach (pop. 3,000) entice winter visitors to become permanent residents when they retire. White sand beaches, great fishing, and friendly neighbors are persuasive arguments that help retirees make up their minds about Alabama's Gulf Coast. Luxury retirement villages are making an appearance

GULF SHORES WEATHER

	IN DEGREES FAHRENHEIT				ANNUAL	
	Jan.	April	July	Oct.	RAIN	SNOW
Daily highs	61	78	91	79	64"	—
Daily lows	41	58	73	56		

to accommodate newcomers. The largest charter-boat fleet on the Gulf Coast is located in Orange Beach. There is an emphasis on golf communities, with seven golf courses within a 20-minute drive. As one resident put it, "We're becoming a mini–Myrtle Beach, minus the traffic, noise, and flash."

An interesting diversity of retirees gives Gulf Shores and Orange Beach a cosmopolitan flavor not common in smaller resort towns. Because retirees come from all parts of the country, they bring a rich mixture of interests and talents. Year-round residents love to participate in art shows, theater, concerts, and other cultural pursuits. Winter tourists bring a blessing to Gulf Coast businesses: This means seasonal part-time jobs are available for those who want them.

Even though the population is small, health care is adequate. Because of the number of elderly tourists each season, this area has an unusual number of paramedics, perhaps the highest per capita in the nation. A hospital is located in nearby Foley, just 5 miles from Gulf Shores. Foley, by the way, is a popular place because of its manufacturers' outlet stores of the shop-till-you-drop genre. For big-ticket items Pensacola is just a 30-mile drive, and Mobile is about an hour away.

Dothan

Before we discovered some of Alabama's better retirement locations, we kept hearing about a town called Dothan (pronounced DOE-than). Readers would ask, "Why don't you mention Dothan in your books?" We checked our Alabama road map and were puzzled why a place in the corner of southeast Alabama should have something special going for it. We received so many inquiries that we decided to take a look for ourselves. We're glad we did.

Dothan (pop. 67,000) and its neighboring communities combine a pleasant Alabama location with an unusually diverse retiree population.

Folks come from all over the world to settle here. This is partly due to nearby Fort Rucker, home of the world's largest international helicopter-training center; military families from around the world remember Dothan when making retirement plans. Post exchange privileges and access to military medical services make it a natural.

But there's another interesting source of Dothan's unique diversity: a growing colony of civilian retirees from the Panama Canal Zone. Between 100 and 120 families have moved to Dothan to begin (or resume) their retirement careers. With the canal now having been transferred to Panama, more families are on the way.

How did such an unlikely place as southeast Alabama become a Mecca for folks who lived much of their lives in tropical Panama?

It started some years back when a retiring canal zone employee convinced his wife to consider his home state of Alabama instead of staying in Panama, as many others did when retiring. When the couple returned to Panama for visits, they talked so much about the charms and advantages of Dothan that others began visiting. Many eventually moved here. The treaty between Panama and the United States, which returned control over the canal to Panama, really started the ball rolling. With an unclear future ahead and no roots in any place outside of Panama, many decided to look more closely into Dothan, where friends were retiring.

The Dothan area supports the usual outdoor recreational opportunities, including hunting, fishing, and golf. Golfers are pleased that one of the new Robert Trent Jones 36-hole golf courses is located here. When I asked our chamber of commerce guide what her husband does, she replied, "Oh, he plays golf nine days a week." The city sponsors 37 public tennis courts and many parks.

Providing medical care to the cities of Enterprise, Ozark, and Dothan are four hospitals plus the medical facility at Fort Rucker. Ozark has Dale Medical Center, with 92 beds. The Enterprise Medical Center is a fully

DOTHAN WEATHER

	IN DEGREES FAHRENHEIT				ANNUAL	
	Jan.	April	July	Oct.	RAIN	SNOW
Daily highs	57	77	91	77	49"	—
Daily lows	36	53	72	53		

accredited hospital with 135 beds and has recently added all the newest high-tech equipment. Dothan has two hospitals: Southeast Alabama Medical Center and Flowers Hospital.

Alexander City/Lake Martin

Back in the mid-1920s the Alabama Power Company decided to place a dam across the Tallapoosa River. Residents at that time were devastated and totally convinced that the rising waters would create swamps and breeding grounds for flotillas of mosquitoes and armies of bugs. Resigned to disaster, they sold out at $5 to the acre, feeling lucky to get anything at all for such worthless land. Little did they realize! Lakeshore lots now go for a minimum of $25,000, up to more than $500,000!

Today travel writers describe Lake Martin as one of the most beautiful recreational lakes in the South. It's also become one of east-central Alabama's prime retirement destinations, having received numerous recommendations by retirement and relocation experts. Scattered around the lake are 9 or 10 developments, which range from relatively inexpensive places nestled among the woods to elegant gated communities with private golf courses. Almost 22,000 people make their homes on the 750 miles of shoreline—on sandy beaches, in secluded coves, or on rocky knolls with magnificent views. Officially designated one of Alabama's cleanest lakes, residents proudly refer to Lake Martin as "44,000 acres of pure drinking water." Golf, boating, waterskiing, and fishing—the lake has it all. Residents rave about the quality of their new surroundings. With golf and water recreation the central focus, newcomers have a wide choice of lifestyles, from exclusive golf-course developments where homes cost a small fortune, to a mobile-home park. Don't expect super bargains in real estate, however; after all, if you live on a lake as pretty as this, you'll pay for the privilege. Strict building codes ensure that the housing is high quality—no shacks or fish shanties are permitted.

Nearby Alexander City (pop. 15,000) is an alternative for those who would like to be near the lake, but prefer more inexpensive housing in town. "Alex City" (as people here call it) is a charming place in its own right. Just 50 miles from the state capital in Montgomery and 30 miles from Auburn University, the Alexander City–Lake Martin area is conveniently located for occasional big-city shopping and cultural fixes. Birmingham is a 70-mile drive via super-highway.

ALEXANDER CITY/LAKE MARTIN WEATHER

	IN DEGREES FAHRENHEIT				ANNUAL	
	Jan.	April	July	Oct.	RAIN	SNOW
Daily highs	56	76	91	77	58"	—
Daily lows	36	55	70	54		

Quite naturally, recreation here centers on golf and water sports. Swimming, fishing, waterskiing, and boating are favorites. Many residents keep powered pontoon boats tied at their lakefront homes, ready for fishing, loafing, or a trip across the water to dine at a first-class restaurant. The original championship golf course at Willow Point has 13 of its 18 fairways edging the lakeshore. Two other courses are similarly located on the water. Alexander City also has an 18-hole municipal golf course.

The cultural and entertainment offerings of Montgomery and Birmingham are within an easy drive; however, Alexander City provides its own entertainment. There's a little theater group that stages several productions a year, and the Alexander City Arts Council uses the Central Alabama Community College facilities to bring plays, musicals, and concerts to the community. The college has special programs, free to students age 60 and older.

Russell Hospital, in Alexander City, is a modern, nonprofit, 75-bed hospital with 24-hour, acute-care facilities. For military retirees there's a regional hospital at Maxwell Air Force Base in Montgomery, about an hour's drive.

Anniston/Oxford

From the moment of its inception, Anniston was a planned model city. Back in 1879 two entrepreneurs decided this is where they would build their textile mills and blast furnaces. They needed a town and commercial center to go with their enterprises, so they hired a team of well-known architects to design a company town. They insisted that the new town must be modern as well as pleasing to the eye. Of course, "modern" in those days meant Victorian, and that's what we see today. Most of these historic structures are still in use, well preserved and reflecting Anniston's rich heritage.

Immediately adjacent, the city of Oxford has another 10,000 residents. The two cities form the major shopping center for the surrounding area's total population of 120,000. Thirteen miles away, not quite close enough to be considered an Anniston suburb, the town of Jacksonville provides a university setting. Including students, Jacksonville has a population of 11,000. The university has continuing-education programs as well as Elderhostel programs for folks from all over the country. Because the region is centrally located between Atlanta and Birmingham, the local slogan is "Near Atlanta. Near Birmingham. Near Perfect."

We particularly liked Oxford as a retirement possibility. Originally it was called Lick Skillet, but when time came to incorporate into a town, residents wanted a more dignified name. Can you get more dignified than *Oxford?* Essentially part of Anniston, Oxford has several unusually attractive neighborhoods that appear to be ideal for retirement living. The Calhoun County medical community includes more than 100 physicians, 45 dentists, and three hospitals.

Fort McClellan, a US Army base occupying 15,000 acres of prime land, is one of the military installations that was decommissioned. It's a beautiful place of woods and landscaped grounds. At the moment the federal government, the State of Alabama, and city officials of the surrounding cities are trying to decide what to do with the valuable land. One purpose that seems fairly certain is to devote a percentage of the surplus property to retirement housing.

Anniston and its neighboring city, Gadsden, both have enthusiastic retirement attraction committees ready to assist newcomers. The headquarters for the retirement committees is located at a golf development at Silver Lakes, between the two cities. Silver Lakes is a gorgeous setting of rolling terrain and lakes near the edge of Talladega National Forest. An experiment in retirement attraction, this is the first time one of Robert Trent Jones's Golf Trail courses has ever been placed within a private development. This is a 36-hole, world-class golf complex, and it's always open for public play.

SOUTHERN ALABAMA WEATHER

| | IN DEGREES FAHRENHEIT | | | | ANNUAL | |
	Jan.	April	July	Oct.	RAIN	SNOW
Daily highs	57	77	91	77	49"	—
Daily lows	36	53	72	53		

Gadsden

Gadsden (pop. 37,000) is located in the southern foothills of the Appalachian Mountains, where Lookout Mountain and the Coosa River meet. This is probably Alabama's most successful city when it comes to recruiting out-of-state retirees. Some years ago Gadsden realized that it was losing its industrial base. It needed something to replace the disappearing factories but didn't want to "chase smokestacks." Joining with several other cities in Etowah and Calhoun Counties, Gadsden's retirement committee set a goal of attracting 50 retired couples a year. The first year they exceeded their goal; 63 couples moved to town. The next year 48 couples joined the party. Gadsden has been growing ever since, with more than 4,000 newcomers, many of them retirees.

The impact of new residents on Gadsden's economy has been a dramatic textbook example of how communities benefit from out-of-state relocation. Because of the newcomers, jobs were created for health care specialists, construction workers, and retail businesses. Restaurants, motels, and service businesses blossomed. These new jobs were of a clean, nonpolluting, "smokeless industry" nature. This helped the area to free itself of dependency on a handful of manufacturing facilities.

The downtown's pride and joy is the huge, 44,000-square-foot Gadsden Center for Cultural Arts. When a downtown department store closed its doors—a victim of strip-mall syndrome—Gadsden decided to do something with the large multistory building. Rather than allow the edifice to disintegrate, they converted it into the Center for Cultural Arts, one of the most impressive downtown monuments to rehabilitation we've seen. Besides expansive rooms for community meetings, private parties, school proms, dances, and concerts, the center has an experimental arts programs in which kids from a nearby housing project are paid to study art.

Two popular residential areas on Gadsden's outskirts are the towns of Rainbow City and Attalla. Attalla has a population of approximately 7,000 and a thriving commercial center. This was the bedroom community for employees of Gadsden's heavy industries before they closed some years ago. Much affordable housing is available here. For a while Attalla's downtown section all but died. Then city officials encouraged the establishment of antiques shops and specialty boutiques. This seems to have turned the corner economically for Attalla, because folks come from miles around to shop, and storefronts are beginning to find tenants once again.

Rainbow City is slightly larger, with 9,000 inhabitants, and the residential areas are a bit more upscale. When Gadsden's industrial life was booming, this is where the white-collar and executive employees lived. Some exceptionally lovely homes are located here. Both towns are within minutes of downtown Gadsden. Two hospitals serve the communities, with almost 500 beds between them.

Gadsden State Community College, Alabama's largest two-year college, and the University of Alabama–Gadsden Center provide educational opportunities. If that's not enough, Jacksonville State University is about 18 miles away.

Gadsden Chamber of Commerce: 1 Commerce Square, Gadsden, AL 35901; (256) 543-3472; etawahchamber.com.

MISSISSIPPI

For most folks from outside the South, Mississippi comes as a pleasant surprise. They expect cotton fields and dreary farming communities where "outsiders" might not be welcome. For the most part, these stereotypes fade away upon your first visit to Mississippi. You'll find a delightful landscape of great diversity, from picturesque Appalachian foothills in the northeast to sandy beaches on the sunny Gulf of Mexico. In between are affluent towns and cities graced with lovely pre–Civil War mansions on landscaped grounds, as well as contemporary houses, ranch-style homes in golf-course communities, and developments situated on fishing lakes or surrounded by

Mississippi Tax Profile

Sales tax: 7% to 10%; drugs exempt

State income tax: 3% to 5%; can't deduct federal income tax

Income brackets: lowest, $5,000; highest, $10,000

Property taxes: average 1%; $60,000 exemption for over age 65

Social Security taxed: no

Pensions taxed: no

Inheritance tax: no

Gasoline tax: 18.4¢ per gallon, plus local taxes

MISSISSIPPI WEATHER

	IN DEGREES FAHRENHEIT				ANNUAL	
	Jan.	April	July	Oct.	RAIN	SNOW
Daily highs	51	75	93	76	56"	2"
Daily lows	31	50	69	49		

---

forested hills. The backwoods small-town communities exist, of course, but you'll not likely be searching them out.

Mississippi's cities jealously preserve their Old South heritage of lovely homes to complement modern subdivisions and tasteful commercial centers. Classic university campuses and medical centers are just as prominent as graceful residential districts and upscale restaurants and shopping. In short, the state of Mississippi has everything most retirees might need for a successful and pleasant retirement. I suppose you could find cotton fields if you look hard enough, but, offhand, I don't recall seeing any.

The state of Mississippi is acutely aware of the benefits of retirees choosing to retire in the state, and actively manages a state program called Hometown Mississippi Retirement. The program is designed to help potential retirees investigate various options in participating communities. On the community level hometown residents follow through with a well-considered program to welcome new individuals into each community. It's worthwhile to contact the local chamber of commerce to find out whether a retiree-welcoming committee is active.

To further enhance Mississippi's status as a retiree-friendly place, the legislature voted to exempt qualified retiree income, such as Social Security and income from 401/403 IRAs, from state income tax. Along with low property taxes and favorable living costs, this provides more dollars to be spent on recreation, travel, or investments. Moreover, for those over age 65 or disabled, the first $60,000 of the assessed value of their home is exempt from property taxes.

MISSISSIPPI'S GULF COAST

Long a favored retirement destination, the area around Gulfport and Biloxi manages to combine a summer carnival atmosphere with sedate, Old South values. Many military couples choose to retire here because of convenient medical and PX privileges at nearby Kessler Air Force Base. Most of these military retirees, at one time or another, were stationed in the area and developed a fondness for the beaches and the climate.

The complex of beach cities stretches between Florida and Louisiana and has a total population of around 90,000. The towns are so closely connected that it's sometimes difficult to tell where one ends and another begins.

It's obvious why this is such a tourist attraction. Vast stretches of sugary beach with gentle waves lapping at the sand are complemented by streets arched over by branches of majestic oak and magnolia trees, fine restaurants, and lots of sunshine. Large, formal estates survey the scene with southern majesty. Here was—and is—the mansion where Jefferson Davis chose to live out his days, writing memoirs of his days of glory as president of the Confederacy.

A string of glittering gambling casinos energizes the coastline with bright lights, slot machines, blackjack, and roulette—plus entertainment and fine food. Gambling provides tourists from surrounding states an additional excuse to congregate here: golfing and sunning on the beaches by day, and shouting at the dice by night. In the winter regular tourists are replaced by snowbird tourists, a large percentage of them Canadians, who don't mind the cooler water and occasional nippy days. Compared to Montreal or Moose Jaw winters, the Gulf Coast's coldest days are a tropical paradise.

Don't let gambling prevent you from considering Mississippi's Gulf Coast, because the way things are going, gaming palaces, riverboat casinos, and even oceangoing gaming ships are popping up all over the Gulf Coast, Mississippi River towns, and Florida ports. You're not going to avoid them. Gambling's effect on the local economy brings a mixed bag of assets and deficits. Gambling has created more than 5,000 jobs in the Gulfport-Biloxi area (including much part-time work for retirees) and has warmed the hearts of many local businesses. Although traffic and tourism can be very busy on the beaches in front of the casinos, and traffic is sometimes congested on the streets near the casinos, the crowds disappear in residential neighborhoods just a few blocks from the beach.

Many retirees prefer to settle just a short distance from Gulfport-Biloxi, in two small towns: Long Beach and Pass Christian. These two towns are quiet and peaceful, yet only a short drive to where the "action" is. Residents enjoy the convenience of good hospitals and other emergency

MISSISSIPPI GULF COAST WEATHER

	IN DEGREES FAHRENHEIT				ANNUAL	
	Jan.	April	July	Oct.	RAIN	SNOW
Daily highs	61	77	90	79	61"	—
Daily lows	43	59	74	60		

facilities in nearby Gulfport-Biloxi. A bonus is exceptionally low crime rates in these towns—according to FBI statistics, among the lowest in the country.

Long Beach (pop. 12,000) is a former farming community to the west of Gulfport, whose quiet residential areas attract retirees who enjoy the quality neighborhoods. You'll find an interesting mixture of homes here, varying from extraordinarily inexpensive to amazingly extravagant. The quiet and peaceful small-town atmosphere is one of the first qualities that local residents proudly point out. "Gulfport-Biloxi is too crowded and too honky-tonk," said one retiree we spoke with. "Here, away from the crowds, we have miles of quiet beach, all to ourselves."

Pass Christian (pop. 4,000), long a vacation center for wealthy New Orleans residents, is rich in history and past opulence. At one time steamboats regularly made the 55-mile voyage from New Orleans, bringing high-society families to their second homes. The original families are gone, but their homes remain, as do the gracious lifestyles of the last century. Mansions with manicured lawns line the beachfront, and invitations for afternoon tea indicate social standing. (Unfortunately many of these historical gems suffered damage or destruction in the 2005 hurricane.)

Gulf Coast Chamber of Commerce: 11975 Seaway Rd., Gulfport, MS 39503; (228) 604-0614; mscoastchamber.com.

Oxford

Were this writer to rank the "best places for retirement," Oxford, Mississippi, would surely be among the top 10. I confess that, as an author, I could be biased by a certain mystical literary connection between Oxford authors and the outside world. Oxford has fostered and developed writers from its very beginning as a university town—even before William Faulkner made his home base here—continuing today with several best-selling authors choosing to bask in Oxford's nurturing literary climate. It seems as if every third person we meet in Oxford has published a book!

As an aside, just after this writer was born, my father was looking around for a small-town newspaper to buy. He tried to purchase the newspaper in Oxford but couldn't close the deal and ended up buying a newspaper in a town near St. Louis. Had my father bought in Oxford, I might have become a famous fiction writer instead of an ordinary nonfiction writer. (My wife consoles me with her belief that most everything I write is fiction anyway.)

Snuggled amid the forested hills of northern Mississippi, Oxford is a picture-book example of a gracious southern university town. Handsome antebellum mansions—partially concealed by flowering wisteria, redbud, and creeping ivy—hold court under ancient magnolias and magnificent oak trees. Oxford is positively saturated with history and Old South traditions. Quiet, tree-shaded streets, with silence broken only by the joyous song of a mockingbird and occasional barking of a dog in the distance, recall an era long forgotten in today's frantic rush toward urbanity.

Yet Oxford shows its modern side with a large shopping mall and all the usual businesses and home developments—mercifully located toward the outskirts of town. The outskirts, by the way, aren't all that far away. With a population of about 20,000, the town doesn't spread out to eternity. Oxford appears larger than it is because university students more than double the population. An additional 20,000 people live in the surrounding countryside.

The University of Mississippi's presence takes Oxford into another realm of cultural ambience. Affectionately known nationwide as "Ole Miss," the school has a strong influence on the community. This unique mixture of students and retirees creates a remarkable consumer demand: quality shopping, restaurants, and entertainment at affordable prices.

Oxford's charming downtown square is a perfect illustration of how the presence of a university can preserve the character of a town. Commerce generated by students and residents keeps downtown enterprise alive and healthy instead of abandoning it to strip malls and shopping centers on the highways, as happens in many small towns across the nation. Downtown Oxford looks the way a downtown should look. A classic 120-year-old courthouse, with massive columns and centuries-old oak trees, dominates the scene, complete with the obligatory statue of a Confederate soldier standing guard—a statue which in recent years has become a source of local protest.

Across from the Confederate soldier's statue is a well-known Oxford tradition, the Square Book Store, which features a second-floor veranda that looks out over the square, where friends meet to sip cappuccino and talk about literature. The 25,000-volume collection, on every subject imaginable, makes you aware that the owner operates the store with a respect for books and literature rather than an eye for quick turnover and high profits—which seems to be the trend elsewhere. On the staircase you'll find stacks of autographed copies of books by local authors. The Square Book Store's presentations by well-known authors who discuss their works are favorite happenings.

Among the benefits of living in a university town like Oxford are the cultural attractions that have become a tradition with the community. Residents of all ages are invited to participate in school activities. Those over age 65 can take up to four classes free per semester. Many of the university's concerts, lectures, and drama productions are open to the public at no charge. Of course, not all activities here are intellectual. Bass and crappie fishing in nearby Sardis Lake, outstanding basketball and football games at the school, and two public golf courses take care of outdoor recreation.

The Baptist Memorial Hospital is the regional health care center. More than 70 physicians at the hospital represent 30 specialty areas of medicine to meet the specialized needs of individuals and families.

Oxford Chamber of Commerce: 299 W. Jackson Rd., Oxford, MS 38655; (662) 234-4651; oxfordms.com.

Natchez

Stately Natchez sits on a scenic bluff overlooking the mighty Mississippi River on land that was originally a tribal center of the Natchez. The French, after forcing out the Natchez in 1716, constructed a fort here, making Natchez one of the oldest European settlements on the Mississippi.

Very early the town blossomed as a prosperous cotton-raising and -exporting center. By the time of the Civil War, Natchez had become one of the South's wealthiest cities—possibly the richest city in the entire nation. Today's large number of surviving antebellum homes and awesome mansions testify to this. When war between North and South threatened, most Natchez plantation owners were staunchly opposed to secession. They fully realized that war would be a financial disaster as well as a tragic spilling of blood. Therefore, when war descended upon the nation, Natchez's support was less than enthusiastic. When the first Yankee gunships drifted downriver, ready to bombard Natchez, they were greeted by a huge white flag of surrender fluttering on the bluff. The City of Natchez negotiated a peace that guaranteed the preservation of the magnificent mansions that graced the city. Union troops agreed not to burn the city in return for peaceful cooperation.

After the war, its economy devastated, Natchez drifted into the doldrums. This had the further effect of preserving the antebellum homes from the catastrophe of modernization and urban renewal. Today Natchez is practically a museum of southern aristocratic architecture. Approximately 500 antebellum homes grace the quiet streets of the city, some dating to the eras of Spanish and French rule. Throughout the expansive historic district, lovely Victorian homes add to the feeling of stepping back in time. The interesting thing is that asking prices for proud antebellum homes aren't much higher than ordinary homes in most other Old South towns.

Today Natchez is a quiet town of 16,000 friendly people with well-cared-for neighborhoods and affordable quality housing. Newer subdivisions and apartments are found on the fringes of town and even in the thickly forested surrounding countryside—some on acre-size lots carved out of the woods.

The wealthy aristocrats had their homes on the high ground, but the rough-and-tumble steamboat crowd, rogues, and river pirates strutted their stuff down by the riverbank, called Natchez Under-the-Hill. This was a district of docks, saloons, and bordellos famous for gambling and illicit excitement. Today at least some of the excitement has returned to Natchez Under-the-Hill in the form of riverboat gambling. In addition to a casino and gambling aboard the ship, several unique restaurants have been embellished to keep alive the wicked 1800s decor. Even if not your choice for retirement, Natchez, with all its antebellum glory, is well worth a visit.

In keeping with southern traditions, the social scene in Natchez revolves around several "garden clubs." These usually exclusive, upper-strata social groups have less to do with gardening than with social activities and organizing civic events. Charities and volunteer work fall under the domain of these organizations. We were told to advise newcomers to seek an invitation to join. (Some of the more exclusive garden clubs probably require that your grandmother was a member.) However, a quicker way to meet new friends is to contact the Retire Partnership (natchezretirement.net), a group specially dedicated to attracting retirees to the area and making them feel at home. Inquire at the local chamber of commerce.

Two modern, full-care hospitals and a large group of medical professionals serve the medical needs of Natchez. Between them the hospitals have 250 beds and employ the latest in medical technology. In addition to the hospital staff, 54 physicians practice in the area.

Natchez Chamber of Commerce: 211 Main St., Natchez, MS 39120; (601) 445-4611; natchezchamber.com.

Madison

A charming suburb of Jackson, the state capital, caught our eye during two research trips: the small city of Madison. Located a short distance from where the Natchez Trace skirts to the north of Jackson, Madison (pop. 17,500) is actively welcoming retirees into the community. Homes and developments are tops in quality as well as price; residents have the highest per capita income in the state. Shopping districts and outlying residential development clearly show this affluence.

One of the first things you'll notice about Madison is the lack of strip-mall clutter—no blinking signs, flashing lights, or bright plastic decor. Strict regulation of signs and business architecture should make Madison a model for other small cities—an example of how downtowns should be kept alive and well. Unfortunately it's too late for most towns. Their depressed downtowns are filled with closed shops and painted-over display windows. Shops, markets, and businesses were forced to go out of business or join the movement to the highway on the edge of town. I urge city planners to visit Madison to see how disaster can be avoided.

The city complex now includes more than 60 carefully planned subdivisions, some of them among the most upscale (and expensive) in Mississippi. As a planned community, Madison places emphasis on safety, comfort, and maintaining a quality small-town atmosphere.

Madison is also a favorite spot for antiques shoppers. Those in search of something special from a bygone era will fall in love with the pieces of antebellum and Victorian grandeur found in Madison's shops. Twice a year 30,000 crazed antiques shoppers descend upon the Madison area for the Canton Flea Market, which features more than a thousand vendors of arts and crafts, antiques, and collectibles.

One result of restrictive zoning and building codes is a dearth of low-cost housing. You won't find mobile-home parks or inexpensive tract homes here. Apartment rentals are all but nonexistent, and we saw no condominiums. The average price of houses sold here will be higher than in most Mississippi communities. But if you can afford higher prices, you definitely get your money's worth. Madison has eight golf courses, three of them public.

Madison Chamber of Commerce: 2023 Main St., Madison, MS 39130; (601) 856-7060; madisonthecitychamber.com.

Tupelo

When Hernando de Soto's expedition entered northeast Mississippi in the 1500s, present-day Tupelo was the site of a large Chickasaw Indian village. No longer a village, Tupelo has become a prosperous town of 36,000 inhabitants, where warm smiles and hometown hospitality are the rule, not the exception. This place has one of Mississippi's most enthusiastic retiree welcoming committees eagerly waiting to bring you into the fold, to make sure you get settled in your new home and are introduced all around. They'll have you working on a community project before you know what happened.

Nestled in the scenic beauty of northeastern Mississippi's rolling countryside, Tupelo sits on the Natchez Trace, about halfway between Natchez and Nashville. Memphis is an hour-and-a-half drive via I-78, and Mississippi's lovely state capital of Jackson is a pleasant 3-hour drive along the scenic Natchez Trace. The Trace, by the way, is a nature wonderland you'll not want to miss. You'll see wild turkeys, deer, and a variety of birds, and enjoy light motor traffic (no trucks allowed). A leisurely drive along the

Natchez Trace is truly a pleasure. We've driven this road many times, occasionally pausing for a picnic or a hike along one of the historic pathways that branch off from it.

Twice named an All-American City by the National Civic League, Tupelo enjoys a prosperous base as a manufacturing, retail, and distribution center, and its furniture industry rivals that of North Carolina. Our impression is that this is an exceptionally pleasant place to live, with welcoming neighbors and plenty of opportunities for community participation. And in case you didn't already know it, residents will proudly inform you that Tupelo was the birthplace of Elvis Presley.

Six public and three private golf courses plus relatively mild winters make for golfing pleasure year-round; there's also excellent golf at the Tupelo Country Club. The city maintains tennis courts in abundance, staffed with instructors available to help you learn or sharpen your game. The 1,600-mile-long Tennessee-Tombigbee Waterway is minutes away, providing outdoor fun in the form of fishing, boating, picnicking, or camping.

Tupelo has two colleges: a branch of the University of Mississippi and the Itawamba Community College. Those over age 65 do not have to pay tuition. In addition to continuing-education opportunities at the colleges, the Lee County Library offers year-round lecture series and "brown bag luncheons" (informal presentations for workers on their lunch break and retirees on their shopping break).

Tupelo has a wide range of homes in a variety of comfortable neighborhoods. From stately, older homes to new residential construction, Tupelo provides choices for every budget and lifestyle. Neighborhoods are peaceful and tend to be closely knit, with residents benefiting from well-trained, professional fire and police protection.

North Mississippi Medical Center, a 726-bed hospital, is the major facility in the Tupelo region.

Tupelo Chamber of Commerce: 398 E. Main St., Tupelo, MS 38804; (662) 842-4521; cdfms.org.

LOUISIANA

If you're looking for Gulf Coast beach property in Louisiana, you are out of luck. Except for a short stretch of sand in the western part of the state—humorously referred to as the Cajun Riviera—most of coastal Louisiana is swamps, mudflats, and bayous. People in Texas claim they can tell Louisianans by the high-water marks on their legs. Beaches don't start until you get to Texas, and Texans feel smug about that. Of course, Louisianans enjoy making snide remarks about Texans, so they're even.

The area was very much in the news in 2005 when Hurricane Katrina hit with the full force of a Category 5, making it the most expensive and one of the most deadly hurricanes in American history. The story of New Orleans is well known: More than 75 percent of the city was flooded, leaving an incredible number of homes damaged beyond repair. Strong winds were felt inland as far as 100 miles from the coast. The force of the storm weakened, however, as the winds moved inland. Most towns listed here as preferred retirement spots suffered little or no damage, but there has been some economic impact on those towns that accepted a significant number of refugees from New Orleans. This has created a temporary shortage in low-rent housing. Presumably more and more people will return as New Orleans becomes livable again.

> ### Louisiana Tax Profile
>
> **Sales tax:** 4% to 10.75%; drugs, food taxed
> **State income tax:** graduated from 2% to 6%; federal income tax deductible
> **Income brackets:** lowest, $12,500; highest, $50,000
> **Property taxes:** local taxes average 1.15% of market value
> **Social Security taxed:** no
> **Pensions taxed:** private pensions taxable, $6,000 exemption
> **Inheritance tax:** no
> **Gasoline tax:** 20¢ per gallon, plus sales tax

Nowhere in the United States can you find such a rich diversity of people, customs, and worldviews as in Louisiana. These differences aren't imaginary. You can travel 50 miles in almost any direction and you'll hear distinct accents, slang, music, and different languages. The cuisine is different, too. With eight ethnic groups tracing their ancestors back through Louisiana's history, it isn't surprising that many people here are bilingual, sometimes with English as their second tongue. Visiting Louisiana is almost like visiting a foreign country.

Louisiana has an eclectic collection of nationalities and cultures. Of course, France quite naturally left the strongest influence, as evidenced by

LOUISIANA WEATHER

	IN DEGREES FAHRENHEIT				ANNUAL	
	Jan.	**April**	**July**	**Oct.**	**RAIN**	**SNOW**
Daily highs	62	79	91	79	54"	0.5"
Daily lows	42	58	73	59		

the widespread use of Cajun French. Other artifacts of French influence are the concept of "parish" instead of "county" and Louisiana's legal procedures, which bear a stronger resemblance to the Napoleonic Code than to British common law.

Louisiana's unique property tax system is highly praised by residents who relocate here from other states. This is because the state derives most of its revenues from taxes on petroleum, so there's no need to levy high property taxes on residences. Furthermore, there's a $75,000 deduction from local property tax assessments. Because real estate prices are low, the generous tax exclusion is often equal to the assessed value of the average home. Except for really expensive homes, homeowners often pay little or nothing in the way of property taxes.

Acadiana (Cajun Country)

Louisiana's most famous ethnic group is the Cajuns, descendants of those French Canadians who were evicted from Acadia (today's Nova Scotia) 250 years ago. In 1755 the English authorities—with typical British tact and understanding of the time—insisted that the Acadians not only swear allegiance to the Crown, but that they renounce their Roman Catholic faith and join the Church of England, or get out. The mass exodus that followed was recounted in Henry Wadsworth Longfellow's *Evangeline*. (Somehow I always assumed the Acadians fled Canada rather than submit to English cooking. Haven't you noticed how the Brits boil everything they can't fry?)

The exiles went through terribly difficult times. Some families were shipped to the West Indies, some to the New England colonies, others went back to France. Many wandered, homeless for 20 years, before finding a welcome in the French-speaking environs of Louisiana. They established small farms along the Mississippi River, Bayou Teche, Bayou Lafourche, and other streams and bayous in the territory's southwestern section. The word "Cajun," by the way, comes from a modification of the original French pronunciation of Acadian, describing their French Canadian origins.

From the perspective of someone who loves good food, a big plus for living in Cajun country is Cajun cuisine. A first cousin to the Creole cuisine of New Orleans, Cajun cooking is way ahead in terms of creativity of its dishes and the artistic inspiration of its seasonings. Favorite Cajun dishes include jambalaya, gumbo, *cochon du lait* (suckling pig), *boudin* (a blood, pork, and rice sausage), soft-shell crab, stuffed crab, crawfish étouffée, crawfish bisque, crawfish pie, and shrimp fixed every possible way a Cajun chef can imagine. That's just for starters.

Upscale restaurants all over the world are jumping on the Cajun cooking bandwagon. They've discovered that simply tacking the term "Cajun" to a menu item works miracles. Should the chef make a mistake and burn something, it's advertised as "Cajun Blackened Broccoli," or whatever. One Cajun, angry at worldwide plagiarism of cherished recipes, declared: "My mama never blackened anything in her life and put it on the table! When she blackened somethin' it was a pure mistake and she'd feed it to the dogs!"

Lafayette & Vicinity

Lafayette is often called the "Cajun Capital City," and it offers a full range of activities and services, anything seniors need for quality retirement. Housing of all kinds in all price ranges is available, including several specialized housing developments with independent and assisted-living arrangements, such as Azalea Estates and Courtyard at South College. New developments are under way away from the center of the city, with some impressive "plantation manor" homes on half-acre lots.

For those who feel that Lafayette (pop. 114,000) is too much like a city, there are several delightful choices away from town. Southwest of Lafayette the charming little city of Abbeville (pop. 13,900) is known for its two quaint town squares. Abbeville claims to be the "most Cajun place on Earth." Then there's New Iberia (pop. 33,000) to the east, set among the breathtaking plantations and gardens of Shadows-on-the-Teche. Another major center of Cajun culture is Opelousas (pop. 23,000), the third-oldest city in Louisiana, famous as the site of Jim Bowie's residence and well known for having produced many fine Creole and Cajun chefs. The nearby towns of Marksville, Bunkie, Simmesport, Bordelonville, and others are wonderfully steeped in history, yet lie quietly and unpretentiously as places for a peaceful yet fascinating lifestyle among delightful neighbors.

Lafayette and the surrounding Cajun heartland offer horse racing, boat tours of the Atchafalaya Basin Swamp, and facilities for golf and tennis. Nearby Abbeville is known for excellent duck and goose hunting, hosting a duck festival every Labor Day. Golf courses, although not numerous, are scattered throughout Cajun country, so that you can play if you don't mind a 30-minute or so drive.

Besides a branch of Louisiana State University, Lafayette has a local community college, affectionately known as "Gumbo U," which provides excellent adult education programs for cultural enrichment. Festivals are big in this area, with one taking place nearly every weekend. There's a crawfish festival in Breaux Bridge, a French music festival in Abbeville, a rice festival in Crowley, even a *boudin* festival (*boudin* is a special Cajun sausage) in Carencro. Lafayette is host to the South's second-largest Mardi Gras, complete with parades, balls, masquerades, and more.

Lafayette has six hospitals, with a total of 1,134 beds. Opelousas General Hospital serves as a referral medical center and offers a comprehensive community health care facility with a wide range of medical specialties and state-of-the-art technology.

Lafayette Chamber of Commerce: 804 East St., Mary Boulevard, Lafayette, LA 70503; (337) 233-2705; oneacadiana.org.

Baton Rouge

Not really in Acadiana, Baton Rouge received its French name well before the Cajuns entered the bayou country. French explorer Pierre Le Moyne (Sieur d'Iberville) organized the first permanent European settlement here back in 1682. The site he selected for the village had a tall, red-painted cypress tree on the riverbank that marked the boundaries of hunting territory between two Indian tribes. The newcomers christened their settlement Baton Rouge, "red stick."

As you might expect of Louisiana's state capital, Baton Rouge (pop. 226,000) is a handsome city. With neat, prosperous-looking neighborhoods, attractive subdivisions, and one of the prettiest university campuses in the country, Baton Rouge fulfills its role as the political and educational center of the state. Its distinctive blend of French, Creole, Cajun, and Old South traditions makes it as much a part of Louisiana as the great Mississippi that flows past the city on its way to the Gulf.

Until the real estate boom pushed up prices, Baton Rouge had one of the lowest costs of living of any city of its size in the country. Living costs and housing prices are now about average for the nation, although real estate prices are a little below average. It's the quality of the setting for the money that makes it a bargain.

Most university towns have plenty to offer retirees. Baton Rouge, the home of Louisiana State University, is no exception. LSU's cultural offerings and its enrichment of the intellectual aspect of the community are quite important. The school attracts scholars, professors, and university employees from all over the country. The narrow, conservative atmosphere of many southern cities is absent in Baton Rouge. Students, faculty, support personnel, and families of these outside people nourish fresh views and lifestyles throughout the community.

My distinct impression is that most Louisianans in this part of the state don't use the thick southern accent you hear in other Deep South locations. This shouldn't be surprising, because so many people come from places where midwestern accents are the norm. Among the natives a slight Cajun touch of pronunciation is common, but, again, this is totally different from conventional southern accents.

The university touches the community in many ways. A slogan here is "Art Is the Heart of Baton Rouge." Using the talent in theater, music, and fine arts that LSU attracts, the community has organized some commendable programs. Every year a 10-block stretch of downtown is blocked off so people can see potters at their wheels, musicians entertaining, and artists at their easels. Mimes entertain the crowds, and craftspeople of all kinds sell their wares. Two ballet groups bring stars from major companies to work with local students. The Baton Rouge Opera, two light opera companies, a symphony orchestra, and a professional theater company round out the cultural offerings. The city is quite proud of its historic past and is taking vigorous steps to preserve and restore two downtown neighborhoods, historic Beauregard Town and Spanish Town.

As a retirement location, Baton Rouge has a lot going for it. It's a cosmopolitan community, and it's centrally located. It's just 70 miles by interstate to New Orleans. You can reach the beaches at Pass Christian in

2 hours by car. Fifty miles to the north is the 19th-century atmosphere of historic Natchez. For riverboat gambling you don't have to go far: Baton Rouge has two riverboat casinos, the *Belle of Baton Rouge* and *Casino Rouge*.

Baton Rouge Chamber of Commerce: 64 Laurel St., Baton Rouge, LA 70801; (225) 381-7125; brac.org.

Natchitoches

Another place we would never have found had it not been for Louisiana's retirement welcoming program, the city of Natchitoches is in the north-central part of the state. We were invited for a several-day stay to become acquainted with the small city of Natchitoches. Strangers always have problems pronouncing the name. They usually try to pronounce it as it's spelled, which brings polite smiles to the faces of natives, if not outright guffaws. It's pronounced NAK-a-tish. This is a Native word meaning "Place of the Paw Paw," or chinquapin nut.

History buffs will find plenty to marvel at in this fascinating little city of 18,000 inhabitants. Natchitoches has one of the most picturesque and authentic downtown sections of any place we've yet seen in this region, reminiscent of the French Quarter in New Orleans. To get an idea of what the town looks like, rent the movie *Steel Magnolias* from your local video store. The picture was produced on location here, using homes in the downtown area as stages and local people as extras.

Natchitoches has the proud distinction of being the oldest permanent settlement in the entire Louisiana Territory. French explorers first made contact with the Natchitoches Indians in 1700 and 14 years later established a trading outpost on the Red River. Natchitoches soon became a bustling river port and an important crossroads. Wealthy planters not only built imposing plantation houses along the river, but also maintained elegant showplaces in town.

Sometime in the 1830s the US government decided to clear the Red River channel so barges could travel upstream to what is now Shreveport. Theoretically this would make Natchitoches even more prosperous. But to the dismay of Natchitoches residents, the Red River changed its course, leaving the once-thriving river town high and dry, several miles from the new course. The town's future as a bustling port town became history as the river became a spring-fed creek. Although this disaster isolated

Natchitoches, it safeguarded its historic buildings from the curse of prog-ress and urban renewal. It also preserved the deeply ingrained traditions of its residents.

Fortunately, Natchitoches came up with a great idea. Why not dam the old channel and create a lake? Today a 26-mile oxbow lake, called Cane River Lake, runs through upscale Natchitoches residential areas and is the showpiece of the downtown National Landmark District. Cane River Lake looks very much like a river but aesthetically is much better. The lake-river doesn't flood or become muddy in rainy weather. It doesn't have a current or carry flotsam and debris from upstream, and it provides a place for peaceful boating and good fishing in its clear, spring-fed waters. Best of all it lends an air of Old South dignity to Natchitoches, with huge oak and magnolia trees arching over the lake's bank and weeping willows trailing branches into the still water.

Natchitoches's rich historical background encompasses French, Span-ish, Native American, African, and Anglo-Saxon influences. Contempo-rary residents take pride in this colorful palette of tradition and carefully maintain their ties with the past by preserving the older part of the city. Large antebellum town homes of cotton planters sit next to ornate Vic-torian houses and substantial homes dating from the early 1800s. Some have been converted to bed-and-breakfast inns. (In all, Natchitoches has 21 B&Bs.)

These historic buildings are more than museum pieces; they are homes of residents who enjoy being within a short walk of the fascinating downtown. At first we suspected that Natchitoches's commercial district might be a clever remodeling project. The brick streets, wrought-iron bal-conies, and storefronts—all in the style of the 1850s—looked too authentic to be real. But several stores display photographs taken of downtown busi-nesses more than a century ago. They clearly show that, indeed, this is how Natchitoches looked in its prime.

Natchitoches's further claim to being a good retirement choice is enhanced by the presence of Northwestern State University. In addition to its symphony, dinner theater, ballet, and other entertainment, the school offers many interesting continuing-education programs for mature adults.

Compared with the national average, Natchitoches's cost of living appears to be considerably below average. Historic homes usually sell for half what similar places would fetch in Charleston or Savannah. But for this region prices are well above average. This is understandable when the setting is considered.

Natchitoches Chamber of Commerce: 780 Front St., Ste. 101, Natchitoches, LA 71457; (318) 352-6894; natchitocheschamber.com.

Leesville/DeRidder

When World War II exploded, the government hurriedly constructed a large army post in an almost deserted part of western Louisiana. They called it Fort Polk. Generals Eisenhower, Patton, and Clark used the region to train several million soldiers. The first draftees pushed through Fort Polk for training retained bad memories of those rustic early days, so it's understandable that the installation acquired a poor reputation among enlisted military. Over the years the government gradually improved conditions. They constructed quality off-post quarters in Leesville and DeRidder and added amenities to the post itself, such as a championship golf course, parklike landscaping, and quality housing. Those who did tours of duty at Fort Polk in later years look back with fond memories of Leesville and DeRidder. One retiree from Klamath Falls, Oregon, said, "The first time I came to Fort Polk, the army dragged me here kicking and screaming. But six years ago, I decided to retire here!"

In line with recent Pentagon policy, Fort Polk has been downsized. Local residents were delighted that the fort wasn't shut down entirely, something that would have been disastrous for the economy. As part of the cutbacks, however, the government ordered all enlisted men to live on base. This created a buyer's market for quality housing in Leesville and nearby DeRidder. A small community of about 6,000 residents, Leesville has well-designed homes, mostly of brick construction and set on generous plots of tree-shaded land. The historic downtown center, off the highway going through Leesville, is undergoing a dramatic renovation. An old theater has been beautifully restored as a special-events place for banquets, proms, parties, and meetings. The older residential section immediately around the town center is stocked with prewar traditional white frame homes, mostly suitable for low-cost housing. There's a potential for restoration here, as well. These places would be suitable for people who like being within walking distance of downtown.

The golf course at Fort Polk is the local pride and joy, and its beautiful 18-hole layout is always open to the public. With all the lakes, rivers, and forests nearby, outdoors people have plenty of opportunity for fishing and hunting or just enjoying a hike or boat ride. Leesville/Fort Polk is also blessed with a branch of Northwestern State University for adult education. The school offers courses in several professional fields in addition to leisure learning classes. Seniors may take one course per semester tuition-free, with an application fee of $15.

Down the highway 20 miles, DeRidder is the larger of the two towns, with a population of approximately 10,000. DeRidder also has a section of elaborate and elegant homes, a legacy from the era of timber barons who benefited from timber harvests back in the early 1900s. These elaborate showplaces attest to the wealth of the timber barons and merchants. Several modern neighborhoods also have upscale housing; some are showplaces in their own right.

While this region might look attractive because of affordable housing, it would need intensive investigation for those retiring from larger communities from outside the South. The main industry and commercial endeavor is a military base, which are famous for evaporating on a whim, and moving personnel on a moment's notice, which could change your neighborhood's character in a heartbeat.

Leesville Chamber of Commerce: 1309 N. 5th St., Leesville, LA 71496; (318) 238-0349; chambervernonparish.com.

Alexandria

Between 1988 and 1995 the US government closed down 536 military bases, handing over a total of 6 million acres to state and local control. This is the largest transfer of land since the Oklahoma land rush. From what we hear this is just 30 percent of the planned closures; more are to come. The big question is: What are we going to do with these multibillion-dollar properties?

Of course, all military bases aren't exactly prime real estate. Many were constructed in deserts, swamps, or inaccessible backcountry. They'll probably sit and gather sagebrush. But many bases are ideally located for residential and industrial development. Over the years the government spent untold billions on these bases, constructing homes for officers and enlisted men and building PX facilities resembling Wal-Mart, top-quality golf courses, swimming pools, and other amenities that made the bases resemble self-contained cities.

However, many localities feel highly threatened by these abandoned housing units. If sold to the public, these units could glut the housing market, causing real estate values to plunge through the floor. Bad enough the military pulled many thousands of consumers from the region without adding more chaos. Yet it's a shame to let all of these expensive amenities go to waste.

One solution to this dilemma: Convert base housing to senior housing and bring in folks age 55-plus (and their money) from outside the community to rejuvenate the local economy. The incoming retirees would occupy homes that would otherwise be left to deteriorate, while boosting the economy to boot.

When England Air Force Base, on the outskirts of Alexandria (pop. 15,000), was decommissioned, the city turned the airfield into its major commercial airport, renaming it Alexandria International Airport. Warehouses and repair facilities were leased to manufacturers, and some buildings were converted to offices and warehouses.

This left a large collection of housing, mostly two- and three-bedroom homes, in good shape and ready for occupancy. Because the redevelopment authority didn't want to damage the local real estate and rental markets, they decided to restrict the base housing to two categories of tenants: retirees and employees of businesses located on the former air-base property. They named the complex England Oaks, because of the live oak trees that abound here. As an experiment, it was decided that the homes should be leased, rather than sold (as is the case in most other senior developments).

Therefore England Oaks is aimed at a distinct niche in the retirement market: an independent-living facility for middle-income seniors who don't care to invest a lot of money in their retirement homes. Advantages for retirees are security and convenience that go with a maintenance-free lifestyle. Retirees can combine suburban home life with group social and recreational activities without sacrificing comfort, space, and privacy. Social life in England Oaks is centered around the development's clubhouse (the former officers' club), where regular meetings, potlucks, and social hours are held.

The two- and three-bedroom homes (formerly noncommissioned offi-cers' housing) have been remodeled with a view to attracting active seniors whose health is such that assisted living is somewhere down the road. Homes are equipped with emergency-response systems, safety features for the elderly, and even telephones with large, easy-to-read push buttons and a voice that echoes back the number so that a person with poor eyesight can know he or she has made the right connection. This is a pleasant, secure neighborhood of homes shaded by oak and pecan trees, with a golf course, hiking and biking trails, and a gated community that gives you a feeling of security. An arrangement like this especially appeals to retired military because they're familiar with military retirement complexes like Air Force Village in San Antonio and elsewhere.

Three good-size hospitals serve the region, plus a 299-bed veterans' facility.

Alexandria Chamber of Commerce: 1118 Third St., Alexandria, LA 71309; (318) 442-6671; cenlachamber.org.

7

The Midsouthern Hills

If you look at a map of the United States, you'll notice a curious east–west line that cuts the country almost in two. From the point where Nevada, Arizona, and Utah intersect, state boundaries form a line that runs eastward until it hits the Atlantic Ocean near Norfolk, Virginia. This line bisects the nation, separating Virginia from North Carolina, Kentucky from Tennessee, Missouri from Arkansas, Kansas from Oklahoma, Colorado from New Mexico, and Utah from Arizona. Except for a slight deviation around the southern edge of Missouri, the demarcation is almost perfectly straight.

Why the line runs as it does is something only historians or geographers can explain. A long stretch runs through what I call the "Midsouthern Hills"—through the heart of the Appalachians, the Tennessee-Kentucky hill country, the Ozark Mountains of Missouri and Arkansas, and into Oklahoma's Ozark section. Straddling this line is an interesting swath of woodlands, hills, plains, and mountains, places that offer prime retirement conditions for those who like four seasons and a woodsy and slow-paced lifestyle. A low cost of living, inexpensive housing, and high personal safety are bonuses.

Industry and modern agriculture characterize the country to the north of this strip of semi-wilderness. Below is the Deep South. Life in the Midsouthern Hills moves at its own pace, always a little out of sync with the rest of the nation. Until World War II this was one of the most poverty-stricken segments of the nation. Cartoonist Al Capp located his imaginary town of Dogpatch here, the home of indigent Li'l Abner, his family, and his girlfriend, Daisy Mae. Although the cartoon strip amused folks who didn't have to live in Dogpatch, real-life circumstances were anything but funny. Roads were often gravel and dirt. Subsistence farmers lived in flimsy shacks as they raised families and tried to coax a living from the rocky soil.

By the way, this very first wave of baby boomers will probably be the last of those who might remember those *Li'l Abner* cartoons of long ago. Even then perhaps only because Al Capp, the strip's creator, was very supportive of the Vietnam War, and made fun in his comic strip of those protestors (today's retirees) who were against the war. Those who matured after the 'Nam conflict was settled probably won't remember *Li'l Abner!*

The change in living standards since the war years has been nothing less than miraculous. Change began with the government building dams and water-power projects to provide cheap electricity. Manufacturing industries and businesses relocated to take advantage of inexpensive power as well as low labor costs. Local people no longer had to move to the North to find employment.

Fortunately, progress didn't destroy the Midsouthern Hills's natural beauty; it actually improved things. With the dams came lakes—hundreds of them. The combination of Ozark and Appalachian scenery with new lakes—perfect for fishing, boating, waterskiing, and just plain looking—created an overnight tourist sensation. Vacationers brought money, and retirees brought even more dollars, which further contributed to economic growth. Today small farms are more often a hobby or a sideline than a means of survival.

Because of its porous limestone base, the Ozark formation is honeycombed with caves, sometimes storing so much water that rivers gush from the subterranean depths as if by magic. One example: In Missouri's Big Spring Park, a full-fledged river surfaces at the rate of 286 million gallons a day! Ozark soil—typically rock-studded, rust-red in color, and nutrient-poor—doesn't lend itself easily to plows or farm machinery. For this reason large portions of this country escaped agricultural development; they remain rustic, unspoiled, and delightful places for retirement hideaways.

Most retirees we interviewed here emphasize the four-season climate as a major plus. "I like to know what time of year it is," said one lady who had lived in California before retirement. "Here I get the feeling of seasons. Summer is nice and hot, fall is beautiful and colorful, winter is short and merciful, and then comes spring!" She sighed in ecstasy.

Make no mistake: Winter does bring chilly winds, creeks ice over, and your furnace gets a workout. Still, it doesn't begin to compare with winters farther north. Summers are humid but not unbearable, with 90-degree highs normal. Enough rain falls in the summer to keep the landscape looking green and fresh, streams flowing, and fishing good to excellent year-round.

As mentioned earlier in this book, many small towns lack intercity bus service and air transportation. This is particularly common in the Mid-southern Hills region. Without intercity buses or passenger trains, you are totally dependent upon an automobile. The nearest airport could be 75 miles away. When the grandkids come to visit, how do they get to your place from the airport? If you don't drive, and if you're used to public transportation, don't take it for granted when looking for a retirement destination. Make it a point to determine the situation before locking yourself in.

KENTUCKY

The first region west of the Allegheny Mountains settled by American pioneers, Kentucky epitomizes America's rugged frontier heritage. This is the country of Daniel Boone, the Hatfields and McCoys, and good ol' mountain music. Today it's much more than that. With up-to-date services, neighborly people, and modern shopping everywhere, Kentucky is a great choice for relocation.

The Mississippi River marks Kentucky's western border, and deep valleys and rugged gorges of the Appalachians delimit its eastern border. In between you'll find a wide selection of environments from which to choose: everything from gently rolling farmland to magnificent panoramas of the Blue Ridge Mountains; from quiet, rural crossroads communities to sophisticated cities and university towns. Modern-day transportation, with modern highways crisscrossing the state, has opened the backcountry to the world. No longer are large parts of the state isolated and populated with illiterate mountaineers and moonshiners. Kentucky today is too open for that. This opening of the state also created retirement opportunities

---

Kentucky Tax Profile

Sales tax: 6%; food, drugs exempt
State income tax: 2.0% to 6.0%
Income brackets: lowest, $3,000; highest, $75,000
Property taxes: 1.35% on 100% assessed value
Social Security taxed: no
Pensions taxed: excludes $41,110
Inheritance tax: based on federal estate tax law
Gasoline tax: 18.4¢ per gallon

KENTUCKY WEATHER

	IN DEGREES FAHRENHEIT				ANNUAL	
	Jan.	April	July	Oct.	RAIN	SNOW
Daily highs	41	68	88	69	43"	14"
Daily lows	24	46	67	46		

that didn't exist previously. Yet Kentucky certainly hasn't become a carbon copy of middle America. Many charming areas back in the hills are almost as rustic and unspoiled as ever. And because most Kentucky counties have opted for prohibition, you can bet many of those piney hills still conceal moonshine stills.

Kentucky is particularly attractive for midwestern and northern retirees who see advantages in retiring close to their prior homes, in inexpensive, low-crime surroundings. The relatively mild, four-season weather easily satisfies requirements for those who insist on colorful autumns, invigorating winters, and glorious springs.

Bowling Green

About an hour's drive north of Nashville (65 miles by I-65) and the Nashville International Airport is the delightful little city of Bowling Green. Because of its central location (within one day's drive of three-fourths of the US population), this is becoming a popular retirement location for fugitives from crowded northern cities. The interstate, a major north–south artery, facilitates transportation and makes it easy for the grandchildren to visit. Today's population is about 60,000.

Originally the town was called the Barrens, after the Barren River that runs through the site, but in 1797 it was renamed something a bit more descriptive of the area: Bowling Green. The second name derived from the habit of court officials and visiting attorneys amusing themselves between trials by lawn bowling beside the old courthouse. The surrounding countryside is as green as the name—lush, with rolling meadows surrounded by white fences, and thoroughbred horses munching away at the Kentucky bluegrass. Bowling Green looks exactly as one imagines Kentucky should look.

Because of its location, Bowling Green serves as a regional hub for retail shopping and medical services. And because this is the only place between Louisville and Nashville where alcohol is served, Bowling

Green's higher-quality restaurants attract folks from miles around for celebrating that special occasion. According to a chamber of commerce survey, Bowling Green has more restaurants per capita than any other US city except San Francisco. Understand, that comes from the chamber of commerce, but no question, there are plenty of restaurants scattered around.

Another factor in maintaining an upscale atmosphere is the presence of Western Kentucky University, with almost 20,000 students adding intellectual variety. The university maintains a symphony orchestra and two theater groups, and it hosts frequent visits from touring artists and entertainers. Other cultural offerings are presented by the Capitol Arts Center and the Public Theatre of Kentucky. Participation in university affairs is made easy by Kentucky's policy of senior-citizen scholarships that pay the full cost of tuition. This is true for both full-time and part-time students and applies toward either graduate or undergraduate courses. Numerous continuing-education programs are also offered, ranging from the history of American presidents to motorcycle training.

Bowling Green's vibrant economy is due in large part to the General Motors Corvette plant and the wages that boost business and commercial interests. The city takes pride in being the "Home of the Corvette"; a 1,200-employee plant builds these sleek, sports-styled speedsters. Since 1981 every Corvette made was produced in Bowling Green.

Although Bowling Green is a fine example of a larger Kentucky town, it's not big enough to suffer from big-city problems. Crime rates here are low, pollution is almost nonexistent, and the cost of living is slightly below the national average. Housing costs are usually low, with homes selling well below national averages.

Bowling Green Chamber of Commerce: 710 College St., Bowling Green, KY 42101; (270) 781-3200; bgchamber.com.

Murray

Murray (pop. 18,000) is a city that consistently garners recommendations from retirement writers as a good place to relocate. It's also an excellent example of how good things can happen to a community when retirees move in. A few years ago Murray received a rash of national publicity when a popular retirement guide designated it as the country's "top-rated" place for retirement. Publicity of this nature creates an enormous amount of interest among folks planning relocation—so much interest that some 250 couples immediately made the move to Murray. The real estate market zoomed out of the doldrums and soon exhausted its inventory. Suddenly there was a housing shortage! Building construction increased to keep pace. Before long five new housing developments were under way. The median sales price of housing made a satisfying leap upward.

This retiree immigration proved to be an economic bonanza for the community—in the short term, at any rate. The boost in the price of real estate turned out to be temporary. In their exuberance developers overbuilt, depressing the market and dropping asking prices. The extra retirees, however, were enough to push the city into enlarging the senior citizens' center and adding more services. The staff at the local center, by the way, is dedicated and enthusiastic about plans for the facility's future.

So what were the lasting bad effects? Apparently none. Today real estate is still a bargain, selling well below national averages, much the same as other communities in the region. People moving into the mid-South from other parts of the country still feel like bandits as they sign the escrow papers.

A volunteer worker at the senior center pointed out that Murray has a California Club composed of others like her who had chosen Kentucky for retirement. When I asked why Kentucky, she explained that it was mostly to live near her children, who were in St. Louis and Nashville. Murray is only a few hours' drive to either place. What were the drawbacks? She had to admit that snow and ice took some getting used to. What did they miss most from their California lifestyle? The lack of good restaurants. It turns out that Murray is in a dry county, and when restaurants can't make the extra profits from serving drinks, there is no reason to serve gourmet meals.

Murray is home of the largest public hospital in the lakes area (west of Kentucky Lake and Lake Barkley): the Murray/Calloway County Hospital. Serving the west Kentucky and northwest Tennessee region, the hospital is a 366-bed facility with resident physicians representing 26 medical specialties.

Murray Chamber of Commerce: 805 N. 12th St., Murray, KY 42071; (270) 753-5171; mymurray.com.

Danville

Kentucky's bluegrass region is world famous for its green pastoral beauty, picturesque horse farms, and wooded countryside. The college town of Danville (pop. 16,000) is an excellent example of bluegrass-country life-styles. The cultural and business center of the region, Danville is a place of wide, tree-lined streets, low crime, light traffic, and no parking meters. Its downtown is alive and well, convenient for those who live near the city center, and a great place for strolling and greeting friends.

Danville's historic town center is well preserved. Stately mansions, some dating to the early 1800s, grace the shady streets of the district known as Beaten Biscuit Row. You'll find antiques shopping, quaint restaurants, and charming bed-and-breakfast inns in this neighborhood, as well as many old homes that would be great for retirement living.

Senior citizens are a vital part of the Danville community. A well-equipped senior citizens' center has recently been added to the area. The newly built structure includes an activity room, exercise room, and dining room. The facility offers lunches, speakers, shopping excursions, daylong outings, dancing and fitness sessions, and crafts.

Were it not for Danville's Centre College, the town wouldn't have been included in this book. Like any college town, the school changes the dynamics. Among other things it provides the community access to internationally recognized performing artists and world-class exhibitions in its Norton Center for the Arts. The school was the site of a presidential debate during the Bush-Gore campaign. In addition to multiple cultural offerings at the school, Danville has several theaters, including an outdoor dinner theater, and several art galleries in the heart of its historic downtown.

Housing in Danville ranges from historic homes around the town center to newer homes toward the city's edge and tranquil rural homesteads on rolling farm and forest land. Even the most secluded regions of the county are only minutes away from shopping. Because of the college, a good supply of apartment and home rentals are available. Lakeside and golf-course homesites are found just minutes from Danville. Real estate prices are well below national averages.

Old Bridge Golf Club on Lake Herrington has an 18-hole course open to public play, reputed to be one of the best courses in the region. The country-club setting includes an Olympic-size pool and lighted tennis courts. Danville is in a dry county, but there is a country club where you are allowed to bring your own wine and liquor. The city of Lexington, 35 miles away, does allow liquor sales.

Medical needs are served by a 160-bed, acute-care hospital. The facility offers comprehensive care representing more than 20 medical specialties, backed by state-of-the-art technology. Emergency care is staffed 24 hours a day.

Danville Chamber of Commerce: 109 E. Walnut St., Danville, KY 40422; (859) 236-2361; danvilleboylechamber.com.

TENNESSEE

Tennessee is somewhat of a mirror image of Kentucky to the north and Arkansas to the west. Eastward, the land slopes gradually upward until the foothills finally become the Appalachian Mountains. They grow ever more rugged, reaching their highest peaks in eastern Tennessee, near the state's border with North Carolina.

With the Appalachians providing a scenic backdrop, the state maintains a mild climate, with four distinct seasons. Summers are usually warm and humid, with somewhat cooler temperatures in the mountains. Summer temperatures range from an average high near 90 degrees to an average low of 65. Winter temperatures range from an average high of 44 to an average low of 30 degrees. Rainfall commonly averages 50 inches a year. With comfortably warm days and cool summer nights, the Smoky, Blue Ridge, and Appalachian Mountains can be ideal places for relocation.

Near the Mississippi River, plains of fertile bottomland alternate with dense hardwood forests. King Cotton once ruled this domain, a land steeped in the genteel traditions of the Old South. Flat-to-rolling land covers much of the eastern portions of Tennessee, with rich agricultural fields hedged with rows of trees,

Tennessee Tax Profile

Sales tax: 6% to 8.5%; food, drugs exempt
State income tax: on interest and dividends only, exemption for over 65
Property taxes: vary from 1.46% to 2.37%
Social Security taxed: no
Pensions taxed: no
Inheritance tax: no
Gasoline tax: 26.4¢ per gallon

TENNESSEE WEATHER

	IN DEGREES FAHRENHEIT				ANNUAL	
	Jan.	**April**	**July**	**Oct.**	**RAIN**	**SNOW**
Daily highs	46	71	90	72	48"	11"
Daily lows	28	48	69	48		

neat and prosperous-looking farmhouses, barns, and silos. Most smaller towns here look pretty much like any in Middle America. Memphis and Nashville are the large cities.

Like the other Midsouthern states discussed here, Tennessee is in general an inexpensive place to live, with living costs running 5 percent to 15 percent below national averages. Tennessee has no income tax on salaries, wages, Social Security, IRAs, and pensions. There is, however, a tax on interest and dividends, with a $16,200 exclusion for those over age 65, though those who have a total income of less than $37,000 for a single filer or $68,000 for a joint filer are also exempt. Living in Tennessee could require as little as half the budget of living in a major metropolitan area such as New York City or Los Angeles.

Clarksville

Located on Tennessee's northern border, next to Kentucky, Clarksville sits conveniently near an interstate highway that whisks you to the big city of Nashville in less than 45 minutes. This is one of our favorite Midsouthern Hills locations. Clarksville combines an atmosphere of small-town living with city and urban conveniences.

Don't misunderstand—Clarksville is no small town. An estimated population of 133,000 places Clarksville into the realm of a good-size city, yet it somehow manages to maintain the flavor of small-town life. This is a place where friends are constantly honking greetings to each other as they drive around town. Yet shopping malls and complexes are as large and complete as you could hope for in a much bigger city.

For those who cannot live without hauling fish out of the water or killing ducks, this is a great place to be, with all the conveniences of a city plus great hunting and fishing nearby. The Land Between the Lakes recreational area is 35 miles away, with 170,000 acres of public lands for hiking, camping, fishing, and seasonal scheduled hunting. The peaceful

Cumberland River flows through Clarksville; pleasure boats cruise where huge paddle-wheelers once carried tobacco and cotton for European ports. A half-hour drive from pleasant residential neighborhoods can take you to thick forests or rich farms and bluegrass meadows where horse breeding is a major industry. This is where the Tennessee Walking Horse breed was developed.

For big-city life nearby, Nashville offers fine restaurants, museums, and its famous Grand Ole Opry along with a booming music scene filled with undiscovered artists. Seems as if every country-and-western star from Minnie Pearl to Conway Twitty has a museum dedicated to him or her. But to me the most interesting museum is the home of President Andrew Jackson, where his original log cabin homestead still stands behind the stately Hermitage, his Greek revival mansion.

Clarksville differs from many other Midsouthern Hills towns in the large number of out-of-state folks who retire here. This happens whenever you combine a pleasant area with a large military base like Fort Campbell, which straddles the Tennessee-Kentucky state line adjacent to Clarksville. The base covers 105,000 acres, mostly in Tennessee, but because the post office is in Kentucky, that state claims Fort Campbell as its own. Military retirees enjoy base PX privileges and medical benefits. The fort, almost a city in itself, has a peacetime population of 38,000, with a PX as large as a shopping center, plus seven on-post schools for military dependents.

The early-day prosperity of the tobacco plantations shows clearly in the beautiful antebellum mansions in town. Set back from the street among magnificent oak and magnolia trees, surrounded by acres of lawn, these old homes are among the best preserved in the South. This notion of large lawns carries over into modern housing. Big lots are in. Even humble two-bedroom homes sit on enormous lots with awesome expanses of lawn—awesome because of the amount of energy spent in keeping the grass mowed. Yet folks here will tell you with straight faces, "I really enjoy yard work. Cutting grass is relaxing." (Yes, of course it is. That's why rich people are so tense; they hire someone else to mow their lawns.)

Our previous research showed Clarksville to be one of the housing bargains of the nation. Median sales prices are consistently below the national average. If anything, the cost of living is even lower today. Economic conditions change here depending upon what happens at Fort Campbell. When world conditions are peaceful, Fort Campbell operates with full staff and demand for housing is up. But when military problems arise somewhere in the world, troops here are among the first to go. When this happens, vacancies become easy to find and For Sale signs sprout on lawns.

Clarksville offers a large range of activities. Austin Peay State University is located here, complete with an active theater department that produces five shows a season ranging from comedy to serious theater and even musicals. A jazz festival is held in March and a spring opera in May. Guest-artist recitals are offered throughout the year, with free admission. Fort Campbell has an entertainment-services office, and it produces seven theatrical productions a year, open to the public.

Clarksville Chamber of Commerce: 25 Jefferson St., Ste. 300, Clarksville, TN 37040; (931) 647-2331; clarksvillechamber.com.

Crossville

East from Nashville along I-40 brings you to the foothills of the Blue Ridge Mountains and Crossville, a town with a population of about 12,000. While doing research in Crossville, we noticed that it looked somehow different from similar Tennessee towns. Much of the downtown construction seemed to be fairly recent, with fewer pre-Civil War–era buildings than one might expect. Farms surrounding the town lacked older-looking houses and barns, the kind built in the mid-1800s. When we asked about it, a young lady who worked in a local business disagreed that the buildings are fairly recent, saying, "No sir, Crossville is a very old town. Almost nothing hereabouts is new." When we asked, "How old?," she replied, "Well, I understand that a few buildings here date all the way back to the days of the Franklin D. Roosevelt administration." We had to agree that was indeed ancient history.

It turns out that until the Great Depression Crossville was pretty much woods and empty countryside. Despite rich soil and abundant rainfall, the district had been all but ignored. FDR's New Deal administration, searching for worthwhile projects to bootstrap the country out of the Depression, seized upon a plan to develop the Crossville region as a model agricultural center. Government workers cleared forests, and homesteaders were given loans and seed money to get started. The plan evidently worked, because this is a very prosperous area today. Cheap electricity from the Tennessee

Valley Authority project lured industry into the area, adding jobs and even more prosperity.

As do most larger-size towns in the South, Crossville enjoys friendly neighbors and inexpensive housing. The level of services for senior citizens is as good as anywhere in the state, with enthusiastic and imaginative folks running programs.

The town is dry, with residents routinely making the trek to Knoxville for alcohol—a 70-mile drive each way. When I expressed dismay that drunks should be freewheeling down the interstate for their supplies, residents cheerfully assured me that bootleggers are plentiful in Crossville. "Why, you can buy anything you want, right here!" This weird custom of a community supporting prohibition and bootleggers at the same time never fails to puzzle me.

Property is quite affordable in Crossville and environs. Homes in town are usually on large lots with plenty of mature shade trees. On the town's outskirts larger lots are the rule, with small farms commonly used as retirement homes.

Fairfield Glade

When retirement writers speak of Crossville, often they have one of the special country-club developments in mind. There are several. Fairfield Glade is the oldest and the largest in the area, possibly the largest in the entire state. It's about 15 miles from Crossville and has been under development for two decades. Its year-round population is between 4,500 and 5,000, but thousands more enjoy the facilities on a part-time retirement basis or while on vacation. The corporation that put the package together has lots of experience—they have similar operations throughout the retirement areas of the nation.

Over the years Fairfield Glade has matured gracefully. It changed from a glitzy promotion into a series of pleasant neighborhoods scattered throughout the development's 12,000 acres. Eleven lakes and four championship golf courses with all the adjuncts—such as tennis courts, swimming pools, and restaurants—uphold the original country-club tradition.

Unlike some developments, all promised facilities seem to have materialized. A large gymnasium offers everything from basketball to billiards to bicycle rentals. A riding stable presents complete equestrian facilities and miles of hiking and riding trails. There is a fully functional shopping mall (20,000 square feet under one roof) and a range of good-quality restaurants. Of course, the better establishments serve cocktails to members of Fairfield Glade.

Homes surrounding this lake/golf-course complex are well built, attractively priced, and architecturally pleasing. Acres of wooded and green space separate the various tracts. The closer to the golf course, the more expensive the homes.

Holiday Hills

Closer to Crossville, just a few miles from the downtown section, is the retirement development of Holiday Hills. It spreads over 1,200 prime acres around a lake and a golf course. Apparently this one also started as a time-share resort, but retirement homes have become the style. The tennis and clubhouse facilities are excellent.

Holiday Hills is newer than Fairfield Glade and more convenient to town. Homes are priced comparably to those in Fairfield Glade, and its natural setting is just as beautiful. An interesting feature is the Cumberland County Playhouse, located just outside the development's main gate. Dramas, musicals, and ballets draw visitors from all over the nation.

Nearby is another retirement development, a no-frills place called the Orchards. In recognition of retirees' propensity for recreational-vehicle travel, they build carports high enough to accommodate RVs. The Crossville area attracts retirees from Indiana, Ohio, and Illinois, but the hottest place of origin is Michigan, particularly the Detroit area.

A possible drawback for those with health issues is the lack of a hospital in Crossville and nearby communities. The nearest hospitals require either a 25-mile drive to the town of Sparta or 26 miles to Harriman. Thirty-one miles away is the larger 217-bed hospital in Cookeville.

Crossville Chamber of Commerce: 34 S. Main St., Crossville, TN 38555; (877) 465-3861; crossville-chamber.com.

Cookeville

A tranquil and comfortable little city located about 80 miles east of Nashville and 100 miles west of Knoxville on I-40, Cookeville nestles in an area known as the Upper Cumberland region, a place of hills, valleys, waterfalls, and scenic country. The population here is nearly 28,000, augmented by numerous "commuters" who live in nearby small communities or on rural properties and who travel to Cookeville each day to work, go to school, receive health care, and participate in leisure-time activities.

Cookeville often scores high in popular retirement guides as one of the better retirement "off-the-beaten-track" destinations. Not long ago the city was featured in a *Where to Retire* magazine article: "Six Great Low-Cost Towns." Cookeville and surrounding areas are always well below the national average, with real estate selling for at least 15 percent below average. According to local people, Cookeville also experiences Tennessee's lowest crime rate and lowest property taxes.

Five rivers, seven state parks, and three major lakes—all within minutes of Cookeville—offer camping, picnicking, hiking, and fishing. Cane Creek Park, a 260-acre facility with a 56-acre lake, is closest to Cookeville. Twelve golf courses, all within a few minutes' drive, cater to golfers of varying abilities, and Cookeville Community Center has a half-dozen tennis courts available for public play.

The campus of Tennessee Technological University serves as a cultural center for residents of Cookeville and the Upper Cumberland region, offering concerts, operettas, and recitals by professional artists. The school's Bryan Fine Arts Center hosts a symphony orchestra, art shows, lectures, music, and dance. The Cookeville Drama Center sponsors touring companies, as well as local performers belonging to two grassroots theater groups.

Cookeville Regional Medical Center has been the health care provider for the Upper Cumberland region since 1950. This 227-bed hospital has a staff of more than 90 physicians with specialties in 28 fields of medicine. A recent $20 million expansion added a comprehensive cancer treatment center and an open-heart surgery center.

Cookeville Chamber of Commerce: 1 W. First St., Cookeville, TN 38501; (800) 264-5541; cookevillechamber.com.

ARKANSAS

A major beneficiary of today's retirement trends, Arkansas is one of the fastest-growing states in number of new residents over age 65. Throughout the state almost one in five inhabitants is older than 60, with percentages much higher in popular retirement locations. The areas described here are communities we considered to have a good percentage of retirees from other parts of the country. This means you'll probably have a better chance to "fit in" your new neighborhood. Newcomers from Chicago or Indianapolis find it easy to make friends, because they find that many of their neighbors have relocated from the same part of the country, have similar interests, and have common things to talk about. This is convenient because, believe it or not, many Arkansas natives have never even heard of the Chicago Cubs, much less spend time discussing their pennant possibilities for the season.

What is the attraction here? Arkansas's mild, four-season climate, low taxes, and personal safety. Inexpensive housing and friendly people figure into the picture, but the catalyst for retirees settling in Arkansas is the glorious Ozark environment. These low, ancient, thickly forested mountains symbolize many retirement dreams. The Ozarks represent a rebirth of simplicity, a purging of city life, and a new mode of relaxation.

Arkansas Tax Profile

Sales tax: 6.5%, plus 5.5% possible county tax
State income tax: 1% to 7%
Income brackets: lowest, $4,299; highest, $35,300
Property taxes: average 3.9% at 20% of appraised value
Social Security taxed: no
Pensions taxed: excludes $6,000 for retired military
Inheritance tax: no
Gasoline tax: 21.8¢ per gallon

Besides clear-running streams, squeaky-clean air, and lakes swarming with fish, many retirement dreams also picture an isolated cabin with a boat dock at the back door and lazy days of casting for largemouth bass or lake trout. But don't worry—even non-anglers enjoy the Ozark's beautiful surroundings.

The southern part of Arkansas, below the Ozarks, is rarely the choice of folks coming from other states. They prefer the northern half, above Hot Springs and Little Rock. This is important to know. Without a substantial number of out-of-state retirees or other outsiders for neighbors, you could find yourself isolated among folks with whom you have little in common. Not that people would be anything but friendly and neighborly, but unless your cultural background is basically agricultural and small town, you could have a difficult time adjusting.

ARKANSAS WEATHER

	Jan.	April	July	Oct.	ANNUAL RAIN	SNOW
	IN DEGREES FAHRENHEIT					
Daily highs	48	74	94	76	40"	7"
Daily lows	27	49	71	49		

Following are some northern Arkansas towns we've visited and that we feel have potential for retirement. All have a significant number of nonnatives living there. Some places are small, but none is totally isolated from medical and other important services. Intercity transportation is often a problem, something you'll have to take into consideration if you aren't fond of driving an automobile.

Fayetteville

Up in the northwest corner of Arkansas's Ozark Mountains, several great candidates for senior relocation await your consideration. On either side of 28,000-acre Beaver Lake, Eureka Springs and Fayetteville both have received favorable publicity as great places for relocation. North of Fayetteville is the small city of Rogers, and a bit farther north is one of the earliest planned developments in Arkansas: Bella Vista. This part of Arkansas shares in some of the most beautiful Ozark scenery in the entire region. It starts just a few miles from downtown Fayetteville.

Fayetteville is the largest of these candidates, a city of about 75,000 residents, plus almost 18,000 students at the University of Arkansas. One way you can tell you're in a college town: Look for a collection of ethnic restaurants and eateries with offbeat names. Fayetteville has 'em all. Besides a tempting selection of Japanese, Mexican, and barbecue restaurants, there's Gumbo Joe's Cajun Grill, Penguin Ed's, Armadillo Grill, and Schlegel's Bagels. I can't imagine a restaurant named Penguin Ed's located in a rural Arkansas town, such as Resume Speed, Arkansas. The chef would be arrested and handcuffed by the local sheriff before the first penguin-on-rye sandwich ever left the grill. (They might accept armadillo, however, if served with red-eye gravy and biscuits.) When Bill Clinton was first running for Congress back in 1974, he and his campaign committee used to meet at a popular dining spot in Fayetteville called the D'Lux Cafe.

The University of Arkansas is Fayetteville's heart and soul. The school, its students, and professors add excitement and vigor to the city. To fully savor the magnetism of the resident student community, you must visit Dickson Street, near the campus. This colorful, entertaining street is filled with bistros, restaurants, and art galleries. It's a place to dance the night away to your favorite music. (Doesn't sound like Arkansas, does it?) Dickson Street is also home to the splendid Walton Arts Center.

Fayetteville's downtown is a delightful combination of a healthy business sector and a well-preserved historic district, which local residents refer to as "the Square." Commercial and residential buildings have been lovingly restored to their 19th-century glory. They contrast nicely with contemporary architecture containing shops and offices. Local farmers and craftspeople are encouraged to bring their wares to the laid-back farmers' market on the square, which takes place three times a week. A tourist trolley provides free transportation for shoppers and visitors to move around Fayetteville's downtown on their leisurely errands.

Homes around the Fayetteville historic district are very much in demand, with potential buyers asking to have their names placed on a waiting list. Most homes have been completely renovated and are large, from 2,500 to 4,000 square feet. Downtown historic homes can be relatively expensive compared with other towns with historic districts. By way of contrast, a few blocks away is Wilson Park, a safe, homey neighborhood with houses built in the 1950s and 1960s with much lower price tags. A dozen attractive areas around town, farther away from the city center, offer affordable housing in secure-feeling neighborhoods. Seven upscale developments are in place. One of these is a golf-course subdivision, with residents' backyards touching the greens. In short, the range of real estate is wide here, from Arkansas-inexpensive to more than you'd like to pay.

Bella Vista

About 20 miles north of Fayetteville is the planned community of Bella Vista. One of the earlier experiments in Ozark development, Bella Vista started 40 years ago and now has more than 25,000 year-round residents and thousands of seasonal visitors. It was created by the same developers as Hot Springs Village, employing the same concepts, although it's older. Originally intended as a retirement and vacation resort, it became popular with commuters to Fayetteville who didn't mind the drive over the new four-lane highway. When you buy into Bella Vista, you automatically belong to four country clubs and recreational complexes. Residents have access to tennis courts, swimming pools, eight lakes, and seven golf courses.

For health care in Fayetteville and Bella Vista, the Lincoln County Hospital in Fayetteville offers a 350-bed facility.

Fayetteville Chamber of Commerce: 21 W. Mountain St., #300, Fayetteville, AR 72701; (479) 521-1710; fayettevillear.com.

Eureka Springs

This delightful town in northwest Arkansas started with a retirement boom more than a century ago. Eureka means "I have found it," and this is how many visitors felt when they decided to convert their vacation visits into permanent relocation here. The population of year-round residents is about 2,400. Yes, it is a small town, but what a delightful setting!

People started coming to Eureka Springs around the turn of the 20th century because of the "magical" healing qualities of the spring waters that gushed out of the canyon's grottoes. Perhaps the mineral water helped, but getting away from the crowds and squalor of the city, breathing the pure mountain air, and seeing the lovely Ozark surroundings probably had more than a little to do with the miracle cures.

The miracle waters were known and appreciated by Native Americans long before the white settlers muscled into the region. The pale-faced newcomers really began arriving in large numbers in the 1880s, when the Frisco Railroad ran a line into town to carry visitors from Chicago, St. Louis, and Kansas City. Several luxurious hotels accommodated the crowds. Wealthy families built ambitious Victorian mansions that duplicated their big-city homes. Before long the town's winding streets were lined with houses, hotels, and commercial buildings, still displaying the fancy gingerbread styles of that era.

During World War I, for some reason, visitors stopped coming to Eureka Springs. The town's bonanza was put on hold; its popularity declined as new residents moved away or died. Lovely homes were boarded up and forgotten as absentee owners lost interest in the town. The Great Depression was the final blow; Eureka Springs almost became a ghost town. At the time townsfolk must have viewed this abandonment as extreme misfortune, but today's residents see it as a stroke of luck. Otherwise Eureka

Springs would have suffered from modernization, with the old buildings gradually replaced. This temporary loss of popularity created a time capsule of Ozark Victorian architecture.

Your first glimpse of Eureka Springs is a guaranteed surprise. Solid limestone and brick buildings, wrought-iron fancywork, and gracefully styled mansions with winding carriageways make the town a fascinating window into yesterday. Boutiques, restaurants, art galleries, and other businesses occupy the downtown's street-level stores, with second- and third-floor apartments for those who live downtown. Majestic private homes line streets that twist and climb the mountainside above the business district. This incredible collection of Victorians rivals the quality and variety that San Francisco has to offer. Some places seem to be out of time-sync, with fluted columns rising three stories in front of dignified brick facades and wrought-iron balconies—homes that look as if they belong on the set of *Gone with the Wind*. And more than just stately mansions have survived. Many small, one-bedroom cottages built by ordinary people sit next to large Victorians of the wealthy. It's difficult to describe Eureka Springs without slipping into clichés, because the entire town is a cliché, a magic peek into yesterday.

The town and environs offer all the amenities retirees seek: good medical facilities, a quaint, artistic cultural atmosphere, friendly neighbors, recreational opportunities, and inexpensive real estate. Eureka Springs has become both a retirement mecca and an artist colony.

An interesting aspect of Eureka Springs is that you often can buy a historic Victorian for about what you'd pay for an ordinary tract house in some parts of the country—even less. Several retired couples have converted their spacious old mansions into charming bed-and-breakfast inns. These antique homes are exceptional bargains, but there is plenty of conventional housing on the town's outskirts, similarly priced well below national averages.

Holiday Island

A half hour's drive from Eureka Springs takes you to an ambitious golf/country-club resort known as Holiday Island. Located on Table Rock Lake, the resort is set on 5,000 acres of natural beauty. The lake is narrow at this point, following the twists and turns of an old riverbed, thus creating a large number of lakefront lots. There are two golf courses (one with a

9-hole layout), a number of tennis courts, two swimming pools, and most of the facilities expected of a resort community. Ninety percent of the residents are from other states, mostly from Illinois, Missouri, and Texas.

Golf seems to be excellent here, so much so that enthusiastic golfers purchase inexpensive lots and pay the annual assessment just to enjoy unlimited use of the two 18-hole courses. Owners of lots also have the right to stay in Holiday Island's campground and use all facilities.

Eureka Springs Chamber of Commerce: 44 Kingshighway, Eureka Springs, AR 72632; (800) 638-7352; eurekaspringschamber.com.

Mena

Small towns have the reputation of being exceptionally low-crime areas. However, crime waves can strike anywhere, at any time. Not long ago a serial auto thief struck the western Arkansas town of Mena. Faced with an emergency, the local sheriff asked the local radio station to broadcast a warning: "Don't leave your car keys in the ignition! Someone is stealing cars!" Fortunately the culprit was apprehended—and turned out to be a high school student who liked joyriding. A good thing, too, because Mena citizens aren't used to heavy-duty crime waves. They'd never get accustomed to removing their car keys.

Sitting in a valley surrounded by western Arkansas's Ouachita (pronounced WAH-shi-taw) Mountains, Mena is a pleasant town of 5,600 in a county of 17,000. It's not far from the Oklahoma border, about 77 miles west of Hot Springs, and 85 miles south of Fort Smith. Local boosters call their town "the pride of the Ouachitas." (Why they aren't called the "Ozarks" is a puzzle, but local people insist that although they appear to be part of the same geological formation, *their* mountains deserve their own name: Ouachitas.)

Mena is surprisingly prosperous looking, with several upscale neighborhoods with housing selling at scandalously low Arkansas prices. Another surprise: Mena is a college town. Students and faculty always brighten a community, adding a touch of energy and spirit. The college influence shows in the way the downtown is still alive and breathing: The old railroad station, refurbished and restored, is now a museum and chamber of commerce office. Stores, businesses, and restaurants are open and thriving, not boarded up and collecting cobwebs as in some small Arkansas towns.

Part of Mena's economic well-being is due to local industries that employ skilled workers and consequently pay better-than-average wages. US Motors, a division of Emerson Electric, provides a large number of jobs. Another skilled-worker employer is a large facility that repairs and maintains aircraft for major US and Canadian airlines. Its technicians are all FAA qualified and can work just about anywhere in the world they choose. But they like it here in Mena. One man said, "We were looking for a good place to raise our children, and we couldn't find a better place than Mena."

Good wages have a multiplier effect on the economy in precisely the same way retired people's incomes do. When spent in the community, wages and incomes turn into profits and wages for other residents. They, in turn, have more money to spend, which benefits still others. The money goes 'round and 'round. Mena's community leaders understand this very clearly. That's exactly why they are so enthused about sharing their community with retirees rather than going after marginal, minimum-wage industries as many other Arkansas cities have done.

The town is surrounded by 1.5 million acres of the Ouachita National Forest, the South's oldest and largest national forest. These mountains look exactly like the Ozarks to me, but local boosters claim it's a different mountain range, so I defer to their expertise. Thirty-two recreational areas are scattered throughout the forest, where residents enjoy picnicking, camping, hiking, horseback riding, mountain biking, swimming, fishing, hunting, and boating.

For a small town Mena surprised us by having two public golf courses as well as a private golf course at the local country club. Like most Arkansas small towns, Mena is in a dry county; however, for those who enjoy a glass of vintage grape with their steak and a cocktail after dinner, the local country club has a permit to serve alcohol. Also the Oklahoma state line is less than 10 miles away, where liquor stores are open for business. Ironically, Oklahoma was one of the last states to permit legal sale of liquor, yet now it's the first place people from neighboring states go to stock up their liquor cabinets.

Rich Mount, Mena's college, is a small school but has lots of get-up-and-go about it. The school's library has 20 computers, plus three computer labs, which the community is welcome to use between classes. Free tuition is offered to anyone over age 60, for either credit or audit.

Housing costs in Mena are pretty much standard for Arkansas. (That means very low.) The difference between Mena and the average Arkansas small city is a higher number of affluent neighborhoods than you'd normally expect. One couple I interviewed (retirees from Wisconsin) were absolutely delighted with their home: a three-bedroom, two-bath, modern log cabin sitting on 9 wooded acres with a stream flowing through. "We always wanted to live in a log cabin," they said, "and we absolutely fell in love with this one. When the seller told us he was only asking $65,000 for everything, we didn't even think about making a counter-offer. Then we found out taxes were only $300 a year!" (Of course, this happened a few years ago, so don't expect prices and taxes quite that low today!)

Mena Chamber of Commerce: 524 Sherwood Ave., Mena, AR 71953; (479) 394-2912; menapolkchamber.com.

Greers Ferry Lake Area

About 60 miles north of Little Rock, the Greers Ferry Lake area is another of Arkansas's retirement success stories. Three towns share in this success: Heber Springs, Greers Ferry, and Fairfield Bay. They sit on the shores of a 40,000-acre lake created by an Army Corps of Engineers dam. (One of President Kennedy's last official acts was to dedicate Greers Ferry Dam while on his way to Dallas.)

This 300 miles of wooded shoreline—encompassing a lake filled with bass, stripers, walleye, catfish, and lunker trout—soon caught the attention of folks considering an Ozark retirement. Inexpensive property, low taxes, a temperate climate, and an almost nonexistent crime rate added to the attraction of retirement here. Folks from Chicago and St. Louis paid particular attention, for the lake wasn't so far from their grandchildren and old friends that they couldn't go home for a visit whenever they pleased.

In a matter of 25 years, Heber Springs, the largest of the communities, zoomed from a population of 2,500 to 7,500. The vast majority of newcomers were retired couples from northern states. Their pension incomes and savings pumped up bank deposits more than twentyfold. This extra purchasing power boosted retail sales, created jobs, and generated tax money for local improvements. Home-building activity continues today, with lovely new neighborhoods materializing in low-density clusters, often hidden in wooded, lakeshore settings.

Actually the area's population increased much more than the figures indicate. Most small neighborhoods are located outside town limits, nestled in wooded glades, often invisible from major roads and highways. Typically a development consists of a grouping of from 10 to 50 homes, sometimes with lake views. This arrangement cuts the expense of utility installation as well as construction costs. There could be as many as 150 of these mini-neighborhoods scattered through the forests, raising the population without showing in the official census of the towns. Although building lots are usually half an acre or more, the setting creates a sense of closeness among the neighbors. "We never worry about leaving our home vacant during the winter," remarked one resident, "because our friends watch the place for us."

Construction quality is high, most homes are of brick, and low labor costs keep the selling prices affordable. Properties on the lake are priced higher, but not remarkably so. Lakeside homes enjoy the view, but so do places set farther back. Unlimited water access is provided by public docks, ramps, and marinas. A unique type of retirement development that appeals to those who fly small planes is Sky Point Estates, where you can build your home next to an airstrip.

For even smaller small-town retirement, Greers Ferry (pop. 1,000) sits invitingly on the other side of the lake. The community provides all the basic services needed for day-to-day living, yet it's so small and uncongested that traffic lights seem to be unnecessary. Greers Ferry has grocery stores, craft shops, and three branch banks. As a consideration for retirees' health care, the community has three full-time doctors, and free ambulance service to Cleburne Hospital in Heber Springs is provided.

One of the advantages of living in the Greers Ferry Lake area is its proximity to Little Rock, an hour's drive away. With a metropolitan-area population of nearly 250,000, Little Rock provides the health services that smaller towns cannot. Libraries, museums, and other cultural attractions fill a void for those who are used to larger cities. Little Rock is also the closest place to stock up on wine and beer to serve your guests, for like most rural Arkansas areas, this area is in a dry county.

Housing prices here are traditionally way under national trends. A typical remark by new residents is, "Our new home is twice the size as the one we sold back home, and it cost half the money." Property taxes come as a pleasant shock when new residents receive tax bills just a fraction of what they paid back home.

At the far end of the lake is Fairfield Bay, a more upscale setting where newcomers can buy a modern ranch home on or near a golf course. This resort/retirement community features round-the-clock security plus all the advantages of an exclusive, gated complex. Fairfield Bay's parent company has built several similar developments around the country.

Greers Ferry Chamber of Commerce: 8101 Edgemont Rd., #4, Greers Ferry, AR 72067; (501) 825-7188, (800) 825-7199; greersferry.com.

Bull Shoals/Mountain Home

In the north-central part of Arkansas, along the Missouri border, a forested area of lakes and rivers has become a miniature melting pot, with retirees moving here from all over the country. Even traditional retirement areas such as California and Florida are represented by new arrivals taking advantage of an exceptionally low crime rate, inexpensive living, and gorgeous scenery.

Bordered on three sides by water, Bull Shoals and Lakeview sit on the shore of a lake that stretches for almost 100 miles. Its deep blue waters are legend among bass anglers, and the rivers and streams feeding the lake are considered premier spots for rainbow trout fishing, which in the spring and summer can even be done at night under lights. There are no closed seasons here; you can fish year-round. Sports aren't restricted to fishing or hunting; several challenging golf courses in the area will test your skills, whether you're a pro or a duffer.

The lake's shore is off-limits to construction up to the high-water mark, but the public has free access to both lakes and rivers. This restriction protects the lake's pristine quality, keeping it from being cluttered with sagging docks and scruffy-looking boats. The shoreline always looks clean and natural. Public marinas will house your boat for as little as $400 a year, so you don't have to keep pulling your boat out of the water after every fishing trip.

Mountain Home is 15 miles from Bull Shoals and Lakeview, over a highway that winds through picturesque Ozark woods. This small city of about 13,000 is the commercial center for the lake communities and the surrounding county of nearly 40,000 inhabitants. Mountain Home has a real downtown area, including an archetypal, old-fashioned town square. Major shopping and consumer businesses are located on the highway and around the major intersections. Stores here supply any consumer goods anyone could reasonably need. A community college serves the area, and retiree organizations offer opportunities for volunteer work. A hospital accommodates the area's population, and an airport runs shuttle flights to the nearest large cities. The Area Agency on Aging operates a local bus service.

The county in which Mountain Home is located allows the sale of package liquor, and cocktails are permitted to be served in at least one restaurant. On the other hand, Bull Shoals is dry except for one private club.

According to couples who retired in this area, major attractions are mild winters and low living costs. One couple from just north of Chicago said, "We cut our property taxes by $2,000 a year by coming here, and we cut our heating bills by more than half. The money we save makes the difference between struggling to stay within our budget and having money to spend for luxuries."

Providing medical care for the surrounding smaller towns is Baxter Regional Medical Center, with 263 beds, located in Mountain Home.

Mountain Home Chamber of Commerce: 1337 Hwy. 62 W., Mountain Home, AR 72653; (870) 425-5111; enjoymountainhome.com.

Hot Springs

Situated partially within Hot Springs National Park, the city of Hot Springs (pop. 38,000) is one of the more attractive retirement possibilities in Arkansas. Hot Springs combines the spirit of a 1920s resort with that of a 21st-century small city. It is as different from the previously described towns as can be, yet its rustic setting on the lower edge of the Ouachita Mountains lends it an Ozark feeling.

The old part of town sits in a canyon with buildings and homes clinging to the sloping-to-steep sides of the ravine. During the decades before, during, and shortly after World War II, Hot Springs maintained a reputation as a lively nightlife town. Roulette, blackjack, and slot machines were as much an attraction as the gushing hot springs. Nightclubs and fancy restaurants flourished in a kind of mid-country Monaco atmosphere. Wealthy and famous citizens rubbed elbows with ordinary workers and the elite of the crime syndicates. Gambling, drinking, and dancing the night away preceded health-restoring soakings in the hot springs the next morning.

During its heyday Hot Springs was considered as sumptuous a resort as Las Vegas or Palm Springs is today.

Casino gambling and nightclubs are just memories. The action now is bathing in the soothing waters and enjoying the quiet atmosphere of the Ozark Mountains. After casino-style gambling was prohibited, the old town, in the steepest part of the canyon, gradually fell into disrepair. When high rollers stopped visiting, money ceased flowing. Local folks preferred to shop in the malls away from downtown. But a new wave of retirees and a revival of tourist interest in the hot springs stirred a renewal of the downtown. Once-abandoned buildings now sport fine restaurants, art galleries, and quality shopping. The motif is turn of the 20th century, with antique globe streetlamps, Victorian trim, even horse-drawn carriages for sightseeing. A new breed of visitors comes to Hot Springs today, bringing retirement money instead of casino gambling money, and they tend to stay permanently.

Hot Springs's residential areas are all located on higher levels, where the land is rolling and hilly but not steep. A good thing, too, because the narrow canyon is subject to flash floods. Several years ago newspapers reported that a 6-foot wall of water crashed its way down the canyon and a main business street, flooding stores and wreaking havoc. Hot Springs business people are used to this. After cleaning out the mud, the bathhouses, boutiques, and restaurants opened for business with little delay.

Of course, the town's name comes from the volcanic springs that issue steaming hot water from grottoes and crevices in the canyon floor. Neither drought nor rainy seasons seem to affect the water's copious flow. For generations the elderly and infirm praised the water's healing and revivifying powers. The young and healthy (unaware of what revivification entails) simply enjoy sitting in the hot water and relaxing. The bonus for all is the fresh mountain air and the smell of pines and sassafras trees. The bewitched waters are reputed to heal everything from rheumatism to dandruff.

Residential neighborhoods fall into two distinct categories: Victorian and modern. The older sections have ample yards and large homes— often with enormous lawns and large shade trees. Other neighborhoods are more modern, with conventional bungalows, duplexes, and low-profile apartment buildings. There are several new, quality senior citizens' developments and some excellent mobile-home parks. Not only is the cost of living well below national averages, but often homes can be found for as much as 30 percent below the national average!

Medical care is covered by St. Joseph's Health Center, with 275 beds, which serves the entire region.

Hot Springs Village

Fifteen miles from the city, you'll find one of the more impressive retirement complexes in Arkansas. Hot Springs Village, with almost 10,000 full-time residents, is one of those Florida-style, self-contained, guarded enclaves. The assurances and dreams of the promoters have been realized here; the promised improvements are in place, including a shopping center that would do justice to a good-size town.

Property in Hot Springs Village is not inexpensive, at least not for Arkansas, but it is certainly first class and returns full value for the money. House and town house prices would compare favorably with similar developments we've investigated in Florida, Arizona, and California. Yet for Arkansas they might be considered pricey.

Comprising 26,000 acres of rolling-to-steep Ozark foothill wilderness, the property is covered with a hardwood forest of oaks, hickories, and a scattering of evergreens. Roughly one-third of the property has been converted into lakes and golf courses. There are four par-72 golf courses and one par-62 layout, each with its own clubhouse, restaurant, and pro shop. Another third of the land is devoted to homesites, and the remaining third is natural forest.

Hot Springs Village is not exclusively a retirement complex; many people who work in the nearby city of Hot Springs commute from here. Because there are no schools here (residents voted down a school tax to avoid having schools), families with younger children rarely purchase property. According to the salespeople, the majority of the residents come from large cities in Illinois, Missouri, and Kansas.

Hot Springs Chamber of Commerce: 659 Ouachita Ave., Hot Springs, AR 71901; (501) 321-1700; hotspringschamber.com.

MISSOURI

Ozark hills and forests do not stop at the Arkansas border. They extend into Oklahoma on the west and about halfway up the state of Missouri before fading into plains and prairie country. Although the Ozarks indiscriminately bestow beauty upon all three states, Missouri's share is the largest, with 33,000 square miles of low mountains, verdant valleys, and rolling plateaus. The Missouri River marks the northern boundary of the Ozark range, Springfield the western edge, and the mountains taper out before they reach the Mississippi River in the east. Even in the midst of the mountains, plateaus can stretch for miles, with flat-to-rolling country reminiscent of the prairie to the north and west.

Missouri Tax Profile

Sales tax: 4.225%; food taxed at 1.225%
State income tax: 1.5% to 6%
Income brackets: lowest, $1,000; highest, $9,000
Property taxes: average 1.1%
Social Security taxed: half of benefits taxable for higher incomes
Pensions taxed: excludes $6,000
Inheritance tax: no
Gasoline tax: 17.4¢ per gallon

One of the more scenic areas is the 86,000-acre Current and Jacks Fork River country, set aside as the Ozark National Scenic Riverways. This writer personally cherishes fond childhood memories of camping along the Current River and watching my father fly fish for trout. (I don't remember him ever catching one.) Memories like this are partly why people dream of retiring in an angler's paradise such as the Ozarks.

Several Missouri Ozark rivers have been impounded by dams, forming long chains of lakes. They sprawl and twist through wooded valleys, covering a great part of both Missouri and Arkansas with water. The largest lakes are the Lake of the Ozarks—in the middle of the Missouri mountain range—and the Table Rock–Bull Shoals–Lake Taneycomo complex on the Missouri-Arkansas state line.

Lake of the Ozarks/Osage Beach

The largest lake in the Ozarks originated with the construction of Bagnell Dam across the Osage River in the 1930s. Ninety-four miles long, the lake boasts more than 1,000 miles of shoreline for fishing and recreation. Ozark hardwood forests climb from the water's edge, up and over low mountains, as far as the eye can see.

Years ago, before World War II, most outsiders who owned Ozark property expected, and demanded, rustic accommodations. They preferred log cabins for use as summer retreats or as fall hunting lodges. Most cabin owners lived in cities like St. Louis or Kansas City, occasionally coming from as far away as Chicago. City folks prized their backwoods hideaways and wanted to keep things rustic. Ozark natives were few in number and culturally isolated from the outside world. Natives and outsiders had little in common and lived in separate worlds, even though they might be next-door neighbors every summer.

Things have changed around the Lake of the Ozarks. Rustic vacation cabins with kerosene lamps have been replaced by bustling motel complexes, gourmet restaurants, and marinas. And, of course, the inevitable shopping malls lining the four-lane highway. In contrast to sleepy lake towns in other parts of Missouri and Arkansas, Missouri's Lake of the Ozarks is jumping. Kerosene lamps are out, contemporary living is in.

One couple, who retired to Osage Beach from St. Louis, said, "We're used to shopping malls, nice restaurants, and big-city conveniences. We couldn't stand living in a small, isolated village where we would have to settle for whatever the stores *have* rather than what we want. Yet we want to live on a lake and be away from it all." The couple's home is 15 minutes from a shopping mall, but it couldn't be more private. It sits on a large lakefront lot surrounded by a forest of northern red oak, black oak, shagbark hickory, and basswood. They can't see a neighbor in any direction. Because this is not an Army Corps of Engineers lake, a private boat slip is permitted at the lake's edge. Roads follow the lake's twisted arms to reach large, luxurious homes, ordinary houses, and rustic, unsophisticated cabins, most within easy shopping distance of town.

Osage Beach is the largest town on the Lake of the Ozarks and by far the most commercialized, with shopping malls, classy restaurants, and all the other amenities that come with full development. Vacationers, weekenders, and retirees come from all over the Midwest. Newcomers spend dollars that attract more businesses and more employees in a circular growth pattern. Instead of a summer resort with businesses that close every winter, Osage Beach has become a year-round town of around 5,000, the commercial center for an unknown number of lakeside residents and cabin owners outside the town limits. The reported population of the town doesn't take into consideration the thousands who are scattered through the lake area in unincorporated areas.

A few years ago a financial crisis in St. Louis's largest high-tech manufacturing firm caused a large number of employees—executives and factory workers alike—to seek employment elsewhere. This had a profound

MISSOURI WEATHER

	Jan.	April	July	Oct.	RAIN	SNOW
	IN DEGREES FAHRENHEIT				ANNUAL	
Daily highs	42	68	90	71	40"	17"
Daily lows	21	44	66	46		

effect upon real estate prices around the Lake of the Ozarks. Weekend homes were unceremoniously dumped on the market. Bargains were legion, and the real estate market was slow in recovering from the shock.

The University of Missouri (in Columbia) maintains the University Physicians–Lake of the Ozarks Specialty Clinic, with several medical specialties represented. For more serious problems patients go to Columbia for care at the university's high-tech hospital.

Lake of the Ozarks Chamber of Commerce: 1 Wilmore Ln., Lake Ozark, MO 65049; (573) 964-1008; lakeareachamber.com.

Branson

For years Branson, Missouri, south of Springfield near the Arkansas border, has been an enormously popular vacation destination for families living in the midwestern and southern regions. The entire family—kids, parents, and grandparents—enjoy vacationing together in a unique combination of "neon and nature." By day vacationers enjoy nature with three scenic Ozark lakes, including Lake Tanycomo (accessible from the center of Branson), where some can swim, ski, boat, sail, scuba dive, Jet Ski, or parasail while others fish for trout or lunker bass. Evenings are devoted to the neon and bright lights of 40 theaters, with nationally celebrated musicians, singers, and entertainers performing on stage. Thus Branson has become the Ozarks' counterpart to North Carolina's family-friendly Myrtle Beach (with its combination of golf courses, theme parks, and theaters). And like Myrtle Beach, Branson has become a popular locale for retirement. It's a place where grandchildren eagerly anticipate visits with their grandparents.

One feature about the Branson/Lakes area that many retirees appreciate is the opportunity for part- and full-time work. Those who aren't ready for the rocking chair have numerous choices for employment. Jobs are usually there, whether working in the theater box office or as an usher, greeting guests at a hotel, demonstrating a craft skill, or holding one of the many other positions in the retail, restaurant, and hospitality industries. Working is a great way to become acquainted with other residents of the community.

Beyond the recreational, entertainment, and part-time employment opportunities, the moderately priced housing market is a good reason for retirement here. Finding a home on a golf course costing half of what might be asked in other vacation destination cities is an appealing concept. A wide variety of homes and prices can be found, running the gamut from multimillion-dollar lakefront estates to moderately priced, in-town, single-family homes—something for every budget. As a result, the population from 1990 to 2014 more than doubled, from 3,700 to 10,500 inhabitants. Seniors account for a large measure of this growth, with an impressive 32 percent of the population age 55 and older. Revenue from tourism is a factor in keeping city taxes low. The cost of living in Branson is usually about 6 percent below the national average.

A major hospital and several specialty clinics provide a full range of health care services for residents and visitors. The 165-bed Skaggs Community Health Center—recently rated among the top 10 hospitals in Missouri by the Center for Healthcare Industry Performance Studies—offers a full range of medical services. The hospital recently added a $20 million outpatient facility expansion for cardiac rehabilitation.

Branson Area Chamber of Commerce: 410 Gretna Rd., Branson, MO 65616; (417) 334-4084; bransonchamber.com.

Columbia

Although not exactly in the Ozarks, the college town of Columbia is just a short drive from the Ozarks's outdoor recreation and rustic mountain scenery. With a population of 113,000, Columbia is large enough to supply all the amenities and conveniences of a modern city, yet not so large that it suffers from the inherent congestion, crime, and pollution of the big cities.

As a place for relocation, Columbia is popular with folks from large midwestern cities such as St. Louis, Chicago, and Kansas City. Just as visiting the Ozarks is convenient from Columbia, so are visits to places like

Kansas City or St. Louis. Either city is a 2-hour interstate drive, giving Columbia residents access to major-league professional sports, stage plays, major shopping areas, and all the good things offered by a large city. Then they return to the refuge of a safe, quiet, and clean hometown.

Making the decision to retire in Columbia is made easy by a unique program provided through Columbia's chamber of commerce. When we visited there, a few years ago, volunteer retirees were giving newcomers a 90-minute "windshield tour" of the city, visiting residential neighborhoods ranging from economical to deluxe. They drove us past the three colleges in town as well as by the golf courses and hospitals. You'll see the best shopping areas and visit Columbia's delightful downtown. This way potential retirees check out neighborhoods, home styles, and amenities without being pressured by a real estate agent.

Despite Columbia's upscale appearance, housing costs fall below national averages. The most popular retiree housing here is split-level ranch, usually of brick construction, with a large lawn. Condominiums are available for those who don't care for mowing lawns. Because of the college population, apartment rentals are often scarce. During the summer, however, temporary housing is easily found for those who want to savor the atmosphere of Columbia as a final test for livability. At least four developments here specifically target the retiree market. One development features golf-course living.

Columbia's economy is solidly based on education. The city's three major employers are institutions of higher learning: the University of Missouri, Stephens College, and Columbia College. This accounts for the high level of prosperity, stability, and an almost recession-proof economy. (A university isn't forced to lay off employees when the economy slows down.) The academic milieu enhances the city's cultural and social life with school activities that spill over into the community. It seems as if something is always happening for the public to participate in—lectures, concerts, sports events, or celebrations, some of which are free. The huge university library is open to the public for browsing and research, and although you can't check out books, the staff is very accommodating in helping you locate material. As you might guess, Columbia is a great place for continuing education. Many retirees choose Columbia specifically for that purpose; adult education programs reach out to mature residents and encourage them in their quest for lifetime learning.

Education flows through all sectors of the community, even in law enforcement; 90 percent of Columbia police officers are college graduates. That may have something to do with the city's low crime rate, which is sometimes 30 percent below the national average.

The university, with its medical school, confers another blessing on the community by leading the way in health care. In addition to the university hospital, seven other hospitals serve the community along with so many health care personnel that one in five workers in Columbia is employed in a health-related occupation. A unique service provided by the university is the Elder Care Center. Its major goal is to keep patients out of nursing homes by providing activities to help them maintain high functional levels. The daily fee (often covered by Medicaid) is less than half the usual nursing-home cost in the area. University students in physical, occupational, and speech therapy benefit from their experience at the center, and patients benefit from more robust health and postponement of nursing-home care.

Outdoor recreation is more than adequate. Besides two municipal golf courses and two private country clubs, there is the Twin Lakes Recreation Area, complete with boating, fishing, and swimming. A relatively new hiking and recreation trail follows the abandoned MKT Railroad line and will eventually connect with hiking trails that cross the state. This 4.7-mile stretch invites jogging and biking through dense woods, past streambeds, rock cuts, and open meadows—a small escape to the country, yet just yards removed from the surrounding city. For inclement-weather exercise the university hospital has organized a mall walker's club. At 6:30 every morning, long before the huge indoor Columbia Mall opens for business, you'll find several hundred walkers working on their stamina and blood pressure. In 30 minutes you can do two full laps, equaling almost 2 miles of vigorous walking, and you don't get rained on.

Columbia Chamber of Commerce: 300 S. Providence Rd., Columbia, MO 65203; (573) 874-1132; columbiamochamber.com.

OKLAHOMA

When people think of Oklahoma, they imagine flat plains extending to the horizon, perhaps rolling hills studded with oil derricks or farm machinery, and cattle fenced in by barbed wire. True, much of Oklahoma fits that description, for this is a state renowned for cattle, agriculture, and petroleum. But, just as New York state isn't all Manhattan, Oklahoma is not all flat farm country.

Parts of Oklahoma, particularly in the east and north, are hilly and heavily forested, the tail end of the Ozark Mountains. Some places are even less populated than the Missouri and Arkansas Ozarks. You can drive for miles with barely a suggestion that anyone might be living behind the solid mask of forest that lines the highways. Several dams take advantage of deep river valleys to create wide lakes that wiggle and squirm across wooded landscapes and through the hills. The largest, Eufala Reservoir, covers more than 100,000 surface acres. At least 18 lakes, most of them built by the Army Corps of Engineers, provide recreation as well as irrigation and power. This huge complex of water storage changed forever the face of a state that once was in danger of drying up and blowing away during the 1930s.

> **Oklahoma Tax Profile**
>
> **Sales tax:** 4.5%; prescriptions exempt
> **State income tax:** 0.5% to 5.25%
> **Income brackets:** lowest, $1,000; highest, $8,700
> **Property taxes:** Between 11% and 13.5% of fair cash value
> **Social Security taxed:** No
> **Pensions taxed:** excludes up to $10,000
> **Inheritance tax:** no
> **Gasoline tax:** 20¢ per gallon

The desolation of Oklahoma's Dust Bowl, drought, and depression is a well-known piece of history. Those dismal times are far behind as Oklahoma has become a center for aerospace and aviation industries. The latest agricultural technology, conservation, and flood control protect the land from a repeat of the 1930s disaster. Wonder of wonders: A deep river channel utilizing a system of dams and locks links Tulsa with the Gulf of Mexico, making it an important seaport!

John Steinbeck's *The Grapes of Wrath* dramatizes the desperate condition of life in Oklahoma during the Dust Bowl era. The book chronicles a dream of a good life in California and the Joad family's struggle to get to paradise. (Of course, that was well before California suffered from graffiti, drive-by shootings, and multilane, high-speed freeways.)

OKLAHOMA WEATHER

| | IN DEGREES FAHRENHEIT | | | | ANNUAL | |
	Jan.	April	July	Oct.	RAIN	SNOW
Daily highs	46	72	93	75	38"	9"
Daily lows	24	49	72	50		

Today some grandchildren of those refugees who immigrated to California in the 1930s are ready for retirement. After suffering today's hardships of freeway traffic, high taxes, and idiotic politicians, many of the Joad family descendants dream of a good life somewhere else.

Grand Lake o' the Cherokees

A series of lakes runs halfway down the state near the Missouri and Arkansas border. Each lake supports small towns that can be practical for retirement. One of the more popular areas is in the state's northeast corner, named after its largest lake, the Grand Lake o' the Cherokees. Sometimes it's called the Pensacola Dam Project or simply Grand Lake. The contraction "o" does not mean *of*, but *over*, to commemorate the Cherokee burial grounds that lie at the bottom of the lake. Sixty-six miles long, with 1,300 miles of shoreline and 60,000 surface acres of water, this is one of the Ozarks's largest bodies of water. Unlike the practice at many reservoirs created by the government, workers here cleared trees and stumps before impoundment, greatly improving both navigation and aesthetics. The countryside around these lakes is not as rugged as the true Ozark Mountains to the east or to the south in the Tenkiller Lake area, but the charm of the Ozark foothills is still evident.

The lake's wide stretches of water encourage sailboats, even full-fledged yachts capable of cruising in all kinds of weather. Some marinas specialize in sailboat moorings. Fishing is great; bass are so abundant that there's no size limit. Countless coves throughout the many crooks and branches of the lake make great places for picnics, should you become tired of torturing worms by sticking them with fishhooks. Rivers that run into the lake are famous for canoeing, an important tourist activity, with "canoe trails" as part of the Oklahoma park system.

The Grand Lake area supports more population than most Ozark waterways, with houses all along the lakeshore. Also, unlike at many man-made lakes in the Midsouthern Hills, lakefront ownership is not restricted, and private docks are allowed. In addition to simple fishing piers, some folks build flat docks like floating patios; other boat docks are covered and enclosed floating cabins of sorts. For years these lakes were considered the playground of Oklahoma oil patriarchs and big-city vacationers. They have long been popular weekend retreats for residents of northern Oklahoma, Missouri, Kansas, and Arkansas. Lately, however, the area is gaining prominence as a retirement destination.

Grand Lake even has a country club–type development. The 600-acre Coves of Bird Island (actually a peninsula) has a golf course, clubhouse, restaurant, and about 150 homes, mostly owned by retirees. The usual swimming pools, tennis courts, and 24-hour security are provided, a plus for those who like to leave their homes and travel. Don't expect to see mobile homes or trailers here; they're not permitted. Residents do their shopping in nearby Grove or in Langley.

A number of little towns sit on the shore of Grand Lake, the largest being Grove, with a population of 6,500. About twice that number who live nearby consider Grove to be their hometown as well. Without industry to provide employment, most folks either work in service jobs or are retired. An estimated 30 percent of the total population are retired—a very high percentage. Heavy shopping is available in Joplin (Missouri), a 45-minute drive, or 75 miles away in Tulsa. Grove is fortunate to have its own small hospital. Another hospital facility is located in Vinita, a half-hour drive away.

South Grand Lake Area Chamber of Commerce: 420 OK-28, Langley, OK 74350; (918) 782-3214; grandlakechamber.org.

Bartlesville

Not everyone is enamored of the idea of living in Ozark small towns, and many retirees rank hunting and fishing low on their must-have list. Bartlesville is our idea of Oklahoma small-city living, a place consistently given high marks for quality of life by national publications. Located in the gently rolling grasslands of northern Oklahoma, Bartlesville is just 45 minutes from Tulsa International Airport and a short drive to Ozark lake environs.

The city is small enough (pop. 36,000) that newcomers can make friends throughout the community, yet is sufficiently ample in size to afford amenities missing from more rustic sections of Oklahoma. In fact, the showcase entertainment events that Bartlesville stages each year would do honors to a much larger city. Its famous community center, designed by Frank Lloyd Wright, hosts the internationally acclaimed OK Mozart Festival. This occasion lasts 10 days in mid-June, hosting guest artists from all over the world. The entire populace is invited to participate.

The Bartlesville Community Center is not one of those public buildings that sits idle between big-time events. Numerous community-based groups stage art shows, performances, exhibitions, festivals, and parties. My wife and I attended a wedding dinner there—it was a fabulous evening! The 75-piece Bartlesville Symphony is recognized as one of the best in the country. The Bartlesville Civic Ballet offers a mixed palette of music and dance, and the Theater Guild presents year-round entertainment. This is hardly what one would expect to find in small-city Oklahoma!

Bartlesville's overall cost of living varies from 6 to 10 percent below the national average. Housing costs (in normal times) fall 15 percent below the national average, making quality living in nice neighborhoods affordable.

Bartlesville Chamber of Commerce: 201 SW Keeler Ave., Bartlesville, OK 74003; (918) 336-8708; bartlesville.com.

8

Texas: The B-i-i-g State

You don't have to be told that Texas is one enormous state. Give a Texan half a chance and he'll tell you *all* about it. Don't give him a chance and he'll tell you anyway. The truth is Texas is almost as large as Texans claim, and that's pretty darn big. It's bigger than any country in Europe except for Russia, and 10 times larger than many European countries. Not only is Texas spacious, but it boasts some of the prettiest scenery you can imagine, as well as some of the most desolate and boring imaginable. You have a choice. This wide range of climate, scenery, and elevation presents a broad menu of retirement options, something for almost every taste.

Texas's range of climates varies wildly. The subtropical southern tip of the state never sees snow and thinks any temperature below 60 degrees is downright chilly. At the other extreme the high plains of the northern Panhandle region can be one of the coldest conceivable places in the winter, yet it can also be one of the hottest places this side of Death Valley in the summer. The Gulf Coast is as humid as Florida, and west Texas is dry as the proverbial bone. You'll encounter large cities and small villages and medium-size places perfect for retirement. Landscapes vary from plains to deserts to seashores to mountains. Variety is the spice of Texas retirement choices!

ON THE TEXAS COAST

With more than 600 miles of the Texas coast facing the Gulf of Mexico, one would expect beachfront developments galore. The fact is that most of the Texas waterfront is uninhabited. Furthermore, almost all the mainland faces not the Gulf, but offshore islands and narrow peninsulas that effectively shut off the open Gulf waters. For the most part these islands are long and narrow, composed of sand dunes and unexplored beaches. Much of the actual coast is little changed from the days in the early 1800s when the pirate Jean Lafitte used the islands as a base.

Long stretches of these islands, as well as parts of the mainland, are designated as wildlife refuges. Whooping cranes and Kemp's Ridley sea turtles are making a comeback after what once seemed almost certain extinction. Turtle eggs from Mexico planted on the Padre Islands about 30 years ago are beginning to show wonderful results. Hatchlings from the experiment have grown into adult turtles and are returning to their beach of origin to nest in a protected environment. When the new batches of eggs hatch and the baby turtles start for the sea, they are captured and cared for in special pens until they're old enough to have a good chance for survival.

Texas Tax Profile

Sales tax: 6.25% to 8.25%; food, drugs exempt
State income tax: no
Property taxes: about 2.2%, varies with district, can be high
Social Security taxed: no
Pensions taxed: no
Inheritance tax: no
Gasoline tax: 20¢ per gallon

This is an angler's paradise. Both the channel and Gulf sides of the long islands teem with fish. From beaches and piers you can expect to catch redfish, speckled and sand trout, flounder, sheepshead, skipjack, croakers, and drum. (Local people assured us that fish actually *have* those names!) Group boats offer bay and deep-sea fishing, with charter cruisers available for individual or small-party sport. The offshore game includes tarpon, sailfish, kingfish, marlin, mackerel, pompano, ling cod, bonito, and red snapper, among others. By far fishing is the major sport attraction for retirees who have chosen the Texas Gulf Coast for their home.

Galveston

On the entire Texas coast, only one city actually faces the open Gulf: Galveston. With a population of almost 60,000, it occupies one of those long islands and is reached via a lengthy causeway across Galveston Bay. Except for this 32-mile stretch of beach—not all of which is developed—there is little residential construction on the Gulf, just a tiny portion around Corpus Christi and farther south on Padre Island.

Many years ago Galveston was one of our favorite weekend resorts; we visited as often as we could, swimming in the surf, crabbing off the jetties, and driving along the beach with the waves playing at our car wheels. Upon returning, after an interval of almost 30 years, we expected change. To our surprise we discovered that Galveston had changed very little compared with the enormous changes in nearby Houston.

This shouldn't have been so surprising, because the limited space on Galveston Island long ago filled to capacity with homes and businesses. The only new construction possible is replacing old buildings with new, something the local people are reluctant to permit. The old downtown section, instead of being replaced by slick, new, glass-and-steel monsters, has been preserved and restored to a charming, early 1900s state. Old brick and cast-iron fronts with wrought-iron balconies give the area a New Orleans French Quarter feeling. One street has been turned into a pedestrian mall, complete with restaurants, smart shops, and park benches for sunning and people watching.

True, along the beachfront some older homes and buildings slowly give way to newer, more profitable construction focused on tourist dollars. But change is slow in coming. Most of the town is still the same: old-fashioned and comparatively inexpensive. Surf anglers can try their luck almost anywhere along the beach. There are free municipal jetties and rock groin piers at regular intervals. If you fail to catch anything, markets sell the freshest catch found anywhere—right out of the Gulf into your frying pan.

People who don't live here think of Galveston as a weekend or vacation hot spot, a convention site, a place to go and blow off steam. However, there is a surprisingly intellectual air about Galveston. The University of Texas medical school is in the downtown, as well as a branch of Texas A&M and a community college.

Today the beach outside town is no longer deserted and wild, but is lined with often ugly, unpainted summer homes built on 15-foot stilts to avoid high waves during hurricane weather. (All along the Gulf Coast,

TEXAS GULF COAST WEATHER

| | IN DEGREES FAHRENHEIT | | | | ANNUAL | |
	Jan.	April	July	Oct.	RAIN	SNOW
Daily highs	59	73	87	78	40"	—
Daily lows	48	65	79	68		

from Key West to the tip of Texas, you find this stilt construction. Insurance companies insist on new buildings having stilts; it cuts their losses considerably.) Some owners successfully disguise the stilts by screening the lower portions of their houses, turning them into garages and storage spaces. This disguise makes the houses look like attractive two-story homes. But others don't bother, making stretches of beach look as if they had been invaded by spindly-legged monsters.

Galveston Chamber of Commerce: 2228 Mechanic St., Ste. 101, Galveston, TX 77550; (409) 763-5326; galvestoncchamber.com.

Corpus Christi

The only other major city on the Texas coast is Corpus Christi, a fast-growing metropolis of over 300,000 inhabitants. It's actually not on the Gulf, but on a large bay, sheltered from open water by 30-mile-long Mustang Island. A major deepwater port, Corpus is large enough to mask the tourist crowds in all but the most hectic times (college semester breaks). For the most part it looks like an ordinary, contemporary city—pleasant and unusually neat. It even has a modern, high-rise downtown.

A seawall runs along the downtown area, with stairs that lead to the water and a yacht basin. Palm-lined boulevards and cosmopolitan hotels and office buildings complete the picture. Unlike many parts of the coast, which sit exposed to the whims of hurricane-driven tides, Corpus Christi enjoys the relative protection of the seawall and its offshore islands. Actually, hurricanes aren't all that common; the last one hit here in August 1970.

The region enjoys what is described as a modified Mediterranean climate, which is a combination of a tropical and a dry climate. In the summer temperatures range from the lower 80s to the upper 90s. During the winter temperatures typically range from the 50s to the upper 60s.

Because the Corpus Christi area offers the only beach access along many miles of coastline, it has become quite popular as a resort. Not only are there beaches along the bay, but also there are 110 miles of sand and surf on the islands that shelter the mainland. Corpus has become almost as famous as Fort Lauderdale, Florida, for its assemblage of frolicking college students during semester break. As many as 100,000 tourists—an uncounted number of them college students—flock to Corpus Christi and Mustang Island to celebrate every spring.

Corpus Christi is a mecca for anglers from all parts of south Texas. The city is almost surrounded by miles of accessible shoreline and beaches, piers and jetties, and protected bay waters that serve as a year-round hatchery for fish. The most commonly targeted species are spotted sea trout, red drum, and flounder. Two nearby parks, Padre Island National Seashore and Mustang Island State Park, are popular and convenient places to visit for surf casting and small-boat fishing. For deep-sea action, be prepared for a 20- to 50-mile trip into the Gulf.

Because of the region's mild weather, golf is an activity to be enjoyed the entire year. You won't have to travel very far to play, either. Four public or semiprivate golf courses are located within the city limits.

The local business climate is healthier than the national economy. Government and service industries such as hotels are gaining jobs, while manufacturing is losing jobs. The local cost of living is very favorable, with housing costs way below the national average.

Medical services are excellent here, with 11 hospitals as well as the military medical facilities serving the local naval air station. (Numerous retired military families live here.) Educational and cultural needs are met by a two-year college as well as a branch of Texas A&M State University.

Corpus Christi Chamber of Commerce: 602 N. Staples St., #150, Corpus Christi, TX 78401; (361) 881-1800; unitedcorpuschristi chamber.com.

South Padre Island

From time to time travel writers describe the coast between Corpus Christi and the tip of Texas—where it touches the Mexican border—as Texas's Riviera. Nothing could be further from the truth; this is one of the most deserted and unpopulated places in the United States. But that's its charm. Except for one solitary highway approaching the shore, Texas maps show a blank: no roads, no towns, nothing but beach wilderness. A Texas Riviera it is not.

Pavement penetrates North Padre Island for 5 miles; from then on you're looking at untouched dunes and deserted beaches for 75 glorious miles. Picnicking, camping, and driving are permitted on the seashore, except for a 5-mile stretch reserved for pedestrians. Four-wheel-drive vehicles are almost essential here, but they can't be used anywhere except on the beach. (No dune-running, please.) No bridge connects North Padre Island with South Padre Island. When the island terminates, that's it. The wilderness area continues on this neighboring island for many more miles until a highway heads south to the town of South Padre Island.

Approximately the same latitude as Miami Beach, the southern tip of South Padre Island has always stirred the imagination of developers and promoters as the next tourist and retirement bonanza. So far their optimism has been greater than their successes. To be sure, a wealth of condos, hotels, and rental units compete for space with restaurants and souvenir shops, but the expected mass immigration just hasn't happened yet.

Although the town of South Padre Island looks like a city when first viewed from the causeway that crosses the Laguna Madre from Port Isabel, only about 3,000 residents live here year-round. That figure increases impressively during the season, because more than 3,000 condo units are rented out to tourists and visitors, and even in the off-season a good percentage of the rentals are occupied. Unlike nearby Lower Rio Grande Valley, the peak season is summer rather than winter. At the crescendo of the tourist crush, during spring semester break, an unbelievable number squeeze into town. Fortunately, miles and miles of camping on the beaches handle the overflow.

The developed portion of the island covers 6 miles of the southernmost tip, with the remaining 34 miles in deserted dunes and beaches inhabited by RVs, campers, and anglers. The beaches seem endless and gently sloping—great for swimming and surf fishing. By the way, driving the beach is permitted (four-wheel-drive vehicle recommended) as far as Mansfield Pass. This artificial ship channel created two islands out of one. Local people will argue that an artificial channel doesn't make two islands out of one, but in 1964 the State of Texas officially pronounced it to be two islands, so that settles that. All along the beach anglers camp and cast bait into the surf for some really great sport fishing.

The Laguna Madre—those bay waters between the mainland and South Padre Island—is said to be jumping with fish such as sea trout, flounder, sheepshead, redfish, and croakers. In the town of South Padre Island and also in Port Isabel, you can find charter fishing for sailfish, marlin, tarpon, kingfish, and pompano. For those who don't fish, there is plenty to do in the built-up, modern town. Several commercial RV parks accommodate

CORPUS CHRISTI/SOUTH PADRE ISLAND WEATHER

	IN DEGREES FAHRENHEIT				ANNUAL	
	Jan.	April	July	Oct.	RAIN	SNOW
Daily highs	69	82	90	82	28"	—
Daily lows	52	67	75	66		

visitors, and there is a county park, Isla Blanca, where you can park your rig while you beachcomb for lost pirate treasures.

Because South Padre Island is at the most southern latitude of anywhere in the continental United States except for the Florida Keys, you might expect it to have a Florida-like climate, particularly because it enjoys a lower summer humidity. But because the Gulf Stream, the secret to Miami Beach's climate, misses the Texas coast, summers are hotter here and winters cooler. This is more than compensated for by the calm and peaceful atmosphere (except during semester break).

Port Isabel

On the mainland across a short causeway is Port Isabel (pop. 5,500). Many retirees choose to live here and make the 2.6-mile drive across the causeway to enjoy South Padre Island without paying premium prices for property. Like all south Texas towns that attract "winter Texans," Port Isabel each year sees its population rise in proportion to the thermometer's fall in the colder sections of the United States and Canada. RV parks begin filling the last of October and stay packed until spring thaw lures the snowbirds back home. Because this is a year-round resort area, several large parks don't empty as they do in the winter resort areas. Those with self-contained rigs often prefer to boondock on the island beaches because they don't need electric or water hookups. Just north of town, and for miles up the coast, pristine beaches, all but deserted, invite campers and RV boondockers, offering good surf fishing and quiet times for reading or just sitting and contemplating whitecaps on the Gulf's blue waters.

In addition to the climate and beach location, local people point out the low crime rate, lack of rush-hour traffic, and serene living as reasons for retirement here. For traffic jams people need to travel elsewhere.

South Padre Island Chamber of Commerce: 610 Padre Blvd., South Padre Island, TX 78597; (956) 761-7056; spichamber.com.

THE RIO GRANDE VALLEY

After flowing 2,000 miles through Colorado, New Mexico, and Texas, the Rio Grande, the state's most famous river, finally empties into the Gulf of Mexico just below South Padre Island. Winter is why most folks investigate the lower stretches of the Rio Grande Valley. Midwestern farmers have known about it for years. When snow and ice gripped their fields with bitter winter cold, they arranged for someone to feed the cows and hogs, hooked a house trailer behind the old pickup, and headed for the Rio Grande for a winter of leisure and sunshine.

With seemingly endless sunshine, palm trees, and flowering tropical plants gracing city streets, the ambience is unmistakably subtropical. Balmy breezes from the Gulf of Mexico caress the countryside, perfuming the air with the scent of orange and grapefruit blossoms. Meanwhile, back on the farm, winds are whipping snowdrifts and dropping the chill factor to subzero records.

It is no surprise that the Rio Grande Valley is immensely popular with snowbirds in their motor homes and campers. Only here, these seasonal visitors call themselves "winter Texans." With good reason the early retirees referred to this region as the "poor man's Florida." Local people used to joke that "farmers would come here with a five-dollar bill and a pair of overalls and not change either one the whole winter." To this day the Rio Grande Valley is among the more inexpensive places to live in the United States. The overall cost of living is usually about 13 percent below national averages, and housing at one point was a whopping 22 percent below average! Although many thousands of retirees come to this part of Texas in RVs, spend the winter, and move on, please don't get the impression that's all there is to Rio Grande Valley relocation. Let's agree that a vagabond RV lifestyle isn't for everyone. Most retirees insist on the security of a permanent home with an extra bedroom for guests. They want a hometown and a neighborhood where they can interact with the community as permanent residents, not as wandering strangers. So the Rio Grande Valley is not simply about winter retirement. The

LOWER RIO GRANDE VALLEY WEATHER

	IN DEGREES FAHRENHEIT				ANNUAL	
	Jan.	April	July	Oct.	RAIN	SNOW
Daily highs	70	83	93	84	26"	—
Daily lows	51	67	76	66		

year-round population is growing at a healthy rate. According to the US government, a huge number of Social Security checks are being sent to this region.

Because of its hot summers, the lower Rio Grande Valley would seem unlikely to be a popular retirement location for year-round living. The coolest part of the evening or night rarely falls below 75 degrees. You can routinely expect high 90s during the day. Like anywhere in the country where folks trade cool summers for warm winters, air-conditioning comes to the rescue. You leave your air-conditioned home to enter your air-conditioned auto and drive to the air-conditioned mall for shopping. And so on. Golf or bicycling is done early in the morning, since they haven't invented a way to air-condition a golf course.

Two cities are among the more popular relocation places for out-of-state retirees: Harlingen and Mission.

Mission/Harlingen

"Home of Winter Texans" is one of the ways Mission advertises itself, but the town can't seem to make up its mind, because it also claims the title of "Home of the Grapefruit." It's said that Texas's first citrus orchard started here when mission priests planted trees in 1824 (hence the name Mission). The area is indeed famous for its groves of Texas Ruby Red grapefruit. In addition to the sweet aroma of citrus blossoms in December, residents enjoy a particularly colorful Christmas because of the abundance of poinsettias throughout town. The joyful theme of "Tropical Christmas" is celebrated with profuse displays of these colorful plants in public buildings, parks, and private homes.

The Mexican city of Reynosa sits across the river from Mission. A popular shopping place for valley residents, Reynosa offers much the same attractions as Matamoros. Some excellent restaurants here serve cuisine rarely found in US restaurants—wild game, for example. As is the case in all the border towns, be sure that you have proper documentation for smooth crossing.

About 30 miles from Brownsville, the town of Harlingen is somewhat smaller, with a population of around 65,000. Like the rest of the Rio Grande Valley, Harlingen sees its population climb dramatically during the winter. This city stands out because of its local beautification campaigns and recycling efforts. Thanks to the hard work of its citizens, Harlingen won the All-American City award from the National Civic League. A recent survey by *Money* magazine ranked the city the 20th-best place to live in the United States.

This is an area of truck farms, orange groves, and more of the prized Texas Ruby Red grapefruit. With a year-round growing season, one crop or another is ready to be harvested at any given time. Harlingen's appearance is similar to that of Mission, with palm trees, colorful bougainvillea, and poinsettias brightening the warm Christmas season.

Overall Harlingen is a nice place for winter retirement, even though it requires a longer drive for shopping in Mexico. The city also boasts four PGA championship golf courses, plus a 27-hole municipal course and several par-3 layouts.

In a comparison of lower Rio Grande Valley housing and year-round rentals, Harlingen turns out to be the most economical of the towns mentioned here. Housing costs are among the lowest in the country.

Mission Chamber of Commerce: 202 W. Tom Landry Rd., Mission, TX 78572; (956) 585-2727; missionchamber.com.

SOUTH-CENTRAL TEXAS

San Antonio

It's difficult to think of San Antonio (pop. 1,373,000) as being in the south-central part of Texas, because it looks like west Texas to me. Only 28 inches of rain per year falls on San Antonio, compared with Houston's 45 inches or Galveston's 52 inches. Dry range country with thorny bushes starts not far from the city limits. Certainly, from here westward, we are looking at the kind of country one expects from the western United States, with brush, cactus, and sandy soil. I figure, if the West doesn't start in San Antonio, then where?

When white settlers first came here, a Coahuilecan Indian village occupied the bank of a beautiful river, where present-day downtown San Antonio is located. The river, life-giving and crystal-clear, was shaded by large poplar trees (alamo trees in Spanish). The Coahuilecan called the river Yanaguana, or "refreshing waters." Unfortunately the river didn't retain its pristine state once white men began using it to dump sewage and trash.

Today this river is a symbol of San Antonio's fight against urban decay. The downtown river project is a textbook example of how to remedy central-core blight. The city completely transformed the river—which was little more than a weed-choked garbage dump not so many years ago—and turned it into an elegant shopping and restaurant area. Soaring cypress and cottonwood trees grace the riverbanks, shading shops, restaurants, and hotels. Tourists and residents alike enjoy strolls, boat rides, and nightlife along the riverbanks. The project has revitalized San Antonio's entire downtown. This author can only hope that the Coahuilecan would be proud of the way their river has returned to its "refreshing waters" status.

San Antonio's weather is a plus that retirees constantly brag about. Summers are warm, with highs typically in the low 90s. Yet summer evenings are delightful, with temperatures dropping into the high 60s or low 70s—just right for shirtsleeve evenings and for sleeping without the annoyance of air-conditioning. The humidity is moderate, so swamp coolers work efficiently, and refrigerated air-conditioning isn't absolutely necessary. In the winter temperatures rarely drop below 40 degrees at night, and afternoons are almost always in the mid-60s, even in the coldest months. For all practical purposes there is no winter. Snow? Almost none; every three or four years San Antonio catches enough snow to measure, although in 1985 it snowed 13 inches! Rain? Just enough to keep lawns and shrubbery green.

Previous editions of *Where to Retire* praised San Antonio for its low cost of living. At one time it was the lowest-ranking large city in the country. The area commonly ranks 10 percent below the national average cost of living. Real estate is traditionally inexpensive, and appears to be trending that way in 2019, with below-average prices on homes and rentals. Residential areas flourish on the fringes of the city, with new subdivisions popping

SOUTH-CENTRAL TEXAS WEATHER

	IN DEGREES FAHRENHEIT				ANNUAL	
	Jan.	April	July	Oct.	RAIN	SNOW
Daily highs	62	80	95	82	28"	0.7"
Daily lows	39	59	74	59		

up everywhere. Most newcomers prefer to live in the outer ring of newer subdivisions, near one of several large shopping centers. These areas have comfortably high levels of personal safety, as opposed to the inevitably higher crime rate found closer to a city's center.

Medical care here is awesome. The University of Texas Health Science Center is located here, with schools in medicine, dentistry, and nursing, and research programs in cancer, cardiology, and other problems endemic to the elderly. This is one of only six sites in the nation that is approved for patients to try experimental cancer drugs. The South Texas Medical Center, a 700-acre complex, encompasses eight major hospitals, clinics, laboratories, and a cancer research and therapy center. Also there's the world-renowned Burn Unit at Brooke Army Medical Center at Fort Sam Houston, which receives burn victims from all over the world.

Since its beginning as a Spanish presidio almost three centuries ago, San Antonio has maintained a military tradition. Four Air Force bases circle the city: Brooks, Kelly Field, Lackland, and Randolph, plus Fort Sam Houston, a US Army post. Brooks Air Force Base is famous in military circles for having one of the finest medical facilities in the country. This alone is an attraction for military retirees and would bring them here even if San Antonio weren't such a nice place to live. Our understanding is that almost 70,000 service personnel and families live in the San Antonio area and at least twice that many retirees. This may well be the largest population of military retirees in the country.

San Antonio Chamber of Commerce: 602 E. Commerce St., San Antonio, TX 78206; (210) 229-2100; sachamber.org.

Texas Hill Country

The picture most of us have of west Texas is flat or rolling stretches of eternity, sparsely covered with prairie grass or low brush that extends to meet the distant horizon. Sometimes wheat replaces grass; occasionally a lethargic steer can be seen munching cactus. Nothing moves except the up-and-down rocking of oil pumps or perhaps a distant windmill. Texas flatlands do indeed flow pretty much undisturbed by mountains, except for the extreme western portion, where the Rocky Mountains march southward through Big Bend National Park.

This bleak picture is more or less accurate, with a notable exception: the Texas Hill Country. A geological formation known as the Balcones Fault has pushed the land a thousand feet above the surrounding plains, creating a mini-mountain range. This not only changes the geography of Texas, but it also profoundly affects the state's climate. Moisture-laden breezes from the Gulf of Mexico can't easily lift over the Hill Country, so they release their rain on the southeastern part of the state and leave the western part arid. You can easily see this, for the great southwestern desert begins on the other side of the Texas Hill Country.

This special part of Texas is a wonderland of large, limestone-cropped hills not quite large enough to be called mountains, mostly wooded and intersected by half a dozen clear rivers, spring-fed creeks, and lakes. Perhaps 50 small, friendly towns and cities are scattered throughout the lightly populated countryside, many of them holding great retirement potential. Because much of the Texas Hill Country is rocky, with high concentrations of limestone and caliche, the soil isn't suitable for extensive farming operations. Most of the land is left in its natural state, covered by juniper thickets and wild cherry, gnarled oak, native pecan, and mountain laurel trees. Along the slow-moving rivers, magnificent cypress and elms shade the banks and provide cover for wild creatures. Cattle and sheep share the wilderness with white-tailed deer, turkey, javalina (wild pigs), and imported Russian boar.

The Texas Hill Country is as different from our usual view of Texas as can possibly be. Long considered one of the better living areas in the state, the region has been enjoying nationwide attention through retirement publications. One thing that makes it so different from other parts of west Texas is its year-round rainfall. The Hill Country receives more than 30 inches of rain each year, several times that of many Southwest locations. This accounts for its green, sometimes lush vegetation. The rain falls every month of the year, helping to keep things looking fresh.

Kerrville

Often considered the capital of the Hill Country, Kerrville is the largest city in the hills. With a population of almost 23,000, Kerrville is the Hill Country's major shopping destination; the county population is more than 45,000. Some residents find it convenient to commute to jobs in San Antonio, about 45 minutes away on I-10. Thus Kerrville fulfills two roles: as a place to retire and as a bedroom community.

Kerrville shares in the Hill Country's panoramic views and is further blessed by the Guadalupe River flowing softly through the heart of town. Kerrville's location at 1,600 to 1,800 feet above sea level, the highest in the Hill Country, contributes to its good climate, providing cooler summers and more clearly defined seasons than in Austin or San Antonio. Local people are happy with July and August days, always several degrees cooler than the lowland cities. One source of retirees stems from those summer residents who later decide to move to the Hill Country when embarking on new careers as retirees.

Because of the area's growing population of retirees (almost 30 percent of county residents are over age 65), many Kerrville social and business events focus on seniors. The local chamber of commerce is one of the few we've seen that really goes all out for retirees and deserves high praise. An interesting example is the annual Senior Job Opportunity Fair that the chamber of commerce conducts. One recent year local businessmen and more than 200 seniors joined in a half-day seminar to explore employment possibilities. Together they worked out ways to create a large number of part-time and permanent jobs for retirees and supplied valuable employees for area businesses.

Kerrville holds a reputation as the Hill County's preeminent art colony. The picturesque surroundings naturally encourage artistic development and act as a magnet to draw working artists, many of whom display works in local galleries and boutiques. One of Kerrville's galleries, the Cowboy Artists of America Museum, is the nation's only museum whose exhibitions are restricted to America's western and cowboy artists. Culture isn't restricted to the visual arts; there are also outdoor theater productions and a performing arts group that brings concerts and other live shows.

Another popular attraction is the annual Kerrville Folk Festival, held in late spring. Residents and tourists enjoy 18 days of musical events, which include original works performed by artists in an outdoor theater, evening concerts around campfires, and a songwriters' competition. The Scott Schreiner Municipal Golf Course underwent $1.8 million in renovations not too long ago and is open for public play. Within a 13-mile drive from Kerrville, you'll find four other public golf layouts.

Camp Verde, 11 miles south of Kerrville, was the eastern terminus of a camel route that stretched all the way to Yuma, Arizona. This was part of an experiment in overland transportation, an idea whose time never quite arrived.

Kerrville Chamber of Commerce: 1700 Sidney Baker, #100, Kerrville, TX 78028; (830) 896-1155; kerrvilletx.com.

Wimberley

Wimberley is another Hill Country town that has been basking in the warm light of national publicity as a new discovery in retirement destinations. Its photogenic qualities make wonderful color layouts for magazines. This is where the clear, cool waters of Cypress Creek join the warmer waters of the slow-moving Blanco River, a place where large trees and old homes of native stone hark back to another era. This was a popular getaway during World War II, when rich folks from Houston and San Antonio didn't have enough gasoline to travel to their second homes in the Blue Ridge Mountains. So they built summer homes—"camp houses" as they called them—in Wimberley. When they retired, these summer places became permanent homes, thus starting a retirement trend. As a result, Houston transplants are well represented here. It's properly called a "village," because it's never been incorporated, and folks hereabouts like it that way.

Wimberley is strategically located between Austin and San Antonio, not far off I-35. The population is a little more than 8,000 (including adjacent crossroads communities), large enough for essential services, but Wimberley enjoys a small-town atmosphere, with low crime and friendly neighbors. Because it's only 12 miles to San Marcos, that's where most heavy-duty shopping is done, or 45 miles (about an hour) away in Austin. San Marcos is also the nearest place to purchase bottles of wine or liquor; local restaurants do serve wines and cocktails by the drink.

Although there is no Greyhound bus service, the county sponsors a service called CARTS, which takes disabled and senior citizens to medical appointments and even into Austin for shopping and special medical needs. A volunteer ambulance group takes emergency cases to the hospital in nearby San Marcos.

Wimberley sits at an altitude of 1,100 feet—twice as high as Austin— and therefore enjoys slightly cooler summers and a few inches more rainfall, with an average of 300 days of sunshine a year. Snow is a rarity.

Homeowners choose among properties on rivers or hills, on city-size lots or acreages, with homes selling for slightly less than national averages. Nearby Woodcreek is a planned community with an 18-hole golf course (open to the public), tennis courts, clubhouse, and other amenities.

A summer community tradition is an outdoor movie theater (bring your own chairs). The Blanco River, lined with huge old cedars and oak trees, passes one edge of town and intersects with Cypress Creek on the other. The rivers are crossed by one-lane bridges, which residents refuse to widen because that would mean cutting some beautiful cypress trees. The Blanco River's turquoise waters are excellent for swimming, tubing, fishing, and canoeing.

Wimberley Chamber of Commerce: 14100 Ranch Rd. 12, Wimberly, TX 78676; (512) 847-2201; wimberley.org.

AUSTIN

The capital of Texas, Austin sits 80 miles north of San Antonio on I-35. Austin (pop. 850,000) is about half the size of San Antonio, but even more charming. Its downtown centers on an ornate state capitol and its extensive grounds.

Not as level as most Texas cities, Austin sits on the fringe of the Texas Hill Country and is surrounded by a circle of low hills. Unlike San Antonio, which developed from a haphazard grouping of trails converging at a river crossing, Austin began as a carefully planned city designed to be the state's capital. The downtown has an interesting mixture of modern and older buildings, creating an air of informality. In recent years the city has become somewhat of a tech hub, with companies from Silcon Valley setting up satellite campuses in the surrounding areas.

Austin combines a culturally rich environment enjoyed by a well-educated and creative population. Contributing to this is a large student population and many talented musicians and artists. The city is famous for the live music playing almost every evening near the city center, including some blues, rock, country, and jazz. Austin is also becoming widely known as a country music center, second only to Nashville. Everything from jazz to reggae can be heard in the clubs around the city, particularly on Sixth Street, the renovated 19th-century historic district. The city is also proud of its reputation as a cultural center in arts other than music. Museums, theaters, and art galleries are well attended throughout the city. A symphony, ballet, and lyric opera fill out the cultural offerings. Medical services are more than adequate, with a dozen hospitals and numerous specialists in attendance.

Austin is also known for its universities and colleges. The University of Texas at Austin is the largest in the state system. Adult education classes are widely available. In addition to the university, Austin Community College has seven campus sites in greater Austin. Each year it enrolls an amazing 30,000 students in its programs. The city provides outstanding recreational and outdoor activities. The city maintains over 27,000 acres of public land, which includes 191 parks and, throughout the city, a number of public facilities, including over 40 swimming pools, more than 100 tennis courts, and 6 golf courses. Almost 20 golf courses are open to the public, plus another 15 private clubs, the mild climate permitting fairway use throughout the year.

For health care the university's Breckinridge Hospital, with 248 beds, and Seton Medical Center, with 423 beds, are among the top 100 hospitals in the United States.

Highland Lakes

Austin's outdoor recreation centers on the Highland Lakes area. This has long been considered one of the better retirement areas in the state. With 150 miles of water wonderland, a series of lakes stair-step down toward Austin. The lakes area offers abundant fishing and boating as well as wonderful scenery for retirement living. Buchanan Dam (pop. 3,000) is a small resort and retirement community that grew at the construction site of the lake by the same name. This is the largest of the lakes and also the highest. The altitude is 1,025 feet (approximately 500 feet higher than Austin), high enough to be cooler in the summer but not so high as to have heavy winter snows. Roads circle the lake, giving access to retirement homes, RV parks, and rental properties.

Another retirement possibility, Marble Falls (pop. 6,500) takes its name from the dam that created this particular lake. Sheer bluffs of limestone, granite, and marble encompass the lake at this point. Hunting, fishing, and camping are popular activities. White-tailed deer and wild turkey are said to be plentiful. Nearby Granite Mountain is the source of the distinctive pink-and-red granite used to construct the state capitol in downtown Austin. Other lakes in the area are Travis, Austin Town Lake, Canyon Lake, and Lake Georgetown.

Austin Chamber of Commerce: 535 E. 5th St., Austin, TX 78701; (512) 478-9383; austinchamber.com.

Georgetown

Although sometimes billed as the "Gateway to the Hill Country," Georgetown is at an altitude of only 750 feet—not much higher than Austin—so it can't technically be considered Hill Country. That doesn't detract from its charm, however. Only 27 miles from Austin on the interstate, the community lies within easy commuting distance from the city. This makes it convenient for residents to enjoy Austin's amenities, such as shopping, college sports events, and continuing-education opportunities. Georgetown is home to Southwestern University, founded in 1840, one of the South's premier liberal arts institutions and the oldest university in the state.

With a population of a little more than 49,000, Georgetown is proud of its history and delights in its wealth of Victorian architecture. The centerpiece is old Courthouse Square, with antiques stores and boutiques. Residents take great care in the restoration and preservation of this historic town, with 180 homes and commercial structures designated as having historical significance. Some are now in use as restaurants and bed-and-breakfast inns.

In addition to the 14 parks maintained by the city, Lake Georgetown offers picnic, swimming, fishing, and boating areas maintained by the Corps of Engineers. Residents enjoy walking the 5-mile hiking and biking trail, which begins at Blue Hole Park and travels along the riverbank, ending in beautiful San Gabriel Park. Six public golf courses are located within 9 miles from Georgetown's civic center.

As an indication of faith in Georgetown's future as a retirement location, the Del Webb Corporation constructed one of its famous Sun City developments here. Sun City Georgetown is now the largest active-adult community in Texas.

The development's 5,300-acre planned community features two scenic creeks meandering through fields of Texas wildflowers and stands of native pecans, walnuts, and majestic live oaks. Interspersed are three 18-hole golf courses. Other recreational facilities include swimming pools, tennis courts, and extensive hiking and biking trails. Eventually 9,500 homes will be built, with 45 percent of the land remaining as open space and natural areas. At present the number of homes is 7,500.

Georgetown Chamber of Commerce: 1 Chamber Way, Georgetown, TX 78626; (512) 930-3535; georgetownchamber.org.

9

Western Mountains and Deserts

From New Mexico to eastern California, from the Mexican border to Colorado, the Southwest is a geological and scenic wonderland. Distinctive, dramatic arrangements of earth, water, and sky blend together, creating landscapes of unforgettable beauty. Sprawling, forest-covered plateaus scarred by awesome canyons contrast with endless expanses of sand, cactus, and sagebrush; great man-made lakes sparkle like aquamarine jewels in stark red settings. Badlands, with enormous monoliths, arches, and chiseled buttes, imitate mythical cities, while snowcapped peaks preside over all. This is what draws retirees to the Southwest (in addition to sometimes snow-free, warm winters).

It isn't all unspoiled natural paradise. Modern cosmopolitan cities have risen over the shards of ancient Indian ruins, and old ghost towns are disappearing. Huge retirement developments with golf courses and Olympic-size swimming pools (that look as if they've been magically transported from Florida) compete with small, comfortable localities of a few hundred homes. Anglo, Spanish, and Native American cultures blend to create a spicy potpourri of something distinctly southwestern.

The word "desert" incorrectly conjures images of Sahara-like dunes and desolate sweeps of barren land. True, North American deserts can be like that, but rarely are. Over eons plants and animals have adapted to living in dry country—even in places with 4 or 5 inches of rain per year. Trees and bushes survive on little water, flourishing miraculously in a dry desert or mountain environment. The first spring storm makes the desert bloom with an unforgettable explosion of colorful flowers and a profusion of green, all of which disappear when the plants withdraw into their water-conserving mode for the summer. Plants and animals have adapted quite nicely to living in the desert climate. The reptiles and mammals often survive hot summers by conserving body energy during the heat of the day and foraging and exercising in the cooler hours of the morning and evening. Therefore, it should come as no surprise that the famous species *Snowbirdus americanus* has also adapted to dry mountain and desert living. In the midst of the day, they conserve body energy in air-conditioned homes and autos. They forage in enclosed shopping malls and play golf in the cooler hours of the morning and evening. Midday is for naps.

NEVADA

Because a high mountain range, the Sierra Nevada, extends along the California-Nevada border, cutting off rain-bearing winds from the Pacific Ocean, Nevada is one of the driest of the southwestern states. Extensive deserts cover most of the land, with most residents choosing to live in or near one of Nevada's major towns. In fact, more than half of the population resides in the vicinity of either Las Vegas or Reno. Most rainfall occurs in the spring, at which time barren deserts become a riot of color with the blossoms of cactus, sagebrush, and wild iris.

Of all the western states, Nevada most represents the Old West to me. With new settlers arriving daily, Nevada feels like a frontier, a place of new beginnings. Something about Nevada's wide-open spaces stimulates a spirit of adventure and go-for-broke attitude. It's a place where string ties, boot-top jeans, and snakeskin boots feel like natural apparel, a place where you might even be tempted to wear a Stetson hat, confident you won't look downright foolish.

Perhaps a hangover from the era of frontier gambling and gold rushes, a definite atmosphere of excitement hovers over Nevada. Gambling casinos are everywhere, and slot machines are often strategically located in gasoline stations, drugstores, and supermarkets. Sometimes you'll even find them in restrooms—the gambling syndicates don't want to miss a bet. This is a state where lucky gamblers made a stake and lucky miners made fortunes. This is evident today: Prospecting for precious metals is a big hobby in Nevada, another way of gambling, and, believe me, it's addictive. It's like pulling the handle of a slot machine: There's always that chance that the next rock you crack open with a hammer will expose a gleaming streak of gold. (This writer has spent many a day in the desert smashing rocks with his prospector's hammer—but so far all he's found were smashed rocks.)

Yet there's plenty of room to grow, because 87 percent of the land is public property, owned by the US government. Newcomers aren't strangers here, because their neighbors come from all over North America, just as you do. In Nevada casinos you'll notice that blackjack dealers, bartenders, and security guards traditionally wear name tags that tell you where they came from, sometimes without names, just their hometowns.

Warning! Seriously, should you or your spouse have a tendency to go overboard on gambling and succumb to the irresistible fever of chance, then forget Nevada! Go around it, fly over it, or run in the opposite direction! The round-the-clock excitement is just too much for some folks. They end up throwing household money on the tables in increasing amounts in a desperate attempt to recoup their losses. The sad thing is that if they do hit a lucky streak and win a bundle, the fever won't let them quit. They'll play until they are broke again. It's eerie how some people can become as addicted to gambling as others become addicted to heroin or cocaine.

On the other hand, most retirees handle gambling quite well, taking advantage of all the freebies and bargains the clubs offer to lure customers inside. Some never put even a nickel in the machines but have a great time anyway. Prime rib dinners and buffet tables laden with salads, entrees, and desserts at almost giveaway prices are designed to lure gamblers into the casinos. Lounge entertainment with music, dancers, and comedians is often free, although you're encouraged to buy drinks. Some casinos even present free circus acts, complete with animals, high-wire performers, and clowns.

Nevada Tax Profile

Sales tax: 6.85% to 8.75%; food, drugs exempt
State income tax: no
Property taxes: approximately 1% of appraised value
Social Security taxed: no
Pensions taxed: no
Inheritance tax: no
Gasoline tax: 23.8¢ per gallon

However, all is not upbeat in Nevada. Up until 2009 this was the country's fastest-growing state, with an almost unbelievable population increase of 60 percent over a little more than a decade. Then suddenly, in 2009, the trend began to reverse itself. Nevada is now battling a 14 percent unemployment rate. Families who moved here for economic opportunity suddenly began to leave the state. For the first time in years, Nevada has been losing jobs, big time, and the population is decreasing as unemployed families return to their home states. Between 2009 and 2014 the state lost about 70,000 inhabitants! While this trend is expected to correct its direction, this does create opportunities for those who don't *have* to be employed during retirement.

Las Vegas

Not so long ago the city of Las Vegas (pop. 641,000 and growing) was a fascinating and glittering curiosity: a flashy carnival of gambling, cabaret shows, and gaudy casinos. This desert oasis was a powerful magnet for Los Angeles high rollers and fun-seekers from all over the world. People came, spent their money, and went home. Others stayed to take lucrative jobs offered in the growing metropolis. Las Vegas was the epitome of a modern western boomtown. Suddenly, in 2009, the boom came to a screeching halt.

The recession cut sharply into the region's gambling and resort revenue. Jobs were eliminated as businesses cut back. The tremendous construction industry faltered, leaving homes, new casinos, and residential developments half built. As of early 2010, the number of Las Vegas homes "underwater" (more money owed than the property's value) increased to a mind-blowing 80 percent. Forty-seven percent of all Las Vegas home sales in September 2010 were foreclosures! Of course, since then the situation has been gradually improving.

While a slumping economy is bad news for long-term residents, those who *don't* need to work during retirement might find an opportunity to move into a Las Vegas where home values have fallen dramatically since their peak in May 2006. Since 2010 the city has been making strong strides toward a healthy recovery. As of our last visit, in early 2018, things were looking up, with employment and home prices on the upswing.

Traditionally, Las Vegas casinos, restaurants, and hotels depend on part-time employees to supplement the regular staff. Retirees are ideal for these jobs, which usually pay much higher than just minimum wage. Workers who need full-time jobs don't usually bother with this type of employment. Casinos, restaurants, and hotels often give special consideration to hiring senior citizens. The percentage of older employees is impressive.

Well, except for the cocktail waitresses, that is, who tend to be young and buxom. This is clearly age discrimination, but then, you wouldn't care to run around scantily dressed, delivering drinks to a bunch of gamblers anyway, would you?

Many people who normally might choose Phoenix for retirement are trying Las Vegas instead. When asked why, they usually provide various reasons in addition to low property costs, casino entertainment, and gaming excitement. No state income tax and proximity to Southern California head the list. (Las Vegas is a 5.5-hour drive from Los Angeles, compared with Phoenix's 7.5 hours. Before long a privately financed super-train could link Las Vegas and Southern California, moving millions of visitors at a fantastic 250 miles per hour!) State taxes are low, because about 50 percent of all state tax revenues come from the resort, tourism, and casino industry. Because of this easy income, Nevada doesn't depend so much on corporate or personal income tax revenue, and its property taxes are among the lowest in the West.

All those questioned about their choice of Las Vegas as a retirement destination included weather in one form or another. Make no mistake, summers in Las Vegas are hot—yet those who retire here maintain that they love it that way. Of course, since they spend most of their time in air-conditioned casinos, what do they know?

Because of low humidity and the absence of freezing weather, mobile homes are quite practical. Inexpensive evaporative coolers do a fine job during the warm months, although nowadays just about everybody uses air-conditioning or heat pumps. Mobile-home parks present a wide choice of options, from inexpensive to super-luxurious. During the winter RV parks fill with fugitives from cold weather, who, as expected, depart for cooler climes come summer. But unlike in some desert cities, retirees in Las Vegas form a steady year-round population as opposed to the floating second-home group found around Lake Havasu.

LAS VEGAS WEATHER

	IN DEGREES FAHRENHEIT				ANNUAL	
	Jan.	April	July	Oct.	RAIN	SNOW
Daily highs	56	77	104	82	4"	1"
Daily lows	33	50	76	54		

Las Vegas has several active senior citizens' groups as well as the usual volunteer organizations like the Retired Senior Volunteer Program (RSVP). Local newspapers run regular features covering news and activities of interest to retirees. Because this is a city instead of a town, senior citizens' centers aren't small and intimate as you might expect in a smaller place, but they certainly offer a wide range of activities to keep active folks busy and happy. (And hopefully, keep them out of the casinos!)

Las Vegas Chamber of Commerce: 575 W. Symphony Park Ave., #100, Las Vegas, NV 89106; (702) 641-5822; lvchamber.com.

Henderson

Originally a housing camp for workers on the Hoover Dam back in the 1930s, the town faded away when the project was completed. Then Henderson staged a comeback during World War II. Because of an urgent need for magnesium for the war effort, the government constructed an enormous magnesium-processing plant in Henderson. In the process they built homes for thousands of employees. When the national emergency was over, the plant was closed. The town, all but abandoned, was offered for sale as "war surplus." At this point the State of Nevada decided to buy the town site and 13 square miles of desert land.

As recently as 35 years ago, the population was only 9,000—still not much more than a wide spot in the highway on the way between Las Vegas and Lake Mead, a place to top off your gas tank before pushing on into the desert. Over the past few years, Henderson has been one of the fastest-growing cities in the country, with a growth rate of 25 percent since the 2000 census. It now has more than 260,000 inhabitants! Henderson has pushed Reno out of its slot as Nevada's second-largest city.

Although considered part of the Las Vegas metropolitan area, Henderson is an incorporated city with its own city services, its own shopping malls, and its own distinct, glittering casinos. It has its own personality and identity, with a large collection of neighborhood developments, each different from the next. The vast majority of newcomers are from out of state. A large number of residents come here as retirees, of course, but don't get the impression that this is an old-folks retirement scene. The median age is only 36 years. That means the vast majority of Henderson's residents are working families with children. However, the residents here do not depend on gambling and tourism to the same extent as Las Vegas and Reno. Therefore, the community wasn't hit quite as hard by the 2009 economic downturn.

Henderson is situated on level desert terrain. There are at least 12 public golf courses and another half-dozen semiprivate or resort courses. Several upscale golf-course residential communities are in place, including one encompassing 560 acres that features a golf layout designed by Jack Nicklaus. Another gated golf-course community is building an ambitious 2,277 residential units on 600 acres. With the addition of Lake Las Vegas, Del Webb's Anthem, MacDonald Highlands, and the custom homes at Seven-Hills, custom and semicustom home availability has increased substantially.

Henderson Chamber of Commerce: 400 N. Green Valley Pkwy., 2nd Floor, Henderson, NV 89074; (954) 565-8951; hendersonchamber.com.

Pahrump

Las Vegas and Reno are examples of fast-growing cities in the desert, where the emphasis is on entertainment and big-city conveniences. Dozens of other smaller communities throughout the state offer somewhat the same attractions as Las Vegas and Reno, although on a much smaller scale. And some towns, like Pahrump (about 60 miles and a world away from Las Vegas), are popular just for being desert places to live in. Yes, Pahrump has a tiny casino or two, but you get the feeling gambling isn't the essential part of the scene. (This writer once hit a quarter jackpot there, and the bartender immediately hung an out-of-order sign on the machine!)

In a remarkably short time, Pahrump has grown from little more than a couple of taverns, a handful of stores, and some cotton farms into a small, widely scattered city. Complete with a senior citizens' center, a library, a medical facility, a bowling alley, and a community center (with swimming pool), Pahrump has moved from the category of crossroads settlement to a viable retirement community. In fact, about 40 percent of the residents are retired. The town has grown at an astounding 15 percent per year for the last several years to its present size of 36,000.

A caveat about desert lifestyles: They aren't for everyone. That's particularly true with a community such as Pahrump, where homes and businesses are scattered around with plenty of wide-open space. Some people love not having neighbors within a hundred yards; others get lonely for the sound of neighbors arguing and loud music.

Travelers are often unaware exactly when they've entered the town of Pahrump, because its inhabitants are scattered over an area of 25 square miles. A feeling of spaciousness is enhanced by homes sitting on large parcels, mostly 1 acre in size—sometimes 10 to 20 acres—and as far off the main highway as possible. Because desert land is inexpensive, folks see no need to crowd themselves. Pahrump also lacks a compact, traditional downtown center so characteristic of other communities its size. Like residential homes, businesses tend to locate on large pieces of land, spaced apart from competitors. There's never a problem finding a parking space here! Several small shopping centers host a collection of stores grouped about a supermarket but with plenty of open space between the complex and other businesses. Because everyone drives a car here, sidewalks are absent, adding to the rural feeling of western desert living.

The major drawing cards in this valley are sunshine, low-cost land, and friendly neighbors. Pahrump ranks just below Yuma, Arizona, as one of the places with the most sunny days in the United States. Its low humidity makes even the hottest days bearable, if not comfortable. Yet water supplies are not a problem because Pahrump sits on the third-largest underground supply of water in the United States.

Medical care in Pahrump and surrounding residential areas used to depend on local physicians or else a 40-mile drive to Las Vegas for hospitalization. Something new is the Desert View Hospital, with an emergency room and plans for a 70-bed hospital facility.

Pahrump Valley Chamber of Commerce: 1301 S. Hwy. 160, Floor 2, Pahrump, NV 89041; (775) 727-5800; pahrumchamber.com.

Reno

Although Las Vegas and Lake Tahoe try to be as formal and glitzy as possible, places like Reno tend to be more informal and relaxed. Except in some of the newer Reno hotel-casinos, neckties and cocktail dresses are rare; western wear—cowboy hats, ornate boots, and string ties—are seen about as frequently. This is changing in Reno to some extent, because the Las Vegas–Atlantic City gambling corporations are attempting to duplicate their luck in Reno. New elaborate and classy casinos seem to be appearing like magic, yet I suspect this will have little effect upon the Reno of the non-tourist resident.

Reno is an old town in a picturesque setting with a backdrop of snow-fringed peaks looming in the distance. This is a town proud of its rowdy gold- and silver-mining past—demonstrated by its deliberately preserved Old West atmosphere. Originally Reno's major business was supplying the booming mining camps that flourished nearby. About the time the mines played out, a new industry arose in the form of quickie divorces. Reno divorces were once considered the only practical way to go for an uncomplicated marriage dissolution. As other states liberalized their divorce laws, legalized gambling became the leading industry. Ironically, today Reno has become a quickie marriage center, with wedding chapels scattered around town like fast-food restaurants. Marriages in Reno outnumber divorces by a 10-to-1 ratio.

Like Las Vegas, Reno underwent an extended building boom, with the city expanding outward at a rapid pace. Including the adjoining city of Sparks, the population has climbed past the 230,000 mark, making Reno a good-size city. Yet folks here still cling to Reno's self-bestowed title of "The Biggest Little City in the World." While Las Vegas construction imitates Southern California modern style—stucco, sprawling ranch houses, and tile roofs—Reno prefers houses built of honest red brick. The older neighborhoods are of solidly built, no-nonsense homes—a settled, mature city—but the desert around the city is constantly sprouting subdivisions of modern designs.

Reno also offers 24-hour entertainment and glitter. But there's something hometown about the downtown gaming palaces that escapes Lake Tahoe, Las Vegas, and Laughlin. This hometown feeling was deliberately cultivated when gambling was legalized during the Great Depression. Harold Smith, the founder of Harold's Club, decided to go after local money instead of depending upon infrequent tourist visitors. He instituted the practice of giving free drinks and double odds on crap tables. He cashed paychecks without charge and tried to make people feel at home. Harold's Club also started the practice of preferential hiring of local people and senior citizens. Retirees work at everything from dealing blackjack to making change.

As a retirement center, Reno is one of our favorites. Because of the large number of retirees, the level of services for senior citizens is exceptionally high. Retiree clubs and organizations are unusually active. At least

RENO/CARSON CITY WEATHER

	IN DEGREES FAHRENHEIT				ANNUAL	
	Jan.	April	July	Oct.	RAIN	SNOW
Daily highs	45	63	91	70	7"	24"
Daily lows	20	29	48	31		

13 apartment complexes specialize in assisted housing for the elderly, physically handicapped, and disabled. In addition there are three large, full-service retirement facilities. Private programs such as Meals on Wheels and Care and Share are active, as are several run by the government. There's a senior citizens' employment service, and a senior citizens' law center provides free assistance with wills, Social Security, leases, and things of that nature.

The cost of living is not cheap, but compared with most urban locations, it is reasonable. The Reno area has all the facilities necessary for good retirement: hospitals, colleges, cultural events, and community services.

Some choose Reno retirement for excitement, but everyone likes its extraordinary climate. The 4,440-foot altitude and very low humidity keep the weather pleasant year-round despite its apparent low temperatures. For those who cannot stand hot summer weather, Reno is perfect. Expect to enjoy about 300 sunny days a year here. Even though July and August temperatures usually approach 90 degrees by midafternoon, you will sleep under an electric blanket every night; the thermometer always drops into the 40s. Even in the middle of winter, the high temperatures are about the same as the summer lows!

Reno is the medical center for the western Nevada–eastern California area. Washoe Medical Center has an important cardiac rehabilitation facility and is the hospital where other hospitals send patients when serious problems arise. St. Mary's and four other hospitals serve the Reno area.

Reno-Sparks Chamber of Commerce: 4495 Virginia St., Reno, NV 89501; (775) 337-3030; thechambernv.org.

Carson City

For those who feel Reno-Sparks is too much of a big city, an alternative is Carson City and its numerous developments of moderately-sized and priced homes. Even though it has a population of less than 60,000, Carson City is Nevada's state capital and the state's fifth-largest city. The downtown's antique buildings give you a feeling for Carson City's historic past and rich western heritage. The old state legislature building and the courthouse probably look much the same as they did back in the days when Mark Twain worked as a newswriter and typesetter in nearby Virginia City. Even though gambling is big business here, the city's expansion seems to be directed out into the desert rather than upward with tall casinos. Tourist demand for large, luxurious casinos hasn't hit Carson City as it has Reno and Las Vegas, so the funky old downtown changes slowly over the years. This is one of the city's charms: a comfortable, slow-paced, almost non-tourist atmosphere. Subdivisions fan away from the city with both upscale and moderate construction. All neighborhoods enjoy views of nearby mountains, and the clear air seems to magnify their majestic presence.

Carson City Chamber of Commerce: 1900 S. Carson St., Carson City, NV 89701; (775) 882-1565; carsoncitychamber.com.

NEW MEXICO

With its inventory of scenic deserts, lush forests, and high mountain ranges, New Mexico clearly lives up to its nickname: "Land of Enchantment." The state has an arid to partly dry climate not particularly different from other southwestern desert regions. A combination of low humidity, high altitude, and abundant sunshine makes this a pleasant and healthy place to live. Summer days are hot, but nights in New Mexico are always cool. Many localities commonly find that temperatures may register 90 degrees on a sunny day and then fall to 50 degrees in the evening. Although daytime air-conditioning may be popular in some areas, most of the time you'll sleep under blankets at night. Rainfall varies from 8 inches per year in some places to as much as 24 inches in some mountainous areas. Yearly snowfall ranges from almost nothing to as much as 300 inches near Ruidoso.

About a third of New Mexico's residents refer to themselves as Hispanic, as opposed to Latino or Mexican American, and are quite proud of their heritage. Why? Because they trace their family histories to the early *Spanish* explorers and colonists (rather than *Mexican*). These were the first white settlers in this area. The Hispanic founders were farming and building towns and villages in New Mexico a full generation before the first Pilgrim ever set foot on Plymouth Rock. So don't make the mistake of referring to New Mexican Hispanics as "Mexicans," or you'll run the risk of dirty looks and sarcastic remarks. After all, some Hispanic families were living here more than two centuries before Mexico was a nation! People often converse in a slightly archaic form of Spanish, the cultured manner of speaking that was in vogue in Spain back in the 16th and 17th centuries. Some words in their vocabulary

---

New Mexico Tax Profile

Sales tax: 5% to 8%; no exemptions

State income tax: 1.7% to 4.9%; can't deduct federal income tax

Income brackets: lowest, $5,500; highest, $16,000

Property taxes: about 7%

Social Security taxed: no

Pensions taxed: excludes up to $2,500, depending on income level

Inheritance tax: related to federal estate tax

Gasoline tax: 18.9¢ per gallon, plus possible local taxes

---

might not be understood in Mexico. They've been isolated so long that their customs, cuisine, and worldviews are different from those of Mexico. And although New Mexico shares a border with Mexico, no highways, railroads, or connections with Mexico exist along the desolate southern frontier other than one minor border crossing at Columbus. Historically, Mexican immigration (legal and illegal) tended to bypass New Mexico, moving into California, Arizona, or Texas instead.

Albuquerque

High in the desert, sitting on the east bank of the Rio Grande at an altitude of more than 5,000 feet, Albuquerque (pop. 554,000) is a fast-growing retirement area. Its combination of high altitude, dry air, and mild temperatures is exactly what many people look for in a place to live. The thermometer rarely hits 100 degrees and never sees zero. With afternoon humidity typically a low 30 percent, the weather seems even milder than charts might indicate. July's average highs of 90 degrees usually drop into the 60s at night.

Rainfall averages a scant 8 inches per year, which means lots of brilliant, sunny weather. And the best part is that the winter months of December and January are the sunniest. It's a two-season year, with about 11 inches of snow expected every winter. It doesn't stick around for long, though, because winter days usually hit 50 degrees by noon. Muggy days and long, drizzling spells are just about unknown in Albuquerque. Summers can become quite dry, however, causing the mighty Rio Grande to dwindle to a muddy trickle. Once when Will Rogers was giving a talk in Albuquerque, he cracked, "Why, you folks ought to be out there right now irrigating that river to keep it from blowing away!"

Albuquerque's biggest drawback is that its name is difficult to spell. The problem with spelling started in 1706 when the Spanish Duke of Alburquerque decided that this spot, where the old Camino Real crossed the Rio Grande, would be a great place to have a town named after himself. But when they put up the city limits sign, somebody left an *r* out of his name. And school kids have had trouble spelling it ever since. (Shouldn't there be at least one *k* somewhere in Albuquerque?)

The city has taken pains to preserve its historic sector. Preservation was possible partly because the coming of the railroad in 1880 moved the downtown away from the original plaza, thus sparing it from development. Today the area, now known as Old Town, offers fine restaurants and shops and maintains the historical flavor of the Old West. Venerable adobe buildings and museums cluster around the Duke of Albuquerque's village.

The downtown section is clean, modern, and prosperous looking. Everything seems polished and tastefully designed. A pedestrian mall completes the picture of a pleasant city center. The rest of the metropolitan area is also quite pleasant, with many homes designed in an adobe style and lots of huge shade trees in the older areas of town.

The metropolitan hub of New Mexico, Albuquerque is also a high-technology center of the Southwest. As such, it attracts people from all over the country to work and live there. The University of New Mexico (enrollment 25,000) accounts for much of the rich cultural offerings of

SOUTHERN NEW MEXICO WEATHER

	IN DEGREES FAHRENHEIT				ANNUAL	
	Jan.	April	July	Oct.	RAIN	SNOW
Daily highs	47	71	93	72	8"	11"
Daily lows	22	39	65	43		

the city. There's a full calendar of lectures, concerts, drama, and sporting events, as well as numerous classes of interest to senior citizens.

Skiing is great, with more than 11 facilities within striking distance. Sandia Peak (15 miles northeast of Albuquerque) has lifts that rise higher than 10,000 feet. Hunting, fishing, prospecting, and rock hunting are all great outdoor pastimes. But all outdoor activities don't require going into the wilderness. Horse-racing fans will find seven racetracks in New Mexico, with the season starting in January at the Downs at Albuquerque.

Rio Rancho

As an example of Albuquerque retirement away from the city's congestion, let's look at Rio Rancho, 20 minutes from downtown Albuquerque and 45 minutes from Santa Fe. It's a comfortable, safe area of mixed new and older homes. Originally started as a mail-order retirement scheme to sell parcels of worthless desert landscape, Rio Rancho targeted New Yorkers, and, as a result, many residents come from that state. Some folks were skeptical about the project, and they were surprised when it actually took off; it hasn't stopped since.

Today about 89,000 people live on ranch land that 35 years ago supported fewer than 200 cows. Rio Rancho ranks among the fastest-growing communities in the country. Although many retirees are buying new and older homes here, a recently opened Intel Company facility brought high-tech workers from all over the world. It's a great place for retirees, but it's basically a multigenerational community. With five public golf courses and a panorama of the Sandia Mountains in the distance, Rio Rancho is a blend of Southwest desert and middle-class suburb.

Albuquerque Chamber of Commerce: 115 Gold Ave. SW, Albuquerque, NM 87102; (505) 764-3700; abqchamber.com.

Roswell

The town came into being in the mid-1870s as a trail crossing, where springs provided cattle herds with water as they were being guided toward the railhead, on their way to be made into Kansas City T-bone steaks. In 1875 the famous Chisholm Trail was inaugurated when New Mexico rancher John South Chisholm sent 11,000 head over this route, stretching from Roswell to Las Cruces. (The trail approximately follows modern I-10.)

Later, around 1890, a vast artesian water supply was discovered beneath Roswell. To this day this underground reservoir provides irrigation water to sustain the thriving agricultural base that boosts the regional economy.

A bustling community of 100,000 inhabitants, Roswell is situated at an elevation of 3,700 feet, surrounded by ranch country and farms. It was once described by Will Rogers as "the prettiest little town in the West," and local residents insist that Roswell is still one of the prettiest, as well as one of the most welcoming little towns in the West. They may have a point, because this exceptionally neat and attractive town has the honor of twice being selected as an All-America City by the National Civic League. The local chamber of commerce claims that this is an accomplishment achieved by only a few other towns in America. The downtown historic district features wide streets, large trees, and some old homes and grounds, reviving memories of the early days, when the Chisholm Trail flourished.

Roswell's real estate market peaked along with other places around the nation and began its downward spiral a few years ago, but since it started from a very low price bracket in the first place, the downward spiral has been gentle compared with similar small cities in other parts of the country. The average home selling price in Roswell (at the time of writing) is 17 percent below the national average. Of course, it's difficult to tell how many foreclosures are involved in that average.

One of the region's claims to fame occurred in July 1947, when an unidentified flying object crashed near Roswell. According to reports, the bodies of several aliens were found near the wreckage of a "spaceship." In some versions of the incident, one or more of the aliens survived for a period of time. The government denies the claim, but local residents are convinced of the UFO's authenticity because of numerous local witnesses and subsequent contradictory government press releases. The quick transfers and disappearance of key witnesses further raised suspicions that an extraordinary event was being covered up. Every year Roswell keeps the interest up with a world-famous UFO Festival that attracts between 60,000 to 70,000 visitors. To learn more about this, you can visit Roswell's International UFO Museum and Research Center, which is open to the public.

Since the sun seems to shine just about every day in New Mexico, a wealth of outdoor activities is available to Roswell residents. You have your choice of fishing, boating, or sailing on one of several convenient lakes, or camping, hiking, or horseback riding in nearby state and national parks. In town there's swimming, golf, or tennis and, afterward, dinner at the country club. There's an 18-hole municipal golf course, 30 public tennis courts, and several fitness and health centers. A 5-mile bike/walking trail wanders from the zoo through the city's parks, and if the town is experiencing one of its two or three light snowfalls, the Roswell Mall provides indoor opportunities for keeping fit.

For a small city Roswell offers an unusual array of cultural happenings. For over 38 seasons the troupe of talented performers with Roswell Community Little Theater has staged excellent dramatic productions. The community's symphony orchestra has held performances for over 39 seasons.

Health care is above average as well. Roswell's 162-bed medical center was recently completed, having invested over $25 million in renovations. This entitles Eastern New Mexico Medical Center to claim to be the largest, most comprehensive, and technically advanced health care facility in southeast New Mexico.

Roswell Chamber of Commerce: 131 W. Second St., Roswell, NM 88202; (505) 623-5695; roswellnm.org.

Las Cruces

Las Cruces was once home to Apaches, early Spanish settlers, and Wild West characters such as Billy the Kid. Today, with its mild, high-desert climate and majestic views of soaring mountains and the Rio Grande Valley, Las Cruces is attracting the attention of city-folk easterners who are searching for relocation possibilities.

Combining the cultural influences of New Mexico State University and its 23,000 students, scientists and high-tech workers at nearby White Sands Missile Range, and the diversity of a border town, Las Cruces is a perfect candidate for a new hometown. Today it's the second-largest city in New Mexico, with about 100,000 inhabitants. It's only a 45-minute drive to El Paso via I-10, so you have the convenience of a nearby large city. Many people commute to El Paso, taking advantage of Las Cruces's low property taxes as well as New Mexico's overall low tax burden. Retirement is popular here but is far from a predominant trend.

Nestled in the fertile Mesilla Valley, which draws irrigation water from the Rio Grande, the city is in the center of a prosperous farming district, producing cotton, pecans, and chile peppers. Mountains rising to higher than 9,000 feet surround Las Cruces and block some of the northern winter winds to produce a mild, low-humidity winter. Summers are warm, similar to El Paso's, although the large amount of irrigation raises the summer humidity somewhat. The mild weather permits fishing year-round in nearby Elephant Butte and Caballo Reservoirs. Las Cruces has three public golf courses and a private country club. Eighteen lighted tennis courts make for comfortable play on hot summer evenings.

Las Cruces is an unusually attractive setting with a distinctive, Old West pueblo character. Apparently city planners try to channel architecture toward the pueblo style of Santa Fe, with soft, earthy tones. Yet Las Cruces has avoided a regimented, stiff adherence to this style, permitting pastels and bright colors to break up the muted earth tones. We looked at a display of exceptionally imaginative homes of elegant, Old West style. They were set on landscaped, low-maintenance lots that incorporated natural shrubs and cactus. We guessed their value at $100,000 more than the asking price.

New Mexico State University brings the community together by inviting the public to join in cultural and entertainment activities, such as drama presentations and orchestral concerts. Seniors are welcome to take regular courses or occasional classes at the weekend college, a program just for seniors offering scholarly mini-courses on subjects ranging from local history to opera appreciation.

Medical care here is exceptional, with one of the best-equipped hospitals in the state, the 286-bed Memorial Medical Center. Las Cruces is the medical hub of a five-county region. Even larger medical facilities in nearby El Paso are just a short drive down the interstate.

Las Cruces Chamber of Commerce: 150 E. Lohman Ave., Las Cruces, NM 88001; (505) 524-1968; lascruces.org.

LAS CRUCES/EL PASO WEATHER

	IN DEGREES FAHRENHEIT				ANNUAL	
	Jan.	April	July	Oct.	RAIN	SNOW
Daily highs	58	79	95	78	8"	6"
Daily lows	31	49	70	49		

Ruidoso

Ruidoso bursts upon travelers as an absolute surprise; it's a setting you don't expect to find in New Mexico. Almost magically the landscape changes from dry desert, covered with brush and patches of carrizo grass, into a gorgeous, winding river canyon graced with majestic evergreens perfuming the breezes. Cool mountain air and lush vegetation make Californians imagine they're at Lake Tahoe. Easterners might recall Maine forests or Canadian mountain vistas.

Of course, this isn't news to west Texans; they knew about the Ruidoso Upper Canyon for decades as an excellent place to escape blazing Texas summers. The crystal-clear river cascading through the tree-shaded canyon made for a wonderful escape and family fun. Summer cabins sprang up among the large ponderosa pines and along the small river. By the way, *ruidoso* is Spanish for "noisy," an apt description of the sound of the river's cascading water.

With the opening of the racetrack at Ruidoso Downs in 1947, people started thinking of Ruidoso as a resort instead of merely a summertime mountain getaway. More than 35 years ago, the Mescalero Apache tribe, with the help of a Texas oilman, developed a ski run high up on Apache Peak, a part of the Mescalero Apache Reservation. They called it Ski Apache and established Ruidoso's second career as a winter resort. The 12,000-foot ski run immediately attracted the attention of ski buffs from all over the country. This is the southernmost place to ski in the Southwest, and because of its exceptionally high location, skiing lasts long after many other areas have closed down, providing some of the best warm-weather powder skiing in the world. A popular skiing magazine rates Ruidoso as one of the 10 best ski towns in which to live.

Skiing did more than simply bring tourists and increase employment opportunities; it brought visitors and allowed them to observe the area under winter conditions as well as summer. Visitors were pleasantly surprised to discover relatively mild winters here and to learn that fall and spring are delightful seasons as well. This launched Ruidoso upon yet another career as a center for year-round residence and retirement.

Summer cabins were enlarged, and larger homes started springing up for both retirees and working families. This continuing growth provides employment for even more new residents and encourages more businesses to open. Today Ruidoso has blossomed into a pleasant town of about 9,200 inhabitants and is still growing, with the county population over 13,000. The area supports many more shops, stores, restaurants, and businesses of all kinds than you might expect of a town this size. Because Ruidoso draws visitors and tourists all year long, small businesses flourish, and you'll find an astonishing selection of excellent restaurants serving almost any kind of cuisine imaginable, from French to Chinese, and from prime rib to Indian squaw bread. According to local business owners, the only slow time is in April, when they manage to squeeze in their vacation time. April, by the way, is an excellent time of the year to investigate Ruidoso as a retirement destination. You'll not only find less traffic and off-season rates for motels, but you'll also experience Ruidoso's spring, one of its best seasons.

The tall forest makes a proper setting for Ruidoso real estate, with homes shaded by a thick green canopy. Elegant homes can sit next door to small cottages, log cabins, and, occasionally, mobile homes. The higher end of the housing scale, at the northern edge of town, is also at the highest elevation.

The local hospital is the Lincoln County Medical Center, with 25 beds. The nearest larger facility is at Alamagordo, a 35-mile drive from Ruidoso.

Ruidoso Valley Chamber of Commerce: 720 Sudderth Dr., Ruidoso, NM 88345; (505) 257-7395; ruidosonow.com.

Santa Fe

Fifty-nine miles northeast of Albuquerque, the town of Santa Fe sits like an antique jewel in the picturesque Sangre de Cristo Mountains, perched at an altitude of 7,000 feet. A sense of history pervades the streets and byways of this oldest capital city in the United States. Settled in the year 1610, Santa Fe was a bustling town and commercial center 10 years before the Pilgrims set foot on Plymouth Rock! Santa Fe has been a capital city for more than 375 years. Today's population is about 74,000.

Here you'll find the oldest private house in the United States and the oldest public building in the country, the Palace of the Governors. This building became General Kearney's headquarters in 1846, when his troops captured Santa Fe during the Mexican War. Incidentally, this was the first foreign capital ever captured by US armed forces.

Santa Fe is a town steeped in history and culture, and its residents work hard at keeping it that way. Strict building codes insist that all new construction be of adobe or adobe-looking material; all exteriors must be in earth tones. This preserves the distinctive Spanish pueblo style for which Santa Fe is famous. Occasionally one sees a home that was built in the days before zoning codes, and the blue or white building sticks out like the proverbial sore thumb. At first the mandatory shades of sand, brown, and tan can seem a bit somber, but after a while one grows to appreciate the way they complement the setting.

Along with tourism and retirement, artistic endeavors are one of Santa Fe's prime industries. Art affects the everyday lives of Santa Fe residents, with hundreds of painters, artists, and craftspeople doing their thing and almost 200 galleries exhibiting their treasures. The old plaza in the heart of the city is usually lined with street artisans displaying jewelry, paintings, leather goods, and all kinds of quality artwork. Local Native Americans bring intricate silver and turquoise jewelry to sell in the plaza. A highly regarded opera company performs in a unique outdoor theater. Fortunately, Santa Fe's weather seldom interferes with the performances, because only about 15 inches of rain falls each year. A year-round calendar of events includes concerts by the Orchestra of Santa Fe, the Chorus of Santa Fe, the Desert Chorale, and the Santa Fe Symphony, as well as Native American festivals and celebrations. Numerous theater and drama presentations come from the New Mexico Repertory Theatre, the British American Theatre Institute, the Armory for the Arts, the Santuario de Guadalupe, the Community Theatre, and the Greer Garson Theater. There's even a rodeo every summer. Of course, the thoroughbreds race at famous Santa Fe Downs from May to Labor Day.

"When I get up in the morning, I know there's going to be sun," said a man who retired in Santa Fe after living most of his life in northern Illinois. "It makes a big difference in my life." Santa Fe is almost tied with Albuquerque for sunshine; almost 300 days a year are guaranteed to be at least partly sunny. Remember that the altitude here is 7,000 feet, so expect a four-season climate. Santa Fe gets more rain than Albuquerque, though, and three times as much snow—about 33 inches annually. This keeps Santa Fe greener. Be prepared to wear a sweater on summer evenings; the temperature occasionally drops to below 50 degrees at night.

Folks who can afford to buy a second house anywhere they like tend to buy one here. That should tell us something about Santa Fe's quality. The problem is that Santa Fe has such a reputation as a retirement and artist center that outsiders have bid up real estate to an unusual level. "It's getting so we natives can't afford to live here anymore," lamented one hometown resident. Yet housing is curiously mixed in price. Generally it's more expensive than Albuquerque, particularly for nicer housing. But there are also many inexpensive places. Several high-end developments are under way, at least one with its own private golf course. A couple of attractive, full-care retirement residences are located in Santa Fe, one without any endowment or entrance fees—but there could be a waiting list.

An active senior citizens' program, Open Hands, offers services and an opportunity to volunteer for satisfying and worthwhile community projects. Hospital care is provided by the Christus St. Vincent Medical Center, a 180-bed facility.

Santa Fe Chamber of Commerce: 1644 St. Michaels Dr., Santa Fe, NM 87505; (505) 988-3279; santafechamber.com.

Silver City

For a thousand years the mountains around Silver City have been a source of valuable minerals. Early Native Americans mined outcrops of copper to fashion ornaments and spear points. In the 1790s Spanish miners worked the copper deposits, loading the ore on the backs of burros and hauling it south into Chihuahua for smelting. But Silver City itself wasn't established until returning California forty-niners discovered silver ore a few miles north of the present town site. This kicked off a typical mining-boom scenario, with a tent city being replaced by substantial brick buildings and optimistic expansion.

Western-history buffs might be interested to know that Silver City is where the famous outlaw Billy the Kid grew up, went to school, committed his first crime, was arrested for the first time, and made his first of several escapes from jail. Billy the Kid's first arrest was for robbing clothes from a Chinese laundry when he was 15. Had to start somewhere.

Silver City's 6,000-foot altitude provides cool, dry weather and beautiful, forested mountain vistas. With a population of a little over 12,000, the city is large enough to supply most services but still small enough to escape big-city crowding, crime, and pollution.

The town's architectural style clearly reflects the time of its development. The downtown is rich with the Victorian brick buildings so popular in western mining towns during the last century. In fact, Silver City's historic district boasts the largest concentration of Victorian homes in southern New Mexico.

The presence of Western New Mexico University takes Silver City out of the category of an ordinary mining town and is responsible in part for inspiring a fast-growing artist colony. An astonishing number of galleries, studios, and workshops are open to art lovers, either regularly or by invitation.

Outdoor enthusiasts will find much to do within a short distance from Silver City, which is surrounded by the 3.3-million-acre Gila National Forest. Five fishing lakes offer good catches of bass and crappie, and there are rivers and streams with trout. Five tennis courts and an 18-hole golf course augment the 10 parks and two swimming pools in Silver City.

Affordable real estate is one of the attractions that draws retirees here. In nearby Tyrone the Phelps-Dodge company decided to move some of its company housing by marketing the workers' homes as retirement locations. Homes were refurbished and sold starting at $40,000. Those days are long gone, of course. In 2008, just before the real estate crash, Silver City's median residence price was about $140,000. At the time of writing, the estimated median home value is around $123,000.

The Gila Medical Center is the only hospital within about a 50-mile radius. The facility has 68 beds and has a favorable rating among local residents.

Silver City Chamber of Commerce: P.O. Box 1028, Silver City, NM 88062; (800) 548-9378; silvercity.org.

Taos

Farther up the road from Santa Fe, the picturesque town of Taos sits in the heart of the Sangre de Cristo Mountains. A bustling village, quiet retreat, art colony, ski resort—these are but a few of Taos's many faces. Its 55 art galleries and numerous art programs hint at the large number of artists in residence. Famous for its picturesque adobes, narrow, winding streets, and the ancient Pueblo village on the town's outskirts, Taos provides awesome inspiration for the artistic set.

The population is very small (about 5,600), so resident artists and other inhabitants tend to form a closely integrated group. The successful and well-known mingle with the unsuccessful and rank amateurs much more freely than they would in large-scale Santa Fe. One person told us, "We permanent residents of Taos achieve social equality that you seldom find elsewhere. Some very wealthy, successful people here prefer to drive rusty pickups instead of Mercedes and wear blue jeans and boots instead of city dress. I've attended cocktail parties where starving artists, multimillionaires, and local businesspeople mix as if they were at class reunions."

Bear in mind that Taos is a tourist destination. Skiing at nearby Ski Valley draws snow enthusiasts beginning at Thanksgiving. Ski Valley averages 321 inches of snow each year, so the season lasts into the middle of April. Then, just when ski traffic thins out, camera-toting tourists take up the slack. They come to photograph the ancient adobes in Taos and, of course, the very ancient Pueblo Indian village—one of the most-photographed sites in the West. The main complaint you'll hear from permanent residents is the amount of tourist traffic, and the business community's dependence upon tourism for survival.

Real estate falls into two categories here: the surprisingly expensive (especially for the old adobes) or average to substandard. Because Taos is a popular place and because there are so few properties on the market, buyers can often get their asking prices, especially when selling to seasonal residents. Part-time residents are divided between wealthy folks who can afford a summer getaway residence, or perhaps a winter ski home, and those who come to rent a condo for a few months to experience the magic of the area.

Hospital care is provided by Holy Cross Hospital, a small general medical facility with 46 beds.

Taos Chamber of Commerce: 1139 Paseo Del Pueblo Sur, Taos, NM 87571; (575) 751-8800; taoschamber.org.

UTAH

Utah is the fourth-fastest-growing state in the nation, with an increase in population of more than 30 percent over the last 25 years. Part of this growth can be attributed to Utah's having one of the country's largest concentrations of computer software firms and a growing biomedical industry. As a result, the state attracts young working people who come here for jobs. According to the latest census, Utah has the nation's youngest population as well as the highest birthrate of any state.

Few states can compete with Utah when it comes to sheer beauty of spectacular landscapes. Visitors are overwhelmed by sights of fantastic canyons carved in brilliant red sandstone, lush mountain forests teeming with wildlife, and sapphire lakes brimming with trout. For contrast Utah also displays enormous stretches of uninhabitable desert, sagebrush, and barren alkaline flats. Utah's best-known landmark, of course, is the Great Salt Lake. Actually an inland sea, the water is so salty that few ocean fish could survive in it. In the midst of a desert, hundreds of miles from the Pacific Ocean, it seems strange to see swarms of seagulls and pelicans. Most of Utah's gorgeous and scenic panoramas are places that lack drinkable water, so few people choose to dwell there. Other than scattered farms and an occasional village, most people live in areas with more abundant rainfall or near facilities for irrigation.

For that reason about three-quarters of the population is concentrated around Salt Lake City and other medium- to small-size cities in the north, and around Cedar City and St. George in the south. The rest of the state consists of small towns and villages, where few outsiders settle. These smaller communities would require in-depth research and understanding before considering relocating there, because of Utah's unique social structure. In small rural Utah towns, everyday living is greatly influenced by religion—much more so than in southern Bible Belt communities. In many, if not most, small towns, you'll find only one church: the Church of Jesus Christ of Latter-Day Saints (also known as the LDS, or Mormons). Occasionally there will be an alternative, perhaps a Baptist or Catholic denomination in town, but in all cases non-Mormons will be a tiny minority.

Other religious denominations do thrive in the larger cities, which is why most non-Mormons seek out places like Salt Lake City, Cedar City, and St. George—places where the population is mixed. The larger the town or city, the larger the percentage of residents who are not LDS members. For example, the last time we inquired, there were only two Jewish rabbis in the state, both living in Salt Lake City, and the only synagogue outside Salt Lake City was in Ogden.

Mormons are known to be warm and loving, showing deep concern for each other's welfare. However, to members of other faiths, Mormons often appear to be polite but somewhat aloof and distant. Even some converted

Mormons complain of discrimination because they were not born into the church. As an indication of how religion permeates Utah life, around 90 percent of the state's politicians are active members of the Mormon Church.

Having said this, and emphasizing that this is strictly my opinion, I can also say that many non-Mormons tell me that they haven't found religion much of an obstacle. "It's only a problem if you let it be one," said one newcomer to St. George. "We've had no trouble making friends, and our neighbors are quite gracious."

One member of the church, whom we interviewed, disputed the existence of discrimination and explained it this way: "What many folks don't understand is that being a member of our church isn't just a Sunday thing. Our everyday lives often involve the church in one way or another. So when Mormon families in a neighborhood all get on a bus to go to a church activity or a picnic, the uninvited neighbors might feel left out. We don't mean to snub our neighbors. It just isn't appropriate that they join in our church affairs any more than if we would participate in their church activities."

In this chapter we highlight three locations—places popular with out-of-state retirees—places where the populations are somewhat heterogeneous: Salt Lake City, St. George, and Cedar City.

Utah Tax Profile

Sales tax: 4.75% to 6.23%; drugs exempt
State income tax: flat rate of 5%; federal income tax 50% deductible
Property taxes: average 1.38% based on 100% of assessed value
Social Security taxed: half of benefits taxable for higher incomes
Pensions taxed: excludes up to $7,500
Inheritance tax: no
Gasoline tax: 30¢ per gallon

Salt Lake City

In 1847 the church leader Brigham Young led a band of Mormons westward across the plains and mountains in search of freedom from religious persecution. When the travelers looked down from mountains overlooking the valley of the Great Salt Lake, Brigham Young announced that this was the Promised Land where they would live. They set to work tilling the soil that same day and began transforming the dry and desolate land into beautiful, well-planned Salt Lake City.

Located at an altitude of 4,400 feet, Salt Lake City is the capital of Utah and one of the largest cities in the Rocky Mountain region, with a population of almost 200,000. The city sits in a valley bordered to the north and east by mountains, near the southeastern shore of the Great Salt Lake. This is also the world capital of the Church of Jesus Christ of Latter-Day Saints. Surrounded by beautifully landscaped grounds, the chief buildings of the Mormon Church anchor the city center. Other buildings of note in the city are those of the University of Utah, the state capitol, the city and county building, the museum, the exposition buildings, and two former residences of Brigham Young. In Temple Square the centerpiece is the famous Sea Gull Monument, a memorial to the flocks of seagulls that saved the crops of the early settlers in the Salt Lake Valley during the summer of 1848.

At first the city's growth depended on the inflow of Mormon converts from Europe and America. Later, industrial and business expansion attracted many gentiles, or non-Mormons, who now make up almost half the population. This makes for a more cosmopolitan community than is found in most areas of Utah, where non-Mormons are pretty much the minority.

Recreation and cultural opportunities abound here. The region's low humidity and abundance of sunshine makes golf a year-round sport, with eight courses open for play. Hiking and bicycling in the nearby mountains are popular recreational activities. Salt Lake City is the home base of the Utah (formerly New Orleans) Jazz professional NBA basketball team. Skiing in nearby Park City, home of the US Ski and Snowboard Team and other winter sports, draws snow enthusiasts in the winter. Utah's snow is unusually dry powder—ski areas receive as much as 400 inches a year—and it is considered by many skiers to be the world's best. Seven ski resorts are less than an hour's drive from Salt Lake City.

Part of Salt Lake City's rich quality of life derives from its enthusiastic support of the arts. Residents have daily choices of performances, exhibits, and events for entertainment or enrichment. A world-class symphony orchestra, the Utah Opera Company, and one of the country's largest ballet companies attract professionals from around the world. Five major universities are within an hour's drive from Salt Lake City, as are several community colleges.

The overall cost of living in Salt Lake City is slightly above average, alleviated in part by exceptionally low utility costs. A robust, diverse economy

SALT LAKE CITY WEATHER					
IN DEGREES FAHRENHEIT				**ANNUAL**	
Jan.	April	July	Oct.	**RAIN**	**SNOW**
Daily highs 37	61	93	67	15"	58"
Daily lows 20	37	62	39		

attracts newcomers and has created an increase in real estate prices over the past few years. Salt Lake City, once below the national cost of living, now ranks about average among other similar-size cities. Some of the major employers here are Intel, Gateway, Myriad Genetics, and the University of Utah.

Seven major medical facilities serve this area, making it one of the premier places for health care in the West. Altogether Salt Lake City has 13 hospitals, and Provo, about 40 miles to the south, is currently served by two excellent hospitals.

Salt Lake City Chamber of Commerce: 175 E. University Blvd., #600, Salt Lake City, UT 84111; (801) 364-3631; slchamber.org.

St. George

The largest city in southern Utah, St. George works hard to attract retirees and has acquired a strong reputation as a retirement community. It consistently receives top recommendations from national magazines and retirement guides as a place to retire, often ranking number one in the West.

Because of St. George's relatively mild winters, boosters like to refer to the area as Utah's "Dixie." The truth is the designation is derived partly from the town's southernmost location in the state, but more from the early-day cotton fields that brought prosperity to the pioneer community. However, it is also true that a lower elevation—only 2,840 feet—blesses St. George with warmer winters than its nearby retirement counterpart, Cedar City. The tradeoff is hotter summer temperatures, but evenings are always cool enough to sleep under blankets.

Conveniently located on I-15, a little more than 2 hours' drive from Las Vegas, St. George isn't as isolated as it might seem. The city's population of about 72,000 is large enough to provide adequate services, and the community stands on its own commercially.

St. George's picturesque surroundings are some of the more dramatic of any retirement destination described in this book. Stark red cliffs loom over the town, sometimes rising vertically from residents' backyards. You get the feeling that you're living on the set of a Western movie. In its own way St. George is as spectacular as Sedona, Arizona, although on a smaller scale.

According to locals, St. George has more golf course facilities per capita than any place this side of Palm Springs. I'm not sure that's true, but golfers do enjoy 12 golf courses, all but two of them public—open year-round—all within a 15-minute drive from town. There's even a 1,800-square-foot indoor golf facility to help you find out why your slice is so messed up.

This combination of beauty, relatively mild winters, and great golfing draws more retirees from outside Utah than do other Utah communities. This is important for non-Mormons, because outsiders dilute the religious majority, and newcomers won't be so likely to feel like outsiders. In fact, St. George has 24 community churches besides those of the Mormon faith. These range from Roman Catholic to Jehovah's Witnesses, as well as Baptist, Episcopal, Lutheran, Presbyterian, Methodist, and several we've never heard of. Of course, the majority of residents are Mormons, but it looks as if there's plenty of room for others.

Settled in 1861 by 309 Mormon families, St. George was transformed from a forbidding alkali flat into a livable town in the space of a decade. Some of the original homes survive and are treated with reverence by local residents. Included is the house where Brigham Young spent a few of his last years. Streets are wide and tree lined, and homes are as neat and orderly as Brigham Young would have wished.

As the health care center for the surrounding area, St. George is noted for providing quality care, with top facilities and at lower costs than the national average. The 130-bed Dixie Medical Center is a progressive, regional referral facility that serves the health care needs of nearly 100,000 in a tri-state area of southern Utah, southern Nevada, and northeastern Arizona.

St. George Chamber of Commerce: 136 N. 100 E., St. George, UT 84770; (435) 628-1658; stgeorgechamber.com.

ST. GEORGE/CEDAR CITY WEATHER

	IN DEGREES FAHRENHEIT				ANNUAL	
	Jan.	April	July	Oct.	RAIN	SNOW
Daily highs	54	76	101	80	11"	5"
Daily lows	26	44	66	45		

Cedar City

Many communities we've visited in the state of Utah present a pleasant, old-fashioned look—neat as a starched shirt, as the saying goes. Mormon Church members claim that the religious commitments of church followers are responsible for this, as well as for the state's exceptionally low crime rate. This could be the subject of debate, but the fact remains that tranquility and safety are the norm in most Utah communities. Cedar City is typical of Utah's small cities and always ranks low in crime, according to FBI statistics.

This small university town of 30,000 offers many advantages for retirement living. Sheltered in the foothills just a few miles from some of the most spectacular landscapes in the world, Cedar City combines the cultural atmosphere of an active university with some of the best skiing and outdoor sports to be found anywhere. The 5,800-foot altitude guarantees a vigorous, four-season climate. According to residents, they usually get four good snowfalls every winter, but warm afternoons and plenty of sunshine make quick work of melting them away.

Cedar City is located on I-15, which gives it easy access to St. George, 52 miles south, and to Salt Lake City, 270 miles north. Las Vegas is little more than 3 hours away.

Even though a huge majority of Cedar City residents are members of the Mormon Church, Cedar City also has a respectable percentage of non-Mormons as well (there are 13 other traditional Christian churches in town). This is partly due to workers moving into the community with manufacturing companies that have relocated here. Cedar City has a low cost of living, usually about 10 percent below its sister city of St. George. Housing costs are usually somewhat lower as well.

Because of an exciting variety of cultural presentations, Cedar City calls itself the "Festival City." Now in its 26th season, the Shakespeare Festival here is famous throughout the West and draws fans from far and wide. Each year Southern Utah University presents four Shakespeare plays plus another stage play and a musical, running from the last week in June through Labor Day. Another interesting festival is the yearly Jedediah Smith High Mountain Rendezvous. This follows an old-time western theme, assembling would-be trappers, traders, and mountain men for a nostalgic festival of frontier contests and camaraderie. Southern Utah University's campus is the focus of many other community events such as music festivals, ballet, and the Utah Summer Games.

Valley View Medical Center is a 48-bed, full-service facility with some secondary-level services. It has an intensive-care/cardiac-care unit.

Cedar City Chamber of Commerce: 510 W. 800 S., Cedar City, UT 84720; (435) 586-4484; chambercedarcity.org.

10

The Pacific Northwest

Oregon and Washington offer a dramatic collection of varied landscapes providing a broad range of choices for retirement living. There's something here for everyone. Rugged seascapes and coastal mountains contrast nicely with inland valleys and fertile plains. High-mountain passes of the Oregon Cascades resolve into the lava beds and ponderosa pines of the high desert, then into the magnificent waterfalls and cliffs of the Columbia River Gorge. You can test your luck with salmon, steelhead, sturgeon, or bottom fishing—from the banks of a river, an ocean boat, or in a sunny forest glade. The nice thing is that the overwhelming majority of acreage in the Pacific Northwest is publicly owned, with national forests and deserts open to everybody for hiking, camping, and general outdoor enjoyment.

This northwestern portion of the continent is somewhat different, socially and culturally, from the opposite coast of America. (In our opinion.) The mindset here also differs from California, the other Pacific coast state. The causes are accidents of history.

The first Europeans to enter what is now the United States—on the northeast and southern coasts—can be described socially as wealthy families and aristocrats. In the 1600s it was very expensive to join a group of investors whose aim was to settle the fabled "new world," to found a colony, and hopefully make lucrative returns from the investments. Those immigrants who came later—who weren't wealthy—were either unemployed laborers or petty criminals exiled as indentured labor in the colonies.

In contrast, the Northwest Territory was discovered in the 1830s and 1840s by fur traders who blazed wagon trails to return their bounty of precious furs. Occasional immigrant wagon trains of farming families and laborers began following these trails in the early 1840s, finding wonderfully fertile and unclaimed lands. When the California gold rush participants of the late 1840s and 1850s began their migrations, the wagon trains discovered something just as precious as gold: an exceptionally mild climate, free farmland, and an opportunity to start over.

The point is that these settlers came mostly from the northern and midwestern parts of the country. They were not wealthy or socially upper class. (In those days wealthy people traveled by stagecoach or ship, not by prairie schooner.) So from the beginning the Pacific Northwest was settled by farmers, laborers, and merchants. A tradition of equality and mutual assistance developed, and it can be felt today.

It is our observation and belief that the Pacific Northwest has its own distinct culture and worldview. We believe that while people here are exceptionally open to newcomers and eager to make friends when new neighbors enter their neighborhoods, there is also a strong association with community and city. This can also lead some who are long established to keep outsiders at an arms distance until newbies have proven they are there to stay. It is an odd dichotomy to navigate upon entry. (By the way, both authors have lived in the Pacific Northwest.)

WEST COAST WEATHER

The conventional image of Oregon and Washington is a place of continual rain, where long-term residents develop duck feet and where ducks wear galoshes. The land is perceived as full of green, verdant mountains towering over lush river valleys with misty waterfalls and leaping trout. However, some of the eastern parts of Washington are practically treeless, with rolling hills of wheat, scrub grasses, and occasional thirsty-looking sagebrush as far as the eye can see.

An interesting thing about Washington and Oregon weather is that places 50 miles apart can have climates and topography so different it's hard to believe you're in the same state. The extreme eastern parts are high-mountain country, with tall evergreen trees, harsh winters, snow-covered peaks, and great skiing. The central portions have scanty rainfall—about half that of Kansas—with a mild, four-season climate and light snowfalls. The Pacific coast catches enough rain to keep everything perpetually green—even though it may snow occasionally. The ocean moderates temperatures far inland, because the warm Japan Current flows by the coast, sending temperate breezes inland and keeping freezing weather to a minimum. With a steady, year-round mildness, the climate approaches perfection for those who detest hot, sweltering summers. All but the higher elevations escape the Montana-like winters you might expect at this latitude. There's even a conifer and fern rain forest on the Olympic Peninsula, the only one in the Northern Hemisphere. Annual rainfall here is as much as 140 inches! (Eleven feet of rain!)

Despite Washington and Oregon's reputation for rain, statistics show that Olympia, Washington, has about the same yearly rainfall as Orlando, Florida (51 inches), and Portland, Oregon, averages 37 inches of rain each year, about the same as Buffalo, New York (except that Buffalo also receives 92 inches of snow). Rainfall in places like Ashland or Grants Pass is approximately 30 inches a year or less—about the same as San Antonio, Texas, and only half as much as most parts of Florida.

Having defended Oregon's weather so strongly, we must admit that sometimes it feels like some parts of the state get much more rain than statistics indicate. This is because rain tends to fall gently upon the landscape here, slowly, mostly in the winter, and over long periods of time while it builds up the accumulated totals. This rain keeps everything beautifully green, even through the winter months, in many locations. Along the coast low clouds can hang around for days on end, even when it isn't raining, giving the impression of dampness.

OREGON

When it comes to taxes in Oregon, we must rely on a favorite expression: "good news and bad news." The good news is: Oregon has no state sales tax. But the bad news is: Property taxes are high to make up the deficit. The good news: About 35 years ago a state referendum sent outraged property owners to the polls to support a reduction in property taxes to a maximum of $15 per $1,000 valuation, with a prohibition against raising assessed values to make up for lost revenue. The bad news: Voters didn't notice that the prohibition applied only to commercial property; private homes could be (and were) reappraised. It turns out that the tax-reduction proposition was the brainstorm of business-property owners.

We happened to own a home on the Rogue River at that time, which we bought for $145,000 the year before the vote. Our property was promptly reassessed at $185,000. At the end of the third year, the assessed value was $230,000! Our "tax cut" amounted to a 30 percent increase in tax payments. When it comes to tax reduction, it seems like we just can't win.

Another bit of "good news" is the comfortable mix of out-of-state folks choosing Oregon for retirement. In some of the smaller towns, the natives are often outnumbered by retirees from all over the United States and Canada. The wonderful choice of mild climates draw retirees from all over the country.

Oregon's Inland Valleys

As it traverses the state from south to north, I-5 travels through a string of exceptionally desirable retirement locations, from Ashland near the California border to Portland on the Columbia River at Oregon's northern edge. From our point of view, this entire region offers more of what retirees say they want than any other part of the nation. Yet few people outside the West Coast ever hear much about this part of the country. Californians, of course, have heard of it—much to Oregonians' chagrin—and they come here with open checkbooks, snapping up bargain retirement homes like alligators on a duck pond. Of course, this pushes up prices.

The landscape changes quickly as you cross into Oregon from California. Suddenly everything looks green, even in the middle of summer when most of California turns golden tan. Tall pines cloak the hills, and meadows are lush with grass; there are cows standing knee-deep in clover. It's easy to imagine the early pioneers' amazement as their covered wagons rumbled along the Oregon Trail to California. We understand why so many of them stayed right here! Although rainfall in most inland valleys averages only 25 to 37 inches, enough moisture falls in the summer to keep things fresh. Without heavy frost in winter to kill the grass, fields are greenest in December through March, because that's when more rain falls.

The operative climate word here is "mild." Although an occasional light snow may fall, it seldom stays around more than a few hours because

> ### Oregon Tax Profile
>
> **Sales tax:** no
> **State income tax:** 5% to 9.9%; federal income tax deductible to $5,000
> **Income brackets:** Lowest, $3,350; highest, $125,000
> **Property taxes:** rates are set by counties and special levies
> **Social Security taxed:** no
> **Pensions taxed:** generally, retirement income is subject to tax
> **Inheritance tax:** based on federal inheritance tax
> **Gasoline tax:** 34¢ per gallon, plus possible local taxes

of warm afternoon temperatures. January lows are typically around 30 to 40 degrees, with highs of 50 to 60 degrees. Because it rarely freezes, few homeowners bother to insulate their water pipes. A recent cold snap caught them by surprise, however, giving plumbers scads of overtime work.

Outdoor recreation is accessible year-round. Golf courses never close; fishing is possible in all seasons; bicycling and walking will lure you outdoors to do healthy things instead of watching television. Summers are mild, with average highs in the 80s, although July and August do have their share of 100-plus-degree days in the inland valleys. These are tempered by a low, 38 percent relative humidity.

Ashland/Medford

These two cities are about 15 minutes apart along I-5. They share a pleasant countryside of gently rolling hills, with sporadic remnants of the thick forests that once covered the area. Rich farmland and dairy farms spread out beginning at the edges of the towns. Off in the distance, about 30 miles to the east, the forest-covered mountains of the Cascade Range are sometimes covered with snow in the winter, with Mount McLaughlin rising majestically in white-frosted splendor. To the south, another 30 miles distant, is Mount Ashland, which dominates the Siskiyou Mountain Range. Skiing is available there from Thanksgiving through April, with up to 22 runs operating (snow permitting). Elk, deer, and other wildlife abound in the area. With 13 lakes only a short drive in any direction from Ashland and Medford, recreational activities are abundant.

Medford (pop. 77,000) and Ashland (pop. 21,000) are traditional retirement choices not only for Californians but for folks from all over the country who appreciate a blend of culture, year-round outdoor activities, and affordable housing costs. Medford is the commercial center, Ashland its academic counterpart. This area enjoys a very low crime rate, with Ashland usually ranking in the top 25 percent of towns nationally in personal safety. Here you'll find small-town living combined with city conveniences.

Ashland is one of our all-time favorite college retirement towns. Set in a pleasant countryside of gently rolling hills at an elevation of 1,800 feet, the town enjoys a very mild climate, with low rainfall and very little to no snow. Much of the town is beautifully landscaped and graced with lovingly

SOUTHERN OREGON WEATHER

	IN DEGREES FAHRENHEIT				ANNUAL	
	Jan.	April	July	Oct.	RAIN	SNOW
Daily highs	45	64	91	69	20"	8"
Daily lows	30	37	54	40		

restored early 1900s homes. Victorians that would look at home in San Francisco command views on the hills overlooking the valley and mountain peaks in the distance.

As usual, when you combine a large number of students, professors, and support staff with an array of young retired couples, you create a demand for quality shopping, restaurants, and services at reasonable costs. The result is Ashland's charming downtown area. Residents from Oregon towns near and far journey here to dine in restaurants serving French country cooking, wood-fired pizza, or Thai cuisine; to browse in used-book stores; or try on tweed fashions imported from Scotland.

Part of the rich cultural atmosphere of Southern Oregon State College and the school's outreach into the community is Ashland's nationally acclaimed Shakespeare Festival. This is a year-round production in three theater facilities, with contemporary theater and other popular entertainment in addition to classic presentations. Local residents enjoy volunteering in theater production, costuming, ushering, or even acting, as part of their social activities. Tourists are delighted to encounter costumed actors wandering about town, having a snack in a restaurant, and discussing their roles in the current theater production.

A bonus for Ashland retirement is the city's unusually low crime rate, with violent crimes at 50 percent of normal. At one time Ashland was one of the country's undiscovered real estate bargain places. Today prices have risen along with the number of retirees moving into town. Even though the average sales price of real estate is always higher than in similar-size Oregon towns, the overall cost of living is several points below national averages.

The wonderful, mild climate here makes outdoor sports possible year-round. Fishing in nearby rivers with crystal-clear waters produces catches of salmon and steelhead trout, and five lakes within a half-hour drive of Ashland are favorites for swimming, waterskiing, and picnics. Golf at seven public courses in Ashland and Medford is played throughout the four seasons.

Ashland Chamber of Commerce: 110 E. Main St., Ashland, OR 97520; (541) 482-3486; ashlandchamber.com.

Grants Pass/Rogue River

Downriver toward Grants Pass, the scenic Rogue River flows through several small towns and communities where retirement is a pervasive theme. Mobile-home parks and cozy-looking houses sit in close proximity to the river, allowing anglers to enjoy record steelhead and salmon fishing just a few yards from their back doors.

Eight miles to the south of Grants Pass is the city of Rogue River (pop. 2,200), a delightful little community sitting where I-5 and the Rogue River intersect. Quiet streets, shaded by mature trees, provide inexpensive homes, condos, and small apartments for those who prefer to be within walking distance of stores and the library. To the east a vast countryside of small farms and forested homesites captivates the get-away-from-it-all crowd.

The river wends its way downstream to Grants Pass, a traditional retirement area for Southern Californians. With about 36,000 people living within the city limits, Grants Pass supports enough commerce to take it out of the realm of a small town. Yet it is surprising how often residents drive 45 minutes to Medford for heavy-duty shopping.

Houses in town are predominantly older frame buildings, mostly single family, neat, well cared for, and affordable. Newer houses tend to be away from downtown, built on an acre or so, with trees and natural shrubbery planted as low-maintenance landscaping devices. As is the case in the Rogue River area, a great number of retirees choose to retire out in the more rustic places. Oregon becomes mountainous at this point, with forests and rugged hills covering much of the landscape. A 15-minute drive from the Grants Pass downtown takes you to wonderfully secluded and wild-looking properties where you will be plagued by deer eating your flowers and black bears raiding your garbage cans.

After the river leaves Grants Pass on its way to the ocean, the going gets rough. Whitewater enthusiasts who have braved rapids all over the world will tell you that rafting Oregon's Rogue River is the ultimate whitewater experience because of its incredible beauty and varying levels of difficulty. Congress designated it as the first of the nation's protected rivers under the Wild and Scenic Rivers Act of 1968. Here is where Zane Grey chose to build his home and to write many of his famous Western novels. Many scenic descriptions in his books were inspired by the picturesque Rogue River country. Moviemakers have found inspiration as well, with Hollywood crews making the trek to the Grants Pass region to take advantage of the scenery. Although Grants Pass has many practical neighborhoods suitable for retirement, most newcomers are attracted more toward the picturesque and lightly settled countryside to the west of Grants Pass. Follow the Rogue River downstream and you'll find numerous rural homes, half-hidden on forested lots, many of them, perhaps most, owned by retirees. Some properties hug the riverbanks; others perch on hills overlooking the Rogue River Valley, sheltered by tall pines; and many sit as close to the rippling trout and salmon water as possible.

Three Rivers Community Hospital, with 155 beds, serves the medical needs of the region. About 25 miles down I-5 is the Rogue Valley Medical Center, with 291 beds and plenty of specialist doctors.

Merlin/Galice

The town of Merlin (pop. 4,000) is about 20 miles downriver from Grants Pass, and a favorite put-in location for river rafts and kayaks. From this point on downstream to the ocean, the river is federally designated as a Wild and Scenic River. Merlin's town center is sprawled along the road that follows the river; houses and small businesses are strung along the highway for several miles. Side roads fan out from the town center, with a surprising number of small farms and private homes located on multi-acreage lots in the forest. Some are within a stone's throw of the road; others are almost buried in the forest, often with a cow or two and a horse munching grass. Those residents who aren't retired are usually connected with river occupations in some way or another.

It is surprising how the retiree population along the river seems to come predominantly from other parts of the United States, with native Oregonians seemingly in the minority. The mild weather, fantastic fishing, and beautiful scenery with a movie-set ambience are the draw. Some are hobby farmers, some raise horses, some just practice being retired—but all seem to love fishing and kayaking through the Rogue River rapids.

For several miles downriver from Merlin, the highway provides tantalizing views of whitewater rapids and steep canyon walls. The narrow highway wends its way through Galice, a tiny community with a fascinating history. In the mid-1850s a French doctor named Louis Galice was trying his luck at prospecting for gold. A few miles below Hellgate Canyon, Dr. Galice discovered gold nuggets in the creek that now bears his name. High above the river valley, prospectors discovered an ancient riverbed rich in nuggets. Rumor has it that a 9-pound gold nugget was found there. This was the beginning of a frantic gold rush. Ten years later about 2,000 men were at work along the creek and the river, many claiming 200-foot sections of creek and riverbank to pan for gold. Twenty years later Galice was all but deserted.

Today the attraction is beautiful scenery of cliffs and pines on the canyon sides, and fishing boats finding opportunities to bring in record-size steelhead trout and salmon. Just about all permanent Galice residents seem to be either retired, working as river guides, or both.

This writer and his wife once owned a vacation home here. It was on a tree-shaded, 2-acre lot, right on the river. Our house was one of several homes scattered along the riverbank. It was a perfect place for trout and salmon fishing, with deer wandering through the woods and an occasional mama bear and her cubs investigating our garbage can. About 65 families were living there (about 20 years ago), almost all retired couples. Of all the residents at that time, only one couple claimed to be native Oregonians. They argued that since they had moved to Galice 20 years previously—from Montana—they were entitled to native status!

Today, however, the quiet little village has become a beehive of activity. Dozens of new homes have popped up in the area, and many more are scattered on either side of the town's center. While Galice isn't exactly like it was 20 years ago, it's still a delightful place for retirement among friendly neighbors.

Grants Pass Chamber of Commerce: 1995 NW Vine, Grants Pass, OR 97526; (541) 476-7717; grantspasschamber.org.

Cave Junction

Some folks love small towns and rural life and can't stand the thought of living in a city, even a small one. These folks might direct their attention toward any number of small settlements tucked away in the hills and low mountains surrounding Grants Pass. While doing research in this part of Oregon's interior valleys, we made a minor discovery in Cave Junction, a crossroads town of 1,500 inhabitants with the distinction of being one of the most affordable places in the state.

Cave Junction is just one of several similar communities scattered along the scenic highway that winds its way across the mountains toward the ocean at Crescent City. This area is known as the Illinois Valley, named after the Illinois River that runs through here. You'll find several "wide-spot-in-the-road" communities, such as O'Brien, Kirby, and Selma. Because there is neither industry nor jobs, most residents seem to be retired. Their younger neighbors have to commute to Grants Pass for work. Most homes hereabouts are placed on generous plots of land. They are mostly of modest construction, often built by the owners themselves. Manufactured homes are permitted by zoning, so you may buy acreage and place a large mobile home on it.

Cave Junction sits in the heart of Illinois Valley and the center of one of Oregon's famous wine-producing regions. Three small, family-owned wineries operate in the Cave Junction area, places where you have to beep your horn to alert someone that you want to visit the tasting room. The town calls itself the gateway to the Oregon Caves, a fascinating complex of nearby limestone caverns.

People living here forfeit the benefits of city life, accepting instead the solitude and charm of country living. However, realize that to fit into this rustic world, you have to bring a certain amount of country mentality with you. You'll not find Greyhound buses zipping through here, and the nearest airport is 58 miles away (Medford). You'll have to adapt to local norms; you cannot expect your neighbors to change to your way of thinking. But that's part of living in the country.

But it isn't so rustic that civilized amenities are absent. The Illinois Valley Golf Club is a 9-hole, regulation-length layout. Hunting and fishing are big here. Bird hunters go after pheasant, quail, pigeon, geese, and ducks. The Illinois, Rogue, and Applegate Rivers provide salmon, steelhead, and rainbow trout, while Selma's 160-acre, man-made Lake Selmac is the state's premier trophy bass lake. A 55-mile drive to the coast affords surf casting, rock fishing, and deep-sea adventures.

For medical emergencies it isn't necessary to travel to Grants Pass; Cave Junction has a small medical clinic and an ambulance service. But for advanced medical care, you will have to make the trip to Grants Pass, about 24 miles away.

Cave Junction Chamber of Commerce: P.O. Box 312, Cave Junction, OR 97523; (541) 592-3326; cavejunction.com.

Eugene/Springfield

Located halfway up the state at an elevation of 426 feet above sea level, the twin cities of Eugene and Springfield are separated by the Willamette River as it runs through the heart of the metropolitan area. Enjoying a typically mild Oregon climate, the Eugene area catches about 40 inches of rainfall a year—about what you would expect in most East Coast towns—but very little snow. Summers are gloriously sunny, with only 15 days a year reaching temperatures of 90 degrees or higher. The city of Eugene counts about 158,000 inhabitants, whereas Springfield has a little more than 60,000.

The biggest "industry" here is the University of Oregon, with an enrollment of nearly 18,000 students. Like Ashland, university life and the excitement of learning and culture spill over into the community. Locals are die-hard football fans, rooting for the "Ducks," and sporting events become citywide affairs. Ongoing schedules of lectures, concerts, and plays, many of which are free, provide a constant source of interest for the retirement community. The Hult Center for the Performing Arts houses two theaters: a concert hall and a playhouse, which feature plays, concerts, and performances by local, regional, and national talent.

Eugene's business center features a large pedestrian mall for a pleasant shopping experience. Popular with students and residents alike, the center is well stocked with excellent restaurants and upscale shops. A large old building known as the Fifth Street Market houses a family of unique crafts and specialty retailers, bookstores, and restaurants, all of which make shopping in Eugene a treat. Toward the outskirts, two large shopping malls—one enclosed, the other open-air—offer shoppers a vast array of goods, food, and services. Eugene's open-air Saturday market is a popular, ongoing event from April to Christmas. Housing prices in Eugene are usually higher than in similar-size Oregon towns.

Across the river in Springfield, housing costs are usually about 10 percent lower than in Eugene, and its downtown makes up for lack of size with extra charm. By the way, Springfield supports one of the best senior centers

CENTRAL OREGON WEATHER

	IN DEGREES FAHRENHEIT				ANNUAL	
	Jan.	April	July	Oct.	RAIN	SNOW
Daily highs	46	60	82	65	40"	6"
Daily lows	33	34	50	41		

we've encountered in Oregon, or anywhere, for that matter. Facilities are excellent, the staff is dedicated, and retirees are unanimously pleased with their center.

Much outdoor activity centers on the Willamette River, which provides trout fishing, picnicking, miles of bicycle trails, and river walks. For ocean fishing, clamming, and beachcombing for driftwood or Japanese glass fishing floats, the Pacific beaches are just a 90-minute drive west through beautiful, low-mountain country and the Siuslaw National Forest. A short drive in the opposite direction is the Deschutes National Forest, crowned by the Mount Washington and Three Sisters Wilderness Areas. To the north similar towns suitable for retirement await your investigation, places such as Corvallis, Albany, and Salem (Oregon's capital). Some of the state's best trout fishing can be enjoyed toward the east after a scenic drive to the Diamond Lake area.

Eugene Chamber of Commerce: 1401 Willamette St., Eugene, OR 97401; (541) 484-1314; eugene-chamber.com.

Salem

Sometimes called the "Cherry City," Salem is known for flowering orchards in the surrounding countryside. Fertile soil brings bountiful crops of strawberries, raspberries, pears, filberts, and walnuts. The region is becoming known for wine, especially pinot noir, riesling, and chardonnay.

Salem is the third-largest city in Oregon, with a population of 160,000, and its appearance gets a double boost from being both the site of Oregon's state capital and the home of Willamette University. These institutions help keep the downtown alive and thriving. A great deal of commerce and business is generated by both entities. The city has one of the best libraries we've ever seen, not only for its book collection, but also for the public conference rooms available for residents to use for meetings, classes, lectures, and social events. The library is one of the focal points of the community for many retirees, a place to meet people and make friends. As you might expect of a state capital, the downtown center is vibrant, with nice restaurants, shopping, and excitement in the air, yet with an informality not expected in a capital city. During our last research trip to Salem, a retired couple invited us to one of the local microbreweries for a snack. The place is famous for good hamburgers in addition to its homemade beer. While we were ordering our hamburgers, a couple walked in and sat at the table next to us. They turned out to be Oregon's governor, John Kitzhaber, and his wife, Sharon. Both were dressed casually; he wore his accustomed blue jeans, sport coat, and tie. Our friends exchanged pleasantries with the governor, and we returned to our conversation.

By the way, Governor Kitzhaber was a good friend to retirees. He is a medical doctor and the architect of Oregon's unique health care program, which is often mentioned as a possible health care model for the nation. In 1997, during the governor's first term, the Death with Dignity Act was passed, legalizing physician-assisted dying (commonly referred to as "physician-assisted suicide"). Certain restrictions prevent abuse of the law. Thus Oregon became one of the first jurisdictions in the world that permits terminally ill patients to determine the time, place, and manner of their end of life.

For a fairly large city, Salem manages to retain a vestige of small-town atmosphere. Some friends of ours who retired here from Los Angeles said, "We thought we'd have a difficult time making friends and keeping busy here. First thing we did was join a social group and register for senior citizen classes at the university. Before long we had too much to do and more friends than we had before we retired." Willamette University's contribution to senior learning is another example of why college town retirement is such a good idea. Called the Institute for Continued Learning, this program costs $80 per person for the entire year and includes summer sessions; participation in all twice-weekly seminars; use of the gym, swimming pool, and exercise equipment; free tickets to Willamette athletic events; and the use of the copy and learning resource centers. Seminars and lectures are given by noted scholars on a wide variety of subjects, such as literature, music, art, history, philosophy, and current events. Taking classes in a university environment is an excellent way for newcomers to meet friends with common interests and ideas.

NORTH OREGON WEATHER

	IN DEGREES FAHRENHEIT				ANNUAL	
	Jan.	April	July	Oct.	RAIN	SNOW
Daily highs	44	60	80	64	16"	6"
Daily lows	34	41	56	35		

Salem is the major medical care center for many surrounding communities. The largest hospital is a 454-bed facility with a large skilled-care center. The hospital is augmented by a large rehab center.

Salem Chamber of Commerce: 1110 Commercial St. NE, Salem, OR 97301; (503) 581-1466; salemchamber.org.

Portland

Reno, Nevada, bills itself as "The Biggest Little City in the West." Portland turns this around, claiming the title of "The Biggest Small Town in the West." And it is big, with a million people living in its urban area; the city limits alone includes about half a million in population. Portland's influence spreads from the foothills of Mount Hood to the plains of the Coast Range, covering a four-county area.

As an important West Coast seaport, Portland has always supported industry—everything from lumber to light manufacturing. But over the past decade, the city has evolved into a major high-tech center. A number of technology companies are located here. In addition to several software firms, electronic companies such as Hewlett-Packard, Epson, and NEC have plants in the Portland area. Intel, the high-tech giant, employs a large number of workers. This makes Portland especially popular with aging computer and Internet specialists who are looking at retirement with possible part-time job opportunities.

Portland works hard to maintain its small-town atmosphere and its second motto, "City of Roses." Fortunately the city's founding fathers incorporated a large number of parks, some quite large, which contribute to a feeling of spaciousness. Rolling hills and lots of shade trees extend this feeling into Portland's neighborhoods.

Unlike many American cities, where shopping malls have destroyed downtowns by luring consumers into the suburbs, Portland has managed to keep its central core alive and well, a pleasant place to visit or shop. During the 1970s the city built a transit system and instituted a system of free public transportation in a 340-block downtown area known as Fareless Square. A combination of pedestrian-only streets and free buses makes shopping downtown Portland a pleasure. Well-preserved buildings, upscale shops and restaurants, and good law enforcement complete the picture of a delightful "small-town big city." On Saturday an open-air, outdoor market by the river offers local artist wares, live music, and an array of exotic foods.

Because Portland's cool climate, sophisticated setting, and hilly picturesqueness are reminiscent of San Francisco, Portland draws many retirees from that area. Coming here from one of the most expensive parts of the country is a pleasant surprise for ex–San Franciscans. Lovely Victorian homes, which would cost a fortune where they came from, can be purchased for California tract-home prices. (You realize, of course, that some California tract homes can be expensive.) At least one San Francisco publisher and several authors we know of have made the switch to Portland from the San Francisco Bay area.

Portland has a reputation for rainy weather, but truthfully, the region gets much less than most places in the eastern United States, less than 40 inches (compared with Miami's 60 inches). Northwestern Oregon just seems to have more rain because it mostly falls in the winter months in a long, lazy drizzle rather than in vigorous showers. Winter rains can sometimes drag on for several days. But glorious spring, summer, and fall weather makes amends for wet winters. (Not to mention an almost total absence of snow!)

Retirees who live in the Portland area love the convenience of their location. A short drive in one direction takes you to beautiful Pacific beaches. Go the other way and you are in Oregon's famous wine country. Mountains are nearby, with lush forests and rushing trout streams. Not much farther east you'll find yourself in desert country and rugged lava beds.

According to FBI reports on Oregon cities, Portland ranks just below Grants Pass for personal safety. Nationally it ranks about average for cities of similar size. That's not to suggest that Portland is crime-free by any means; like all large cities, its suburbs are generally tranquil, with more crime found on the fringes of downtown.

And although many people prefer living in the various neighborhoods near central Portland—again reminiscent of San Francisco's charming neighborhood settings—more retirees like the sections on the fringe of the city. There are too many charming suburbs and adjoining towns to list all of them here, but we'll mention a couple of the most popular.

On the west side of the river, and bordered on one side by Forest Park, Portland's Northwest District is an area densely populated by 1920s-era apartments, renovated Victorian homes, and older bungalows. The Northwest District's commercial area is endowed with upscale retail shops, restaurants, coffeehouses, theaters, microbreweries, and bookshops. Housing may be a bit on the expensive side, but rentals are plentiful and not outrageous. The Northwest District is a neighborhood for those who like to be in the middle of lots of activity.

The area known as Southwest Hills is a scenic neighborhood that embraces some of the most expensive property in the area. Thirty percent of the residents are said to earn more than $100,000 per year, and housing costs reflect this affluence. Although Portland's city center is just a short drive from Southwest Hills, the district's quiet streets and almost crime-free atmosphere make downtown seem leagues away. Prices of homes drop as you move south from the hillier parts.

Portland Business Alliance Greater Portland Chamber of Commerce: 200 SW Market St., Ste. 1770, Portland, OR 97201; (503) 224-8684; portlandalliance.com.

The Dalles/Hood River

The drive up the Oregon side of the Columbia River from Portland is another scenic marvel that attracts potential retirees. A half-dozen historic little towns space themselves along the highway, with the huge river flowing past, carrying fishing boats, cargo barges, and windsurfers. Two places in particular make wonderful retirement locations: Hood River (pop. 7,500) and The Dalles (pop. 13,500).

The Dalles received its name from French Canadian voyagers who used to "shoot the rapids" here instead of tediously unloading their boats and dragging them around the narrow rapids (which are now buried beneath a dam). The French used the word *dalle* to refer to a place where waters were constrained between high rock walls. They called this exciting stretch of river *la grande dalle de la Columbia,* "the great rapid of the Columbia." Those traveling the Oregon Trail who floated downriver to this point had to portage around the rapids for the final leg of the trip. Others arrived with their wagons and either had to build rafts and float their belongings downriver or detour inland around Mount Hood. Some weary travelers decided to give it up and settle in The Dalles, making it one of the earliest towns in the state. Later, steamboats made their way up the Columbia as far as The Dalles—the trip taking 12 hours and the fare costing $1 round-trip.

Today The Dalles is the center of a thriving agricultural region, with wheat fields and orchards fringing the town limits. It's definitely dry here, with less than half the rainfall of Portland just 100 miles downriver. The Dalles catches about 14 inches of rain (about the same as Los Angeles) and a couple of inches of snow two or three times each year. Summers are warm, often in the 90s, but it's a dry heat, with lots of breeze off the river and almost no rain during July and August.

In the historic downtown shopping district, streets run parallel with the river and are full of substantial brick buildings of late 1800s vintage. The town center seems to be active and spared from traffic by the interstate that bypasses The Dalles. Most major shopping retailers are represented on the edge of town. Residential neighborhoods climb the rather steep hillside behind the town, each street enjoying panoramic views of the Columbia River Gorge and Dallesport Peninsula. At the very top the Columbia Gorge Community College and the large Sorosis Park command the final view across the river into the state of Washington.

Residential neighborhoods sit on streets that stair-step up the steep hillside. Most homes, therefore, enjoy great views of the river and of the state of Washington in the distance. Residential neighborhoods vary from elegant to economical, something for every pocketbook.

When the community of Hood River was settled in 1854, early residents called it Dog River, but under pressure by housewives the name was changed. This was one of the first places along the Oregon Trail where pioneers found enough rain to grow some of the same kinds of crops they were used to back east. Some of the first things planted were apple trees and strawberries. Today the region is famous for pear and apple orchards.

It's interesting how just a little distance between The Dalles and Hood River (22 miles) makes a real difference in the climate. Hood River gets 30 inches of rain and lots more snow than The Dalles. This extra precipitation makes a big difference in the vegetation as well. Everything is green, even through the summer, and much more lush. Still, Hood River gets less precipitation than Portland (about the same as Des Moines or Detroit).

The downtown business center, varying from 1 to 3 blocks wide, follows along the river. It seems to be holding up well against the heavy shopping competition on the highway leading out of town. Several interesting restaurants and historic buildings with specialty stores draw downtown shoppers. Residential neighborhoods close to the town center vary from comfortable to not-quite-elegant, and most older homes are shaded by large trees. The newer homes away from downtown can be quite upscale and command great views of the Columbia River. Many places, either up or down the river, combine views and acreage. Behind Hood River, ascending the mountain slopes toward Mount Hood, a series of small communities and towns adds to Hood River's regional population—such places as Odell, Dee, and Parkdale.

Hood River Chamber of Commerce: 720 E. Port Marina Dr., Hood River, OR 97031; (800) 366-3530; hoodriver.org.

Oregon Coast

A wonderful, often overlooked retirement area is found along Washington and Oregon's Pacific coast. North along US 101, an inviting series of small towns dots the shore, starting with Brookings, just across the California state line, to Astoria, on Oregon's northern border, and on up to Washington's Grays Harbor. *National Geographic* named northwest Oregon's Cannon Beach "one of the world's 100 most beautiful places."

Ask people who retire along this picturesque stretch of coast, and they'll most likely give "wonderful year-round climate" as a major reason for their decision. Forget about air-conditioning and snow shovels. Because it seldom freezes, sweaters or windbreakers are the heaviest winter clothing required. Because midday summer temperatures rarely top 75 degrees, folks here sleep under electric blankets year-round.

However, it's this stretch of Pacific coast that earns Oregon and Washington a reputation for being rainy. Gold Beach is perhaps the wettest of all, with almost 80 inches per year. Most of it falls in the winter; it would fall as snow somewhere else. The summers are often sunny and dry, although low clouds are also common. This is a great place for part-time retirees,

OREGON COAST WEATHER

	IN DEGREES FAHRENHEIT				ANNUAL	
	Jan.	April	July	Oct.	RAIN	SNOW
Daily highs	53	54	67	63	39"	1"
Daily lows	41	44	52	49		

those seeking to escape Arizona's scorching July and August or Florida's muggy summers.

Overcrowding? Coast residents have plenty of elbow room. Along Washington and Oregon's 500-mile stretch of Pacific coastline, you'll only find about 20 towns plus a scattering of villages. Most have between 1,000 and 5,000 friendly residents. The only cities are Coos Bay, Astoria, and Aberdeen, and they are just barely large enough to be called cities. Most beaches are deserted, with unrestricted public access guaranteed by state law. A 5 or 10 minutes' drive inland takes you to low mountains, the Coast Ranges, with thousands of square miles of wilderness—almost all publicly owned or in national forest.

Good fishing, both ocean and river, is another plus. Steelhead, chinook salmon, and rainbow trout lurk in streams flowing from nearby mountains. Clamming, crabbing, and whale watching are popular activities. The open countryside is perfect for camping, picnicking, or beachcombing, as well as golf and horseback riding. White-tailed deer are plentiful, and you might see an occasional black bear or cougar. A large proportion of beachfront is dedicated to public parks and campgrounds, in the midst of the most beautiful seascapes to be found anywhere in the world.

Brookings/Harbor

Just across the California-Oregon state line are the twin towns of Brookings and Harbor. An estimated 30 percent of the population here are retirees. That seems like a low estimate, because retirement is big business along this coast. The total population here is around 15,000, spread over a 15-mile-long stretch of land along the Pacific Ocean beaches. The twin towns appear to be a lot larger than they are because of the long and narrow character of the terrain.

Residents love their unusually mild climate, optimistically referring to the area as Oregon's "banana belt." There's some justification, because flowers bloom all year; about 90 percent of the country's Easter lilies are grown here. Rhododendrons and azaleas bloom wildly in the late spring, and an Azalea Festival is held every Memorial Day. But let's face it, bananas don't grow well at all in this banana belt.

Like all Oregon coastal towns, Brookings and Harbor have plenty of things for retired folks to do, both organized and do-it-yourself. The main problem, as far as we are concerned, with these smaller towns is the distance from large shopping centers. People who live here insist there's an adequate supply of hardware stores, grocery markets, and the like, but we suppose some of us are spoiled and want huge selections of everything.

Brookings-Harbor Chamber of Commerce: 16330 Lower Harbor Rd., Brookings, OR 97415; (541) 469-3181, (800) 535-9469; brookings harborchamber.com.

Gold Beach

The mighty Rogue River empties into the ocean at Gold Beach. A road follows its course for a few miles inland, passing many retirement places favored by anglers who prize the steelhead and salmon that pass their doors every day. Some folks just can't choose between ocean and river fishing. They have to have both. Behind the town stretches mile after mile of forested wilderness, with trout, steelhead, and salmon streams, and deer hunting. The town's population is smaller than it appears, since most of the town is concentrated on the highway that hugs the coast. Gold Beach only has about 2,300 inhabitants. Its commercial district is larger than normal, because it serves the population scattered to the north and south of town, as well as inland residents along the river.

Gold Beach has an interesting history. It derived its name from an incident that started a frantic gold rush back in the forty-niner days. A prospector passing through the area discovered a small quantity of gold mixed in with beach sand. He panned a tiny bit of color and casually mentioned the fact to some other miners. As the word spread, the story expanded until gold-mining camps all over California and Oregon fluttered with news of a place where the ocean's waves deposited nuggets of gold in the sand, the beach strewn with riches, there for the gathering. Mining camps in California's Mother Lode all but emptied as miners frantically rushed to the "gold" beach.

Actually, gold is rather common on Oregon and California beaches, usually found in black streaks of magnetite sand mixed in with beach terraces. The problem is that it is very fine and difficult to separate from the coarser sand. Back during the Great Depression, when many people had nothing else to do, a lot of gold was gleaned from the beaches, but it was tedious work.

The gold stampede in Gold Beach was short-lived, but some miners, tired of jumping from place to place in search of riches, decided to retire from gold panning and settle down. They started the first retirement community on the Oregon coast. The tradition continues today, with retirement becoming a significant industry.

Single-family homes, cottages, and mobile homes are the general rule, with people living in multigenerational communities rather than strictly adult developments. A small hospital with an emergency room takes care of Gold Beach's medical needs.

As you drive north along the Oregon coast and catch a glimpse of the coast at Port Orford, you will see the ultimate picture-postcard scene. Dramatic rock formations jut from the sea, catching the force of waves, sending spray flying, and then the swells continue on to become gentle breakers on the sandy beach. Beaches here are known for semiprecious stones such as agates, jasper, and jade, as well as being places to look for redwood burls.

Gold Beach Chamber of Commerce: 29692 Ellensburg Ave., P.O. Box 489, Gold Beach, OR 97444; (541) 247-0923; goldbeachchamber.com.

Newport

The entire Oregon coast, from the California border to the Columbia River, is sprinkled with small towns and villages that make great retirement choices. We can heartily recommend towns such as Port Orford and Bandon as places with great potential for a coastal retirement. Other choices are Florence, Seaside, and Astoria. Some places have retiree populations equal to or greater than those still working. The requirements for living here are a distaste for extreme hot or frigid weather and a love of ocean beaches. An affordable cost of living is the bonus.

Of all these Oregon coast towns, the little city of Newport is our own personal favorite. One reason we like it here is the town's rich diversity of cultural interests and local arts that make it a stimulating place to explore your own creativity. The Newport Performing Arts Center is a vibrant arts community of working artists, talented young people and senior citizens, exuberant volunteers, and dedicated audiences who have developed a year-round season of theater, music, dance, exhibitions, readings, and lectures.

With about 10,000 inhabitants, Newport strikes a balance between being a village beach community and being large enough to provide all services. The larger city of Corvallis is a 52-mile drive east, not too far to go shopping for the day, and Portland is 119 miles away.

Yaquina Bay and the ocean beaches offer an endless array of recreational activities to revitalize and recharge your batteries. Fishing, crabbing, clamming, boating, canoeing, bike riding, kite flying, tide-pooling, or taking long walks on the beach are favorite activities, and there's a public golf course at Agate Beach (9 holes, par 36).

Newport's homes are a curious mixture, from older cottage styles in the historic Nye Beach District to beautiful custom-built homes with views. You'll also find condominiums, manufactured homes, retirement villages, and homes on wooded parcels hidden away in the quiet countryside. An especially interesting part of Newport is the old port area, "below the bridge," where interesting restaurants, seafood markets, and old buildings remind you of Newport's marine history. Every now and then a filmmaker uses the many colorful spots in and around Newport as a shooting location.

Newport living alternatives offer unique ocean, bay, and river properties with dramatic sandy beaches, breathtaking rocky shorelines, and hillsides with colorful landscapes and magnificent views.

Newport Chamber of Commerce: 555 SW Coast Hwy., Newport, OR 97365; (541) 265-8801, newportchamber.org.

Oregon High Country

On the sunny side of Oregon's spectacular Cascade Mountains, the high-desert country basks in a moderate climate boasting 263 days of sunshine a year. Rainfall is low enough to call this region a desert, but the sun doesn't get so hot that it discourages vegetation growth, as happens in many desert regions. The high-desert country is not only a place of four seasons, it's a place where winter makes its presence known. Most moisture falls in the winter, much of that in the form of snow. Because it only takes an average of 1 inch of rain to make 1 foot of snow, the white stuff can really pile up here in the cold season! Snowfall averages 38 inches, with occasional heavy overnight buildups. Unlike most of Oregon, snow tends to stick around here in the high desert. Summers are quite pleasant, almost always sunny, with an average of only 15 days a year with temperatures higher than 90 degrees. Rarely is 100 degrees reached.

Bend

A passion for outdoor recreation lures uncounted tourists to Oregon's high-desert city of Bend, located almost exactly in the center of the state. Shielded by the nearby Cascade Mountain range, Bend enjoys four distinct seasons, including a livable winter. Tourists enjoy fantastic trout and steelhead fishing, downhill skiing, and rafting through the exciting triple waterfalls of the Deschutes River. They love golfing at one of 26 nearby courses, as well as hiking, camping, and exploring the weird lava fields in the region.

As might be expected, regular vacationers often become retirees, choosing retirement homes in or near the city of Bend. They join the influx of younger newcomers who were attracted by the area's booming job market. For a while it was being claimed that only Las Vegas, Nevada, was growing at a faster rate than Bend, Oregon. Bend's population is now pegged at 79,000 (up from 25,000 not too many years ago), a very livable town with lovely residential areas and inexpensive country properties just a few minutes from the city center. True, the town suffers from main-artery traffic congestion, especially at the height of the tourist season, but a parkway and a traffic bypass promise to alleviate the problem. All in all, Bend manages to blend high growth and urban sophistication with a relaxed quality of life. It's interesting that the largest growth in newcomers are those in the 50- to 60-year-old age group—many work, at least part-time, as consultants or telecommute via their Internet connections. Most newcomers admit that they come here to work or retire primarily because of the nearness of outdoor recreation and the beautiful mountain and forest surroundings.

Although tourism and retirement revenues nourish Bend's expanding economy, local planners work diligently at enticing "living-wage" industries to relocate here, further enhancing the affluence of the region. The city has also done wonders with its old city center. All but abandoned a few years

OREGON HIGH COUNTRY WEATHER

	IN DEGREES FAHRENHEIT				ANNUAL	
	Jan.	April	July	Oct.	RAIN	SNOW
Daily highs	37	56	84	62	10"	46"
Daily lows	18	30	54	34		

ago as businesses moved to the strip malls, Bend's riverside downtown has become transformed into a pleasant place for shopping, with boutiques, first-class restaurants, and specialty shops of all descriptions. Sometimes an old-fashioned horse-drawn coach offers to show you the turn-of-the-20th-century buildings and other highlights of downtown Bend. Wide stretches of green grass along the Deschutes River bestow a restful counterpoint to the old brick and masonry buildings that compose Bend's once-dying business area.

Continuing education, important for today's retirees, is provided by Central Oregon Community College, a popular school that has more non-credit students enrolled than regular students. A large percentage of students are older and take classes for personal growth rather than to achieve occupational goals. The college library is open free of charge to district residents.

Although economical housing is available, prices have risen dramatically over the past few years. Even with the slump in housing prices since the 2008 debacle, average home prices will still be above average for similar central Oregon communities. Property values outside the city of Bend are determined to a large extent by the availability and quality of water.

The Bend area has a total of four hospitals, with an emergency air-ambulance service. The hospital serving Bend is St. Charles Medical Center—a comprehensive facility with 261 beds and 250 physicians on call. The facility maintains a trauma center and an upgraded intensive-care unit.

Bend Chamber of Commerce: 777 NW Wall St., Ste. 200, Bend, OR 97701; (541) 382-3221; bendchamber.org.

Sunriver

An upscale alternative to living in Bend is Sunriver, a resort retirement community a 20-minute drive away. A self-contained community on 3,300 acres, Sunriver has 1,300 homes, ranging from relatively inexpensive condos to ultra-deluxe homes with airstrip access for the family Cessna. An expansive shopping mall, an emergency medical center, and a full complement of services make Sunriver nearly self-sufficient.

At Sunriver most homes have plenty of land separating it from the next, so even condos don't seem crowded. Hiking paths and 80 miles of paved bike trails seem to pass by each living unit. Three 18-hole golf courses, 26 tennis courts, two swimming pools, hot tubs, stables, and a racquet club provide summer sports for active retirees. Winter sports are skiing at nearby Mount Bachelor and cross-country skiing over the hiking trails and golf courses.

Of the 1,700 full-time residents, better than half are retired, most coming from other states. Retired couples are even more strongly represented among the many part-time owners. They spend part of the year there—whichever is their favorite season—and rent their property for other seasons. A close family friend owns a house here but spends most of her time in Monterey, California. "One of the advantages of owning," she said, "is that if my kids don't want to use the place in the winter ski season or for summer golf, I just call the management company and they generally find tourists who are happy to pay $160 a day for my place." The winter ski tourists and the summer fishing and golf enthusiasts just about cover our friend's payments. This is done through one of several management companies that advertise the rentals, collect the rent, and clean after each tenant leaves.

Retirement in a resort community such as Sunriver—where a large percentage of homeowners stay only for the skiing season, while many other homeowners live here only during spring and summer—might appear to make full-timers feel lonely and isolated. For much of each winter and summer, a large percentage of the homes will be vacant. Yet an interview with a couple from Connecticut who retired at Sunriver painted a different picture of retirement in a resort. They said, "We discovered that we didn't just buy a house, we bought into a neighborhood!" It turns out that the full-time residents eagerly seek out newcomers who plan to live in Sunriver full-time. The Connecticut couple found themselves being appointed to committees and besieged with invitations to dinners, barbecues, playing tennis, and so forth.

Something that needs to be stressed about places like Sunriver: It isn't a full-service retirement community. Sunriver isn't a place where you can expect assisted-living or round-the-clock home-care workers to look after you. Instead, this is a place for active and alert people—the kind who won't mind an occasional 2 feet of snow during winter and who might like to try cross-country skiing. Why is this any different from places in Idaho and Montana? Because, despite the snow, the Oregon high country doesn't get severe low temperatures, spring comes earlier, and fall stays longer.

Sunriver Chamber of Commerce: 56825 Venture Ln., #110, Bend, OR 97707; (541) 593-8149; sunriverchamber.com.

Klamath Falls

An often overlooked retirement area—but not overlooked by bargain-hunting California retirees—is Klamath Falls. About 18 miles from the California border, Klamath Falls offers a high-desert climate similar to that of Bend, some 137 miles to the north. Fishing and hunting are great, with camping, nature trails, and sailing on the huge Klamath Lake providing a full range of outdoor activities. Landlocked salmon and steelhead grow to outstanding sizes. Local anglers claim that the average trout taken from the water measures 21 inches. (Would local anglers lie?)

Sitting at an altitude of 4,100 feet, Klamath Falls enjoys a dry climate with 280 days of sunshine and crisp, cold winters. This region experiences much less snow than Bend. In fact, the nearest ski resort is about a 2-hour drive from here because of this low snowfall. The countryside is definitely a desert environment, with fewer trees (and those you do see are more stunted) until you get into the nearby mountains. The city of Klamath Falls has a population of approximately 21,000, with an additional 28,000 more living in the surrounding county. The town looks much larger than that because it spreads far out into the countryside from its old-fashioned, low-key city center. Shopping centers on the southern edge of town have lured away many businesses.

One of Klamath Falls's unique features is a natural underground supply of geothermal water used to heat homes and businesses. This heating source is completely sustainable, nonpolluting, and inexpensive. It warms downtown sidewalks and bridges to keep them frost-free in the winter.

The big drawing card for most retirees (besides excellent trout fishing) is affordable real estate. Housing prices are as low as anywhere we've investigated, and considering the quality of the area, it's perhaps one of the best buys in the country. Another economic benefit here is an unusually low cost of utilities, more than 25 percent below national averages. This helps offset higher heating bills in the winter.

Klamath Falls's Sky Lakes Medical Center serves the Klamath Basin's health care needs with 176 beds, more than 85 physicians, and 860 employees. It has cancer and heart centers and a family practice residency program. There are also a number of smaller clinics, home health care operations, and several emergency services.

Klamath Chamber of Commerce: 205 Riverside Dr., Ste. A, Klamath Falls, OR 97601; (541) 884-5193; klamath.org.

WASHINGTON

Oregon has traditionally attracted more West Coast retirees than Washington State; however, this is changing. More and more retirees are traveling just a little farther to see what Washington has to offer. The state's electronics, bio-tech, and aerospace industries have been bringing skilled workers from all parts of the country to join the steady stream of Californians who have been leapfrogging over Oregon to land in Washington. They are pleased to find pleasant living conditions, a mild climate, and moderate housing costs when compared to California prices.

Worthy of special mention is Washington's philosophy on state income taxes: It's one of the few states in the country that does *not* collect them! Furthermore, it's one of those states with laws prohibiting other states from placing liens to collect taxes owed to that other state. Another good idea here is property-tax breaks for the elderly. Under state law retirees age 61 and older with incomes less than $35,000 are entitled to a full exemption from special assessments. Widows and widowers at least 57 years old whose spouses qualified for exemption at the time of death, and those who are disabled at any age, are also eligible for the property-tax exemption. Retired persons over age 61 with less than $40,000 total income, as well as those who are disabled at any age, can defer property tax indefinitely. When the tax liability reaches 80 percent of the home's equity value, the liability becomes a lien on the property, payable when it is sold or probated.

The other side (perhaps downside) of Washington State's no income tax policy is that money has to come from somewhere, and that somewhere turns out to be property and sales tax. Sales taxes start at approximately 6.5 percent, and property is taxed at 1.8 percent of its appraised value. Because property values were increasing at a rapid rate over the last 10 years, the burden is growing.

The most popular retirement locations in the state are found in high-quality towns near Seattle and on Puget Sound's network of bays, coves, straits, and inlets. Because so much of Washington's coast is in Puget Sound, the total length of shoreline is almost twice that of Oregon. This large mass of water moderates temperatures, which rarely drop below freezing or rise above 80 degrees.

Places like Shelton, Sequim, and Port Townsend share Seattle's climate and scenic beauty but also offer the benefits of small-town living. Equally charming are the communities set on islands, large and small, in and around the sound, among them Whidbey Island, Fidalgo Island, and the San Juan Islands. These quaint coastal towns nestled in forests of Douglas fir remind us of New England fishing villages. One drawback is that both Olympic National Park and the San Juan Islands attract tourists by the thousands, which can mean waiting in line for several hours to board a ferry during the summer and on weekends year-round.

> ### Washington Tax Profile
>
> **Sales tax:** 6.5% to 9.5%; food, drugs exempt
> **State income tax:** no
> **Property taxes:** average 1.8% of assessed value; exemptions for age 62 and over
> **Social Security taxed:** no
> **Pensions taxed:** no
> **Inheritance tax:** replaced with estate tax
> **Gasoline tax:** 49.4¢ per gallon, plus possible local taxes

All around Puget Sound, however, the cost of living is relatively high. In some places, especially the San Juan Islands, it can be extremely high. More affordable living can be found farther south in seaside communities such as Grayland and Long Beach on the Pacific coast.

Seattle Area

Seattle offers all the advantages of a large city, as well as all the disadvantages. Its setting—between Puget Sound and Lake Washington, with magnificent mountain views in all directions—helps make it one of the more beautiful cities in America. Lofty evergreens shade its parks and

WESTERN WASHINGTON WEATHER

	IN DEGREES FAHRENHEIT				ANNUAL	
	Jan.	April	July	Oct.	RAIN	SNOW
Daily highs	44	59	76	61	49"	4"
Daily lows	33	41	53	45		

suburbs, which blend into the surrounding forest. Its location—on the water and sheltered from Pacific storms by the mountains of the Olympic Peninsula—keeps winters mercifully mild and summers pleasantly cool. There is an all-pervasive community spirit such as is found in few other major cities. As you might expect from a big city, crime rates are a little higher than in surrounding communities, but for an urban area the safety factor here is reassuring. Most local neighborhoods in Seattle are as safe as you can find anywhere.

It's the high-quality towns near Seattle or on Puget Sound's network of bays, coves, straits, and inlets that make this area such a great retirement choice. Places like Bellingham, Burlington, or Olympia—to name just a few—share in Seattle's climate and scenic beauty, but also offer the benefits of small-town living. Anacortes, for example, located on a peninsula jutting out into the bay, enjoys one of the lowest crime rates in the country. Edmonds is another attractive area, sitting between Seattle and Everett; its downtown is right on the water, with a beach and ferry terminal at the end of the main shopping street.

The San Juan Islands must also be accessed by ferryboat and are among the more popular, albeit expensive, retirement places of the Puget Sound. Real estate prices are a bit high compared with some of the other island complexes nearby, but the quality lifestyle possible here makes it worthwhile. Whidbey Island, another favorite retirement area, has the advantage of being accessible by highway bridges rather than ferryboats.

Bainbridge Island

Nearly half of Bainbridge Island's workforce commutes to Seattle to work, according to David Harrison, a senior lecturer at the University of Washington's Evans School of Public Affairs and an 18-year islander. On the plus side the trip is predictable, and it can even be productive, thanks to wireless Internet access.

One of Seattle's most exclusive suburban neighborhoods, Bainbridge Island is linked to the peninsula by a highway bridge and to Seattle by a ferry route. Here you'll find many gracious homes secluded on large estates hidden from casual view by stands of evergreens. The 48-square-mile island is home to 22,000 people. Another island connected to the peninsula, Vashon Island, has a part bucolic, part artsy population of 10,000 and is linked by ferry to Tacoma.

The most intriguing communities on the peninsula are those farthest from the ferries that carry commuters to the urban side of the sound. Poulsbo, a waterfront community 16 miles north of Bremerton, got its start in the 1880s as a fishing village of Norwegian immigrants. The Scandinavian heritage lives on along the town's main street, now filled with arts and crafts galleries, antiques shops, and waterfront cafes, as well as in annual events ranging from the Viking Fest in May and the Midsommarfest in August to a traditional lutefisk dinner in October and the Christmastime Yule Fest. Hartstene Island, connected by a bridge to the southeastern corner of the Kitsap Peninsula, has forests, beaches, and meandering roads that provide access to hundreds of residences concealed deep in second-growth forest.

Bellingham

If any area of the northwestern Washington coast can claim to be "undiscovered," it is Whatcom County, which stretches along the Canadian border from the Straits of Georgia shoreline to the crest of the North Cascades. The population center is Bellingham, with 80,000 inhabitants.

Situated on bluffs overlooking Bellingham Bay, the city has the Cascade Mountains, temperate rain forests, and 10,000-foot Mount Baker as a scenic backdrop that is hard to beat. Many neighborhoods enjoy views of the San Juan Islands across the water to the west. Local boosters like to point out the varied cultural mix of college students, aging hippies, and Native Americans that makes Bellingham a stimulating relocation possibility.

Many neighborhoods here have parks, and although Bellingham is situated just off I-5, a mere 90-minute drive north of Seattle, its historical charm has never been overwhelmed by the growth boom that has transformed other cities to the south.

Over the years Bellingham has developed an intriguing cultural mix. Through much of the 20th century, the town's economy depended mainly on Canadians from Victoria and Vancouver, British Columbia, who came south to buy US-made goods duty-free. Though the North American Free Trade Agreement is gradually eliminating import tariffs between Canada and the United States, you still see about as many British Columbia license plates as Washington ones in shopping mall parking lots.

As the site of Western Washington University, Bellingham has a college student population of nearly 13,000. It is also one of the favorite communities in Washington among aging hippies and enlightenment seekers. Smaller neighboring villages retain distinctive Dutch and Scottish influences from early settlement days. In addition approximately 5,000 Lummi and Nooksack Indians make their homes on two nearby reservations.

Senior residents find that it's hard to get bored in Bellingham. The exceptionally active senior center offers more than 60 classes, health programs, and social events each week. Additional activities are offered by AARP and the Older Women's League (OWLS). Whatcom County Senior Services sponsors low-cost boat, train, and bus trips to destinations throughout Washington, Oregon, and even Alaska. Independent-living apartments including dinner, transportation, and social activities are available at the Willows Retirement Community near St. Joseph's Hospital.

Bellingham Chamber of Commerce: 119 N. Commercial St., Ste. 110, Bellingham, WA 98225; (360) 734-1330; bellingham.com.

Olympia

When Olympia was established back in 1846, it was the first settlement in the region. The founding fathers had a vision that the town someday would become the capital of the future state, so they provided a hilltop site for the future capitol building. The vision became reality seven years later when Olympia became the capital of the newly formed Washington Territory. The town was modeled after the New England towns where the pioneers came from, with the obligatory town square and wide, tree-lined streets.

Today Olympia proudly sits on the shore of South Puget Sound, with the rugged Olympic Mountains rising in the distance across the water and the dome of Washington's capitol soaring above the town. In our opinion Olympia ranks as one of America's loveliest cities. Over the years the city has maintained the kind of dignified, not-too-big atmosphere that every state capital should have.

Recent population growth in Washington has resulted in a rapidly expanding state government and a resulting job boom in this region. In the process Olympia has grown to a comfortable-size city of almost 48,000. It's the commercial center for the neighboring towns of Tumwater and Lacey, which have expanded until they've become almost contiguous. More than half of the area's almost 200,000 residents live in outlying rural areas, which are full of small ranches, vegetable farms, and homes on large acreage.

As the seat of Washington's government, Olympia serves as a proving ground for social programs, including several new intergenerational programs designed to bring together elders and young people. The Grand-folks Brigade places seniors from area retirement communities as mentors in elementary schools, and the Synergy Intergenerational Arts Program fosters creative collaborations between older adults and schoolchildren. One experimental program brings local third-grade students to adult day-care centers as companions to elderly and fragile seniors.

Retired military personnel who discovered the area while stationed at nearby Fort Lewis or McChord Air Force Base account for a sizable segment of Olympia's active senior community. It's an especially good place for military retirees because it's convenient to commissaries and base hospitals. Another medical facility that serves the Olympia area is St. Peter Hospital, with 290 beds and 450 physicians. The facility can perform all major procedures except heart transplants.

The weather here is typically Pacific coast mild, although Olympia receives a bit more rain and fog than Seattle and other Puget Sound communities farther to the north. It usually doesn't rain hard, but it rains often, with an average of 230 cloudy days a year. There is more than a trace of rain on 147 of those days and fog on 75 of them.

Olympia Chamber of Commerce: 809 Legion Way SE, Olympia, WA 98501; (360) 357-3362; thurstonchamber.com.

Port Angeles

The largest town on the Olympic Peninsula, Port Angeles (pop. 19,000) is the main gateway to Olympic National Park. This fact alone makes it an appealing choice for nature lovers. Besides limitless hiking trails and unparalleled wildlife watching, the park has special programs that provide volunteer opportunities for senior citizens. The city has also seen increased tourist popularity due to the fact that it and its small, neighboring town of Forks served as a setting for the popular *Twilight* book series.

Port Angeles itself is a busy town that stretches along the waterfront. Its two parallel main streets and the downtown area, small enough for walking, are complete with early 1900s architecture in need of a fresh coat of paint. A long waterfront park has paved hiking trails and well-groomed woodlands. Growth has been slow and steady, so residential areas contain a mix of older and contemporary homes.

Homesteaders came to the mountain valleys around Port Angeles long before the creation of the national forest and national park, so the fringe areas around the park are a patchwork quilt of federal and private land. You'll find houses of every description, from rustic log cabins to contemporary custom-built homes, many of them secluded down miles of unpaved forest roads. The area's rural residents actually outnumber the population of Port Angeles itself.

Recreation and hiking enthusiasts will find hundreds of miles of trails of every length and difficulty in Olympic National Park. The park is also one of the best places in Washington for wildlife viewing. The Port Angeles area is a great place for saltwater and freshwater fishing, with four public boat launches inside the city limits. Favorite catches are black-mouth salmon and halibut. Clams, crabs, and shrimp are also abundant in offshore waters. Anglers cast in dozens of nearby rivers and lakes for steelhead, cutthroat, and rainbow trout. Fishing charters and river float trips are available in season.

Port Angeles Chamber of Commerce: 121 E. Railroad Ave., Port Angeles, WA 98362; (360) 452-2363; portangeles.org.

San Juan Islands

The San Juan Islands, in the northern portion of Puget Sound, are one of the scenic wonders of the entire country. The islands, with rocky shorelines, coves, and bays, are covered with tall evergreens and are often separated from their neighbors by narrow channels. More than 400 islands compose this group, but only 60 are inhabited and only four have ferry service. These four islands—San Juan, Orcas, Lopez, and Shaw—have about 12,000 residents altogether, an estimated half of them retired.

The San Juan Islands are not for everyone; they appeal to a special type who values scenery over conveniences. Because ferry service is very slow, often involving long waits, commuting to a job is hardly practical. The islands are basically residential, with almost no available jobs for newcomers, other than those that can be done by Internet connections. Residents tend to be either retired, writers or artists, or else those wealthy enough to afford a place here as a second home. Those who choose to settle here must enjoy cool weather, because the average July high temperature is only 70 degrees. Finally, because island property is becoming more expensive as time goes by, those who retire here must be able to afford the housing costs. Those who do fit this profile clearly feel that the high-quality lifestyle, tranquility, and beautiful surroundings make it all worthwhile.

One possible drawback about living here is health care. At the time of writing, there is neither a hospital nor an around-the-clock medical facility. For quick fix emergencies there is the PeaceHealth Peace Island Medical Center, a critical-care center in Friday Harbor; for more serious problems you might have to take a helicopter to a mainland hospital. For routine health care there are medical centers on San Juan, Lopez, and Orcas Islands.

Real estate is among the most costly in the Northwest. Property is priced in three categories, depending upon location. The most expensive category is waterfront, where you can have a dock and a boat. Next is view property, with prices depending on how gorgeous the view of the water and nearby islands (these can be spectacular). And the third category is "inland, no view." But even these can be expensive. Rentals and condos are almost nonexistent.

San Juan Island Chamber of Commerce: 165 1st St. S., Friday Harbor, WA 98250; (360) 378-5240; sanjuanisland.org.

Whidbey Island

Whidbey Island was known as a retirement area long before the first senior citizen thought of moving to Sequim. Langley, a residential community on the southwest shore of the island, is nicknamed "Port of the Sea Captains" because it has been a favorite retirement spot for mariners for more than a century.

Measuring 55 miles from north to south, Whidbey Island is the longest island in the United States—a distinction it gained in 1985 when the US Supreme Court ruled that Long Island, New York, was actually a peninsula. It has the advantage of being accessible by a highway bridge, but only from the north. Frequent ferries carry vehicles and passengers from terminals on the island to both Mukilteo, north of Seattle, and Port Townsend on the Olympic Peninsula.

Whidbey Island is predominantly rural in character, with three towns and a scattering of tiny villages along the protected coast that faces the mainland across Skagit Bay and the Saratoga Passage. The biggest town on the island is Oak Harbor, with a population of 23,000, including many personnel from nearby Whidbey Naval Air Station; however, the county seat of Island County (Whidbey Island, that is) is little Coupeville, an old-fashioned, Victorian-era port town of 1,900. For the most part Whidbey Island residents live on small dairy and truck-produce farms nestled in the fir trees that line a seemingly endless labyrinth of nameless little paved roads.

Whidbey Island is the place to go if the ultimate in peace and quiet is your goal. Any kind of excitement is highly unlikely here; in fact, retirees we've talked to in such laid-back places as Sequim, Port Townsend, and Anacortes dismiss the prospect of life on Whidbey Island as "too boring." Boredom gives way to congestion on sunny weekends and during the summer months, when day-trippers from the Seattle area arrive as fast as the ferries can carry them and clog the island's only highway with bumper-to-bumper traffic bound for Deception Pass State Park and other popular recreation areas.

Whidbey Island/Coupeville Chamber of Commerce: P.O. Box 152, Coupeville, WA 98239; (360) 678-5434; coupevillechamber.com.

Vancouver, Washington/Portland, Oregon

Two hundred years ago, in 1806, explorers Meriwether Lewis and William Clark passed through this area as they made their way to the Pacific Ocean. In his daily journal Lewis noted, "indeed the only desirable situation for a settlement which I have seen on the West side of the Rocky Mountains." Nineteen years later Vancouver became the first nonnative settlement in the Pacific Northwest when the Hudson's Bay Company established Fort Vancouver.

Sitting on the north bank of the magnificent Columbia River, the city of Vancouver, Washington, is but a short commute across a scenic bridge to the metropolitan city of Portland, Oregon. Some might consider Vancouver to be one of Portland's numerous bedroom communities, but considering its population of 166,000, that designation is somewhat misleading. The city has grown more than 210 percent in the last 20 years. Vancouver's city center is lively, dynamic, and self-contained. Vancouver's high-tech manufacturing, traditional industry, and small businesses provide ample employment opportunities that do not entail commuting.

One difference between Vancouver and Portland is that Vancouver's residential neighborhoods tend to have larger lots for homes, yet smaller price tags. More than 40 miles of river frontage set the tone for a community that offers recreation and leisure as well as a vibrant, well-balanced economy. Always within view the startling beauty of Mount St. Helens and the challenging ski slopes of Mount Hood are just a short drive away.

As in neighboring Portland, wet, mild winters and moderately dry summers are typical of southwest Washington. With year-round golf and fishing galore, the region offers year-round enjoyment of the beauty that is the Pacific Northwest.

A most significant difference between Vancouver and Portland is the matter of taxes. As mentioned earlier, the state of Washington does not impose a state income tax, whereas the state of Oregon does not collect a state sales tax. As you might imagine, both states make up for the loss of tax revenue by collecting it through property taxes. (Can't win, can we?) But residents of Vancouver can have it both ways. They pay no taxes on income, yet by crossing over the Columbia River Bridge, they can make major purchases in Oregon and avoid sales tax! Property taxes? Well, we can't have everything, can we?

The Vancouver Parks and Recreation Department presents an awesome array of services and programs for seniors. Its Marshall Luepke Center offers a series of tours that would put a travel agency to shame.

Upriver on the Washington side of the Columbia are several delightful little towns strung along a winding, scenic road. Camas, Washougal, and Skamania are close enough to the city for convenience but not so close as

VANCOUVER/PORTLAND WEATHER

	IN DEGREES FAHRENHEIT				ANNUAL	
	Jan.	April	July	Oct.	RAIN	SNOW
Daily highs	44	60	80	64	16"	6"
Daily lows	34	41	56	35		

to feel overwhelmed by it. Streets forming tiers along the river provide scenic views for the towns' homes. There's an exceptionally peaceful air about this stretch of river, a combination of woods, meadows, and steep hills that invites retirement.

Vancouver Chamber of Commerce: 1101 Broadway, Vancouver, WA 98660; (360) 694-2588; vancouverusa.com.

11

The Snowbelt States

We always have been hesitant to recommend places for retirement with harsh winter climates. I have to admit that this is a personal bias on our part, due to our being typical California weather-wimps. Californians tend to get grumpy when winter temperatures drop into the low 40s. Our firm belief is that if we were meant to live in frigid climates, we would have been born with ear muffs.

Don't misunderstand—we can take freezing weather, and actually enjoy short exposures to it. From our California home we can drive up into the Sierra Nevada, downhill ski for 4 hours, and be home in time for dinner and a dip in the swimming pool. Ice and snow are fun, but only in short bursts.

Yes, I fully realize that we Californians are in the minority. Most retirement surveys show that while many people prefer to escape ice and snow, the majority express a preference for a mild, four-season climate. The stress is on the word "mild." They idealize a short winter, with the possibility of a touch of snow for Christmas. When relocating from a place with blustery winters, folks tend to look favorably toward Florida, Arizona, or California. Since our job is to report on and recommend places for retirement, we try to recommend communities where people actually retire, not simply where they *could* retire if they really wanted to.

Unless there is a specific reason, those retiring from Michigan don't often move to Minnesota, North Dakota, or other places that remain frozen 4 to 6 months out of the year. Yes, if they originally came from North Dakota, or if their grandchildren are living there, it might make sense to move there. For years we've seen retirement writers recommend towns such as Camden, Maine, and Burlington, Vermont, as "best places" for retirement. These are towns with genuine winters (though not necessarily of the North Dakota variety), and statistics show that people actually *do* retire there. So we decided to visit and research some popular cold-weather retirement locations and include them in *Where to Retire*.

We started with Camden, Maine, and moved more or less westward, looking for places where most retirees live year-round, and where others enjoy beautiful spring, summer, and fall seasons, then vacation in warm-weather destinations for the winter.

MAINE

Maine's state government is actively encouraging retirees to move to the state. They see them as a potential boon for the economy and a human asset for communities where they settle. One time we attended a retirement conference in Portland, and the governor at that time, Angus King, spoke of the economic benefits brought by out-of-state retirees. He cited figures showing that every retiree household has the equivalent economic effect of 3.7 factory jobs. He also stressed the low crime rates enjoyed by the state. He said, "I seldom lock my house, and I never lock my automobile." After a pause he said, "Well, actually I *do* lock my car in the autumn, especially when it is parked in town. Otherwise I return to find the back seat stuffed full of zucchini."

As far as we are concerned, the only part of Maine that is inhabitable during winter is the coastal area. The ocean moderates the temperatures to lows that are almost always well above zero, as opposed to common *below* zero daily lows. (What would you expect from California writers?) However, most of those retiring in Maine are either from the New England states, where they're somewhat accustomed to cold winters, or else they escape the winters, basking in their part-time Florida condos.

Maine Tax Profile

Sales tax: 5.5%; food, drugs exempt
State income tax: low, 0%; high, 7.95%
Income brackets: lowest, $5,199; highest, $20,900
Property taxes: average 1.6% of assessed value
Social Security taxed: no
Pensions taxed: $6,000 exemption
Inheritance tax: replaced with estate tax
Gasoline tax: 30¢ per gallon

Camden

Camden, Rockport, Bar Harbor, and neighboring towns snuggled among Atlantic seascapes are about as beautiful as it gets along the rugged Maine coastline. Camden is the community we looked at in more depth. Nestled on Penobscot Bay at the foot of steeply sloping hills, Camden is about 60 miles north of Portland and an hour south of Bangor. This quaint coastal community is famous for its beautifully restored Victorian homes and breathtaking ocean views. Settled in 1769, Camden retains much of its 18th-century flavor. Homes with views tend to be expensive, and rightly so, because of the quality of the panorama.

Because of the northern location, winters can get cold, although nothing like the inland regions of Maine. Heavy accumulations of snow are less common here, thanks to the moderating effect of the Atlantic Ocean. (Were it not for the milder than usual climate, we couldn't make a recommendation.) Retirees here say that beautiful springs, mild summers, and stunning autumn scenery outweigh any downside of the winter.

Most retirees here previously lived along the Eastern Seaboard and were frequent summer visitors before deciding to relocate. Approximately 5,500 people live in Camden year-round, but the population triples during the summer season. Almost a third of Camden's residents are age 55 or older. Many have been drawn to the town for its boating, skiing, and other outdoor recreation opportunities. Outdoor recreation isn't limited to summer vacations. You can enjoy golf by the sea in the summer and skiing at a nearby alpine area in the winter. Some go sailing practically from their front yards. Concerts and plays are given year-round.

The nearby University of Maine branch campus presents lecture series and offers noncredit classes in everything from photography to boat-building to wine-making. Many classes are taught by senior volunteers, teaching other retirees. Penobscot School offers intensive courses in foreign languages. This would be the place to brush up on your French for the next trip to Europe.

Volunteer opportunities for seniors are plentiful, including working with the Longstreet Society, a historic preservation organization, and Habitat for Humanity, a group that builds homes for lower-income folks. The town also has a reputation as an artist colony, with more than 20 art galleries and museums. Not far from town is the 5,000-acre Camden Hills State Park, at the foot of Mount Battie. This is popular for picnicking and

COASTAL MAINE WEATHER

| | IN DEGREES FAHRENHEIT | | | | ANNUAL | |
	Jan.	April	July	Oct.	RAIN	SNOW
Daily highs	32	45	78	55	45"	35"
Daily lows	13	32	60	39		

wildlife watching in the summer and cross-country skiing in the winter. Winter sports include a 400-foot toboggan chute and cross-country and alpine skiing.

The Penobscot Bay Medical Center, a full-service regional hospital, has 106 beds and 80 physicians.

Camden-Rockland Chamber of Commerce: 1 Park Dr., Rockland, ME 04841; (207) 236-4404; camdenrockland.com.

VERMONT

Vermont, tucked in the northeast corner of the United States, is the second-smallest state in the nation, with a population of less than one million. The state capital, Montpelier, with a population of well under 10,000, is one of America's smallest state capital cities. When French explorer Samuel de Champlain arrived, the region was populated by various indigenous peoples of the Algonquin, Iroquois, and Abenaki nations. Modern-day names of towns, lakes, and rivers are often derivatives of old Native names. Back then Vermont's hills were filled with wildlife, and fish were bountiful in the many rivers, ponds, and lakes. Today the situation remains pretty much the same.

Known as the Green Mountain State, Vermont has long been a vacation destination for residents of New England and the northeastern part of the country. The region

---

Vermont Tax Profile

Sales tax: 6% to 7%; drugs exempt
State income tax: 3.6% to 9%
Income brackets: lowest, $37,450; highest, $411,501
Property taxes: average 1.05% plus municipal assessments
Social Security taxed: no
Pensions taxed: no
Inheritance tax: no
Gasoline tax: 31.2¢ per gallon

experiences four distinct seasons, with temperatures averaging in the mid-70s in summer and in the low 20s during winter. The glorious summers draw refugees from the bustling and crowded eastern cities, and winter season brings 'em back for skiing. From 100 inches to more than 250 inches of snow falls during the winter, depending on elevation. Cross-country ski and snowmobile trails provide paths into parts of the Vermont woods you can't easily get to at other times.

Considering all this, it isn't surprising that when thinking of retirement relocation, many aficionados of the outdoors consider Vermont. Our experience when researching the state was centered in Burlington, and oddly enough our informants were born and raised Californians, who chose to semiretire in this city on beautiful Lake Champlain.

Burlington

For years smaller and quieter areas of New England have offered popular relocation destinations for many people living and working in that huge megalopolis that stretches from Boston to Washington. The legendary tranquility and lovely scenery of Vermont's towns and small cities make possible an enviable retirement or semiretirement lifestyle. A benefit is that retirees needn't be so far away from friends and family in northeastern cities, and not far from their favorite Florida winter getaways. Vermont natives refer to these newcomers as "flatlanders." This isn't necessarily a pejorative term, merely a description of those who have suffered the misfortune of being born someplace other than Vermont.

Our favorite place in Vermont happens to be a college town, as usual. Burlington, with a population of just under 43,000, happens to be the largest city in the state. That should give you an idea of the state's population density. Perched on a hillside overlooking the eastern shore of Lake Champlain, between the Adirondack and Green Mountains, Burlington is only 95 miles from Montreal. It regularly receives awards as one of America's most livable cities. Numerous public beaches line the lakeshore, with a bike path/walking trail that stretches for 10 miles along the shoreline.

The downtown outdoor mall of Church Street Marketplace is a perfect picture of old New England architecture, with that pleasing mixture of restaurants, cafes, and entertainment found only in a college town. The town center supports a thriving cultural and music scene with offerings ranging from rock and roll, to jazz, to folk, to classical, creating a vibrant nightlife

BURLINGTON AREA WEATHER

	IN DEGREES FAHRENHEIT				ANNUAL	
	Jan.	**April**	**July**	**Oct.**	**RAIN**	**SNOW**
Daily highs	27	54	82	57	33"	79"
Daily lows	10	34	60	40		

that is well known throughout the region. We have a semiretired friend from California who relocated to Burlington, teaching mathematics in the local college and playing jazz and rock guitar on weekends. He said that what he and his wife enjoy most are the low traffic and laid-back pace of life. According to him, "The rush hour here only lasts 15 minutes."

Because of its freshwater access to the ocean, via Canada's St. Lawrence River, Burlington at one time was an important port and shipping point for the lumber industry. Today the town's economy focuses on tourism and education. This is the home of the University of Vermont, its campus over-looking the shores of Lake Champlain, with the Green Mountains looming in the background. Established in 1791, the school today has 12,000 gradu-ate, undergraduate, and medical students, plus more than 1,100 faculty members. That's not all. Two private colleges plus a community college add to the academic population. These three schools play an important part in the community's social life and everyday activities. Vermont resi-dents receive discounts on tuition, and many school activities are open to the public.

Of course, Burlington is clearly not one of the mild climate locations we usually recommend as retirement destinations. This region experi-ences a full three months or more of real winter every year, with plenty of snow (and skiing opportunities). But this is compensated for by delight-ful spring and mild summer weather, and unforgettable autumns. Five ski lifts are within an hour's drive, and a long ski run just 40 minutes from Burlington. In the winter Lake Champlain freezes over, to the delight of ice-skaters. This is a climate for those who thoroughly enjoy year-round recreation. Alternatively, Vermont is a place for those who have a second home or other warm-weather escape hatch.

As you might expect from a town that has a university medical school, health care here is more than adequate. The medical school has the larg-est teaching hospital in the state. Doctors in all specialties are working as well as teaching in a newly renovated hospital under excellent conditions. Fletcher Allen Health Care runs the 420-bed Medical Center of Vermont.

Burlington Chamber of Commerce: 60 Main St., #100, Burlington, VT 05401; (802) 863-3489; burlington-chamber.com.

MASSACHUSETTS

Massachusetts, in the heart of New England, is the region's most populous state. Lively urban areas, picturesque seaside communities, and tiny rural towns offer a unique ambience. A drive through the Massachusetts countryside is like being in an outdoor museum, with galleries of brick mansions dating from before the Revolution and nostalgic mills by rushing creeks. This is where modern American history began—with the Boston Tea Party, Lexington and Concord, and Bunker Hill; you are continually reminded of the events that launched a nation.

Our country practically began with Massachusetts. The Pilgrim colony at Plymouth was the second permanent English settlement in the New World. Many other Massachusetts towns were founded by colonists from England in the 1620s and 1630s. During the 18th century, Massachusetts became known as the "Cradle of Liberty" when Boston became the fuse that lit off the American Revolution. Probably no other state can equal this region for historic sites to visit.

Massachusetts Tax Profile

Sales tax: 6.25%; food, drugs exempt
State income tax: 5–12% of federal tax
Income brackets: lowest, $4,350; highest, $17,350
Property taxes: average 1.6% of assessed value
Social Security taxed: no
Pensions taxed: no
Inheritance tax: limited estate tax
Gasoline tax: 26.5¢ per gallon

Originally dependent on fishing, agriculture, and trade with Europe, Massachusetts was transformed into a manufacturing center and led the way during the Industrial Revolution. Archaic textile mills and factory buildings dating from the 1800s add to the quaintness of mid- and small-size towns. During the 20th century the economy shifted away from manufacturing. This time the pioneering is on higher education, high-tech development, health care technology, and financial services.

Amherst

We chose to profile Amherst in the picturesque western part of the state because of our introduction by a longtime friend from California and her husband, who decided *this* was the place to live. They aren't exactly retired—Greta is a well-known artist, and her husband, Peter, teaches drama at the local college—but their enthusiasm and that of other people we interviewed sold us on the idea that retired life here could be all we might want.

As mentioned earlier, Massachusetts has become one of the leaders in college and university education. Amherst is a poster child of this trend. A recent US Census showed that 68 percent of the city's population have at least a four-year college degree, and 47 percent have a post-graduate or professional degree.

Five world-famous colleges and universities are found within an 8-mile radius, in the towns of Amherst, South Amherst, South Hadley, and Northampton. Amherst hosts by far the largest of the schools, the University of Massachusetts. The four others are private schools: Amherst College in Amherst, Hampshire College in South Amherst, Smith College in Northampton, and Mount Holyoke College in South Hadley. As a member of the Five College Consortium, the University of Massachusetts shares a mutually rewarding relationship with the four other institutions. Although the schools are separate entities, they participate in an interschool program called University Without Walls. Enrolled students design their curriculum and may take classes at any of the five schools.

It's almost a cliché to describe Amherst as historic and picturesque. Yet this is one of New England's most delightful towns. Situated in the historic Connecticut River Valley—it's called the Pioneer Valley here—amid forested hills, fertile river plains, with views of distant mountains, Amherst is the classic New England setting. Houses dating from the 1700s are common. The town itself is a living museum. The Emily Dickinson home is on the tourist agenda, as well as the house where Noah Webster lived while compiling his famous dictionary. Robert Frost, Henry Ward Beecher, and Calvin Coolidge all either attended or taught at the University of Massachusetts here, the flagship of the state's university system.

Nearby Hadley, the oldest town in the vicinity, was settled around 1660, and Amherst a few years later. Before long the region began developing an industrial economy because of the abundant water power. It soon became famous for textiles and woolen mills. Over time factories began to migrate toward low-wage southern states and then to even cheaper foreign countries. Fortunately, the Amherst region replaced the disappearing enterprises with a more viable industry: education. The university was established in 1867 and soon became the largest in the state.

Amherst's town center has everything you might expect to find in a college town. It's a lively place with interesting restaurants, fine galleries, boutiques, antiques shops, and bookstores. The neighboring college towns of South Hadley and Northampton also sparkle with culture, art, music, and theater. If there isn't enough to keep you occupied with culture here, an hour's drive west takes you to the Berkshire Hills and Hancock Shaker Village, the Norman Rockwell Museum, and the Massachusetts Museum of Contemporary Art. Regional festivals abound year-round, including the famous Berkshire Theater Festival and the Tanglewood Summer Music Festival.

Individually the three college towns are not very big, but combined they make the equivalent of a small city. Amherst's University of Massachusetts is a major research center, enrolling 24,000 students from all 50 United States and over 100 countries. Consequently the town's population varies from about 37,000 during the academic year to around 25,000 during the summer. Northampton has a population of around 29,000, and South Hadley 17,000.

For outdoor recreation the famous southern Vermont ski slopes are only about an hour away, and several local recreation areas are just minutes from Amherst. The Connecticut River Greenway, one of Massachusetts's newest state parks, connects open spaces, parks, scenic vistas, and archaeological and historic sites along the length of the Connecticut River as it

AMHERST AREA WEATHER

| | IN DEGREES FAHRENHEIT | | | | ANNUAL | |
	Jan.	April	July	Oct.	RAIN	SNOW
Daily highs	37	61	82	67	40"	19"
Daily lows	20	37	62	39		

passes through the state. Twelve miles of permanently protected shoreline and numerous highway access points to the river give local residents entree to outdoor recreation.

Valley Medical Group provides comprehensive and convenient primary and specialty care to residents of the region, with health centers in Amherst, Northampton, and Greenfield. Cooley Dickinson Hospital offers a wide range of inpatient and outpatient services at its main facility in Northampton.

Amherst Area Chamber of Commerce: 35 South Pleasant St., Amherst, MA 01002; (413) 253-0700; amherstarea.com.

COLORADO

When you think of mountain scenery, the state of Colorado often comes to mind. Rugged peaks covered with ice and snow, mountain slopes green with pine and fir forests and golden with fall aspens dominate the landscape, with majestic mountains everywhere. Some of the most gorgeous mountains on the continent are found here, with several passes above 10,000 feet. The highways that cross them are at such high altitudes that some folks often have trouble breathing. When they do catch their breath, the mountain scenery immediately takes it away again.

Much more than a tourist attraction, the mountains are rich in minerals and teem with wildlife—deer, antelope, elk, black bear, and bighorn sheep. One-third of the state is forested: ponderosa pine, spruce, Douglas fir, and, of course, aspen. Mountain streams are the hideouts of rainbow and brown trout, and lakes hold trophy bass and schools of perch. Add to this world-class skiing and hiking, and you'll probably agree that Colorado offers outdoor recreation rivaling that of any other state. Also, some of the best high-tech centers in the nation are located here, with possible employment opportunities for those high-tech folks who take early retirement.

On the other hand, the state isn't all forested slopes and snowcapped peaks. Wide expanses of Colorado are high desert, with equally interesting landscapes. The eastern portion of the state—from Denver to the Kansas state line—is sparsely populated great plains.

Many people choose retirement in Colorado on a seasonal basis. They enjoy the refreshing summers, maintaining homes in high-altitude, picture-postcard locales. Before snow begins to cover the ground, they return to their winter quarters in Phoenix or Yuma. Others come here in the opposite season, to enjoy superb skiing and Colorado winter sports. Although some prefer the ambience of Old West mining towns, modern cities and progressive towns are scattered all over the state, places that provide all the amenities of civilized, cultured retirement. University towns, residential communities, and tourist attractions offer delightful lifestyles for retirees, right next door to Colorado's outdoor wonderlands.

A word about high-altitude living: Those with health problems might want to consult their doctors before considering a move into high elevations. At high altitudes oxygen is less dense, and humidity is 50 to 80 percent lower than at sea level. You need to breathe more deeply to draw enough oxygen into your lungs. Usually your body adjusts to lower oxygen supplies and dryness in the air after 24 to 48 hours. Many people, like this author, experience no altitude symptoms other than drowsiness at altitudes above 11,000 feet. That's no problem; I simply take an extra nap every day until my body adjusts. Then, when my body adjusts to the altitude, I still take extra naps. Hey, I'm *retired*. I nap when I please!

Colorado Tax Profile
Sales tax: 2.9% to 9.9%; food, drugs exempt
State income tax: 4.63% of federal taxable income
Property taxes: average 1.2% of assessed value
Social Security taxed: half of benefits taxable for higher incomes
Pensions taxed: excludes first $20,000; over age 65: $24,000 exemption
Inheritance tax: limited estate tax
Gasoline tax: 22¢ per gallon

Boulder

Boulder has two retirement attractions that make it outstanding: skiing and a college town environment. Even if retirees haven't the slightest interest in continuing education, they find that a university influences a community, serving as an exciting source of entertainment and intellectual stimulation, offering social and cultural activities that wouldn't exist without the school's presence. You don't have to be a registered student to attend lectures or talks (often free) given by famous scientists, politicians, visiting artists, or other well-known personalities. Concerts ranging from Beethoven to boogie-woogie are presented by guest artists as well as the university's music department. You can attend the school's stage plays, musicals, and Shakespearean productions with season tickets that often cost less than a single performance at a New York theater. Some schools allow senior citizens the use of recreational facilities and access to well-stocked libraries.

Therefore, without hesitation, we highly recommend Boulder as one of the better examples of university retirement locations. This wonderfully cosmopolitan city of a little over 100,000 inhabitants is the home of the University of Colorado, whose campus, students, and faculty affect the city's environment in many pleasant ways, carrying the institution's intellectual excitement into the community as a whole. In addition, the city's immediate surroundings are as beautiful as you could imagine. Boulder is about 27 miles northwest of Denver, with the Flatiron Mountains and snow-covered peaks looming in the background and Rocky Mountain National Park just minutes away.

The university's influence is most obvious in the city center, where you can stroll along the renovated downtown pedestrian mall known as Pearl Street. This vibrant historic preservation district is the focal point of the city, its traditional heart and soul. Mimes, jugglers, and musicians mingle with the crowds, adding a touch of magic to the scene, something you'd expect to find in San Francisco or Paris rather than Colorado. All generations mix here to meet for coffee, read a newspaper or magazine, or perhaps browse a bookstore or a boutique. Pearl Street offers a great selection of good restaurants, art galleries, and specialty shops of a variety and quality seldom seen in downtown areas of today's cities. It is abuzz with activities, formal and ad hoc: the site of art festivals, practicing musicians, and birthday celebrations, and a perfect place for people watching and relaxing. In short, downtown Boulder is a delightful place to be.

The University of Colorado encourages retirees to enroll in classes for credit or as auditors. But for those who don't feel up to total immersion in the university's curriculum, an extraordinary senior center operated by Boulder Housing and Human Services gives classes in everything from paper making to computers. It even offers sailboat instruction on Boulder Reservoir and day trips to archaeological sites and theaters in Denver. Coupled with an active volunteer program, this is one of the better senior programs we have seen.

BOULDER AREA WEATHER

| | IN DEGREES FAHRENHEIT | | | | ANNUAL | |
	Jan.	April	July	Oct.	RAIN	SNOW
Daily highs	41	66	88	70	17"	90"
Daily lows	17	45	57	40		

Boulder's winter looks bad statistically—that is, if you consider snow bad—because Boulder catches even more snow than Denver! March and April receive the heaviest blankets of the white stuff, but like in Denver, it doesn't hang around for long; daily temperatures climb high enough to get rid of it quickly. Most days of the year can be spent walking, biking, or pursuing outdoor activities. Summer makes amends by providing gloriously sunny and comfortable days.

The Boulder Community Hospital, with 185 beds, has excellent ratings from the community. Nearby Denver hospitals are also convenient for special needs.

Boulder Chamber of Commerce: 2440 Pearl St., Boulder, CO 80302; (303) 938-8837; boulderchamber.com.

Durango

Tucked away in a horseshoe of the San Juan Mountains in the southwestern corner of the state, Durango has been the gateway to southwestern Colorado's natural riches for more than 100 years. Indians and fur traders, miners and prospectors, ranchers and railroad engineers alike passed through Durango on their way to seek their fortunes. Many found that Durango itself was the treasure they sought. Two million acres of national forest surround the city and provide countless places for outdoor recreation, with hunting, fishing, and hiking opportunities galore.

Although the town is relatively young—established little more than a century ago—the Four Corners region where it is located boasts evidence of ancient glories. Two thousand years ago this was home to a mysterious aboriginal culture known as the Anasazi (the Ancient Ones). For some unknown reason the Anasazi abandoned their sophisticated, several-storied apartment buildings and left the area to the next wave of inhabitants, the

Ute tribes, who arrived a couple of centuries later. They were there to welcome the Spanish, who explored the region in the 1500s.

The town of Durango got its start in 1880 as a depot and roundhouse location for the railroad and grew rapidly into a town of 2,000 residents just a year later. Before long the fledgling town boasted 20 saloons and 134 businesses. Today the population is almost 18,000 and still growing. Retirees make up a sizable percentage of the inhabitants. The business community and residents recognize the treasure of the original buildings, still in use today, that were constructed by Durango's pioneers. Parts of downtown have been named by the Colorado Historical Society as a national historic district, bestowing Durango with Victorian splendor and elegance.

Residents like the town because it's a pleasant and peaceful community with a below-average crime rate and above-average quality of living. A 6,500-foot elevation ensures a four-season climate with bountiful snowfall in the town, yet not so high an altitude that temperatures don't rise above freezing every winter day. With 85 percent solar exposure, snow removal is seldom a problem. You're also guaranteed cool summer evenings without the need of air-conditioning.

Because Durango sits all by itself near the Four Corners area, by necessity it's become a self-contained little city. As Will Rogers once said, "Durango's out of the way and glad of it." Shopping needs are met by commercial development in and around the city. Early-1900s hotels and commercial buildings abound in the business district, and an unusually high number of good restaurants serve a variety of cuisines. The year-round tourist business encourages upscale establishments, to the benefit of year-round residents.

Durango is also gaining recognition as an artist colony. In addition to several well-known painters, half a dozen writers of fiction and nonfiction make this their home, as do a number of essayists, freelancers, and poets. Three galleries here are nationally recognized for quality Native American arts, Navajo weavings, jewelry, paintings, and sculpture.

Skiing at Purgatory Ski Resort, 26 miles away, is reputed to be among the best in the country. Nine lifts and 250 inches of snow annually account for the resort's impressive increase in ski hours. Although the resort has record snowfall, it also has record blue-sky days, which makes for great downhill fun.

DURANGO AREA WEATHER

	Jan.	April	July	Oct.	RAIN	SNOW
	IN DEGREES FAHRENHEIT				ANNUAL	
Daily highs	41	62	85	67	19"	71"
Daily lows	10	29	50	31		

The cost of living here is slightly below national averages, and real estate prices possibly slightly higher than in some other Colorado locations. The reason for this is that there are fewer lower-end starter homes than elsewhere. Contractors prefer to build more upscale places because they sell well.

The Fort Lewis College campus is located on a mesa overlooking Durango, with the 13,000-foot peaks of the La Plata Mountains in the background. Local residents say it has been called one of the most beautiful campuses on the North American continent. In addition to regular classes for its 4,500 students, the school offers continuing-education opportunities for residents.

For health care the community depends on Mercy Medical Center, an 83-bed, acute-care facility.

Durango Chamber of Commerce: 2301 Main Ave., Durango, CO 81301; (970) 247-0312, (800) 525-8855; durango.org.

Fort Collins

This is another city that receives favorable reviews in national publications as a desirable place to live, work, and retire. A scenic place with friendly neighborhoods and almost 150,000 residents, Fort Collins enjoys a panorama of the nearby Rocky Mountains. The Cache la Poudre River runs along the upper edge of the city, a river famous for whitewater rafting, fishing, and just plain scenic enjoyment. The river received its name back in 1836 when a party of French trappers cached an excess cargo of gunpowder (*poudre*) on the river in preparation for a trip into the mountains.

Skiing at world-class ski resorts is a matter of a few hours' drive from Fort Collins. The runs at Loveland Pass, an hour west of Denver, offer free skiing for those older than 70. (One lady I interviewed in Colorado Springs moved here when she was 78 to take advantage of the great skiing.) River

FORT COLLINS AREA WEATHER					
IN DEGREES FAHRENHEIT				ANNUAL	
	Jan.	April	July	Oct.	RAIN	SNOW
Daily highs	43	61	88	67	15"	60"
Daily lows	16	34	59	37		

rafting on the wild and scenic Poudre River can be unlike anything you've ever tried. Although you might get doused with spray and rock and roll as you ride the waves, it's a sport that doesn't require strength or skill—at least not if you go rafting with a guide who will do all the work. If you prefer, you can go with a guide who has the passengers do the work. It's fairly safe, too, because you will be wearing helmets and life jackets.

Hunting and fishing are of course excellent anywhere in Colorado. On the Poudre River, beginning 9 miles northwest of Fort Collins, Colorado's famous "Trout Route" begins. Anglers don't want to miss this. For those who like their outdoor recreation a bit less adventuresome, six public golf courses and plenty of tennis courts provide traditional exercise.

Fort Collins is home to Colorado State, the second-largest university in Colorado with more than 25,000 students, faculty, and staff. Front Range Community College has an additional 3,500 students. The school gives discounts off tuition for those older than 60. You can be sure that the student population makes a difference in the community. One way this manifests itself is in the quality and variety of inexpensive restaurants.

The Poudre Valley Hospital in Fort Collins acts as the regional medical hub for northern Colorado. The facility boasts 235 beds with an intensive- and coronary-care unit.

Fort Collins Chamber of Commerce: 225 S. Meldrum St., Fort Collins, CO 80521; (970) 482-3746; fortcollinschamber.com.

Steamboat Springs

You say you love winter? You can't wait until ski lifts start running? Maybe Steamboat Springs is your town. Snuggled in a high valley at 6,700 feet, the town has an alpine climate, with low humidity, warm summer days, and cool, crisp nights. It also features winter snow—from 170 to 450 inches! Most of that is on the slopes, thank goodness.

This is a charming, upscale place for those who enjoy delightful summers and abundant outdoor winter sports. Although its "champagne powder" skiing brings winter sports enthusiasts from all over the country, Steamboat Springs enjoys wonderful summer weather, just what you might expect from its Rocky Mountain setting. Even in July and August, temperatures rarely climb out of the 80-degree range, and every evening they drop into the 50s.

The town's name came from a mineral spring that made a chugging noise that sounded like a steamboat to the early fur trappers who passed through the area. More than 150 mineral springs are found nearby, supplying medicinal waters for modern-day residents' hot tubs and baths at the public swimming pool.

Abundant wild game and rivers teeming with fish encouraged settlement, and the development of the town as a ski resort brought Steamboat Springs to its present population of approximately 12,000 permanent residents. Its early development is evident in the well-preserved Victorian homes and substantial brick commercial buildings that date from the late 1800s. Folks who have moved here recently say they appreciate the change from the hectic, crime-plagued lifestyle of big cities.

Although it sits on US 40, a major east–west highway, Steamboat Springs is somewhat isolated, being 157 miles from the nearest big city (Denver). However, express shuttles to the Denver airport plus frequent shuttle flights from the local Yampa Valley Regional Airport keep folks in touch with big-city civilization (if they need that sort of thing).

Of course, the major recreational drawing card here is skiing. Steamboat Springs bills itself "Ski Town USA" and has produced more Olympic skiers than any other US town. With 20 lifts, 108 trails, and a 3,600-foot vertical rise to 10,500 feet, this area is recognized as one of the best in the country. The season runs from Thanksgiving to Easter each year. Snowmobiling, sleigh rides, and backcountry skiing are also enjoyed.

STEAMBOAT SPRINGS AREA WEATHER

| | IN DEGREES FAHRENHEIT | | | | ANNUAL | |
	Jan.	April	July	Oct.	RAIN	SNOW
Daily highs	30	52	82	60	26"	60"
Daily lows	01	24	41	24		

The Steamboat Springs Winter Carnival is a tradition that was started in 1914 as a way to help locals with cabin fever during the height of the winter season, and has continued to this day as a way to celebrate winter. In addition to the usual cross-country and downhill skiing races and jumping competitions, there are snowboarding jam sessions, tubing parties, snow chariot racing, and the famous night show extravaganza with huge fireworks displays.

This is not a place to look for bargain real estate; it's an upscale area, and property offerings show this. This higher-priced real estate pulls the overall cost of living up as well. Condos are a big deal here, and practical, because they can be turned into rentals any time you're someplace else.

Yampa Medical Center is the health care provider in Steamboat Springs. The facility has 88 beds and is highly rated by patients who have been treated there.

Steamboat Springs Chamber of Commerce: 125 Anglers Dr., Steamboat Springs, CO 80487; (970) 879-0880; steamboatchamber.com.

Grand Junction

Grand Junction is the largest city in western Colorado, located in a broad valley in the high plateau country west of the Rocky Mountains. Its name came from its location near the junction of the Colorado and Gunnison Rivers (the Colorado was originally called the Grand River). Grand Junction is the center of an urban area of some 87,000 people, although the town itself has a comfortable population of 59,000. Shopping malls, a senior citizens' center, and excellent health care are among the attractions. An abundance of sunshine and a relatively mild winter that permits year-round golf and tennis adds to its desirability for retirement.

Earlier we discussed economic disasters that turned out to be bonanzas for retirees. Here's another story: During the late 1970s, encouraged and subsidized by the government, oil companies began experimenting with the enormous shale oil deposits of Colorado and Wyoming. Thousands of workers flocked there to help develop this potentially valuable natural resource.

Grand Junction participated in this welcome economic boom. New houses, condos, and apartment buildings went up like mushrooms after a

GRAND JUNCTION AREA WEATHER

	IN DEGREES FAHRENHEIT				ANNUAL	
	Jan.	April	July	Oct.	RAIN	SNOW
Daily highs	36	65	94	69	8"	25"
Daily lows	15	38	64	42		

rainstorm. All this new construction still wasn't enough. Exxon developed a nearby flat mountaintop, known as Battlement Mesa, into a spiffy housing development for executives and corporate guests.

After a few years the economic bubble suddenly collapsed. Slumping oil prices made it too expensive to squeeze petroleum from the shale. Almost as quickly as they arrived, oil workers began leaving in search of other employment. This depressed the real estate market, to put it mildly. Many families simply walked away from their homes without looking back. They couldn't even give their properties away. They owed more money on their mortgages than the current market value of the homes. You can imagine how the real estate bargains attracted retirees who did not have to work! More than 30 percent of the buyers came from out of state—many for retirement.

Gradually the economy recovered, in large measure as a result of retirees boosting the economy with their money. Surplus homes were eventually purchased, and the population began rising once more. Today the cost of real estate and the overall cost of living in the Grand Junction area are usually a little below the national average, except for utilities, which are at least 10 percent below average.

Grand Junction Chamber of Commerce: 360 Grand Ave., Grand Junction, CO 81501; (970) 242-3214; gjchamber.org.

IDAHO

What today is the state of Idaho became property of the United States in 1803, when Napoleon sold a vast tract of land stretching from New Orleans to Seattle for the bargain price of $15 million. Even though Napoleon failed to disclose the fact that New Orleans was below sea level, President Jefferson still figured it was a good deal. He immediately commissioned the Lewis and Clark expedition to explore the new territory to see exactly what it was we purchased.

When gold rush fever hit the eastern part of the country in 1849, over 20,000 emigrants hitched up covered wagons and joined the gold rush along the branch of the Oregon Trail through southeastern Idaho. One of the major resting points was Fort Boise (present site of the city of Boise). Heavy emigrant traffic continued along the trail for many years, but few travelers considered settling here. They were in a hurry to push on to the Pacific coast.

Idaho Tax Profile

Sales tax: 6% to 9%; drugs exempt
State income tax: low, 1.6%; high, 7.4%
Income brackets: lowest, $1,451; highest, $210,890
Property taxes: average 1.2% of assessed value
Social Security taxed: no
Pensions taxed: yes
Inheritance tax: no
Gasoline tax: 33¢ per gallon

Idaho is one of the places we've traditionally ignored in this book on retirement destinations. Partly this is because of our belief that retirement should be a year-round life of enjoying the outdoors, rather than spending half the year huddled around the fireplace.

Make no mistake, Idaho is not the retirement choice of the average retired couple. But for those who enjoy winter sports and summer fishing and river rafting, there are possibilities. Of course, there is snow here. But consider the 40 to 70 inches of snow in Michigan, for example, and Boise's winter average of 21 inches seems somewhat mild. The rest of the year, with beautiful spring and fall seasons and mild summers, makes it all worthwhile for those who truly enjoy four-season climates.

Boise

The development of Boise was accelerated a few years ago when job seekers began appearing to take positions in high-tech industries. Several large regional, national, and international companies are headquartered here, including Simplot Corporation, Boise Cascade, Albertsons, Micron Technology, and Hewlett-Packard. In the 1990s these expanding industries drew high-tech employees, programmers, and technicians. Today Boise is not only the largest city in Idaho—the hub of commerce, banking, and government—but it's the third-largest city in the Northwest, right behind

Seattle and Portland. The city of Boise itself (not including the surrounding towns) has a greater population than Salt Lake City, with more than 225,000 inhabitants, or 400,000 if you include nearby towns.

Among the high-tech job seekers who flooded the area in the 1990s were inquisitive, soon-to-be retired people from the West Coast. They were checking around for four-season retirement locations where the cost of living was favorable, real estate affordable, and outdoor recreation opportunities unlimited. They were impressed by the beautiful Boise River Valley, surrounded by rolling hills and mountains in the distance, with the River of No Return Wilderness Area nearby. They had choices ranging from skiing at Bogus Basin Ski Resort, to biking on the 25-mile-long Boise River Greenbelt, to fishing and boating at nearby reservoirs. For outdoor recreation Boise indeed has it all: rugged countryside for hiking, camping, and hunting; rivers and lakes for fishing, kayaking, and rafting; and more than 10 golf courses. Minor-league professional sports teams include the short-season Class A Baseball Boise Hawks and the Idaho Steelheads of the East Coast Hockey League.

Those who decide on retirement here are basically year-round residents. The winter climate is relatively mild for locations this far north, and the snowfall is measured in inches, rather than in feet or yards as is common in many western regions. Boise's elevation of about 2,800 feet wards off truly severe temperatures often found in many parts of Idaho.

Boise's downtown is alive and well, especially because of the presence of Boise State University, the state's largest university, with an enrollment of more than 15,000. The campus is centrally located, just across the river, facing the downtown and near the river greenbelt. The university enlivens the cultural scene, making the city a regional hub for theater and jazz performances. The Gene Harris Jazz Festival is hosted in Boise each spring. You can also find competitive Division I collegiate athletics in action on nearly any given night.

Because of the university's large population of young students and professors, Boise is said to be the most liberal community in Idaho, which has the reputation of being a very conservative state. Also, the area is home to one of the largest concentrations of Basque people outside of Spain and France, with about 20,000 Basque descendants living here. You'll find a vibrant Basque section of the city with great ethnic food. Boise's mayor, as of this writing, is of Basque descent.

BOISE AREA WEATHER

	Jan.	April	July	Oct.	ANNUAL	
IN DEGREES FAHRENHEIT					RAIN	SNOW
Daily highs	36	61	90	64	33"	21"
Daily lows	21	36	57	39		

Because of its two state-of-the-art hospitals, plus four other facilities, Boise has become a regional medical center. There is also a Veterans Affairs health facility, as well as a rehabilitation hospital.

Boise Chamber of Commerce: 1101 W. Front St., Ste. 100, Boise, ID 83702; (208) 472-5205; boisechamber.org.

Coeur d'Alene

About 33 miles east of Spokane, the small city of Coeur d'Alene (population 45,000) is a special place in a gorgeous setting. Sometimes called "the playground of the Pacific Northwest," this resort community was originally a French trading post. Besides being a resort community, Coeur d'Alene is also a college town. The North Idaho College's 45-acre campus is situated on the shore of Lake Coeur d'Alene.

The lake is 25 miles long, with a beautiful shoreline lined with pristine pine forests. Residents take advantage of recreational opportunities here: fishing, swimming, canoeing, and sailing. Along the shores you'll find hiking and horseback trails, and eight public and three private golf courses. The 2,200-foot altitude here isn't high enough to create bitterly cold winters, so outdoor recreation isn't totally out of the question in the winter. After all, Coeur d'Alene has two major ski resorts within easy driving distance: Silver Mountain Resort to the east in Kellogg, and Schweitzer Mountain Ski Resort to the north in Sandpoint. When family and youngsters visit, all will enjoy visiting Silverwood—the Northwest's largest theme park. Your adult visitors will enjoy the Coeur d'Alene tribal casino, which features round-the-clock gambling, seven days a week.

Coeur d'Alene's historic city center is well maintained, with antiques stores, art galleries, and many shops, including jewelers. As can be expected in tourist-college towns, you'll find a wide variety of good restaurants in Coeur d'Alene's town center—everything from brewpubs and pizza parlors with entertainment to gourmet dining, Oriental cuisine, and hamburger havens. This is where visitors and college students mingle.

Kootenai Medical Center is Coeur d'Alene's medical center, also serving the northern Idaho area. With over 1,700 employees, the hospital is the largest employer in the region.

Coeur d'Alene's Chamber of Commerce: 105 N. First St., Coeur d'Alene, ID 83814; (877) 782-9232; cdachamber.com.

Index

About the Authors

John Howells and his wife, Sherry, spent many months of travel by car, motor home, and airplane over the past 25 years, gathering information to produce this book. They interviewed retired folks in all sections of the country, collecting experiences, getting advice, and gaining valuable insights into successful retirement lifestyles. Today Sherry has retired from retiree research. Fortunately John's granddaughter, Teal Conroy, has taken on the task of coauthoring this book.

John has written and co-authored several other books about retirement locations. Among them are the retirement guides *Choose Costa Rica for Retirement* and *Choose Mexico for Retirement*. He writes about retirement and travel for several national publications, occasionally writing for *Where to Retire* magazine. He was one of the original members of the board of directors of the American Association of Retirement Communities. John and Sherry divide their time between Monterey, California, and Playas de Nosara in Costa Rica.

Teal Conroy says she was inspired by her grandfather, John Howells, to travel the world. She lived and traveled in Europe for a time, calling Salzburg, Austria, her home base. She considers Costa Rica and Belize among the most beautiful destinations in the world.

Teal graduated from University of Redlands with a Bachelor of Arts degree in English, creative writing. She published her first children's book, *The Watermelon Queen*, in 2018. She has held a long career in educational advancement while continuing to act as a contributing writer to various printed and web publications. She currently lives in Marin County, California, with her husband, Kevin, her two children, Keagan and Sutton, and her two rescued dogs, Archie and Frankie.